N 26 2004

D0927729

Hyundai Elantra Automotive Repair Manual

by Larry Warren, Mike Stubblefield and John H Haynes
Member of the Guild of Motoring Writers

Models covered:
All Hyundai Elantra models - 1996 through 2001

 (7F1 - 43010)

ABCDE
FGHIJ
KLMNO
PQRS

Haynes Publishing Group
Sparkford Nr Yeovil
Somerset BA22 7JJ England

Haynes North America, Inc
861 Lawrence Drive
Newbury Park
California 91320 USA

Acknowledgements

Wiring diagrams originated exclusively for Haynes North America, Inc. by Valley Forge Technical Information Services

© **Haynes North America, Inc. 2002**

With permission from J.H. Haynes & Co. Ltd.

A book in the Haynes Automotive Repair Manual Series

Printed in the U.S.A.

ISBN 1 56392 451 X

Library of Congress Control Number 2001097037

While every attempt is made to ensure that the information in this manual is correct, no liability can be accepted by the authors or publishers for loss, damage or injury caused by any errors in, or omissions from, the information given.

Contents

Haynes author, mechanic and photographer with 1996 Hyundai Elantra

About this manual

Its purpose

The purpose of this manual is to help you get the best value from your vehicle. It can do so in several ways. It can help you decide what work must be done, even if you choose to have it done by a dealer service department or a repair shop; it provides information and procedures for routine maintenance and servicing; and it offers diagnostic and repair procedures to follow when trouble occurs.

We hope you use the manual to tackle the work yourself. For many simpler jobs, doing it yourself may be quicker than arranging an appointment to get the vehicle into a shop and making the trips to leave it and pick it up. More importantly, a lot of money can be saved by avoiding the expense the shop must pass on to you to cover its labor and overhead costs. An added benefit is the sense of satisfaction and accomplishment that you feel after doing the job yourself.

Using the manual

The manual is divided into Chapters. Each Chapter is divided into numbered Sections, which are headed in bold type between horizontal lines. Each Section consists of consecutively numbered paragraphs.

At the beginning of each numbered Section you will be referred to any illustrations which apply to the procedures in that Section. The reference numbers used in illustration captions pinpoint the pertinent Section and the Step within that Section. That is, illustration 3.2 means the illustration refers to Section 3 and Step (or paragraph) 2 within that Section.

Procedures, once described in the text, are not normally repeated. When it's necessary to refer to another Chapter, the reference will be given as Chapter and Section number. Cross references given without use of the word "Chapter" apply to Sections and/or paragraphs in the same Chapter. For example, "see Section 8" means in the same Chapter.

References to the left or right side of the vehicle assume you are sitting in the driver's seat, facing forward.

Even though we have prepared this manual with extreme care, neither the publisher nor the author can accept responsibility for any errors in, or omissions from, the information given.

NOTE

A **Note** provides information necessary to properly complete a procedure or information which will make the procedure easier to understand.

CAUTION

A **Caution** provides a special procedure or special steps which must be taken while completing the procedure where the Caution is found. Not heeding a Caution can result in damage to the assembly being worked on.

WARNING

A **Warning** provides a special procedure or special steps which must be taken while completing the procedure where the Warning is found. Not heeding a Warning can result in personal injury.

Introduction to the Hyundai Elantra

These models are available in four-door sedan body, four-door hatchback and station wagon body styles.

The transversely mounted inline four-cylinder engines used in these models are equipped with electronic fuel injection.

The engine drives the front wheels through either a five-speed manual or a four-speed automatic transaxle via independent driveaxles.

Independent suspension, featuring MacPherson struts, is used on all four wheels. The power-assisted rack-and-pinion steering unit is mounted behind the engine.

The brakes at the front are discs and either disc or drum at the rear, with standard power assist. Some models are equipped with Anti-lock Braking Systems (ABS).

Vehicle identification numbers

Modifications are a continuing and unpublicized process in vehicle manufacturing. Since spare parts manuals and lists are compiled on a numerical basis, the individual vehicle numbers are essential to correctly identify the component required.

Vehicle identification number (VIN)

This very important number stamped on a plate attached to the dashboard inside the windshield on the driver's side of the vehicle **(see illustration)** It is also stamped on the firewall in the engine compartment and on a plate on the drivers side door **(see illustrations)**. The VIN also appears on the Vehicle Certificate of Title and Registration. It contains information such as where and when the vehicle was manufactured, the model year and the body style.

VIN Engine and model year codes

Two particularly important pieces of information found in the VIN are the engine code and model year code. Counting from the left, the engine code designation is the eighth digit. The model year code is the 10th digit.

Model year codes

T = 1996
V = 1997
W = 1998
X = 1999
Y = 2000
1 = 2001

Engine codes

M = I.8L DOHC four-cylinder engine
F = 2.0L DOHC four-cylinder engine

The engine code number is commonly needed when ordering engine parts. Besides being a component of the VIN, an engine code can also be found on the front (radiator) side of the engine on the right (passenger's side) end below the oil filter.

Transaxle number

The transaxle number is commonly needed when ordering transaxle parts. On

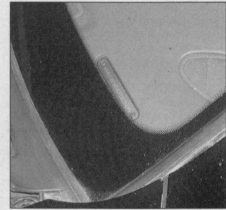

The Vehicle Identification Number (VIN) is stamped into a metal plate fastened to the dashboard on the driver's side - it is visible through the windshield

manual transaxles it's located on the transaxle case. On automatic transaxles, it's found on a tag on the front of the transaxle case.

The Vehicle Identification Number (VIN) is also stamped into firewall in the engine compartment

The VIN can also be found on the end of the driver's door

Buying parts

Replacement parts are available from many sources, which generally fall into one of two categories - authorized dealer parts departments and independent retail auto parts stores. Our advice concerning these parts is as follows:

Retail auto parts stores: Good auto parts stores will stock frequently needed components which wear out relatively fast, such as clutch components, exhaust systems, brake parts, tune-up parts, etc. These stores often supply new or reconditioned parts on an exchange basis, which can save a considerable amount of money. Discount auto parts stores are often very good places to buy materials and parts needed for general vehicle maintenance such as oil, grease, filters, spark plugs, belts, touch-up paint, bulbs, etc. They also usually sell tools and general accessories, have convenient hours, charge lower prices and can often be found not far from home.

Authorized dealer parts department: This is the best source for parts which are unique to the vehicle and not generally available elsewhere (such as major engine parts, transmission parts, trim pieces, etc.).

Warranty information: If the vehicle is still covered under warranty, be sure that any replacement parts purchased - regardless of the source - do not invalidate the warranty!

To be sure of obtaining the correct parts, have engine and chassis numbers available and, if possible, take the old parts along for positive identification.

Maintenance techniques, tools and working facilities

Maintenance techniques

There are a number of techniques involved in maintenance and repair that will be referred to throughout this manual. Application of these techniques will enable the home mechanic to be more efficient, better organized and capable of performing the various tasks properly, which will ensure that the repair job is thorough and complete.

Fasteners

Fasteners are nuts, bolts, studs and screws used to hold two or more parts together. There are a few things to keep in mind when working with fasteners. Almost all of them use a locking device of some type, either a lockwasher, locknut, locking tab or thread adhesive. All threaded fasteners should be clean and straight, with undamaged threads and undamaged corners on the hex head where the wrench fits. Develop the habit of replacing all damaged nuts and bolts with new ones. Special locknuts with nylon or fiber inserts can only be used once. If they are removed, they lose their locking ability and must be replaced with new ones.

Rusted nuts and bolts should be treated with a penetrating fluid to ease removal and prevent breakage. Some mechanics use turpentine in a spout-type oil can, which works quite well. After applying the rust penetrant, let it work for a few minutes before trying to loosen the nut or bolt. Badly rusted fasteners may have to be chiseled or sawed off or removed with a special nut breaker, available at tool stores.

If a bolt or stud breaks off in an assembly, it can be drilled and removed with a special tool commonly available for this purpose. Most automotive machine shops can perform this task, as well as other repair procedures, such as the repair of threaded holes that have been stripped out.

Flat washers and lockwashers, when removed from an assembly, should always be replaced exactly as removed. Replace any damaged washers with new ones. Never use a lockwasher on any soft metal surface (such as aluminum), thin sheet metal or plastic.

Fastener sizes

For a number of reasons, automobile manufacturers are making wider and wider use of metric fasteners. Therefore, it is important to be able to tell the difference between standard (sometimes called U.S. or SAE) and metric hardware, since they cannot be interchanged.

All bolts, whether standard or metric, are sized according to diameter, thread pitch and length. For example, a standard 1/2 - 13 x 1 bolt is 1/2 inch in diameter, has 13 threads per inch and is 1 inch long. An M12 - 1.75 x 25 metric bolt is 12 mm in diameter, has a thread pitch of 1.75 mm (the distance between threads) and is 25 mm long. The two bolts are nearly identical, and easily confused, but they are not interchangeable.

In addition to the differences in diameter, thread pitch and length, metric and standard bolts can also be distinguished by examining the bolt heads. To begin with, the distance across the flats on a standard bolt head is measured in inches, while the same dimension on a metric bolt is sized in millimeters (the same is true for nuts). As a result, a standard wrench should not be used on a metric bolt and a metric wrench should not be used on a standard bolt. Also, most standard bolts have slashes radiating out from the center of the head to denote the grade or strength of the bolt, which is an indication of the amount of torque that can be applied to it. The greater the number of slashes, the greater the strength of the bolt. Grades 0 through 5 are commonly used on automobiles. Metric bolts have a property class (grade) number, rather than a slash, molded into their heads to indicate bolt strength. In this case, the higher the number, the stronger the bolt. Property class numbers 8.8, 9.8 and 10.9 are commonly used on automobiles.

Strength markings can also be used to distinguish standard hex nuts from metric hex nuts. Many standard nuts have dots stamped into one side, while metric nuts are marked with a number. The greater the number of dots, or the higher the number, the greater the strength of the nut.

Metric studs are also marked on their ends according to property class (grade). Larger studs are numbered (the same as metric bolts), while smaller studs carry a geometric code to denote grade.

It should be noted that many fasteners, especially Grades 0 through 2, have no distinguishing marks on them. When such is the case, the only way to determine whether it is standard or metric is to measure the thread pitch or compare it to a known fastener of the same size.

Standard fasteners are often referred to as SAE, as opposed to metric. However, it should be noted that SAE technically refers to a non-metric fine thread fastener only. Coarse thread non-metric fasteners are referred to as USS sizes.

Since fasteners of the same size (both standard and metric) may have different strength ratings, be sure to reinstall any bolts, studs or nuts removed from your vehicle in their original locations. Also, when replacing a fastener with a new one, make sure that the new one has a strength rating equal to or greater than the original.

Tightening sequences and procedures

Most threaded fasteners should be tightened to a specific torque value (torque is the twisting force applied to a threaded component such as a nut or bolt). Overtightening the fastener can weaken it and cause it to break, while undertightening can cause it to eventually come loose. Bolts, screws and

studs, depending on the material they are made of and their thread diameters, have specific torque values, many of which are noted in the Specifications at the beginning of each Chapter. Be sure to follow the torque recommendations closely. For fasteners not assigned a specific torque, a general torque value chart is presented here as a guide. These torque values are for dry (unlubricated) fasteners threaded into steel or cast iron (not aluminum). As was previously mentioned, the size and grade of a fastener determine the amount of torque that can safely be applied to it. The figures listed here are approximate for Grade 2 and Grade 3 fasteners. Higher grades can tolerate higher torque values.

Fasteners laid out in a pattern, such as cylinder head bolts, oil pan bolts, differential

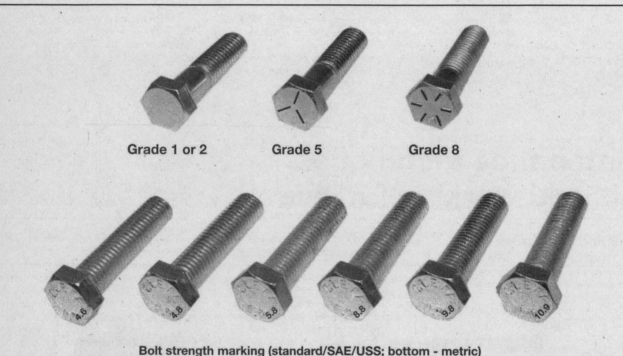

Grade 1 or 2   Grade 5   Grade 8

Bolt strength marking (standard/SAE/USS; bottom - metric)

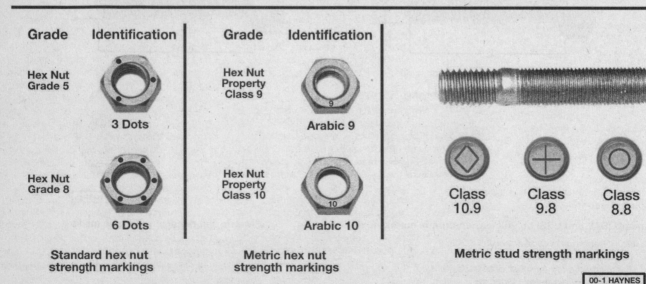

Grade	Identification
Hex Nut Grade 5	3 Dots
Hex Nut Grade 8	6 Dots

Standard hex nut strength markings

Grade	Identification
Hex Nut Property Class 9	Arabic 9
Hex Nut Property Class 10	Arabic 10

Metric hex nut strength markings

Class 10.9   Class 9.8   Class 8.8

Metric stud strength markings

cover bolts, etc., must be loosened or tightened in sequence to avoid warping the component. This sequence will normally be shown in the appropriate Chapter. If a specific pattern is not given, the following procedures can be used to prevent warping.

Initially, the bolts or nuts should be assembled finger-tight only. Next, they should be tightened one full turn each, in a criss-cross or diagonal pattern. After each one has been tightened one full turn, return to the first one and tighten them all one-half turn, following the same pattern. Finally, tighten each of them one-quarter turn at a time until each fastener has been tightened to the proper torque. To loosen and remove the fasteners, the procedure would be reversed.

Component disassembly

Component disassembly should be done with care and purpose to help ensure that the parts go back together properly. Always keep track of the sequence in which parts are removed. Make note of special characteristics or marks on parts that can be installed more than one way, such as a grooved thrust washer on a shaft. It is a good idea to lay the disassembled parts out on a clean surface in the order that they were removed. It may also be helpful to make sketches or take instant photos of components before removal.

When removing fasteners from a component, keep track of their locations. Sometimes threading a bolt back in a part, or putting the washers and nut back on a stud, can prevent mix-ups later. If nuts and bolts cannot be returned to their original locations, they should be kept in a compartmented box or a

Metric thread sizes	Ft-lbs	Nm
M-6	6 to 9	9 to 12
M-8	14 to 21	19 to 28
M-10	28 to 40	38 to 54
M-12	50 to 71	68 to 96
M-14	80 to 140	109 to 154
Pipe thread sizes		
1/8	5 to 8	7 to 10
1/4	12 to 18	17 to 24
3/8	22 to 33	30 to 44
1/2	25 to 35	34 to 47
U.S. thread sizes		
1/4 - 20	6 to 9	9 to 12
5/16 - 18	12 to 18	17 to 24
5/16 - 24	14 to 20	19 to 27
3/8 - 16	22 to 32	30 to 43
3/8 - 24	27 to 38	37 to 51
7/16 - 14	40 to 55	55 to 74
7/16 - 20	40 to 60	55 to 81
1/2 - 13	55 to 80	75 to 108

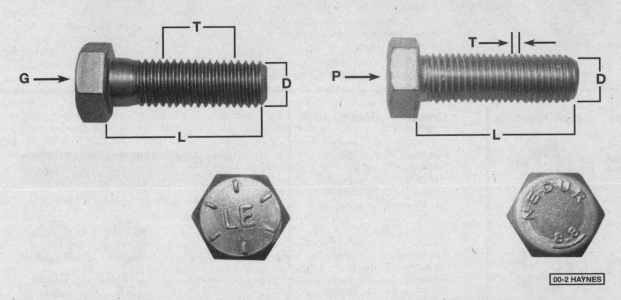

00-2 HAYNES

Standard (SAE and USS) bolt dimensions/grade marks

   G   Grade marks (bolt strength)
   L   Length (in inches)
   T   Thread pitch (number of threads per inch)
   D   Nominal diameter (in inches)

Metric bolt dimensions/grade marks

   P   Property class (bolt strength)
   L   Length (in millimeters)
   T   Thread pitch (distance between threads in millimeters)
   D   Diameter

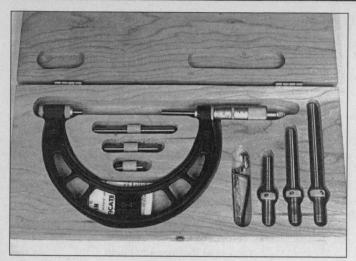

Micrometer set

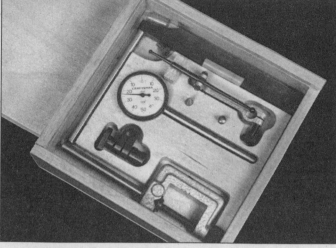

Dial indicator set

series of small boxes. A cupcake or muffin tin is ideal for this purpose, since each cavity can hold the bolts and nuts from a particular area (i.e. oil pan bolts, valve cover bolts, engine mount bolts, etc.). A pan of this type is especially helpful when working on assemblies with very small parts, such as the carburetor, alternator, valve train or interior dash and trim pieces. The cavities can be marked with paint or tape to identify the contents.

Whenever wiring looms, harnesses or connectors are separated, it is a good idea to identify the two halves with numbered pieces of masking tape so they can be easily reconnected.

Gasket sealing surfaces

Throughout any vehicle, gaskets are used to seal the mating surfaces between two parts and keep lubricants, fluids, vacuum or pressure contained in an assembly.

Many times these gaskets are coated with a liquid or paste-type gasket sealing compound before assembly. Age, heat and pressure can sometimes cause the two parts to stick together so tightly that they are very difficult to separate. Often, the assembly can be loosened by striking it with a soft-face hammer near the mating surfaces. A regular hammer can be used if a block of wood is placed between the hammer and the part. Do not hammer on cast parts or parts that could be easily damaged. With any particularly stubborn part, always recheck to make sure that every fastener has been removed.

Avoid using a screwdriver or bar to pry apart an assembly, as they can easily mar the gasket sealing surfaces of the parts, which must remain smooth. If prying is absolutely necessary, use an old broom handle, but keep in mind that extra clean up will be necessary if the wood splinters.

After the parts are separated, the old gasket must be carefully scraped off and the gasket surfaces cleaned. Stubborn gasket material can be soaked with rust penetrant or treated with a special chemical to soften it so

it can be easily scraped off. A scraper can be fashioned from a piece of copper tubing by flattening and sharpening one end. Copper is recommended because it is usually softer than the surfaces to be scraped, which reduces the chance of gouging the part. Some gaskets can be removed with a wire brush, but regardless of the method used, the mating surfaces must be left clean and smooth. If for some reason the gasket surface is gouged, then a gasket sealer thick enough to fill scratches will have to be used during reassembly of the components. For most applications, a non-drying (or semi-drying) gasket sealer should be used.

Hose removal tips

Warning: *If the vehicle is equipped with air conditioning, do not disconnect any of the A/C hoses without first having the system depressurized by a dealer service department or a service station.*

Hose removal precautions closely parallel gasket removal precautions. Avoid scratching or gouging the surface that the hose mates against or the connection may leak. This is especially true for radiator hoses. Because of various chemical reactions, the rubber in hoses can bond itself to the metal spigot that the hose fits over. To remove a hose, first loosen the hose clamps that secure it to the spigot. Then, with slip-joint pliers, grab the hose at the clamp and rotate it around the spigot. Work it back and forth until it is completely free, then pull it off. Silicone or other lubricants will ease removal if they can be applied between the hose and the outside of the spigot. Apply the same lubricant to the inside of the hose and the outside of the spigot to simplify installation.

As a last resort (and if the hose is to be replaced with a new one anyway), the rubber can be slit with a knife and the hose peeled from the spigot. If this must be done, be careful that the metal connection is not damaged.

If a hose clamp is broken or damaged, do not reuse it. Wire-type clamps usually

weaken with age, so it is a good idea to replace them with screw-type clamps whenever a hose is removed.

Tools

A selection of good tools is a basic requirement for anyone who plans to maintain and repair his or her own vehicle. For the owner who has few tools, the initial investment might seem high, but when compared to the spiraling costs of professional auto maintenance and repair, it is a wise one.

To help the owner decide which tools are needed to perform the tasks detailed in this manual, the following tool lists are offered: *Maintenance and minor repair, Repair/overhaul* and *Special.*

The newcomer to practical mechanics should start off with the *maintenance and minor repair* tool kit, which is adequate for the simpler jobs performed on a vehicle. Then, as confidence and experience grow, the owner can tackle more difficult tasks, buying additional tools as they are needed. Eventually the basic kit will be expanded into the *repair and overhaul* tool set. Over a period of time, the experienced do-it-yourselfer will assemble a tool set complete enough for most repair and overhaul procedures and will add tools from the special category when it is felt that the expense is justified by the frequency of use.

Maintenance and minor repair tool kit

The tools in this list should be considered the minimum required for performance of routine maintenance, servicing and minor repair work. We recommend the purchase of combination wrenches (box-end and open-end combined in one wrench). While more expensive than open end wrenches, they offer the advantages of both types of wrench.

Combination wrench set (1/4-inch to 1 inch or 6 mm to 19 mm)
Adjustable wrench, 8 inch
Spark plug wrench with rubber insert

Dial caliper

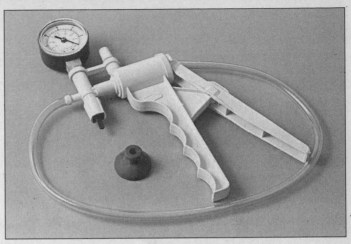

Hand-operated vacuum pump

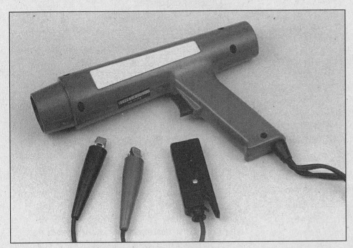

Timing light

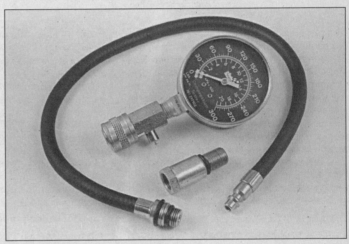

Compression gauge with spark plug hole adapter

Damper/steering wheel puller

General purpose puller

Hydraulic lifter removal tool

Spark plug gap adjusting tool
Feeler gauge set
Brake bleeder wrench
Standard screwdriver (5/16-inch x
    6 inch)
Phillips screwdriver (No. 2 x 6 inch)
Combination pliers - 6 inch
Hacksaw and assortment of blades

Tire pressure gauge
Grease gun
Oil can
Fine emery cloth
Wire brush
Battery post and cable cleaning tool
Oil filter wrench
Funnel (medium size)

Safety goggles
Jackstands (2)
Drain pan

Note: *If basic tune-ups are going to be part of routine maintenance, it will be necessary to purchase a good quality stroboscopic timing light and combination tachometer/dwell*

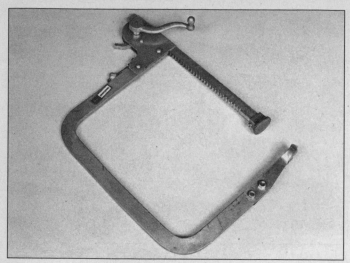

Valve spring compressor

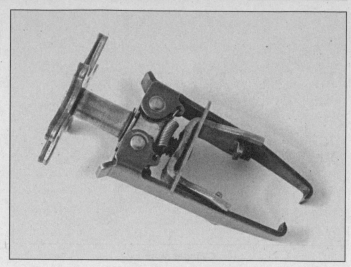

Valve spring compressor

Ridge reamer

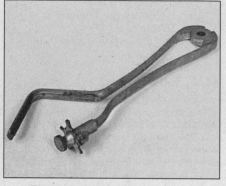

Piston ring groove cleaning tool

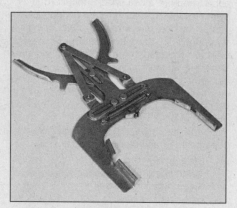

Ring removal/installation tool

Ring compressor

meter. Although they are included in the list of special tools, it is mentioned here because they are absolutely necessary for tuning most vehicles properly.

Repair and overhaul tool set

These tools are essential for anyone who plans to perform major repairs and are in addition to those in the maintenance and minor repair tool kit. Included is a compre-hensive set of sockets which, though expen-sive, are invaluable because of their versatil-ity, especially when various extensions and drives are available. We recommend the 1/2-inch drive over the 3/8-inch drive. Although the larger drive is bulky and more expensive, it has the capacity of accepting a very wide range of large sockets. Ideally, however, the mechanic should have a 3/8-inch drive set and a 1/2-inch drive set.

    Socket set(s)
    Reversible ratchet
    Extension - 10 inch
    Universal joint
    Torque wrench (same size drive as
       sockets)
    Ball peen hammer - 8 ounce
    Soft-face hammer (plastic/rubber)
    Standard screwdriver (1/4-inch x 6 inch)
    Standard screwdriver (stubby -
       5/16-inch)
    Phillips screwdriver (No. 3 x 8 inch)
    Phillips screwdriver (stubby - No. 2)
    Pliers - vise grip
    Pliers - lineman's
    Pliers - needle nose
    Pliers - snap-ring (internal and external)
    Cold chisel - 1/2-inch
    Scribe

    Scraper (made from flattened copper
       tubing)
    Centerpunch
    Pin punches (1/16, 1/8, 3/16-inch)
    Steel rule/straightedge - 12 inch
    Allen wrench set (1/8 to 3/8-inch or
       4 mm to 10 mm)
    A selection of files
    Wire brush (large)
    Jackstands (second set)
    Jack (scissor or hydraulic type)

Note: *Another tool which is often useful is an electric drill with a chuck capacity of 3/8-inch and a set of good quality drill bits.*

Special tools

The tools in this list include those which are not used regularly, are expensive to buy, or which need to be used in accordance with their manufacturer's instructions. Unless these tools will be used frequently, it is not very economical to purchase many of them. A consideration would be to split the cost and use between yourself and a friend or friends. In addition, most of these tools can be obtained from a tool rental shop on a tem-porary basis.

This list primarily contains only those tools and instruments widely available to the

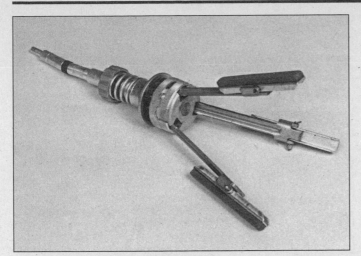

Cylinder hone

Brake hold-down spring tool

public, and not those special tools produced by the vehicle manufacturer for distribution to dealer service departments. Occasionally, references to the manufacturer's special tools are included in the text of this manual. Generally, an alternative method of doing the job without the special tool is offered. However, sometimes there is no alternative to their use. Where this is the case, and the tool cannot be purchased or borrowed, the work should be turned over to the dealer service department or an automotive repair shop.

Valve spring compressor
Piston ring groove cleaning tool
Piston ring compressor
Piston ring installation tool
Cylinder compression gauge
Cylinder ridge reamer
Cylinder surfacing hone
Cylinder bore gauge
Micrometers and/or dial calipers
Hydraulic lifter removal tool
Balljoint separator
Universal-type puller
Impact screwdriver
Dial indicator set
Stroboscopic timing light (inductive pick-up)

Hand operated vacuum/pressure pump
Tachometer/dwell meter
Universal electrical multimeter
Cable hoist
Brake spring removal and installation tools
Floor jack

Buying tools

For the do-it-yourselfer who is just starting to get involved in vehicle maintenance and repair, there are a number of options available when purchasing tools. If maintenance and minor repair is the extent of the work to be done, the purchase of individual tools is satisfactory. If, on the other hand, extensive work is planned, it would be a good idea to purchase a modest tool set from one of the large retail chain stores. A set can usually be bought at a substantial savings over the individual tool prices, and they often come with a tool box. As additional tools are needed, add-on sets, individual tools and a larger tool box can be purchased to expand the tool selection. Building a tool set gradually allows the cost of the tools to be spread over a longer period of time and gives the mechanic the freedom to choose only those tools that will actually be used.

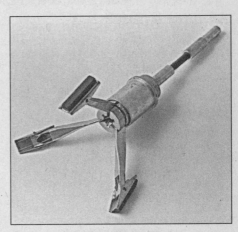

Brake cylinder hone

Tool stores will often be the only source of some of the special tools that are needed, but regardless of where tools are bought, try to avoid cheap ones, especially when buying screwdrivers and sockets, because they won't last very long. The expense involved in replacing cheap tools will eventually be greater than the initial cost of quality tools.

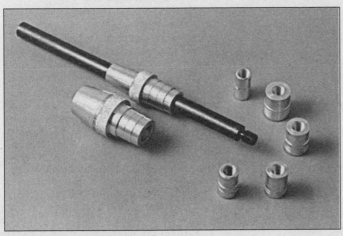

Clutch plate alignment tool

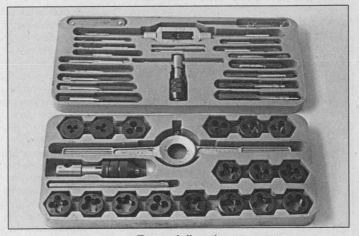

Tap and die set

Care and maintenance of tools

Good tools are expensive, so it makes sense to treat them with respect. Keep them clean and in usable condition and store them properly when not in use. Always wipe off any dirt, grease or metal chips before putting them away. Never leave tools lying around in the work area. Upon completion of a job, always check closely under the hood for tools that may have been left there so they won't get lost during a test drive.

Some tools, such as screwdrivers, pliers, wrenches and sockets, can be hung on a panel mounted on the garage or workshop wall, while others should be kept in a tool box or tray. Measuring instruments, gauges, meters, etc. must be carefully stored where they cannot be damaged by weather or impact from other tools.

When tools are used with care and stored properly, they will last a very long time. Even with the best of care, though, tools will wear out if used frequently. When a tool is damaged or worn out, replace it. Subsequent jobs will be safer and more enjoyable if you do.

How to repair damaged threads

Sometimes, the internal threads of a nut or bolt hole can become stripped, usually from overtightening. Stripping threads is an all-too-common occurrence, especially when working with aluminum parts, because aluminum is so soft that it easily strips out.

Usually, external or internal threads are only partially stripped. After they've been cleaned up with a tap or die, they'll still work. Sometimes, however, threads are badly damaged. When this happens, you've got three choices:

1) *Drill and tap the hole to the next suitable oversize and install a larger diameter bolt, screw or stud.*

2) *Drill and tap the hole to accept a threaded plug, then drill and tap the plug to the original screw size. You can also buy a plug already threaded to the original size. Then you simply drill a hole to the specified size, then run the threaded plug into the hole with a bolt and jam nut. Once the plug is fully seated, remove the jam nut and bolt.*

3) *The third method uses a patented thread repair kit like Heli-Coil or Slimsert. These easy-to-use kits are designed to repair damaged threads in straight-through holes and blind holes. Both are available as kits which can handle a variety of sizes and thread patterns. Drill the hole, then tap it with the special included tap. Install the Heli-Coil and the hole is back to its original diameter and thread pitch.*

Regardless of which method you use, be sure to proceed calmly and carefully. A little impatience or carelessness during one of these relatively simple procedures can ruin your whole day's work and cost you a bundle if you wreck an expensive part.

Working facilities

Not to be overlooked when discussing tools is the workshop. If anything more than routine maintenance is to be carried out, some sort of suitable work area is essential.

It is understood, and appreciated, that many home mechanics do not have a good workshop or garage available, and end up removing an engine or doing major repairs outside. It is recommended, however, that the overhaul or repair be completed under the cover of a roof.

A clean, flat workbench or table of comfortable working height is an absolute necessity. The workbench should be equipped with a vise that has a jaw opening of at least four inches.

As mentioned previously, some clean, dry storage space is also required for tools, as well as the lubricants, fluids, cleaning solvents, etc. which soon become necessary.

Sometimes waste oil and fluids, drained from the engine or cooling system during normal maintenance or repairs, present a disposal problem. To avoid pouring them on the ground or into a sewage system, pour the used fluids into large containers, seal them with caps and take them to an authorized disposal site or recycling center. Plastic jugs, such as old antifreeze containers, are ideal for this purpose.

Always keep a supply of old newspapers and clean rags available. Old towels are excellent for mopping up spills. Many mechanics use rolls of paper towels for most work because they are readily available and disposable. To help keep the area under the vehicle clean, a large cardboard box can be cut open and flattened to protect the garage or shop floor.

Whenever working over a painted surface, such as when leaning over a fender to service something under the hood, always cover it with an old blanket or bedspread to protect the finish. Vinyl covered pads, made especially for this purpose, are available at auto parts stores.

Booster battery (jump) starting

Observe the following precautions when using a booster battery to start a vehicle:

a) *Before connecting the booster battery, make sure the ignition switch is in the Off position.*
b) *Turn off the lights, heater and other electrical loads.*
c) *Your eyes should be shielded. Safety goggles are a good idea.*
d) *Make sure the booster battery is the same voltage as the dead one in the vehicle.*
e) *The two vehicles MUST NOT TOUCH each other.*
f) *Make sure the transmission is in Neutral (manual transaxle) or Park (automatic transaxle).*
g) *If the booster battery is not a maintenance-free type, remove the vent caps and lay a cloth over the vent holes.*

Connect the red jumper cable to the positive (+) terminals of each battery.

Connect one end of the black cable to the negative (-) terminal of the booster battery. The other end of this cable should be connected to a good ground on the engine block **(see illustration)**. Make sure the cable will not come into contact with the fan, drivebelts or other moving parts of the engine.

Start the engine using the booster battery, then, with the engine running at idle speed, disconnect the jumper cables in the reverse order of connection.

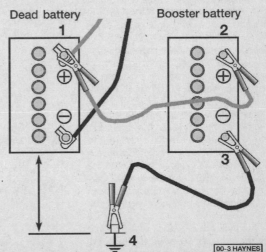

Make the booster battery cable connections in the numerical order shown (note that the negative cable of the booster battery is NOT attached to the negative terminal of the dead battery)

Jacking and towing

Jacking

Warning: *The jack supplied with the vehicle should only be used for changing a tire or placing jackstands under the frame. Never work under the vehicle or start the engine while this jack is being used as the only means of support.*

The vehicle should be on level ground. Place the shift lever in Park, if you have an automatic, or Reverse if you have a manual transaxle. Block the wheel diagonally opposite the wheel being changed. Set the parking brake.

Remove the spare tire and jack from stowage. Remove the wheel cover and trim ring (if so equipped) with the tapered end of the lug nut wrench by inserting and twisting the handle and then prying against the back of the wheel cover. **Caution:** *On some models the wheel cover can't be removed by prying; the wheel nuts must be removed first.*

Loosen, but do not remove, the lug nuts (one-half turn is sufficient). **Note:** *Factory alloy wheels may have one locking nut that requires a special keyed adapter (supplied with the vehicle).* Next, place the scissors-type jack under the side of the vehicle and adjust the jack height until the slot in the jack head engages with the raised portion of the ridge on the vertical rocker panel flange nearest the wheel to be changed. There is a front and rear jacking point on each side of the vehicle.

Turn the jack handle clockwise until the tire clears the ground. Remove the lug nuts and pull the wheel off. Replace it with the spare.

Install the lug nuts with the beveled edges facing in. Tighten them snugly. Don't attempt to tighten them completely until the vehicle is lowered or it could slip off the jack. Turn the jack handle counterclockwise to lower the vehicle. Remove the jack and tighten the lug nuts in a criss-cross pattern.

Install the cover (and trim ring, if used) and be sure it's snapped into place all the way around.

Stow the tire, jack and wrench. Unblock the wheels.

Towing

Vehicles equipped with an automatic transaxle should not be towed with all four wheels on the ground. As a general rule, the vehicle should be towed with the front (drive) wheels off the ground (the best method is to have the vehicle placed on a flat-bed tow truck). If they can't be raised, place them on a dolly.

When towing a vehicle equipped with a manual transaxle with all four wheels on the ground, be sure to place the shift lever in neutral and release the parking brake. The ignition key must be in the ACC position, since the steering lock mechanism isn't strong enough to hold the front wheels straight while towing.

Equipment specifically designed for towing should be used. It should be attached to the main structural members of the vehicle, not the bumpers or brackets.

Safety is a major consideration when towing and all applicable state and local laws must be obeyed. A safety chain system must be used at all times. Remember that power steering and power brakes will not work with the engine off.

The jack fits over the rocker panel flange (there are two jacking points on each side of the vehicle, indicated by notches in the rocker panel flange)

Automotive chemicals and lubricants

A number of automotive chemicals and lubricants are available for use during vehicle maintenance and repair. They include a wide variety of products ranging from cleaning solvents and degreasers to lubricants and protective sprays for rubber, plastic and vinyl.

Cleaners

Carburetor cleaner and choke cleaner is a strong solvent for gum, varnish and carbon. Most carburetor cleaners leave a dry-type lubricant film which will not harden or gum up. Because of this film it is not recommended for use on electrical components.

Brake system cleaner is used to remove brake dust, grease and brake fluid from the brake system, where clean surfaces are absolutely necessary. It leaves no residue and often eliminates brake squeal caused by contaminants.

Electrical cleaner removes oxidation, corrosion and carbon deposits from electrical contacts, restoring full current flow. It can also be used to clean spark plugs, carburetor jets, voltage regulators and other parts where an oil-free surface is desired.

Demoisturants remove water and moisture from electrical components such as alternators, voltage regulators, electrical connectors and fuse blocks. They are non-conductive, non-corrosive and non-flammable.

Degreasers are heavy-duty solvents used to remove grease from the outside of the engine and from chassis components. They can be sprayed or brushed on and, depending on the type, are rinsed off either with water or solvent.

Lubricants

Motor oil is the lubricant formulated for use in engines. It normally contains a wide variety of additives to prevent corrosion and reduce foaming and wear. Motor oil comes in various weights (viscosity ratings) from 0 to 50. The recommended weight of the oil depends on the season, temperature and the demands on the engine. Light oil is used in cold climates and under light load conditions. Heavy oil is used in hot climates and where high loads are encountered. Multi-viscosity oils are designed to have characteristics of both light and heavy oils and are available in a number of weights from 5W-20 to 20W-50.

Gear oil is designed to be used in differentials, manual transmissions and other areas where high-temperature lubrication is required.

Chassis and wheel bearing grease is a heavy grease used where increased loads and friction are encountered, such as for wheel bearings, balljoints, tie-rod ends and universal joints.

High-temperature wheel bearing grease is designed to withstand the extreme temperatures encountered by wheel bearings in disc brake equipped vehicles. It usually contains molybdenum disulfide (moly), which is a dry-type lubricant.

White grease is a heavy grease for metal-to-metal applications where water is a problem. White grease stays soft under both low and high temperatures (usually from -100 to +190-degrees F), and will not wash off or dilute in the presence of water.

Assembly lube is a special extreme pressure lubricant, usually containing moly, used to lubricate high-load parts (such as main and rod bearings and cam lobes) for initial start-up of a new engine. The assembly lube lubricates the parts without being squeezed out or washed away until the engine oiling system begins to function.

Silicone lubricants are used to protect rubber, plastic, vinyl and nylon parts.

Graphite lubricants are used where oils cannot be used due to contamination problems, such as in locks. The dry graphite will lubricate metal parts while remaining uncontaminated by dirt, water, oil or acids. It is electrically conductive and will not foul electrical contacts in locks such as the ignition switch.

Moly penetrants loosen and lubricate frozen, rusted and corroded fasteners and prevent future rusting or freezing.

Heat-sink grease is a special electrically non-conductive grease that is used for mounting electronic ignition modules where it is essential that heat is transferred away from the module.

Sealants

RTV sealant is one of the most widely used gasket compounds. Made from silicone, RTV is air curing, it seals, bonds, waterproofs, fills surface irregularities, remains flexible, doesn't shrink, is relatively easy to remove, and is used as a supplementary sealer with almost all low and medium temperature gaskets.

Anaerobic sealant is much like RTV in that it can be used either to seal gaskets or to form gaskets by itself. It remains flexible, is solvent resistant and fills surface imperfections. The difference between an anaerobic sealant and an RTV-type sealant is in the curing. RTV cures when exposed to air, while an anaerobic sealant cures only in the absence of air. This means that an anaerobic sealant cures only after the assembly of parts, sealing them together.

Thread and pipe sealant is used for sealing hydraulic and pneumatic fittings and vacuum lines. It is usually made from a Teflon compound, and comes in a spray, a paint-on liquid and as a wrap-around tape.

Chemicals

Anti-seize compound prevents seizing, galling, cold welding, rust and corrosion in fasteners. High-temperature anti-seize, usually made with copper and graphite lubricants, is used for exhaust system and exhaust manifold bolts.

Anaerobic locking compounds are used to keep fasteners from vibrating or working loose and cure only after installation, in the absence of air. Medium strength locking compound is used for small nuts, bolts and screws that may be removed later. High-strength locking compound is for large nuts, bolts and studs which aren't removed on a regular basis.

Oil additives range from viscosity index improvers to chemical treatments that claim to reduce internal engine friction. It should be noted that most oil manufacturers caution against using additives with their oils.

Gas additives perform several functions, depending on their chemical makeup. They usually contain solvents that help dissolve gum and varnish that build up on carburetor, fuel injection and intake parts. They also serve to break down carbon deposits that form on the inside surfaces of the combustion chambers. Some additives contain upper cylinder lubricants for valves and piston rings, and others contain chemicals to remove condensation from the gas tank.

Miscellaneous

Brake fluid is specially formulated hydraulic fluid that can withstand the heat and pressure encountered in brake systems. Care must be taken so this fluid does not come in contact with painted surfaces or plastics. An opened container should always be resealed to prevent contamination by water or dirt.

Weatherstrip adhesive is used to bond weatherstripping around doors, windows and trunk lids. It is sometimes used to attach trim pieces.

Undercoating is a petroleum-based, tar-like substance that is designed to protect metal surfaces on the underside of the vehicle from corrosion. It also acts as a sound-deadening agent by insulating the bottom of the vehicle.

Waxes and polishes are used to help protect painted and plated surfaces from the weather. Different types of paint may require the use of different types of wax and polish. Some polishes utilize a chemical or abrasive cleaner to help remove the top layer of oxidized (dull) paint on older vehicles. In recent years many non-wax polishes that contain a wide variety of chemicals such as polymers and silicones have been introduced. These non-wax polishes are usually easier to apply and last longer than conventional waxes and polishes.

Conversion factors

Length (distance)
Inches (in)	X	25.4	= Millimeters (mm)	X 0.0394	= Inches (in)
Feet (ft)	X	0.305	= Meters (m)	X 3.281	= Feet (ft)
Miles	X	1.609	= Kilometers (km)	X 0.621	= Miles

Volume (capacity)
Cubic inches (cu in; in³)	X	16.387	= Cubic centimeters (cc; cm³)	X 0.061	= Cubic inches (cu in; in³)
Imperial pints (Imp pt)	X	0.568	= Liters (l)	X 1.76	= Imperial pints (Imp pt)
Imperial quarts (Imp qt)	X	1.137	= Liters (l)	X 0.88	= Imperial quarts (Imp qt)
Imperial quarts (Imp qt)	X	1.201	= US quarts (US qt)	X 0.833	= Imperial quarts (Imp qt)
US quarts (US qt)	X	0.946	= Liters (l)	X 1.057	= US quarts (US qt)
Imperial gallons (Imp gal)	X	4.546	= Liters (l)	X 0.22	= Imperial gallons (Imp gal)
Imperial gallons (Imp gal)	X	1.201	= US gallons (US gal)	X 0.833	= Imperial gallons (Imp gal)
US gallons (US gal)	X	3.785	= Liters (l)	X 0.264	= US gallons (US gal)

Mass (weight)
Ounces (oz)	X	28.35	= Grams (g)	X 0.035	= Ounces (oz)
Pounds (lb)	X	0.454	= Kilograms (kg)	X 2.205	= Pounds (lb)

Force
Ounces-force (ozf; oz)	X	0.278	= Newtons (N)	X 3.6	= Ounces-force (ozf; oz)
Pounds-force (lbf; lb)	X	4.448	= Newtons (N)	X 0.225	= Pounds-force (lbf; lb)
Newtons (N)	X	0.1	= Kilograms-force (kgf; kg)	X 9.81	= Newtons (N)

Pressure
Pounds-force per square inch (psi; lbf/in²; lb/in²)	X	0.070	= Kilograms-force per square centimeter (kgf/cm²; kg/cm²)	X 14.223	= Pounds-force per square inch (psi; lbf/in²; lb/in²)
Pounds-force per square inch (psi; lbf/in²; lb/in²)	X	0.068	= Atmospheres (atm)	X 14.696	= Pounds-force per square inch (psi; lbf/in²; lb/in²)
Pounds-force per square inch (psi; lbf/in²; lb/in²)	X	0.069	= Bars	X 14.5	= Pounds-force per square inch (psi; lbf/in²; lb/in²)
Pounds-force per square inch (psi; lbf/in²; lb/in²)	X	6.895	= Kilopascals (kPa)	X 0.145	= Pounds-force per square inch (psi; lbf/in²; lb/in²)
Kilopascals (kPa)	X	0.01	= Kilograms-force per square centimeter (kgf/cm²; kg/cm²)	X 98.1	= Kilopascals (kPa)

Torque (moment of force)
Pounds-force inches (lbf in; lb in)	X	1.152	= Kilograms-force centimeter (kgf cm; kg cm)	X 0.868	= Pounds-force inches (lbf in; lb in)
Pounds-force inches (lbf in; lb in)	X	0.113	= Newton meters (Nm)	X 8.85	= Pounds-force inches (lbf in; lb in)
Pounds-force inches (lbf in; lb in)	X	0.083	= Pounds-force feet (lbf ft; lb ft)	X 12	= Pounds-force inches (lbf in; lb in)
Pounds-force feet (lbf ft; lb ft)	X	0.138	= Kilograms-force meters (kgf m; kg m)	X 7.233	= Pounds-force feet (lbf ft; lb ft)
Pounds-force feet (lbf ft; lb ft)	X	1.356	= Newton meters (Nm)	X 0.738	= Pounds-force feet (lbf ft; lb ft)
Newton meters (Nm)	X	0.102	= Kilograms-force meters (kgf m; kg m)	X 9.804	= Newton meters (Nm)

Vacuum
Inches mercury (in. Hg)	X	3.377	= Kilopascals (kPa)	X 0.2961	= Inches mercury
Inches mercury (in. Hg)	X	25.4	= Millimeters mercury (mm Hg)	X 0.0394	= Inches mercury

Power
Horsepower (hp)	X	745.7	= Watts (W)	X 0.0013	= Horsepower (hp)

Velocity (speed)
Miles per hour (miles/hr; mph)	X	1.609	= Kilometers per hour (km/hr; kph)	X 0.621	= Miles per hour (miles/hr; mph)

Fuel consumption*
Miles per gallon, Imperial (mpg)	X	0.354	= Kilometers per liter (km/l)	X 2.825	= Miles per gallon, Imperial (mpg)
Miles per gallon, US (mpg)	X	0.425	= Kilometers per liter (km/l)	X 2.352	= Miles per gallon, US (mpg)

Temperature
Degrees Fahrenheit = (°C x 1.8) + 32

Degrees Celsius (Degrees Centigrade; °C) = (°F - 32) x 0.56

*It is common practice to convert from miles per gallon (mpg) to liters/100 kilometers (l/100km), where mpg (Imperial) x l/100 km = 282 and mpg (US) x l/100 km = 235

DECIMALS to MILLIMETERS

Decimal	mm	Decimal	mm
0.001	0.0254	0.500	12.7000
0.002	0.0508	0.510	12.9540
0.003	0.0762	0.520	13.2080
0.004	0.1016	0.530	13.4620
0.005	0.1270	0.540	13.7160
0.006	0.1524	0.550	13.9700
0.007	0.1778	0.560	14.2240
0.008	0.2032	0.570	14.4780
0.009	0.2286	0.580	14.7320
		0.590	14.9860
0.010	0.2540		
0.020	0.5080		
0.030	0.7620		
0.040	1.0160	0.600	15.2400
0.050	1.2700	0.610	15.4940
0.060	1.5240	0.620	15.7480
0.070	1.7780	0.630	16.0020
0.080	2.0320	0.640	16.2560
0.090	2.2860	0.650	16.5100
		0.660	16.7640
0.100	2.5400	0.670	17.0180
0.110	2.7940	0.680	17.2720
0.120	3.0480	0.690	17.5260
0.130	3.3020		
0.140	3.5560		
0.150	3.8100		
0.160	4.0640	0.700	17.7800
0.170	4.3180	0.710	18.0340
0.180	4.5720	0.720	18.2880
0.190	4.8260	0.730	18.5420
		0.740	18.7960
0.200	5.0800	0.750	19.0500
0.210	5.3340	0.760	19.3040
0.220	5.5880	0.770	19.5580
0.230	5.8420	0.780	19.8120
0.240	6.0960	0.790	20.0660
0.250	6.3500		
0.260	6.6040		
0.270	6.8580	0.800	20.3200
0.280	7.1120	0.810	20.5740
0.290	7.3660	0.820	20.8280
		0.830	21.0820
0.300	7.6200	0.840	21.3360
0.310	7.8740	0.850	21.5900
0.320	8.1280	0.860	21.8440
0.330	8.3820	0.870	22.0980
0.340	8.6360	0.880	22.3520
0.350	8.8900	0.890	22.6060
0.360	9.1440		
0.370	9.3980		
0.380	9.6520		
0.390	9.9060	0.900	22.8600
0.400	10.1600	0.910	23.1140
0.410	10.4140	0.920	23.3680
0.420	10.6680	0.930	23.6220
0.430	10.9220	0.940	23.8760
0.440	11.1760	0.950	24.1300
0.450	11.4300	0.960	24.3840
0.460	11.6840	0.970	24.6380
0.470	11.9380	0.980	24.8920
0.480	12.1920	0.990	25.1460
0.490	12.4460	1.000	25.4000

FRACTIONS to DECIMALS to MILLIMETERS

Fraction	Decimal	mm	Fraction	Decimal	mm
1/64	0.0156	0.3969	33/64	0.5156	13.0969
1/32	0.0312	0.7938	17/32	0.5312	13.4938
3/64	0.0469	1.1906	35/64	0.5469	13.8906
1/16	0.0625	1.5875	9/16	0.5625	14.2875
5/64	0.0781	1.9844	37/64	0.5781	14.6844
3/32	0.0938	2.3812	19/32	0.5938	15.0812
7/64	0.1094	2.7781	39/64	0.6094	15.4781
1/8	0.1250	3.1750	5/8	0.6250	15.8750
9/64	0.1406	3.5719	41/64	0.6406	16.2719
5/32	0.1562	3.9688	21/32	0.6562	16.6688
11/64	0.1719	4.3656	43/64	0.6719	17.0656
3/16	0.1875	4.7625	11/16	0.6875	17.4625
13/64	0.2031	5.1594	45/64	0.7031	17.8594
7/32	0.2188	5.5562	23/32	0.7188	18.2562
15/64	0.2344	5.9531	47/64	0.7344	18.6531
1/4	0.2500	6.3500	3/4	0.7500	19.0500
17/64	0.2656	6.7469	49/64	0.7656	19.4469
9/32	0.2812	7.1438	25/32	0.7812	19.8438
19/64	0.2969	7.5406	51/64	0.7969	20.2406
5/16	0.3125	7.9375	13/16	0.8125	20.6375
21/64	0.3281	8.3344	53/64	0.8281	21.0344
11/32	0.3438	8.7312	27/32	0.8438	21.4312
23/64	0.3594	9.1281	55/64	0.8594	21.8281
3/8	0.3750	9.5250	7/8	0.8750	22.2250
25/64	0.3906	9.9219	57/64	0.8906	22.6219
13/32	0.4062	10.3188	29/32	0.9062	23.0188
27/64	0.4219	10.7156	59/64	0.9219	23.4156
7/16	0.4375	11.1125	15/16	0.9375	23.8125
29/64	0.4531	11.5094	61/64	0.9531	24.2094
15/32	0.4688	11.9062	31/32	0.9688	24.6062
31/64	0.4844	12.3031	63/64	0.9844	25.0031
1/2	0.5000	12.7000	1	1.0000	25.4000

Safety first!

Regardless of how enthusiastic you may be about getting on with the job at hand, take the time to ensure that your safety is not jeopardized. A moment's lack of attention can result in an accident, as can failure to observe certain simple safety precautions. The possibility of an accident will always exist, and the following points should not be considered a comprehensive list of all dangers. Rather, they are intended to make you aware of the risks and to encourage a safety conscious approach to all work you carry out on your vehicle.

Essential DOs and DON'Ts

DON'T rely on a jack when working under the vehicle. Always use approved jackstands to support the weight of the vehicle and place them under the recommended lift or support points.

DON'T attempt to loosen extremely tight fasteners (i.e. wheel lug nuts) while the vehicle is on a jack - it may fall.

DON'T start the engine without first making sure that the transmission is in Neutral (or Park where applicable) and the parking brake is set.

DON'T remove the radiator cap from a hot cooling system - let it cool or cover it with a cloth and release the pressure gradually.

DON'T attempt to drain the engine oil until you are sure it has cooled to the point that it will not burn you.

DON'T touch any part of the engine or exhaust system until it has cooled sufficiently to avoid burns.

DON'T siphon toxic liquids such as gasoline, antifreeze and brake fluid by mouth, or allow them to remain on your skin.

DON'T inhale brake lining dust - it is potentially hazardous (see *Asbestos* below).

DON'T allow spilled oil or grease to remain on the floor - wipe it up before someone slips on it.

DON'T use loose fitting wrenches or other tools which may slip and cause injury.

DON'T push on wrenches when loosening or tightening nuts or bolts. Always try to pull the wrench toward you. If the situation calls for pushing the wrench away, push with an open hand to avoid scraped knuckles if the wrench should slip.

DON'T attempt to lift a heavy component alone - get someone to help you.

DON'T rush or take unsafe shortcuts to finish a job.

DON'T allow children or animals in or around the vehicle while you are working on it.

DO wear eye protection when using power tools such as a drill, sander, bench grinder, etc. and when working under a vehicle.

DO keep loose clothing and long hair well out of the way of moving parts.

DO make sure that any hoist used has a safe working load rating adequate for the job.

DO get someone to check on you periodically when working alone on a vehicle.

DO carry out work in a logical sequence and make sure that everything is correctly assembled and tightened.

DO keep chemicals and fluids tightly capped and out of the reach of children and pets.

DO remember that your vehicle's safety affects that of yourself and others. If in doubt on any point, get professional advice.

Asbestos

Certain friction, insulating, sealing, and other products - such as brake linings, brake bands, clutch linings, torque converters, gaskets, etc. - may contain asbestos. Extreme care must be taken to avoid inhalation of dust from such products, since it is hazardous to health. If in doubt, assume that they do contain asbestos.

Fire

Remember at all times that gasoline is highly flammable. Never smoke or have any kind of open flame around when working on a vehicle. But the risk does not end there. A spark caused by an electrical short circuit, by two metal surfaces contacting each other, or even by static electricity built up in your body under certain conditions, can ignite gasoline vapors, which in a confined space are highly explosive. Do not, under any circumstances, use gasoline for cleaning parts. Use an approved safety solvent.

Always disconnect the battery ground (-) cable at the battery before working on any part of the fuel system or electrical system. Never risk spilling fuel on a hot engine or exhaust component. It is strongly recommended that a fire extinguisher suitable for use on fuel and electrical fires be kept handy in the garage or workshop at all times. Never try to extinguish a fuel or electrical fire with water.

Fumes

Certain fumes are highly toxic and can quickly cause unconsciousness and even death if inhaled to any extent. Gasoline vapor falls into this category, as do the vapors from some cleaning solvents. Any draining or pouring of such volatile fluids should be done in a well ventilated area.

When using cleaning fluids and solvents, read the instructions on the container carefully. Never use materials from unmarked containers.

Never run the engine in an enclosed space, such as a garage. Exhaust fumes contain carbon monoxide, which is extremely poisonous. If you need to run the engine, always do so in the open air, or at least have the rear of the vehicle outside the work area.

If you are fortunate enough to have the use of an inspection pit, never drain or pour gasoline and never run the engine while the vehicle is over the pit. The fumes, being heavier than air, will concentrate in the pit with possibly lethal results.

The battery

Never create a spark or allow a bare light bulb near a battery. They normally give off a certain amount of hydrogen gas, which is highly explosive.

Always disconnect the battery ground (-) cable at the battery before working on the fuel or electrical systems.

If possible, loosen the filler caps or cover when charging the battery from an external source (this does not apply to sealed or maintenance-free batteries). Do not charge at an excessive rate or the battery may burst.

Take care when adding water to a non maintenance-free battery and when carrying a battery. The electrolyte, even when diluted, is very corrosive and should not be allowed to contact clothing or skin.

Always wear eye protection when cleaning the battery to prevent the caustic deposits from entering your eyes.

Household current

When using an electric power tool, inspection light, etc., which operates on household current, always make sure that the tool is correctly connected to its plug and that, where necessary, it is properly grounded. Do not use such items in damp conditions and, again, do not create a spark or apply excessive heat in the vicinity of fuel or fuel vapor.

Secondary ignition system voltage

A severe electric shock can result from touching certain parts of the ignition system (such as the spark plug wires) when the engine is running or being cranked, particularly if components are damp or the insulation is defective. In the case of an electronic ignition system, the secondary system voltage is much higher and could prove fatal.

Troubleshooting

Contents

This section provides an easy reference guide to the more common problems which may occur during the operation of your vehicle. These problems and their possible causes are grouped under headings denoting various components or systems, such as Engine, Cooling system, etc. They also refer you to the chapter and/or section which deals with the problem.

Remember that successful troubleshooting is not a mysterious black art practiced only by professional mechanics. It is simply the result of the right knowledge combined with an intelligent, systematic approach to the problem. Always work by a process of elimination, starting with the simplest solution and working through to the most complex - and never overlook the obvious. Anyone can run the gas tank dry or leave the lights on overnight, so don't assume that you are exempt from such oversights.

Finally, always establish a clear idea of why a problem has occurred and take steps to ensure that it doesn't happen again. If the electrical system fails because of a poor connection, check the other connections in the system to make sure that they don't fail as well. If a particular fuse continues to blow, find out why - don't just replace one fuse after another. Remember, failure of a small component can often be indicative of potential failure or incorrect functioning of a more important component or system.

Engine

1 Engine will not rotate when attempting to start

1 Battery terminal connections loose or corroded (Chapter 1).
2 Battery discharged or faulty (Chapter 1).
3 Automatic transmission not completely engaged in Park (Chapter 7B) or clutch not completely depressed (Chapter 8).
4 Broken, loose or disconnected wiring in the starting circuit (Chapters 5 and 12).
5 Starter motor pinion jammed in flywheel ring gear (Chapter 5).
6 Starter solenoid faulty (Chapter 5).
7 Starter motor faulty (Chapter 5).
8 Ignition switch faulty (Chapter 12).
9 Starter pinion or flywheel teeth worn or broken (Chapter 5).

2 Engine rotates but will not start

1 Fuel tank empty.
2 Battery discharged (engine rotates slowly) (Chapter 5).
3 Battery terminal connections loose or corroded (Chapter 1).
4 Leaking fuel injector(s), faulty fuel pump, pressure regulator, etc. (Chapter 4).
5 Fuel not reaching fuel rail (Chapter 4).
6 Ignition components damp or damaged (Chapter 5).

7 Worn, faulty or incorrectly gapped spark plugs (Chapter 1).
8 Broken, loose or disconnected wiring in the starting circuit (Chapter 5).
9 Broken, loose or disconnected wires at the ignition coil or faulty coil (Chapter 5).
10 Broken or stripped timing belt (Chapter 2).
11 Defective fuel pump relay and/or harness at relay (Chapter 4)

3 Engine hard to start when cold

1 Battery discharged or low (Chapter 1).
2 Malfunctioning fuel system (Chapter 4).
3 Injector(s) leaking (Chapter 4).

4 Engine hard to start when hot

1 Air filter clogged (Chapter 1).
2 Fuel not reaching the fuel injection system (Chapter 4).
3 Corroded battery connections, especially ground (Chapter 1).
4 Malfunctioning EVAP system (Chapter 6).

5 Starter motor noisy or excessively rough in engagement

1 Pinion or flywheel gear teeth worn or broken (Chapter 5).
2 Starter motor mounting bolts loose or missing (Chapter 5).

6 Engine starts but stops immediately

1 Loose or faulty electrical connections at coil or alternator (Chapter 5).
2 Insufficient fuel reaching the fuel injector(s) (Chapters 1 and 4).
3 Vacuum leak at the gasket between the intake manifold and throttle body (Chapters 1 and 4).

7 Oil puddle under engine

1 Oil pan gasket and/or oil pan drain bolt washer leaking (Chapter 2).
2 Oil pressure sending unit leaking (Chapter 2).
3 Valve cover leaking (Chapter 2).
4 Engine oil seals leaking (Chapter 2).

8 Engine lopes while idling or idles erratically

1 Vacuum leakage (Chapters 2 and 4).
2 Defective EGR valve (Chapter 6).
3 Air filter clogged (Chapter 1).
4 Fuel pump not delivering sufficient fuel

to the fuel injection system (Chapter 4).
5 Leaking head gasket (Chapter 2).
6 Timing belt and/or pulleys worn (Chapter 2).
7 Camshaft lobes worn (Chapter 2).

9 Engine misses at idle speed

1 Spark plugs worn or not gapped properly (Chapter 1).
2 Faulty spark plug wires (Chapter 1).
3 Vacuum leaks (Chapter 1).
4 Incorrect ignition timing (Chapter 1).
5 Uneven or low compression (Chapter 2).

10 Engine misses throughout the driving speed range

1 Fuel filter clogged and/or impurities in the fuel system (Chapter 1).
2 Low fuel pressure (Chapter 4).
3 Faulty or incorrectly gapped spark plugs (Chapter 1).
4 Incorrect ignition timing (Chapter 5).
5 Spark plug wires damaged and shorting out (Chapters 1 or 5).
6 Faulty emission system components (Chapter 6).
7 Low or uneven cylinder compression pressures (Chapter 2).
8 Weak or faulty ignition system (Chapter 5).
9 Vacuum leak in fuel injection system (Chapter 4), intake manifold (Chapter 2A) or vacuum hoses.

11 Engine stumbles on acceleration

1 Spark plugs fouled (Chapter 1).
2 Fuel injection system faulty (Chapter 4).
3 Fuel filter clogged (Chapters 1 and 4).
4 Incorrect ignition timing (Chapter 5).
5 Intake air leak (Chapters 2 and 4).

12 Engine surges while holding accelerator steady

1 Intake air leak (Chapter 4).
2 Fuel pump faulty (Chapter 4).
3 Loose fuel injector wire harness connectors (Chapter 4).
4 Defective ECU or information sensor (Chapter 6).

13 Engine stalls

1 Idle speed incorrect (Chapter 1).
2 Fuel filter clogged and/or water and impurities in the fuel system (Chapters 1 and 4).
3 Faulty emissions system components (Chapter 6).
4 Faulty or incorrectly gapped spark plugs (Chapter 1).

5   Faulty spark plug wires (Chapter 1).
6   Vacuum leak in the intake manifold or vacuum hoses (Chapters 2 and 4).
7   Valve clearances incorrectly set (Chapter 1).

14   Engine lacks power

1   Incorrect ignition timing (Chapter 5).
2   Faulty or incorrectly gapped spark plugs (Chapter 1).
3   Fuel injection system malfunction (Chapter 4).
4   Faulty coil (Chapter 5).
5   Brakes binding (Chapter 9).
6   Automatic transaxle fluid level incorrect (Chapter 1).
7   Clutch slipping (Chapter 8).
8   Fuel filter clogged and/or impurities in the fuel system (Chapters 1 and 4).
9   Emission control system not functioning properly (Chapter 6).
10   Low or uneven cylinder compression pressures (Chapter 2).
11   Obstructed exhaust system (Chapter 4).

15   Engine backfires

1   Emission control system not functioning properly (Chapter 6).
2   Ignition timing incorrect (Chapter 5).
3   Faulty secondary ignition system (cracked spark plug insulator and/or faulty plug wires.
4   Fuel injection system malfunctioning (Chapter 4).
5   Vacuum leak at fuel injector(s), intake manifold, air control valve or vacuum hoses (Chapters 2 and 4).
6   Valve clearances incorrectly set and/or valves sticking (Chapter 1).

16   Pinging or knocking engine sounds during acceleration or uphill

1   Incorrect grade of fuel.
2   Ignition timing incorrect (Chapter 5).
3   Fuel injection system faulty (Chapter 4).
4   Improper or damaged spark plugs or wires (Chapter 1).
5   EGR valve not functioning (Chapter 6).
6   Vacuum leak (Chapters 2 and 4).
7   Knock sensor malfunctioning (Chapter 6).

17   Engine runs with oil pressure light on

1   Low oil level (Chapter 1).
2   Short in wiring circuit (Chapter 12).
3   Faulty oil pressure sender (Chapter 2).
4   Worn engine bearings and/or oil pump (Chapter 2).

18   Engine diesels (continues to run) after switching off

Leaking fuel injector(s).

Engine electrical system

19   Battery will not hold a charge

1   Alternator drivebelt defective or not adjusted properly (Chapter 1).
2   Battery electrolyte level low (Chapter 1).
3   Battery terminals loose or corroded (Chapter 1).
4   Alternator not charging properly (Chapter 5).
5   Loose, broken or faulty wiring in the charging circuit (Chapter 5).
6   Short in vehicle wiring (Chapter 12).
7   Internally defective battery (Chapters 1 and 5).

20   Alternator light fails to go out

1   Faulty alternator or charging circuit (Chapter 5).
2   Alternator drivebelt defective or out of adjustment (Chapter 1).
3   Alternator voltage regulator inoperative (Chapter 5).

21   Alternator light fails to come on when key is turned on

1   Warning light bulb defective (Chapter 5).
2   Fault in the printed circuit, dash wiring or bulb holder (Chapter 12).

Fuel system

22   Excessive fuel consumption

1   Dirty or clogged air filter element (Chapter 1).
2   Incorrectly set ignition timing (Chapters 1 and 5).
3   Emissions system not functioning properly (Chapter 6).
4   Fuel injection system malfunctioning (Chapter 4).
5   Low tire pressure or incorrect tire size (Chapter 1).

23   Fuel leakage and/or fuel odor

1   Leaking fuel feed or return line (Chapters 1 and 4).
2   Tank overfilled.
3   Evaporative canister filter clogged (Chapters 1 and 6).
4   Fuel injectors faulty (Chapter 4).

Cooling system

24   Overheating

1   Insufficient coolant in system (Chapter 1).
2   Radiator core blocked or grille restricted (Chapter 3).
3   Thermostat faulty (Chapter 3).
4   Electric cooling fan circuit problem (Chapter 3).
5   Radiator cap not maintaining proper pressure (Chapter 3).
6   Ignition timing incorrect (Chapter 5).

25   Overcooling

1   Faulty thermostat (Chapter 3).
2   Inaccurate temperature gauge sending unit (Chapter 3).
3   Electric cooling fan circuit problem (Chapter 3).

26   External coolant leakage

1   Deteriorated/damaged hoses; loose clamps (Chapters 1 and 3).
2   Water pump defective (Chapter 3).
3   Leakage from radiator core or coolant reservoir bottle (Chapter 3).
4   Engine drain or water jacket core plugs leaking (Chapter 2).

27   Internal coolant leakage

1   Leaking cylinder head gasket (Chapter 2).
2   Cracked cylinder bore or cylinder head (Chapter 2).

28   Coolant loss

1   Too much coolant in system (Chapter 1).
2   Coolant boiling away because of overheating (Chapter 3).
3   Internal or external leakage (Chapter 3).
4   Faulty radiator cap (Chapter 3).

29   Poor coolant circulation

1   Inoperative water pump (Chapter 3).
2   Restriction in cooling system (Chapters 1 and 3).
3   Thermostat sticking (Chapter 3).

Clutch

30   Pedal travels to floor - no pressure or very little resistance

1   No fluid in reservoir (Chapter 1)

2   Faulty clutch master cylinder, release cylinder or hydraulic line (Chapter 8).
3   Broken release bearing or fork (Chapter 8).

31   Unable to select gears

1   Faulty transaxle (Chapter 7).
2   Faulty clutch disc (Chapter 8).
3   Release lever and bearing not assembled properly (Chapter 8).
4   Faulty pressure plate (Chapter 8).
5   Pressure plate-to-flywheel bolts loose (Chapter 8).

32   Clutch slips (engine speed increases with no increase in vehicle speed)

1   Clutch plate worn (Chapter 8).
2   Clutch plate is oil soaked by leaking rear main seal (Chapter 8).
3   Clutch plate not seated. It may take 30 or 40 normal starts for a new one to seat.
4   Warped pressure plate or flywheel (Chapter 8).
5   Weak diaphragm spring (Chapter 8).
6   Clutch plate overheated. Allow to cool.

33   Grabbing (chattering) as clutch is engaged

1   Oil on clutch plate lining, burned or glazed facings (Chapter 8).
2   Worn or loose engine or transaxle mounts (Chapters 2 and 7).
3   Worn splines on clutch plate hub (Chapter 8).
4   Warped pressure plate or flywheel (Chapter 8).
5   Burned or smeared resin on flywheel or pressure plate (Chapter 8).

34   Transaxle rattling (clicking)

1   Release lever loose (Chapter 8).
2   Low engine idle speed (Chapter 5).

35   Noise in clutch area

1   Fork shaft improperly installed (Chapter 8).
2   Faulty bearing (Chapter 8).

36   Clutch pedal stays on floor

1   Faulty clutch master or release cylinder (Chapter 8).
2   Broken release bearing or fork (Chapter 8).

37   High pedal effort

1   Piston binding in bore of clutch master or release cylinder (Chapter 8).
2   Pressure plate faulty (Chapter 8).

Manual transaxle

38   Knocking noise at low speeds

1   Worn driveaxle constant velocity (CV) joints (Chapter 8).
2   Worn driveaxle bore in differential case (Chapter 7A).*

39   Noise most pronounced when turning

Differential gear noise (Chapter 7A).*

40   Clunk on acceleration or deceleration

1   Loose engine or transaxle mounts (Chapters 2 and 7A).
2   Worn differential pinion shaft in case.*
3   Worn driveaxle bore in differential case (Chapter 7A).*
4   Worn or damaged driveaxle inboard CV joints (Chapter 8).

41   Clicking noise in turns

Worn or damaged outboard CV joint (Chapter 8).

42   Vibration

1   Rough wheel bearing (Chapters 1 and 10).
2   Damaged driveaxle (Chapter 8).
3   Out-of-round tires (Chapter 1).
4   Tire out of balance (Chapters 1 and 10).
5   Worn CV joint (Chapter 8).

43   Noisy in neutral with engine running

1   Damaged input gear bearing (Chapter 7A).*
2   Damaged clutch release bearing (Chapter 8).

44   Noisy in one particular gear

1   Damaged or worn constant mesh gears (Chapter 7A).*
2   Damaged or worn synchronizers (Chapter 7A).*

3   Bent reverse fork (Chapter 7A).*
4   Damaged fourth speed gear or output gear (Chapter 7A).*
5   Worn or damaged reverse idler gear or idler bushing (Chapter 7A).*

45   Noisy in all gears

1   Insufficient lubricant (Chapter 7A).
2   Damaged or worn bearings (Chapter 7A).*
3   Worn or damaged input gear shaft and/or output gear shaft (Chapter 7A).*

46   Slips out of gear

1   Worn or improperly adjusted linkage (Chapter 7A).
2   Transaxle loose on engine (Chapter 7A).
3   Shift linkage does not work freely, binds (Chapter 7A).
4   Input gear bearing retainer broken or loose (Chapter 7A).*
5   Dirt between clutch cover and engine block (Chapter 7A).
6   Worn shift fork (Chapter 7A).*

47   Leaks lubricant

1   Driveaxle oil seals worn (Chapter 7).
2   Excessive amount of lubricant in transaxle (Chapters 1 and 7A).
3   Loose or broken input gear shaft bearing retainer (Chapter 7A).*
4   Input gear bearing retainer O-ring and/or lip seal damaged (Chapter 7A).*

48   Locked in gear

Lock pin or interlock pin missing (Chapter 7A).*

* Although the corrective action necessary to remedy the symptoms described is beyond the scope of the home mechanic, the above information should be helpful in isolating the cause of the condition so that the owner can communicate clearly with a professional mechanic.

Automatic transaxle

Note: Due to the complexity of the automatic transaxle, it is difficult for the home mechanic to properly diagnose and service this component. For problems other than the following, the vehicle should be taken to a dealer or transmission shop.

49   Fluid leakage

1   Automatic transmission fluid is a deep red color. Fluid leaks should not be confused with engine oil, which can easily be blown

onto the transaxle by air flow.

2   To pinpoint a leak, first remove all built-up dirt and grime from the transaxle housing with degreasing agents and/or steam cleaning. Then drive the vehicle at low speeds so air flow will not blow the leak far from its source. Raise the vehicle and determine where the leak is coming from. Common areas of leakage are:

a) *Pan (Chapters 1 and 7)*
b) *Dipstick tube (Chapters 1 and 7)*
c) *Transaxle oil lines (Chapter 7)*
d) *Speed sensor (Chapter 7)*

50   Transaxle fluid brown or has a burned smell

Transaxle fluid overheated (Chapter 1).

51   General shift mechanism problems

1   Chapter 7, Part B, deals with checking and adjusting the shift linkage on automatic transaxles. Common problems which may be attributed to poorly adjusted linkage are:

a) *Engine starting in gears other than Park or Neutral.*
b) *Indicator on shifter pointing to a gear other than the one actually being used.*
c) *Vehicle moves when in Park.*

2   Refer to Chapter 7B for the shift linkage adjustment procedure.

52   Transaxle will not downshift with accelerator pedal pressed to the floor

Kick-down solenoid faulty (Chapter 7B).

53   Engine will start in gears other than Park or Neutral

Neutral start switch malfunctioning (Chapter 7B).

54   Transaxle slips, shifts roughly, is noisy or has no drive in forward or reverse gears

There are many probable causes for the above problems, but the home mechanic should be concerned with only fluid level and fluid and filter condition. Before taking the vehicle to a repair shop, check the level and condition of the fluid as described in Chapter 1. Correct the fluid level as necessary or change the fluid and filter if needed. If the problem persists, have a professional diagnose the cause.

Driveaxles

55   Clicking noise in turns

Worn or damaged outboard CV joint (Chapter 8).

56   Shudder or vibration during acceleration

1   Excessive toe-in (Chapter 10).
2   Incorrect spring heights (Chapter 10).
3   Worn or damaged inboard or outboard CV joints (Chapter 8).
4   Sticking inboard CV joint assembly (Chapter 8).

57   Vibration at highway speeds

1   Out of balance front wheels and/or tires (Chapters 1 and 10).
2   Out of round front tires (Chapters 1 and 10).
3   Worn CV joint(s) (Chapter 8).

Brakes

Note: *Before assuming that a brake problem exists, make sure that:*

a) *The tires are in good condition and properly inflated (Chapter 1).*
b) *The front end alignment is correct (Chapter 10).*
c) *The vehicle is not loaded with weight in an unequal manner.*

58   Vehicle pulls to one side during braking

1   Incorrect tire pressures (Chapter 1).
2   Front end out of line (have the front end aligned).
3   Front, or rear, tires not matched to one another.
4   Restricted brake lines or hoses (Chapter 9).
5   Malfunctioning drum brake or caliper assembly (Chapter 9).
6   Loose suspension parts (Chapter 10).
7   Loose calipers (Chapter 9).
8   Excessive wear of brake shoe or pad material or disc/drum on one side.

59   Noise (high-pitched squeal when the brakes are applied)

Disc brake pads worn out (Chapter 9).

60   Brake roughness or chatter (pedal pulsates)

1   Excessive lateral runout (Chapter 9).

2   Uneven pad wear (Chapter 9).
3   Defective disc (Chapter 9).

61   Excessive brake pedal effort required to stop vehicle

1   Malfunctioning power brake booster (Chapter 9).
2   Partial system failure (Chapter 9).
3   Excessively worn pads or shoes (Chapter 9).
4   Piston in caliper or wheel cylinder stuck or sluggish (Chapter 9).
5   Brake pads or shoes contaminated with oil or grease (Chapter 9).
6   New pads or shoes installed and not yet seated. It will take a while for the new material to seat against the disc or drum.

62   Excessive brake pedal travel

1   Partial brake system failure (Chapter 9).
2   Insufficient fluid in master cylinder (Chapters 1 and 9).
3   Air trapped in system (Chapters 1 and 9).

63   Dragging brakes

1   Incorrect adjustment of brake light switch (Chapter 9).
2   Master cylinder pistons not returning correctly (Chapter 9).
3   Restricted brakes lines or hoses (Chapters 1 and 9).
4   Incorrect parking brake adjustment (Chapter 9).

64   Grabbing or uneven braking action

1   Brake pads or shoes worn out (Chapter 9).
2   Malfunction of proportioning valve (Chapter 9).
3   Binding brake pedal mechanism (Chapter 9).

65   Brake pedal feels spongy when depressed

1   Air in hydraulic lines (Chapter 9).
2   Master cylinder mounting bolts loose (Chapter 9).
3   Master cylinder defective (Chapter 9).

66   Brake pedal travels to the floor with little resistance

1   Little or no fluid in the master cylinder

reservoir caused by a leak in the system (Chapter 9).
2   Loose, damaged or disconnected brake lines (Chapter 9).
3   Defective master cylinder (Chapter 9).

67   Parking brake does not hold

Parking brake linkage improperly adjusted (Chapters 1 and 9).

Suspension and steering systems

Note: *Before attempting to diagnose the suspension and steering systems, perform the following preliminary checks:*
a) *Tires for wrong pressure and uneven wear.*
b) *Steering universal joints from the column to the steering gear for loose connectors or wear.*
c) *Front and rear suspension and the steering gear assembly for loose or damaged parts.*
d) *Out-of-round or out-of-balance tires, bent rims and loose and/or rough wheel bearings.*

68   Vehicle pulls to one side

1   Mismatched or uneven tires (Chapter 10).
2   Broken or sagging springs (Chapter 10).
3   Wheel alignment (Chapter 10).
4   Front brake dragging (Chapter 9).

69   Abnormal or excessive tire wear

1   Wheel alignment (Chapter 10).
2   Sagging or broken springs (Chapter 10).
3   Tire out of balance (Chapter 10).
4   Worn strut damper (Chapter 10).
5   Overloaded vehicle.
6   Tires not rotated regularly.

70   Wheel makes a thumping noise

1   Blister or bump on tire (Chapter 10).
2   Worn strut damper (Chapter 10).

71   Shimmy, shake or vibration

1   Tire or wheel out-of-balance or out-of-round (Chapter 10).
2   Loose or worn front hub or wheel bearings (Chapters 1, 8 and 10).
3   Worn tie-rod ends (Chapter 10).
4   Worn lower balljoints (Chapters 1 and 10).
5   Excessive wheel runout (Chapter 10).
6   Blister or bump on tire (Chapter 10).

72   Hard steering

1   Lack of lubrication at balljoints and tie-rod ends (Chapters 1 and 10).
2   Front wheel alignment (Chapter 10).
3   Low tire pressure(s) (Chapters 1 and 10).

73   Poor returnability of steering to center

1   Lack of lubrication at balljoints and tie-rod ends (Chapters 1 and 10).
2   Binding in balljoints (Chapter 10).
3   Binding in steering column (Chapter 10).
4   Lack of lubricant in steering gear assembly (Chapter 10).
5   Front wheel alignment (Chapter 10).

74   Abnormal noise at the front end

1   Lack of lubrication at balljoints and tie-rod ends (Chapters 1 and 10).
2   Damaged shock absorber mount (Chapter 10).
3   Worn control arm bushings or tie-rod ends (Chapter 10).
4   Loose stabilizer bar (Chapter 10).
5   Loose wheel nuts (Chapters 1 and 10).
6   Loose suspension bolts (Chapter 10)

75   Wander or poor steering stability

1   Mismatched or uneven tires (Chapter 10).
2   Lack of lubrication at balljoints and tie-rod ends (Chapters 1 and 10).
3   Worn strut assemblies (Chapter 10).
4   Loose stabilizer bar (Chapter 10).
5   Broken or sagging springs (Chapter 10).
6   Wheels out of alignment (Chapter 10).

76   Erratic steering when braking

1   Front hub bearings worn (Chapter 10).
2   Broken or sagging springs (Chapter 10).
3   Leaking wheel cylinder or caliper (Chapter 10).
4   Warped discs or drums (Chapter 10).

77   Excessive pitching and/or rolling around corners or during braking

1   Loose stabilizer bar (Chapter 10).
2   Worn strut assemblies or mountings (Chapter 10).
3   Broken or sagging springs (Chapter 10).
4   Overloaded vehicle.

78   Suspension bottoms

1   Overloaded vehicle.
2   Worn strut assemblies (Chapter 10).
3   Incorrect, broken or sagging springs (Chapter 10).

79   Cupped tires

1   Front wheel or rear wheel alignment (Chapter 10).
2   Worn strut assemblies (Chapter 10).
3   Wheel bearings worn (Chapter 10).
4   Excessive tire or wheel runout (Chapter 10).
5   Worn balljoints (Chapter 10).

80   Excessive tire wear on outside edge

1   Inflation pressures incorrect (Chapter 1).
2   Excessive speed in turns.
3   Front end alignment incorrect (excessive toe-in). Have professionally aligned.
4   Suspension arm bent or twisted (Chapter 10).

81   Excessive tire wear on inside edge

1   Inflation pressures incorrect (Chapter 1).
2   Front end alignment incorrect (toe-out). Have professionally aligned.
3   Loose or damaged steering or suspension components (Chapter 10).

82   Tire tread worn in one place

1   Tires out of balance.
2   Damaged or buckled wheel. Inspect and replace if necessary.
3   Defective tire (Chapter 1).

83   Excessive play or looseness in steering system

1   Front hub bearing(s) worn (Chapter 10).
2   Tie-rod end loose (Chapter 10).
3   Steering gear loose or worn (Chapter 10).
4   Worn or loose steering shaft joint (Chapter 10).

84   Rattling or clicking noise in steering gear

1   Steering gear loose (Chapter 10).
2   Steering gear defective.

Chapter 1
Tune-up and routine maintenance

Contents

Specifications

Recommended lubricants and fluids

Note: *Manufacturers occasionally upgrade their fluid and lubricant specifications. Check with your local auto parts store for the most current recommendations.*

Engine oil	
Type	API "certified for gasoline engines"
Viscosity	See accompanying chart
Automatic transmission fluid	Dexron III automatic transmission fluid
Manual transaxle lubricant	SAE 75W/90 gear oil
Brake fluid type	DOT 3 brake fluid
Power steering system fluid	
2000 and earlier models	Dexron III automatic transmission fluid
2001 and later models	PSF-3 power steering fluid
Fuel type	Unleaded gasoline, 87 octane or higher
Coolant	50/50 mixture of ethylene glycol for aluminum radiator-based antifreeze and water

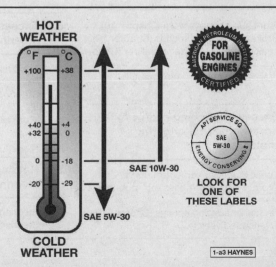

Engine oil viscosity chart - for best fuel economy and cold starting, select the lowest SAE viscosity grade for the expected temperature range

1-a3 HAYNES

Capacities*

Engine oil, with filter change	4.5 qts (4.2 liters)
Automatic transaxle**	8.2 qts (7.7 liters)
Manual transaxle	2.3 qts (2.1 liters)
Coolant	6.4 qts (6.0 liters)

*All capacities approximate. Fill below total capacity, then add as necessary to bring to appropriate level.

**Listed are total new-unit fill capacities (less torque converter). Refill after draining is substantially less. The best way to determine the amount of fluid to add during a routine fluid change is to measure the amount drained.

Ignition system

Spark plug type and gap
2000 and earlier
Type	NGK BKR5ES-11 or Champion RC10YCA
Gap	0.039 to 0.043-inch (1.0 to 1.1 mm)

2001
Type	NGK PFR5N-11 or Champion RC10PYP4
Gap	0.039 to 0.043-inch (1.0 to 1.1 mm)
Spark plug wire resistance	10 K-ohms per 12 inches of length
Engine firing order	1-3-4-2

Ignition timing
2000 and earlier	5 to 15 degrees BTDC
2001	4 to 13 degrees BTDC

Cooling system

Thermostat rating
Starts to open	176 to 183-degrees F (80-degrees C)
Fully open	203-degrees F (94-degrees C)

Accessory drivebelt deflection

Power steering pump	1/4 to 3/8-inch (6.3 to 9.5 mm)
Alternator	1/4 to 5/16-inch (6.3 to 8.5 mm)
Air conditioning compressor	5/16-inch (8 mm)

Brakes

Disc brake pad lining thickness (minimum)	1/16-inch (1.5 mm)
Drum brake shoe lining thickness (minimum)	1/16-inch (1.5 mm)
Parking brake adjustment	8 clicks

Torque specifications

	Ft-lbs (unless otherwise indicated)	Nm
Oil drain plug	25 to 33	35 to 45
Automatic transaxle		
Drain plug	25 to 32	33 to 44
Fluid pan bolts	84 to 96 in-lbs	9.4 to 10.8
Manual transaxle		
Filler plug	33	44
Drain plug	29	39
Spark plugs	168 in-lbs	18
Wheel lug nuts	65 to 80	88 to 108

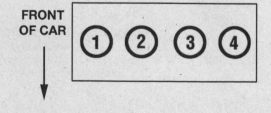

FRONT OF CAR

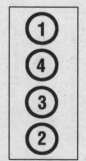

Engine cylinder numbering and coil pack terminal locations

Typical engine compartment layout (2000 and earlier model)

1	Brake master cylinder reservoir	6	Ignition coil pack	11	Engine oil filler cap
2	Fuse/relay panel	7	Spark plug and wire boot cover	12	Windshield washer fluid reservoir
3	Air filter housing	8	Upper radiator hose	13	Power steering fluid reservoir
4	Battery	9	Engine oil dipstick	14	Engine coolant reservoir
5	Automatic transaxle fluid dipstick	10	Radiator cap		

Typical engine compartment layout (2001 model)

1	Brake master cylinder reservoir	6	Ignition coil pack	11	Engine oil filler cap
2	Fuse/relay panel	7	Spark plug and wire boot cover	12	Engine coolant reservoir
3	Air filter housing	8	Upper radiator hose	13	Windshield washer fluid reservoir
4	Battery	9	Engine oil dipstick	14	Power steering fluid reservoir
5	Automatic transaxle fluid dipstick	10	Radiator cap		

Typical engine compartment underside components (2000 and earlier model)

1	Brake line	4	Transaxle drain plug	6	Engine oil drain plug
2	Front brake caliper	5	Exhaust system	7	Engine oil filter
3	Outer driveaxle boot				

Typical engine compartment underside components (2001 model)

1	Brake hose	4	Transaxle drain plug	6	Engine oil drain plug
2	Front brake caliper	5	Exhaust system	7	Brake hose
3	Outer driveaxle boot				

Typical rear underside components (2000 and earlier models)

1	Fuel tank	3	Muffler	5	Stabilizer bar
2	Brake drum	4	Strut and spring assembly		

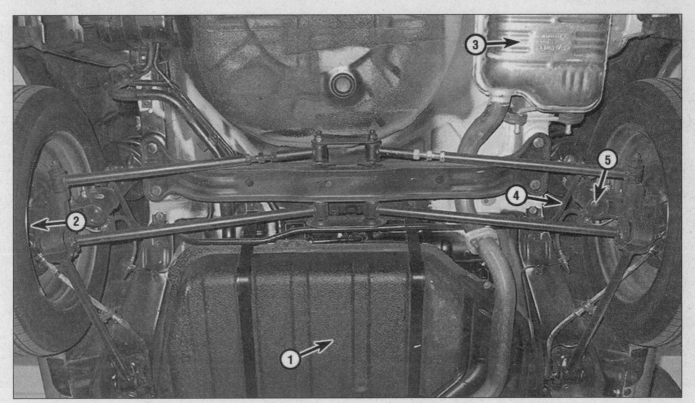

Typical rear underside components (2001 model)

1	Fuel tank	3	Muffler	5	Strut and spring assembly
2	Brake drum	4	Stabilizer bar		

Hyundai Elantra
Maintenance schedule

The maintenance intervals in this manual are provided with the assumption that you, not the dealer, will be doing the work. These are the minimum maintenance intervals recommended by the factory for vehicles that are driven daily. If you wish to keep your vehicle in peak condition at all times, you may wish to perform some of these procedures even more often. Because frequent maintenance enhances the efficiency, performance and resale value of your car, we encourage you to do so. If you drive in dusty areas, tow a trailer, idle or drive at low speeds for extended periods or drive for short distances (less than four miles) in below freezing temperatures, shorter intervals are also recommended.

When your vehicle is new, follow the maintenance schedule to the letter, record the maintenance performed in your owners manual and keep all receipts to protect the new vehicle warranty. In many cases, the initial maintenance check is done at no cost to the owner.

Every 250 miles or weekly, whichever comes first

Check the engine oil level (Section 4)
Check the engine coolant level (Section 4)
Check the windshield washer fluid level (Section 4)
Check the brake and clutch fluid level (Section 4)
Check the tires and tire pressures (Section 5)

Every 3000 miles or 3 months, whichever comes first

All items listed above plus:
Check the power steering fluid level (Section 6)
Check the automatic transaxle fluid level (Section 7)
Change the engine oil and oil filter (Section 8)

Every 7500 miles or 6 months, whichever comes first

All items listed above plus:
Seat belt check (Section 9)
Inspect and replace, if necessary, the windshield wiper blades (Section 10)
Check and service the battery (Section 11)
Check and adjust, if necessary, the engine drivebelts (Section 12)
Inspect and replace, if necessary, all underhood hoses (Section 13)
Check the cooling system (Section 14)
Rotate the tires (Section 15)

Every 15,000 miles or 12 months, whichever comes first

All items listed above plus:
Inspect the brake system (Section 16)*
Check the manual transaxle lubricant level (Section 17)*

Every 30,000 miles or 24 months, whichever comes first

All items listed above plus:
Replace the air filter (Section 18)*
Replace the spark plugs (Section 19)
Inspect and replace, if necessary, the spark plug wires (Section 20)
Check and, if necessary, replace the PCV valve (Section 21)
Service the cooling system (drain, flush and refill) (Section 22)
Replace the brake fluid (Section 23)
Inspect the suspension, steering components and driveaxle boots (Section 24)*
Change the automatic transaxle fluid (Section 25)**
Change the manual transaxle lubricant (Section 26)
Exhaust system check (Section 27)
Inspect the fuel system (Section 28)

Every 60,000 miles or 48 months, whichever comes first

Replace the fuel filter (Section 29)
Replace the timing belt (Chapter 2A and 2B)

*This item is affected by "severe" operating conditions as described below. If your vehicle is operated under "severe" conditions, perform all maintenance indicated with a * at 7500 mile/6 month intervals. Severe conditions are indicated if you mainly operate your vehicle under one or more of the following conditions:*

Operating in dusty areas
Towing a trailer
Idling for extended periods and/or low speed operation
Operating when outside temperatures remain below freezing and when most trips are less than five miles

**If operated under one or more of the following conditions, change the automatic transaxle fluid every 15,000 miles:*

In heavy city traffic where the outside temperature regularly reaches 90-degrees F (32-degrees C) or higher
In hilly or mountainous terrain
Operating in dusty areas
Towing a trailer
Idling for extended periods and/or low speed operation
Operating when outside temperatures remain below freezing and when most trips are less than five miles
In heavy city traffic or where the outside temperature regularly reaches 90-degrees F (32-degrees C) or higher

2   Introduction

This Chapter is designed to help the home mechanic maintain his/her car for peak performance, economy, safety and long life.

The following Sections deal specifically with each item on the maintenance schedule. Visual checks, adjustments, component replacement and other helpful items are included. Refer to the accompanying photos of the engine compartment and the underside of the vehicle for the location of various components.

Servicing your vehicle in accordance with the mileage/time maintenance schedule and the following Sections will provide it with a planned maintenance program that should result in a long and reliable service life. This is a comprehensive plan, so maintaining some items but not others at the specified service intervals will not produce the same results.

As you service your car, you will discover that many of the procedures can - and should - be grouped together because of the nature of the particular procedure you're performing or because of the close proximity of two otherwise unrelated components to one another. For example, if the vehicle is raised for chassis lubrication, you should inspect the exhaust, suspension, steering and fuel systems while you're under the vehicle. When you're rotating the tires, it makes good sense to check the brakes and wheel bearings since the wheels are already removed.

Finally, let's suppose you have to borrow or rent a torque wrench. Even if you only need to tighten the spark plugs, you might as well check the torque of as many critical fasteners as time allows.

The first step of this maintenance program is to prepare you before the actual work begins. Read through all Sections pertinent to the procedures you're planning to do, then make a list of and gather together all the parts and tools you will need to do the job. If it looks as if you might run into problems during a particular segment of some procedure, seek advice from your local parts man or dealer service department.

Owner's Manual and VECI label information

Your vehicle owner's manual was written for your year and model and contains very specific information on component locations, specifications, fuse ratings, part numbers, etc. The Owner's Manual is an important resource for the do-it-yourselfer to have if one was not supplied with your vehicle, it can generally be ordered from a dealer parts department.

Among other important information, the Vehicle Emissions Control Information (VECI) label contains specifications and procedures for tune-up adjustments (if applicable) and sparks plugs (see Chapter 6 for more information on the VECI label). The information on this label is the *exact* maintenance data rec-

4.2 The engine oil dipstick (arrow) is located on the front side of the engine

ommended by the manufacturer. This data often varies by intended operating altitude, local emissions regulations, month of manufacture, etc.

This Chapter contains procedural details, safety information and more ambitious maintenance intervals than you might find in manufacturer's literature. However, you may find procedures or specifications in your Owner's Manual or VECI label that differ with what's printed here. In these cases, the Owner's Manual or VECI label can be considered correct, since it is specific to your particular vehicle.

3   Tune-up general information

The term tune-up is used in this manual to represent a combination of individual operations rather than one specific procedure.

If, from the time the vehicle is new, the routine maintenance schedule is followed closely and frequent checks are made of fluid levels and high wear items, as suggested throughout this manual, the engine will be kept in relatively good running condition and the need for additional work will be minimized.

More likely than not, however, there will be times when the engine is running poorly due to lack of regular maintenance. This is even more likely if a used vehicle, which has not received regular and frequent maintenance checks, is purchased. In such cases, an engine tune-up will be needed outside of the regular routine maintenance intervals.

The first step in any tune-up or engine diagnosis to help correct a poor running engine would be a cylinder compression check. A check of the engine compression (see Chapter 2 Part B) will give valuable information regarding the overall performance of many internal components and should be used as a basis for tune-up and repair procedures. If, for instance, a compression check indicates serious internal engine wear, a conventional tune-up will not help the running condition of the engine and would be a waste of time and money. Because of its impor-

tance, someone should perform compression checking with the proper compression testing gauge and the knowledge to use it properly.

The following series of operations are those most often needed to bring a generally poor running engine back into a proper state of tune.

Minor tune-up

Check all engine related fluids (Section 4)
Clean, inspect and test the battery (Section 11)
Check and adjust the drivebelts (Section 12)
Check all underhood hoses (Section 13)
Check the cooling system (Section 14)
Check the air filter (Section 18)
Inspect the spark plug wires and ignition coil (Section 20)

Major tune-up

All items listed under minor tune-up, plus . . .

Replace the air filter (Section 18)
Replace the spark plugs (Section 19)
Replace the spark plug wires (Section 20)
Check the fuel system (Section 28)

4   Fluid level checks (every 250 miles or weekly)

1   Fluids are an essential part of the lubrication, cooling, brake, clutch and other systems. Because these fluids gradually become depleted and/or contaminated during normal operation of the vehicle, they must be periodically replenished. See *Recommended lubricants, fluids and capacities* at the beginning of this Chapter before adding fluid to any of the following components. **Note:** *The vehicle must be on level ground before fluid levels can be checked.*

Engine oil

Refer to illustrations 4.2, 4.4 and 4.6
2   The engine oil level is checked with a dipstick located at the right rear of the engine **(see illustration)**. The dipstick extends through a metal tube from which it protrudes down into the engine oil pan.

1

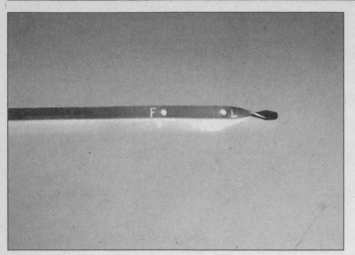

4.4 The oil level should be between the two marks on the dipstick - if it isn't, add enough oil to bring the level to or near the upper line (it takes one quart to raise the level from the lower mark to the upper mark)

4.6 The threaded oil filler cap (arrow) is located on the valve cover - to prevent dirt from contaminating the engine, always make sure the area around this opening is clean before unscrewing the cap counterclockwise

3   The oil level should be checked before the vehicle has been driven, or about 5 minutes after the engine has been shut off. If the oil is checked immediately after driving the vehicle, some of the oil will remain in the upper engine components, producing an inaccurate reading on the dipstick.

4   Pull the dipstick from the tube and wipe all the oil from the end with a clean rag or paper towel. Insert the clean dipstick all the way back into its metal tube and pull it out again. Observe the oil at the end of the dipstick. At its highest point, the level should be between the upper and lower marks **(see illustration)**.

5   It takes one quart of oil to raise the level from the lower mark to the upper mark on the dipstick. Do not allow the level to drop below the lower mark or oil starvation may cause engine damage. Conversely, overfilling the engine (adding oil above the upper mark) may cause oil-fouled spark plugs, oil leaks or oil seal failures.

6   Remove the threaded cap from the valve cover to add oil **(see illustration)**. Use a funnel to prevent spills. After adding the oil, install the filler cap hand tight. Start the engine and look carefully for any small leaks around the oil filter or drain plug. Stop the engine and check the oil level again after it has had sufficient time to drain from the upper block and cylinder head galleys.

7   Checking the oil level is an important preventive maintenance step. A continually dropping oil level indicates oil leakage through damaged seals, from loose connections, or past worn rings or valve guides. If the oil looks milky in color or has water droplets in it, a cylinder head gasket may be blown or the oil cooler could be leaking. The engine should be checked immediately. The condition of the oil should also be checked. Each time you check the oil level, slide your thumb and index finger up the dipstick before

wiping off the oil. If you see small dirt or metal particles clinging to the dipstick, the oil should be changed (see Section 8).

Engine coolant

Warning: *Do not allow antifreeze to come in contact with your skin or painted surfaces of the vehicle. Rinse off spills immediately with plenty of water. Antifreeze is highly toxic if ingested. Never leave antifreeze lying around in an open container or in puddles on the floor; children and pets are attracted by its sweet smell and may drink it. Check with local authorities on disposing of used anti-freeze. Many communities have collection centers, which will see that antifreeze is disposed of safely.*

Note: *Non-toxic antifreeze is now manufactured and available at local auto parts stores, but even this type should be disposed of properly.*

8   All vehicles covered by this manual are equipped with a pressurized coolant-recovery system. A coolant reservoir located in the front corner of the engine compartment is connected by a hose to the base of the radiator filler neck. If the coolant heats up during engine operation, coolant can escape through the pressurized filler cap, then through the connecting hose into the reservoir. As the engine cools, the coolant is automatically drawn back into the cooling system to maintain the correct level.

9   The coolant level in the reservoir should be checked regularly. The level must be between the MAX and MIN lines on the reservoir tank. The level will vary with the temperature of the engine. When the engine is cold, the coolant level should be at or slightly above the lower mark on the dipstick or tank. Once the engine has warmed up, the level should be at or near the upper mark. If it isn't, allow the fluid in the tank to cool, then

remove the dipstick or cap from the reservoir and add coolant to bring the level up to the upper line. **Caution:** *Use only ethylene glycol type coolant and water in the mixture ratio recommended by your owner's manual. Do not use supplemental inhibitors or additives. If only a small amount of coolant is required to bring the system up to the proper level, water can be used. However, repeated additions of water will dilute the recommended antifreeze and water solution. In order to maintain the proper ratio of antifreeze and water, it is advisable to top up the coolant level with the correct mixture. Refer to your owner's manual for the recommended ratio.*

10   If the coolant level drops within a short time after replenishment, there may be a leak in the system. Inspect the radiator, hoses, engine coolant filler cap, drain plugs and water pump. If no leak is evident, have the radiator cap pressure tested. **Warning:** *Never remove the radiator cap or the coolant recovery reservoir cap when the engine is running or has just been shut down, because the cooling system is hot. Escaping steam and scalding liquid could cause serious injury.*

11   If it is necessary to open the radiator cap, wait until the system has cooled completely, then wrap a thick cloth around the cap and turn it to the first stop. If any steam escapes, wait until the system has cooled further, then remove the cap.

12   When checking the coolant level, always note its condition. It should be relatively clear. If it is brown or rust colored, the system should be drained, flushed and refilled. Even if the coolant appears to be normal, the corrosion inhibitors wear out with use, so it must be replaced at the specified intervals.

13   Do not allow antifreeze to come in contact with your skin or painted surfaces of the vehicle. Flush contacted areas immediately with plenty of water.

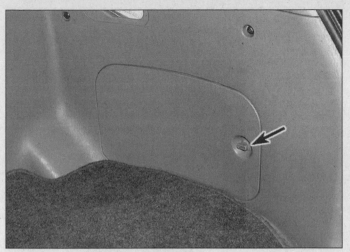

4.14a The rear window washer fluid reservoir is located behind a cover; turn the knob (arrow) to remove it

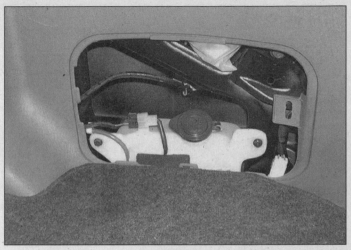

4.14b Flip up the cap to add fluid to the rear window washer reservoir

Washer fluid

Refer to illustrations 4.14a and 4.14

14 Fluid for the windshield washer system is stored in a plastic reservoir, which is located in the front corner of the engine compartment. Check the windshield washer float in the reservoir filler neck to make sure it is near the top of the neck. The rear window fluid reservoir is located behind a panel in the right side of the luggage compartment **(see illustrations)**. Make sure the level is near the top of the filler neck. In milder climates, plain water can be used to top up the reservoir, but the reservoir should be kept no more than 2/3 full to allow for expansion should the water freeze. In colder climates, the use of a specially designed windshield washer fluid, available at your dealer and any auto parts store, will help lower the freezing point of the fluid. Mix the solution with water in accordance with the manufacturer's directions on the container. Do not use regular antifreeze. It will damage the vehicle's paint.

Brake and clutch fluid

Refer to illustration 4.16

15 The brake master cylinder is mounted on the front of the power booster unit and the clutch master cylinder (on manual transmission models) is next to it on the firewall within the engine compartment.

16 To check the fluid level of the brake or clutch master cylinder, simply look at the MAX and MIN marks on the reservoir **(see illustration)**. The level should be between the two marks.

17 If the level is low, wipe the top of the reservoir cover with a clean rag to prevent contamination of the brake system before lifting the cap.

18 Add only the specified brake fluid to the brake or clutch reservoir (refer to *Recommended lubricants and fluids* at the front of this Chapter or to your owner's manual). Mixing different types of brake fluid can damage the system. Fill the brake master cylinder

reservoir to the MAX line. **Warning:** *Use caution when filling the reservoir - brake fluid can harm your eyes and damage painted surfaces. Do not use brake fluid that has been opened for more than one year or has been left open. Brake fluid absorbs moisture from the air. Excess moisture can cause a dangerous loss of braking.*

19 While the reservoir cap is removed, inspect the master cylinder reservoir for contamination. If deposits, dirt particles or water droplets are present, the system should be drained and refilled (see Chapters 8 or 9).

20 After filling the reservoir to the proper level, make sure the lid is properly seated to prevent fluid leakage and/or system pressure loss.

21 The brake fluid in the master cylinder will drop slightly as the brake pads at each wheel wear down during normal operation. If the master cylinder requires repeated replenishing to keep it at the proper level, this is an indication of leakage in the brake system, which should be corrected immediately. Check all brake lines and connections, along with the wheel cylinders and booster (see

Section 16 for more information). A drop in the clutch reservoir level indicates a leak in the clutch hydraulic system (see Chapter 8).

22 If, upon checking the brake master cylinder fluid level, you discover an empty or nearly empty reservoir, the brake system should be bled (see Chapter 9).

5 Tire and tire pressure checks (every 250 miles or weekly)

Refer to illustrations 5.2, 5.3, 5.4a, 5.4b and 5.8

1 Periodic inspection of the tires may spare you from the inconvenience of being stranded with a flat tire. It can also provide you with vital information regarding possible problems in the steering and suspension systems before major damage occurs.

2 Normal tread wear can be monitored with a simple, inexpensive device known as a tread depth indicator **(see illustration)**. Replace the tires before the tread depth reaches 1/16-inch (1.5 mm).

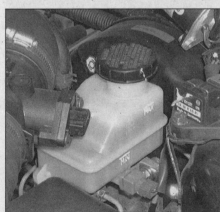

4.16 The brake fluid should be kept between the MIN and MAX marks on the reservoir - turn and lift up the cap to add fluid

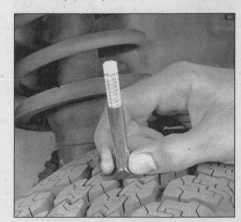

5.2 Use a tire tread depth gauge to monitor tire wear; they are available at auto parts stores and service stations and cost very little

UNDERINFLATION

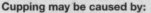

CUPPING

Cupping may be caused by:
- Underinflation and/or mechanical irregularities such as out-of-balance condition of wheel and/or tire, and bent or damaged wheel.
- Loose or worn steering tie-rod or steering idler arm.
- Loose, damaged or worn front suspension parts.

OVERINFLATION

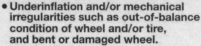

INCORRECT TOE-IN OR EXTREME CAMBER

FEATHERING DUE TO MISALIGNMENT

5.3 This chart will help you determine the condition of the tires, the probable cause(s) of abnormal wear and the corrective action necessary

3   Note any abnormal tread wear **(see illustration)**. Tread pattern irregularities such as cupping, flat spots and more wear on one side than the other are indications of front end alignment and/or balance problems. If any of these conditions are noted, take the vehicle to a tire shop or service station to correct the problem.

4   Look closely for cuts, punctures and embedded nails or tacks. Sometimes a tire will hold its air pressure for a short time or leak down very slowly even after a nail has embedded itself into the tread. If a slow leak persists, check the valve core to make sure it is tight **(see illustration)**. Examine the tread for an object that may have embedded itself into the tire or for a "plug" that may have begun to leak (radial tire punctures are repaired with a plug that is installed in a puncture). If a puncture is suspected, it can be easily verified by spraying a solution of soapy water onto the puncture area **(see illustration)**. The soapy solution will bubble if there is a leak. Unless the puncture is inordi-

nately large, a tire shop or gas station can usually repair the punctured tire.

5   Carefully inspect the inner side of each tire for evidence of brake fluid leakage. If you see any, inspect the brakes immediately.

6   Correct tire air pressure adds miles to the lifespan of the tires, improves mileage and enhances overall ride quality. Tire pressure cannot be accurately estimated by looking at a tire, particularly if it is a radial. A tire pressure gauge is therefore essential. Keep an accurate gauge in the glovebox. The pressure gauges fitted to the nozzles of air hoses at gas stations are often inaccurate.

7   Always check tire pressure when the tires are cold. "Cold," in this case, means the vehicle has not been driven over a mile in the three hours preceding a tire pressure check. A pressure rise of four to eight pounds is not uncommon once the tires are warm.

8   Unscrew the valve cap protruding from the wheel or hubcap and push the gauge firmly onto the valve **(see illustration)**. Note the reading on the gauge and compare this figure to the recommended tire pressure shown on the tire placard on the left door jamb. Be sure to reinstall the valve cap to keep dirt and moisture out of the valve stem mechanism. Check all four tires and, if necessary, add enough air to bring them up to the recommended pressure levels.

9   Don't forget to keep the spare tire inflated to the specified pressure (consult your owner's manual). Note that the air pres-

5.4a If a tire loses air on a steady basis, check the valve core first to make sure it's snug (special inexpensive wrenches are commonly available at auto parts stores)

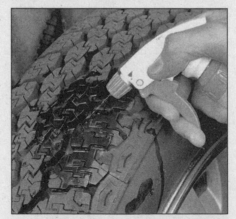

5.4b If the valve core is tight, raise the corner of the vehicle with the low tire and spray a soapy water solution onto the tread as the tire is turned slowly - leaks will cause small bubbles to appear

5.8 To extend the life of the tires, check the air pressure at least once a week with an accurate gauge (don't forget the spare)

7.3 The automatic transaxle dipstick (arrow) is located below the air filter housing

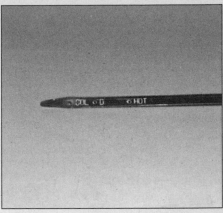

7.5 The automatic transaxle fluid level should be between the two upper marks on the dipstick

sure specified for the compact spare is significantly higher than the pressure of the regular tires.

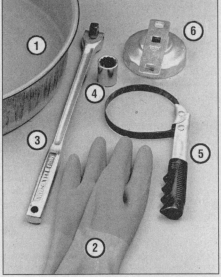

8.2 These tools are required when changing the engine oil and filter

1 **Drain pan** - It should be fairly shallow in depth, but wide to prevent spills
2 **Rubber gloves** - When removing the drain plug and filter, you will get oil on your hands (the gloves will prevent burns)
3 **Breaker bar** - Sometimes the oil drain plug is tight, and a long breaker bar is needed to loosen it
4 **Socket** - To be used with the breaker bar or a ratchet (must be the correct size to fit the drain plug)
5 **Filter wrench** - This is a metal band-type wrench, which requires clearance around the filter to be effective
6 **Filter wrench** - This type fits on the bottom of the filter and can be turned with a ratchet or breaker bar (different-size wrenches are available for different types of filters

6 Power steering fluid level check (every 3000 miles or 3 months)

1 The power steering system relies on fluid, which may, over a period of time, require replenishing.
2 The fluid reservoir for the power steering pump is located on the right inner fender panel near the front of the engine compartment.
3 For the check, the front wheels should be pointed straight ahead and the engine should be off. The fluid should be cold when checking the level.
4 Make sure the fluid level is between the MAX and MIN marks on the reservoir.
5 If additional fluid is required, pour the specified type directly into the reservoir, using a funnel to prevent spills.
6 If the reservoir requires frequent fluid additions, all power steering hoses, hose connections, the power steering pump and the steering gear should be carefully checked for leaks.

7 Automatic transaxle fluid level check (every 3000 miles or 3 months)

Refer to illustrations 7.3 and 7.5
1 The level of the automatic transaxle fluid should be carefully maintained. Low fluid level can lead to slipping or loss of drive, while overfilling can cause foaming, loss of fluid and transaxle damage.
2 The fluid level should only be checked on level ground with the engine idling and the transaxle in Neutral.
3 Remove the dipstick - it's located below the brake master cylinder **(see illustration)**. Check the level of the fluid on the dipstick and note its condition.
4 Wipe the fluid from the dipstick with a clean rag and reinsert it.
5 Pull the dipstick out again and note the fluid level **(see illustration)**. The level should

be between the upper and lower marks on the dipstick. If the level is low, add the specified automatic transmission fluid. Add the fluid through the dipstick opening with a funnel.
6 Add just enough of the specified fluid to fill the transaxle to the proper level. It takes about one pint to raise the level from the lower mark to the upper mark, so add the fluid a little at a time and keep checking the level until it is correct.
7 The condition of the fluid should also be checked along with the level. If the fluid at the end of the dipstick is black or a dark reddish brown color, or if it emits a burned smell, the fluid should be changed (see Section 27). If you are in doubt about the condition of the fluid, purchase some new fluid and compare the two for color and smell.

8 Engine oil and oil filter change (every 3000 miles or 3 months)

Refer to illustrations 8.2, 8.7, 8.12 and 8.14
1 Frequent oil changes are the best preventive maintenance the home mechanic can give the engine, because aging oil becomes diluted and contaminated, which leads to premature engine wear.
2 Make sure you have all the necessary tools before you begin this procedure **(see illustration)**. You should also have plenty of rags or newspapers handy for mopping up any spills.
3 Access to the underside of the vehicle is greatly improved if the vehicle can be lifted on a hoist, driven onto ramps or supported by jackstands. **Warning:** *Do not work under a vehicle which is supported only by a bumper, hydraulic or scissors-type jack.*
4 If this is your first oil change, familiarize yourself with the locations of the oil drain plug and the oil filter. The engine and exhaust components will be warm during the actual work, so try to anticipate any potential problems before the engine and accessories are hot.

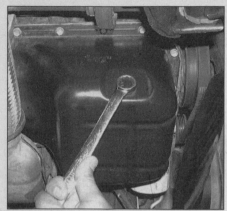

8.7 Use the proper size box-end wrench or socket to remove the oil drain plug without rounding off the corners

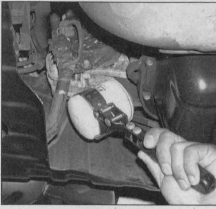

8.12 The oil filter is usually on very tight and will require a special wrench for removal - DO NOT use the wrench to tighten the new filter

8.14 Lubricate the oil filter gasket with clean engine oil before installing the filter on the engine

5   Park the vehicle on a level spot. Start the engine and allow it to reach its normal operating temperature. Warm oil and sludge will flow out more easily. Turn off the engine when it's warmed up. Remove the filler cap from the valve cover.

6   Raise the vehicle and support it securely on jackstands. **Warning:** *Never get beneath the vehicle when it is supported only by a jack. The jack provided with your vehicle is designed solely for raising the vehicle to remove and replace the wheels. Always use jackstands to support the vehicle when it becomes necessary to place your body underneath the vehicle.*

7   Being careful not to touch the hot exhaust components, place the drain pan under the drain plug in the bottom of the pan and remove the plug **(see illustration)**. You may want to wear gloves while unscrewing the plug the final few turns if the engine is hot.

8   Allow the old oil to drain into the pan. It may be necessary to move the pan farther under the engine as the oil flow slows to a trickle. Inspect the old oil for the presence of metal shavings and chips.

9   After all the oil has drained, wipe off the drain plug with a clean rag. Even minute metal particles clinging to the plug would immediately contaminate the new oil.

10   Clean the area around the drain plug opening, reinstall the plug and tighten it securely, but do not strip the threads.

11   Move the drain pan into position under the oil filter.

12   Loosen the oil filter **(see illustration)** by turning it counterclockwise with an oil filter wrench. Once the filter is loose, use your hands to unscrew it from the block. Just as the filter is detached from the block, immediately tilt the open end up to prevent the oil inside the filter from spilling out. **Warning:** *The exhaust system may still be hot, so be careful.*

13   With a clean rag, wipe off the mounting surface on the block. If a residue of old oil is allowed to remain, it will smoke when the

block is heated up. Also make sure that none of the old gasket remains stuck to the mounting surface. It can be removed with a scraper if necessary.

14   Compare the old filter with the new one to make sure they are the same type. Smear some clean engine oil on the rubber gasket of the new filter and screw it into place **(see illustration)**. Because overtightening the filter will damage the gasket, do not use a filter wrench to tighten the filter. Tighten it by hand until the gasket contacts the seating surface. Then seat the filter by giving it an additional 3/4-turn.

15   Remove all tools, rags, etc. from under the vehicle, being careful not to spill the oil in the drain pan, then lower the vehicle.

16   Add new oil to the engine through the oil filler cap in the valve cover. Use a funnel, if necessary, to prevent oil from spilling onto the top of the engine. Pour three quarts of fresh oil into the engine. Wait a few minutes to allow the oil to drain into the pan, then check the level on the oil dipstick (see Section 4 if necessary). If the oil level is at or near the upper hole on the dipstick, install the filler cap hand tight, start the engine and allow the new oil to circulate.

17   Allow the engine to run for about a minute. While the engine is running, look under the vehicle and check for leaks at the oil pan drain plug and around the oil filter. If either is leaking, stop the engine and tighten the plug or filter.

18   Wait a few minutes to allow the oil to trickle down into the pan, then recheck the level on the dipstick and, if necessary, add enough oil to bring the level to the upper hole.

19   During the first few trips after an oil change, make it a point to check frequently for leaks and proper oil level.

20   Used motor oil cannot be re-used in its present state and should be recycled. Oil reclamation centers, auto repair shops and gas stations will normally accept the oil, which can be refined and used again. After the oil has cooled, it can be drained into a

suitable container (capped plastic jugs, topped bottles, milk cartons, etc.) for transport to one of these recycling sites. New or used oil should never be allowed to go into street drains or into the ground.

9   Seat belt check (every 15,000 miles or 12 months)

1   Check seat belts, buckles, latch plates and guide loops for obvious damage and signs of wear.

2   See if the seat belt reminder light comes on when the key is turned to the Run or Start position. A chime should also sound.

3   Seat belts are designed to lock up during a sudden stop or impact, yet allow free movement during normal driving. Make sure the retractors return the belt against your chest while driving and rewind the belt fully when the buckle is unlatched.

4   If any of the above checks reveal problems with the seat belt system, replace parts as necessary.

10   Windshield wiper blade inspection and replacement (every 7500 miles or 6 months)

Refer to illustrations 10.6, 10.7 and 10.8

1   The windshield wiper and blade assembly should be inspected periodically for damage, loose components and cracked or worn blade elements.

2   Road film can build up on the wiper blades and affect their efficiency, so they should be washed regularly with a mild detergent solution.

3   The action of the wiping mechanism can loosen bolts, nuts and fasteners, so they should be checked and tightened, as necessary, at the same time the wiper blades are checked.

4   If the wiper blade elements are cracked,

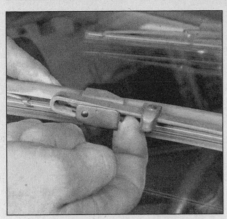

10.6 Press in on the tab and push the blade assembly out of the hook at the end to remove it

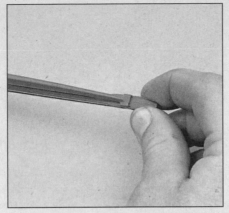

10.7 Squeeze the blade element tabs, then pull the element out of the metal frame and remove it

11.1 Tools and materials required for battery maintenance

worn or warped, or no longer clean adequately, they should be replaced with new ones.
5   Lift the arm assembly away from the glass for clearance.
6   Press in on the lock tab and push the blade assembly down the wiper arm, out of the hook at the end **(see illustration)**.
7   Squeeze the blade element tabs tightly and pull the element out of the metal frame **(see illustration)**.
8   Remove the metal retainers from the element and install them in the new element **(see illustration)**.
9   Insert the element into the frame and push it until the element tabs lock.
10   Place the metal arm assembly in the hook on the wiper arm and press it into place until the lock tab snaps into place.

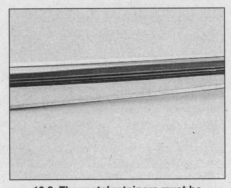

10.8 The metal retainers must be inserted into the slots in the rubber before installation

11 Battery check, maintenance and charging (every 7500 miles or 6 months)

Warning: *Certain precautions must be followed when checking and servicing the battery. Hydrogen gas, which is highly flammable, is always present in the battery cells, so keep lighted tobacco and all other open flames and sparks away from the battery. The electrolyte inside the battery is actually dilute sulfuric acid, which will cause injury if splashed on your skin or in your eyes. It will also ruin clothes and painted surfaces. When removing the battery cables, always detach the negative cable first and hook it up last!*
Caution: *Some models are equipped with an anti-theft radio. Before performing a procedure that requires disconnecting the battery, make sure you have the activation code.*

Check
Refer to illustration 11.1
1   A routine preventive maintenance program for the battery in your vehicle is the only way to ensure quick and reliable starts. But

before performing any battery maintenance, make sure that you have the proper equipment necessary to work safely around the battery **(see illustration)**.
2   There are also several precautions that should be taken whenever battery maintenance is performed. Before servicing the battery, always turn the engine and all accessories off and disconnect the cable from the negative terminal of the battery.
3   The battery produces hydrogen gas, which is both flammable and explosive. Never create a spark, smoke or light a match around the battery. Always charge the battery in a ventilated area.
4   Electrolyte contains poisonous and corrosive sulfuric acid. Do not allow it to get in your eyes, on your skin on your clothes. Never ingest it. Wear protective safety glasses when working near the battery. Keep children away from the battery.
5   Note the external condition of the battery. If the positive terminal and cable clamp on your vehicle's battery is equipped with a rubber protector, make sure that it's not torn or damaged. It should completely cover the terminal. Look for any corroded or loose connections, cracks in the case or cover or loose hold-down clamps. Also check the entire length of each cable for cracks and frayed conductors.

1   *Face shield/safety goggles - When removing corrosion with a brush, the acidic particles can easily fly up into your eyes*
2   *Baking soda - A solution of baking soda and water can be used to neutralize corrosion*
3   *Petroleum jelly - A layer of this on the battery posts will help prevent corrosion*
4   *Battery post/cable cleaner - This wire brush cleaning tool will remove all traces of corrosion from the battery posts and cable clamps*
5   *Treated felt washers - Placing one of these on each post, directly under the cable clamps, will help prevent corrosion*
6   *Puller - Sometimes the cable clamps are very difficult to pull off the posts, even after the nut/bolt has been completely loosened. This tool pulls the clamp straight up and off the post without damage*
7   *Battery post/cable cleaner - Here is another cleaning tool which is a slightly different version of Number 4 above, but it does the same thing*
8   *Rubber gloves - Another safety item to consider when servicing the battery; remember that's acid inside the battery!*

6   Some models with sealed batteries have a battery condition indicator on top of the battery. Compare the color showing in the window to the condition color chart on the battery. You may catch a low-charge battery condition before it strands you on the roadside. If the color indicates a low state of charge, charge the battery and examine the charging system (see Chapter 5 and this Section).

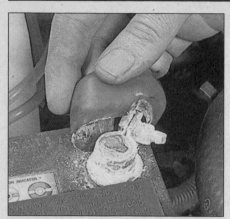

11.7a Battery terminal corrosion usually appears as light, fluffy powder

11.7b Removing the cable from a battery post with a wrench - sometimes special battery pliers are required for this procedure if corrosion has caused deterioration of the nut hex (always remove the ground cable first and hook it up last!)

11.8a When cleaning the cable clamps, all corrosion must be removed

Maintenance

Refer to illustrations 11.7a, 11.7b, 11.8a and 11.8b

7   If corrosion, which looks like white, fluffy deposits **(see illustration)** is evident, particularly around the terminals, the battery should be removed for cleaning. Loosen the cable clamp bolts with a wrench, being careful to remove the ground cable first, and slide them off the terminals **(see illustration)**. Then disconnect the hold-down clamp bolt and nut, remove the clamp and lift the battery from the engine compartment.

8   Clean the cable clamps thoroughly with a battery brush or a terminal cleaner and a solution of warm water and baking soda **(see illustration)**. Wash the terminals and the top of the battery case with the same solution but make sure that the solution doesn't get into the battery. When cleaning the cables, terminals and battery top, wear safety goggles and rubber gloves to prevent any solution from coming in contact with your eyes or hands. Wear old clothes too - even diluted, sulfuric acid splashed onto clothes will burn holes in them. If the terminals have been extensively corroded, clean them up with a terminal cleaner **(see illustration)**. Thoroughly wash all cleaned areas with plain water.

9   Whenever the battery is removed for cleaning or charging, inspect the battery carrier before reinstalling the battery in the engine compartment. If the carrier is dirty or covered with corrosion, clean it in the same solution of warm water and baking soda. Inspect the metal brackets that support the carrier to make sure that they are not covered with corrosion. If they are, wash them off. If corrosion is extensive, sand the brackets down to bare metal and spray them with a zinc-based primer (available in spray cans at auto paint and body supply stores).

10   Reinstall the battery back into the engine compartment. Make sure that no parts or wires are laying on the carrier during installation of the battery. Information on removing and installing the battery can be found in Chapter 5. Information on jump starting can be found at the front of this man-

ual. For more detailed battery checking procedures, refer to the *Haynes Automotive Electrical Manual*.

11   Install a pair of specially-treated felt washers around the terminals (available at auto parts stores), then coat the terminals and the cable clamps with petroleum jelly or grease to prevent further corrosion. Install the cable clamps and tighten the nuts, being careful to install the negative cable last.

12   Install the hold-down clamp and nuts. Tighten the nuts only enough to hold the battery firmly in place. Overtightening these nuts can crack the battery case.

13   Make sure that the battery tray is in good condition and the hold-down clamp bolts are tight. If the battery is removed from the tray, make sure no parts remain in the bottom of the tray when the battery is reinstalled. When reinstalling the hold-down clamp bolts, do not overtighten them.

Charging

Warning: *When batteries are being charged, hydrogen gas, which is very explosive and flammable, is produced. Do not smoke or allow open flames near a charging or a recently charged battery. Wear eye protection when near the battery during charging. Also, make sure the charger is unplugged before connecting or disconnecting the battery from the charger.*

14   Slow-rate charging is the best way to restore a battery that's discharged to the point where it will not start the engine. It's also a good way to maintain the battery charge in a vehicle that's only driven a few miles between starts. Maintaining the battery charge is particularly important in the winter when the battery must work harder to start the engine and electrical accessories that drain the battery are in greater use.

15   It's best to use a one or two-amp battery charger (sometimes called a "trickle" charger). They are the safest and put the

11.8b Regardless of the type of tool used on the battery posts, a clean, shiny surface should be the result (the inside of the clamp is tapered to match the taper on the post, so don't remove too much material)

least strain on the battery. They are also the least expensive. For a faster charge, you can use a higher amperage charger, but don't use one rated more than 1/10th the amp/hour rating of the battery. Rapid boost charges that claim to restore the power of the battery in one to two hours are hardest on the battery and can damage batteries not in good condition. This type of charging should only be used in emergency situations.

16   The average time necessary to charge a battery should be listed in the instructions that come with the charger. As a general rule, a trickle charger will charge a battery in 12 to 16 hours.

12 Drivebelt check, adjustment and replacement (every 7500 miles or 6 months)

Check

Refer to illustrations 12.3 and 12.4

1   The drivebelts are located at the front of the engine and play an important role in the

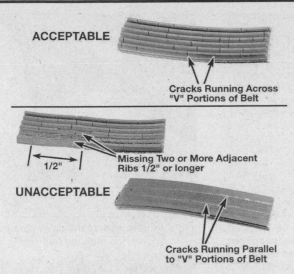

ACCEPTABLE

Cracks Running Across
"V" Portions of Belt

1/2"

Missing Two or More Adjacent
Ribs 1/2" or longer

UNACCEPTABLE

Cracks Running Parallel
to "V" Portions of Belt

12.3 Check the belts for signs of wear like these - if the belt looks worn, replace it

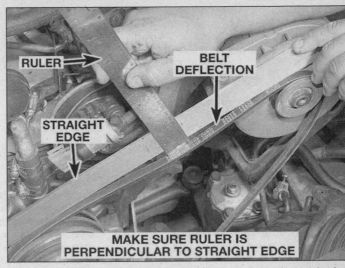

RULER

BELT
DEFLECTION

STRAIGHT
EDGE

MAKE SURE RULER IS
PERPENDICULAR TO STRAIGHT EDGE

12.4 Measuring drivebelt deflection with a straightedge and ruler

overall operation of the vehicle and its components. Due to their function and material make-up, the belts are prone to failure after a period of time and should be inspected and adjusted periodically to prevent major engine damage.

2　The number of belts used on a particular vehicle depends on the accessories installed. Drivebelts are used to turn the alternator, power steering pump, water pump and air conditioning compressor. Depending on the pulley arrangement, more than one of these components may be driven by a single belt.

3　With the engine off, open the hood and locate the various belts at the front of the engine. Using your fingers (and a flashlight, if necessary), move along the belts checking for cracks and separation of the belt plies. Also check for fraying and glazing, which gives the belt a shiny appearance **(see illustration)**. Both sides of each belt should be inspected, which means you will have to twist the belt to check the underside.

4　The tension of each belt is checked by pushing on the belt at a distance halfway between the pulleys. Push firmly with your thumb and see how much the belt moves (deflects) **(see illustration)**. As rule of thumb, if the distance from pulley center-to-pulley center is between 7 and 11 inches, the belt should deflect 1/4-inch. If the belt travels between pulleys spaced 12 to 16 inches apart, the belt should deflect 1/2-inch.

Adjustment

Refer to illustrations 12.5a 12.5b and 12.5c

5　The air conditioner compressor belt tension is adjusted by loosening tensioner pulley bolt and moving the pulley in or out. To adjust the power steering pump belt, loosen the through-bolt and adjuster lock bolt, then move the pump in-or-out to loosen or tighten the belt **(see illustration)**. The water pump and alternator belt tension is adjusted by loosening the alternator adjuster lock bolt

and turning the adjuster bolt **(see illustration)**.

6　After the belts have been adjusted, measure the belt tension in accordance with one of the above methods. Repeat the adjustment procedure until the drivebelt is tensioned properly.

Replacement

7　Follow the above adjustment procedures to loosen the belt, slip the belt off the pulleys and remove it. Since belts tend to wear out more or less at the same time, it's a good idea to replace all of them at the same time.

8　Take the old belts with you when purchasing new ones in order to make a direct comparison for length, width and design. Keep in mind that your old belt may have stretched, and the correct new belt may be slightly shorter. When installing a new ribbed belt, make sure it is centered on its drive pulley.

12.5a Loosen the tensioner pulley lockbolt (1) and turn the tensioner bolt (2) to adjust the air conditioning compressor belt tension

12.5b To adjust the power steering pump belt tension, loosen the pivot bolt (1), then turn the adjustment bolt (2) and move the pump to tighten or loosen the belt

12.5c To adjust the water pump and alternator belt tension, loosen the alternator lockbolt (1), then turn the alternator adjustment bolt (2) clockwise to tighten the belt, or counterclockwise to loosen the belt

9   Install the belt by reversing the removal procedures. When installing a ribbed belt, make sure it is centered on the pulleys, it must not overlap either edge of the pulleys. Adjust the belt as described earlier in this Section.

13   Underhood hose check and replacement (every 7500 miles or 6 months)

Caution: *Replacement of air conditioning hoses must be left to a dealer service department or air conditioning shop that has the equipment to evacuate the system safely. Never remove air conditioning components or hoses until the system has been evacuated and the refrigerant recovered by an air conditioning shop.*

General

1   High temperatures in the engine compartment can cause the deterioration of the rubber and plastic hoses used for engine, accessory and emission systems operation. Periodic inspection should be made for cracks, loose clamps, material hardening and leaks.
2   Information specific to the cooling system hoses can be found in Section 14.
3   Some, but not all, hoses are secured to the fittings with clamps. Where clamps are used, check to be sure they haven't lost their tension, allowing the hose to leak. If clamps aren't used, make sure the hose has not expanded and/or hardened where it slips over the fitting, allowing it to leak.

Vacuum hoses

4   Its quite common for vacuum hoses, especially those in the emissions system, to be color coded or identified by colored stripes molded into them. Various systems require hoses with different wall thickness, collapse resistance and temperature resistance. When replacing hoses, be sure the new ones are made of the same material.
5   Often the only effective way to check a hose is to remove it completely from the vehicle. If more than one hose is removed, be sure to label the hoses and fittings to ensure correct installation.
6   When checking vacuum hoses, be sure to include any plastic T-fittings in the check. Inspect the fittings for cracks and the hose where it fits over the fitting for distortion, which could cause leakage.
7   A small piece of vacuum hose (1/4-inch inside diameter) can be used as a stethoscope to detect vacuum leaks. Hold one end of the hose to your ear and probe around vacuum hoses and fittings, listening for the "hissing" sound characteristic of a vacuum leak. **Warning:** *When probing with the vacuum hose stethoscope, be very careful not to come into contact with moving engine components such as the drivebelts, cooling fan, etc.*

Fuel hose

Warning: *Gasoline is extremely flammable, so take extra precautions when you work on any part of the fuel system. Don't smoke or allow open flames or bare light bulbs near the work area, and don't work in a garage where a gas-type appliance (such as a water heater or clothes dryer) is present. Since gasoline is carcinogenic, wear latex gloves when there's a possibility of being exposed to fuel, and, if you spill any fuel on your skin, rinse it off immediately with soap and water. Mop up any spills immediately and do not store fuel-soaked rags where they could ignite. The fuel system is under constant pressure, so, if any fuel lines are to be disconnected, the fuel pressure in the system must be relieved first (see Chapter 4 for more information). When you perform any kind of work on the fuel system, wear safety glasses and have a Class B type fire extinguisher on hand.*
8   Check all rubber fuel lines for deterioration and chafing. Check especially for cracks in areas where the hose bends and just before fittings, such as where a hose attaches to the fuel filter.
9   When replacing hose, use only hose that is specifically designed for your fuel injection system.

Metal lines

10   Sections of metal line are often used for fuel line between the fuel pump and fuel injection system. Check carefully to be sure the line has not been bent or crimped and that cracks have not started in the line.
11   If a section of metal fuel line must be replaced, only seamless steel tubing should be used, since copper and aluminum tubing don't have the strength necessary to withstand normal engine vibration.
12   Check the metal brake lines where they enter the master cylinder and brake proportioning unit (if used) for cracks in the lines or loose fittings. Any sign of brake fluid leakage calls for an immediate, thorough inspection of the brake system.

14   Cooling system check (every 7500 miles or 6 months)

Refer to illustration 14.4

1   Many major engine failures can be attributed to a faulty cooling system. If the vehicle is equipped with an automatic transaxle, the cooling system also cools the transmission fluid and thus plays an important role in prolonging transaxle life.
2   The cooling system should be checked with the engine cold. Do this before the vehicle is driven for the day or after the engine has been shut off for at least three hours.
3   Remove the radiator cap by turning it to the left until it reaches a stop. Refer to the underhood photographs at the front of this Chapter to locate the radiator cap. If you hear a hissing sound (indicating there is still pressure in the system), wait until it stops. Now

Check for a chafed area that could fail prematurely.

Check for a soft area indicating the hose has deteriorated inside.

Overtightening the clamp on a hardened hose will damage the hose and cause a leak.

Check each hose for swelling and oil-soaked ends. Cracks and breaks can be located by squeezing the hose.

14.4 Hoses, like drivebelts, have a habit of failing at the worst possible time - to prevent the inconvenience of a blown radiator or heater hose, inspect them carefully as shown here

press down on the cap with the palm of your hand and continue turning to the left until the cap can be removed. Thoroughly clean the cap, inside and out, with clean water. Also clean the filler neck on the radiator. All traces of corrosion should be removed. The coolant inside the radiator should be relatively transparent. If it's rust colored, the system should be drained and refilled (see Section 24). If the coolant level isn't up to the top, add additional antifreeze/coolant mixture (see Section 4).
4   Carefully check the large upper and lower radiator hoses along with the smaller diameter heater hoses which run from the engine to the firewall. Inspect each hose along its entire length, replacing any hose that is cracked, swollen or shows signs of deterioration. Cracks may become more apparent if the hose is squeezed **(see illustration).**

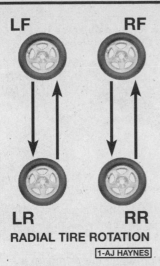

LF   RF

LR   RR

RADIAL TIRE ROTATION

1-AJ HAYNES

15.2 Recommended radial tire rotation pattern for these models

16.7a You will find an inspection window (arrow) in each caliper - the inner brake pad lining thickness can be determined by looking through this window

16.7b To inspect the outer pad thickness (arrow), look at the end of the pad

1

5   Make sure that all hose connections are tight. A leak in the cooling system will usually show up as white or rust colored deposits on the areas adjoining the leak. If wire-type clamps are used at the ends of the hoses, it may be a good idea to replace them with more secure screw-type clamps.

6   Use compressed air or a soft brush to remove bugs, leaves, etc. from the front of the radiator or air conditioning condenser. Be careful not to damage the delicate cooling fins or cut yourself on them.

7   Every other inspection, or at the first indication of cooling system problems, have the cap and system pressure tested. If you don't have a pressure tester, most gas stations and repair shops will do this for a minimal charge.

15   Tire rotation (every 7500 miles or 6 months)

Refer to illustration 15.2

1   The tires should be rotated at the specified intervals and whenever uneven wear is noticed. Since the vehicle will be raised and the tires removed anyway, check the brakes (see Section 16) at this time.

2   Radial tires must be rotated in a specific pattern **(see illustration)**.

3   Refer to the information in *Jacking and towing* at the front of this manual for the proper procedures to follow when raising the vehicle and changing a tire. If the brakes are to be checked, do not apply the parking brake as stated. Make sure the tires are blocked to prevent the vehicle from rolling.

4   Preferably, the entire vehicle should be raised at the same time. This can be done on a hoist or by jacking up each corner and then lowering the vehicle onto jackstands placed under the frame rails. Always use four jackstands and make sure the vehicle is firmly supported.

5   After rotation, check and adjust the tire pressures as necessary and be sure to check

the lug nut tightness. Ideally, lug nuts should be torqued to Specifications with a torque wrench, and rechecked after 25 miles of driving.

6   For further information on the wheels and tires, refer to Chapter 10.

16   Brake system check (every 15,000 miles or 12 months)

Warning: *The dust created by the brake system may contain asbestos, which is harmful to your health. Never blow it out with compressed air and don't inhale any of it. An approved filtering mask should be worn when working on the brakes. Do not, under any circumstances, use petroleum-based solvents to clean brake parts. Use brake system cleaner only! Try to use non-asbestos replacement parts whenever possible.*
Note: *For detailed photographs of the brake system, refer to Chapter 9.*

1   In addition to the specified intervals, the brakes should be inspected every time the wheels are removed or whenever a defect is suspected.

2   Any of the following symptoms could indicate a potential brake system defect: The vehicle pulls to one side when the brake pedal is depressed; the brakes make squealing or dragging noises when applied; brake pedal travel is excessive; the pedal pulsates;

or brake fluid leaks, usually onto the inside of the tire or wheel.

3   Loosen the wheel lug nuts.

4   Raise the vehicle and place it securely on jackstands.

5   Remove the wheels (see *Jacking and towing* at the front of this book, or your owner's manual, if necessary).

Front and rear disc brakes

Refer to illustrations 16.7a, 16.7b, 16.9 and 16.11

6   There are two pads (an outer and an inner) in each caliper. The pads are visible with the wheels removed.

7   Check the pad thickness by looking at each end of the caliper and through the inspection window in the caliper body **(see illustrations)**. If the lining material is less than the thickness listed in this Chapter's Specifications, replace the pads. **Note:** *Keep in mind that the lining material is riveted or bonded to a metal backing plate and the metal portion is not included in this measurement.*

8   If it is difficult to determine the exact thickness of the remaining pad material by the above method, or if you are at all concerned about the condition of the pads, remove the caliper(s), then remove the pads from the calipers for further inspection (refer to Chapter 9).

9   Once the pads are removed from the calipers, clean them with brake cleaner and re-measure them with a ruler or a vernier caliper **(see illustration)**.

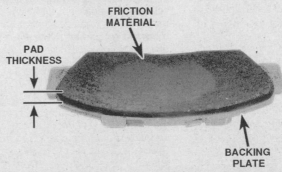

FRICTION MATERIAL

PAD THICKNESS

BACKING PLATE

16.9 If a more precise measurement of pad thickness is necessary, remove the pads and measure the remaining friction material

16.11 Check along the brake hoses and at each fitting (arrows) for deterioration and cracks

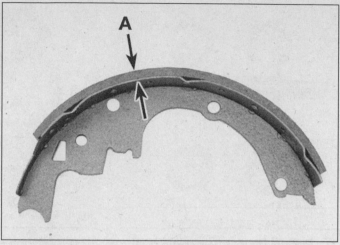

16.15 If the lining is bonded to the brake shoe, measure the lining thickness from the outer surface to the metal shoe, as shown here; if the lining is riveted to the shoe, measure from the lining outer surface to the rivet head

10   Measure the disc thickness with a micrometer to make sure that it still has service life remaining. If any disc is thinner than the specified minimum thickness, replace it (refer to Chapter 9). Even if the disc has service life remaining, check its condition. Look for scoring, gouging and burned spots. If these conditions exist, remove the disc and have it resurfaced (see Chapter 9).

11   Before installing the wheels, check all brake lines and hoses for damage, wear, deformation, cracks, corrosion, leakage, bends and twists, particularly in the vicinity of the rubber hoses at the calipers **(see illustration)**. Check the clamps for tightness and the connections for leakage. Make sure that all hoses and lines are clear of sharp edges, moving parts and the exhaust system. If any of the above conditions are noted, repair, reroute or replace the lines and/or fittings as necessary (see Chapter 9).

Rear drum brakes

Refer to illustrations 16.15 and 16.17

12   On models with rear drum brakes, make sure the parking brake is off. Remove the two screws around the center of the drum (if installed), then tap on the outside of the drum with a rubber mallet to loosen it.

13   Remove the brake drums. If the drums do not pull off easily, apply some penetrating oil to the center of the hub, allow it to soak in, then tap around the center of the drum with a hammer. If it is still on solidly, tap around the outside edge of the drum from the backside.

14   With the drums removed, carefully clean the brake assembly with brake system cleaner. **Warning:** *Don't blow the dust out with compressed air and don't inhale any of it (it may contain asbestos, which is harmful to your health).*

15   Note the thickness of the lining material on both front and rear brake shoes. If the material has worn away to within 1/16-inch of the recessed rivets or metal backing on

bonded type shoes, the shoes should be replaced **(see illustration)**. The shoes should also be replaced if they're cracked, glazed (shiny areas), or covered with brake fluid.

16   Make sure all the brake assembly springs are connected and in good condition, referring to the photographs in Chapter 9, if necessary.

17   Check the brake components for signs of fluid leakage. With your finger or a small screwdriver, carefully pry back the rubber cups on the wheel cylinder located at the top of the brake shoes **(see illustration)**. Any leakage here is an indication that the wheel cylinders should be replaced immediately (see Chapter 9). Also, check all hoses and connections for signs of leakage.

18   Wipe the inside of the drum with a clean rag and denatured alcohol or brake cleaner. Again, be careful not to breathe the dangerous asbestos dust.

19   Check the inside of the drum for cracks, score marks, deep scratches and "hard spots" which will appear as small discolored areas. If imperfections cannot be removed with fine emery cloth, the drum must be taken to an automotive machine shop for resurfacing.

20   Repeat the procedure for the remaining wheel. If the inspection reveals that all parts are in good condition, reinstall the brake drums, install the wheels and lower the vehicle to the ground.

Brake booster check

21   Sit in the driver's seat and perform the following sequence of tests.

22   With the brake fully depressed, start the engine - the pedal should move down a little when the engine starts.

23   With the engine running, depress the brake pedal several times - the travel distance should not change.

24   Depress the brake, stop the engine and hold the pedal in for about 30 seconds - the

pedal should neither sink nor rise.

25   Restart the engine, run it for about a minute and turn it off. Then firmly depress the brake several times - the pedal travel should decrease with each application.

26   If your brakes do not operate as described, the brake booster has failed. Refer to Chapter 9 for the replacement procedure.

Parking brake

27   Slowly pull up on the parking brake and count the number of clicks you hear until the handle is up as far as it will go. The adjustment is correct if you hear the specified number of clicks (see this Chapter's Specifications). If you hear more or fewer clicks, it's time to adjust the parking brake (see Chapter 9).

28   An alternative method of checking the parking brake is to park the vehicle on a steep hill with the parking brake set and the transaxle in Neutral. If the parking brake cannot prevent the vehicle from rolling, it is in need of adjustment (see Chapter 9).

16.17 Check the wheel cylinder boots for leaking fluid indicating that the cylinder must be replaced or rebuilt

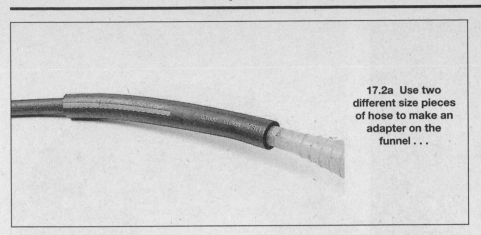

17.2a Use two different size pieces of hose to make an adapter on the funnel . . .

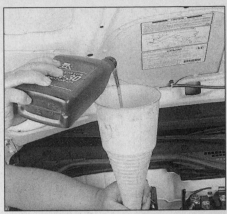

17.2b . . . so you can easily add lubricant to the transaxle from above

17 Manual transaxle lubricant level check (every 15,000 miles or 12 months)

Refer to illustrations 17.2a and 17.2b

1   The manual transaxle does not have a dipstick. To check the fluid level, raise the vehicle and support it securely on jackstands. The vehicle must be level. The check/fill plug is on the front side of the transaxle, and the drain plug is on the bottom edge of the housing. Remove the check/fill plug with a socket or box-end wrench. If the lubricant level is correct, it should be up to the lower edge of the hole. Often, lubricant will leak out when the plug is removed, indicating the level is correct. If lubricant does not leak out when the plug is removed, use your finger as a dipstick to check that it is up to the level of the hole.

2   If the transaxle needs more lubricant (if the level is not up to the hole), use a funnel to add more **(see illustrations)**. Handy lubricant containers with built-in pumps are available from auto parts stores; these provide a still easier method for a moderate extra expense. Stop filling the transaxle when the lubricant begins to run out the hole.

3   Install the plug and tighten it securely. Drive the vehicle a short distance, then check for leaks.

18 Air filter replacement (every 30,000 miles or 24 months)

Refer to illustrations 18.2 and 18.4

1   At the specified intervals, the air filter should be replaced with a new one.

2   Release the air cleaner cover clips **(see illustration)**.

3   Lift the cover up.

4   Lift the air filter element out of the housing and wipe out the inside of the air cleaner housing with a clean rag **(see illustration)**.

5   While the air cleaner cover is off, be careful not to drop anything down into the air cleaner assembly.

6   Place the new filter in the air cleaner housing. Make sure it seats properly in the lower half of the housing.

7   Install the air cleaner cover and tighten the screws securely.

19 Spark plug check and replacement (every 30,000 miles or 24 months)

Refer to illustrations 19.2, 19.4a, 19.4b, 19.5a, 19.5b, 19.8, 19.9 and 19.10

1   The spark plug wires should be checked whenever new spark plugs are installed (see the next Section).

2   In most cases, the tools necessary for spark plug replacement include a spark plug socket which fits onto a ratchet (spark plug sockets are padded inside to prevent damage to the porcelain insulators on the new plugs), various extensions and a gap gauge to check and adjust the gap on the new plugs **(see illustration)**. A special plug wire removal tool is available for separating the wire boots from the spark plugs and may be a good idea if the boots fit very tightly. A torque wrench should be used to tighten the new plugs. It is a good idea to allow the engine to cool before removing or installing the spark plugs.

3   The best approach when replacing the spark plugs is to purchase the new ones in

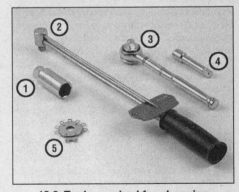

19.2 Tools required for changing spark plugs

1   *Spark plug socket - This will have special padding inside to protect the spark plug's porcelain insulator*
2   *Torque wrench - Although not mandatory, using this tool is the best way to ensure the plugs are tightened properly*
3   *Ratchet - Standard hand tool to fit the spark plug socket*
4   *Extension - Depending on model and accessories, you may need special extensions and universal joints to reach one or more of the plugs*
5   *Spark plug gap gauge - This gauge for checking the gap comes in a variety of styles. Make sure the gap for your engine is included*

18.2 Release all the air cleaner cover clips (arrows)

18.4 Lift up the cover and remove the filter element

19.4a Remove the screws (arrows) and detach the plastic spark plug cover

19.4b With the cover removed the spark plugs are easily accessible

19.5a Spark plug manufacturers recommend using a wire-type gauge when checking the gap - if the wire does not slide between the electrodes with a slight drag, adjustment is required

19.5b To change the gap, bend the side electrode only, as indicated by the arrows, and be very careful not to crack or chip the porcelain insulator surrounding the center electrode

19.8 Because they are deeply recessed, an extension will be required when removing or installing the spark plugs

advance, adjust them to the proper gap and replace the plugs one at a time. When buying the new spark plugs, be sure to obtain the correct plug type for your particular engine. The plug type can be found in the Specifications at the front of this Chapter and on the Emission Control Information label located under the hood. If these two sources list different plug types, consider the emission control label correct.

4   Allow the engine to cool completely before attempting to remove any of the plugs. While you are waiting for the engine to cool, check the new plugs for defects and adjust the gap. Remove the spark plug cover (see illustrations).

5   Check the gap by inserting the proper thickness gauge between the electrodes at the tip of the plug (see illustration). The gap between the electrodes should be the same as the one specified on the Emissions Control Information label or in Chapter 5. The wire should slide between the electrodes with a slight amount of drag. If the gap is incorrect, use the adjuster on the gauge body to bend the curved side electrode slightly until

the proper gap is obtained (see illustration). If the side electrode is not exactly over the center electrode, bend it with the adjuster until it is. Check for cracks in the porcelain insulator (if any are found, the plug should not be used).

6   With the engine cool, remove the spark plug wire as described in the next Section from one spark plug. Pull only on the boot at the end of the wire - do not pull on the wire. A plug wire removal tool should be used if available.

7   If compressed air is available, use it to blow any dirt or foreign material away from the spark plug hole. A common bicycle pump will also work. The idea here is to eliminate the possibility of debris falling into the cylinder as the spark plug is removed.

8   The spark plugs on these models are difficult to reach, so an extension is needed to reach into the deep spark plug recesses. Place the spark plug socket over the plug and remove it from the engine by turning it in a counterclockwise direction (see illustration).

9   Compare the spark plug with the chart

19.9 A light coat of anti-seize compound applied to the threads of the spark plugs will keep the threads in the cylinder head from being damaged the next time the plugs are removed

shown on the inside back cover of this manual to get an indication of the general running condition of the engine. Before installing the new plugs, it is a good idea to apply a thin coat of anti-seize compound to the threads (see illustration).

10   Thread one of the new plugs into the hole until you can no longer turn it with your fingers, then tighten it with a torque wrench (if available) or the ratchet. It's a good idea to slip a short length of rubber hose over the end of the plug to use as a tool to thread it into place **(see illustration)**. The hose will grip the plug well enough to turn it, but will start to slip if the plug begins to cross-thread in the hole - this will prevent damaged threads and the accompanying repair costs.

11   Before pushing the spark plug wire onto the end of the plug, inspect the wire following the procedures outlined in the next Section.

12   Attach the plug wire to the new spark plug, again using a twisting motion on the boot until it's seated on the spark plug.

13   Repeat the procedure for the remaining spark plugs, replacing them one at a time to prevent mixing up the spark plug wires.

20 Ignition system component check and replacement (30,000 miles or 24 months)

Refer to illustrations 20.4 and 20.8

1   The spark plug wires should be checked whenever new spark plugs are installed.

2   Begin this procedure by making a visual check of the spark plug wires while the engine is running. In a darkened garage (make sure there is adequate ventilation) start the engine and observe each plug wire. Be careful not to come into contact with any moving engine parts. If there is a break in the wire, you will see arcing or a small spark at the damaged area. If arcing is noticed, make a note to obtain new wires, then allow the engine to cool and check the ignition coil packs.

3   The spark plug wires should be inspected one at a time to prevent mixing up the order, which is essential for proper engine operation. Each original plug wire should be numbered to help identify its location. If the number is illegible, a piece of tape can be marked with the correct number and wrapped around the plug wire.

4   Disconnect the plug wire from the spark plug. Grasp the rubber boot, twist the boot half a turn and pull the boot free **(see illustration)**. Do not pull on the wire itself.

5   Check inside the boot for corrosion, which will look like a white crusty powder. Light corrosion can be removed with a small wire brush, but replace the wires if corrosion is heavy.

6   Push the wire and boot back onto the end of the spark plug. It should fit tightly onto the end of the plug. If it doesn't, remove the wire and use pliers to carefully crimp the metal connector inside the wire boot until the fit is snug.

7   Using a clean rag, wipe the entire length of the wire to remove built-up dirt and grease. Once the wire is clean, check for burns, cracks and other damage. Do not bend the

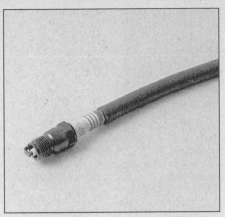

19.10 A piece of rubber hose will aid in getting the spark plug started in the hole

wire sharply, because the conductor might break.

8   Disconnect the wire from the ignition coil pack **(see illustration)**. Pull only on the rubber boot. Check for corrosion and a tight fit. Replace the wire in the coil pack.

9   Inspect the remaining spark plug wires, making sure that each one is securely fastened at the coil pack and spark plug when the check is complete.

10   If new spark plug wires are required, purchase a set for your specific engine model. Remove and replace the wires one at a time to avoid mix-ups in the firing order.

11   Clean the coil pack with a dampened cloth and dry them with a dampened cloth thoroughly.

12   Inspect the coil pack for cracks, damage and carbon tracking. Carbon tracks can usually be removed. If damage exists, refer to Chapter 5 for the replacement procedure.

21 Positive Crankcase Ventilation (PCV) valve check and replacement (every 30,000 miles or 24 months)

Refer to illustration 21.4

1   The Positive Crankcase Ventilation (PCV) system directs blowby gases from the crankcase through the PCV valve and hose back into the intake manifold so they can be burned in the engine. The system consists of a hose leading from the valve cover to the intake duct. The PCV valve, and a hose connecting it to the air intake plenum.

2   The PCV valve is located in the valve cover.

3   Detach the hose from the valve, then unscrew the valve from the valve cover. Reconnect the hose to the valve.

4   With the engine idling at normal operating temperature, place your finger over the valve opening or hose **(see illustration)**. If there's no vacuum, check for a plugged hose, manifold port, or the valve itself. Replace any plugged or deteriorated hoses.

5   Turn off the engine and shake the PCV

21.4 With the engine running at idle, remove the PCV valve and verify that vacuum can be felt at the end of the valve

valve, listening for a rattle. If the valve doesn't rattle, replace it with a new one.

6   When purchasing a replacement PCV valve, make sure it's for your particular vehicle and engine size. Compare the old valve with the new one to make sure they're the same.

7   For further information on the PCV system refer to Chapter 6.

22 Cooling system servicing (draining, flushing and refilling) (every 30,000 miles or 24 months)

Warning : *Do not allow antifreeze to come in contact with your skin or painted surfaces of the vehicle. Rinse off spills immediately with plenty of water. Antifreeze is highly toxic if ingested. Never leave antifreeze lying around in an open container or in puddles on the floor; children and pets are attracted by it's sweet smell and may drink it. Check with local authorities about disposing of used antifreeze. Many communities have collection centers which will see that antifreeze is disposed of safely.*

1   Periodically, the cooling system should be drained, flushed and refilled to replenish the antifreeze mixture and prevent formation of rust and corrosion, which can impair the performance of the cooling system and cause engine damage.

2   At the same time the cooling system is serviced, all hoses and the radiator cap should be inspected and replaced if defective (see Section 13).

3   Since antifreeze is a corrosive and poisonous solution, be careful not to spill any of the coolant mixture on the vehicle's paint or your skin. If this happens, rinse it off immediately with plenty of clean water. Consult local authorities about where to recycle or dispose of antifreeze before draining the cooling system. In many areas, reclamation centers have been set up to collect automobile oil and drained antifreeze/water mixtures, rather than allowing them to be added to the sewage system.

1

22.6 The radiator drain plug (arrow) is located at the bottom corner of the radiator

Draining

Refer to illustrations 22.5 and 22.6

4   Apply the parking brake and block the wheels. If the vehicle has just been driven, wait several hours to allow the engine to cool down before beginning this procedure.

5   Once the engine is completely cool, remove the radiator cap. Also remove the coolant reservoir cap.

6   Drain the radiator by opening the drain plug at the bottom of the radiator **(see illustration)**. If the drain plug is corroded and can't be turned easily, or if the radiator isn't equipped with a plug, disconnect the lower radiator hose to allow the coolant to drain. Be careful not to get antifreeze on your skin or in your eyes.

7   After the coolant stops flowing out of the radiator, disconnect the lower radiator hose from the radiator and allow the remaining coolant in the engine block to drain.

8   While the coolant is draining from the engine block, disconnect the hose from the coolant reservoir and remove the reservoir (see Chapter 3 if necessary). Flush the reservoir out with water until it's clean, and, if necessary, wash the inside with soapy water and a brush to make reading the fluid level easier.

9   While the coolant is draining, check the condition of the radiator hoses, heater hoses and clamps (refer to Section 13 if necessary).

10   Replace any damaged clamps or hoses (refer to Chapter 3 for detailed replacement procedures).

Flushing

Refer to illustration 22.13

11   Once the system is completely drained, remove the thermostat from the engine (see Chapter 3). Then reinstall the thermostat housing without the thermostat. This will allow the system to be thoroughly flushed.

12   Re-connect the lower radiator hose and tighten the radiator drain plug. Turn your heating system controls to Hot, so that the heater core will be flushed at the same time as the rest of the cooling system.

13   Disconnect the upper radiator hose, then place a garden hose in the upper radiator inlet and flush the system until the water runs clear at the upper radiator hose **(see illustration)**.

14   In severe cases of contamination or clogging of the radiator, remove the radiator (see Chapter 3) and have a radiator repair facility clean and repair it if necessary.

15   Many deposits can be removed by the chemical action of a cleaner available at auto parts stores. Follow the procedure outlined in the manufacturer's instructions. **Note:** *When the coolant is regularly drained and the system refilled with the correct antifreeze/water mixture, there should be no need to use chemical cleaners or descalers.*

Refilling

16   To refill the system, install the thermostat, reconnect any radiator hoses and install the reservoir and the overflow hose.

17   Place the heater temperature control in the maximum heat position.

18   Make sure to use the proper coolant listed in this Chapter's Specifications. Slowly fill the radiator with the recommended mixture of antifreeze and water to the base of the filler neck. Then add coolant to the reservoir until it reaches the Full mark. Wait five minutes and recheck the coolant level in the radiator, adding if necessary.

19   Leave the radiator cap and run the engine in a well-ventilated area until the thermostat opens (coolant will begin flowing through the radiator and the upper radiator hose will become hot).

20   Turn the engine off and let it cool. Add more coolant mixture to bring the level back up to the base of the filler neck.

21   Squeeze the upper radiator hose to expel air, then add more coolant mixture if necessary. Replace the radiator cap.

22   Place the heater temperature control and the blower motor speed control to their maximum setting.

23   Start the engine, allow it to reach normal operating temperature and check for leaks.

24   If the coolant temperature rises above normal, there is air trapped in the cooling system. Shut off the engine and allow it to cool completely; the system will automatically vent the trapped air. Repeat the procedure until the engine temperature stays at the normal position on the gauge.

23   Brake fluid change (every 30,000 miles or 24 months)

Warning: *Brake fluid can harm your eyes and damage painted surfaces, so use extreme caution when handling or pouring it. Do not use brake fluid that has been standing open or is more than one year old. Brake fluid absorbs moisture from the air. Excess moisture can cause a dangerous loss of braking effectiveness.*

1   At the specified intervals, the brake fluid should be drained and replaced. Since the brake fluid may drip or splash when pouring it, place plenty of rags around the master cylinder to protect any surrounding painted surfaces.

2   Before beginning work, purchase the specified brake fluid (see *Recommended lubricants and fluids* at the beginning of this Chapter).

3   Remove the cap from the master cylinder reservoir.

4   Using a hand suction pump or similar

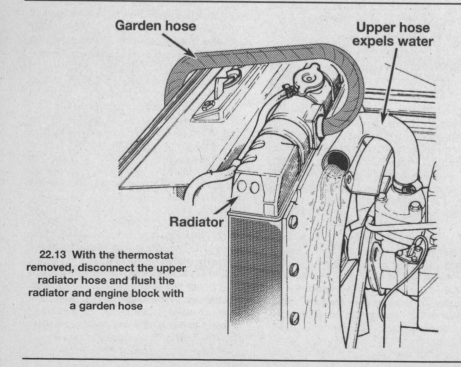

Garden hose

Upper hose expels water

Radiator

22.13 With the thermostat removed, disconnect the upper radiator hose and flush the radiator and engine block with a garden hose

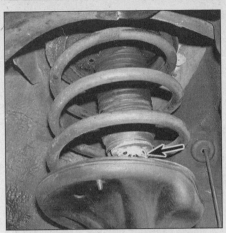

24.6 Check the front and rear shock absorbers for leakage where the rod enters the tube (arrow)

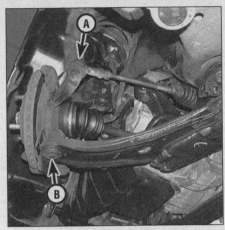

24.9a Inspect the tie rod ends (A) and the balljoints (B) for torn grease seals

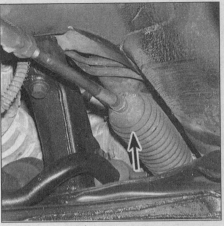

24.9b Check each steering gear boot (arrow) for cracks and leaking steering fluid

1

device, withdraw the fluid from the master cylinder reservoir.

5   Add new fluid to the master cylinder until it rises to the base of the filler neck.

6   Bleed the brake system as described in Chapter 9 at all four brakes until new and uncontaminated fluid is expelled from the bleeder screw. Be sure to maintain the fluid level in the master cylinder as you perform the bleeding process. If you allow the master cylinder to run dry, air will enter the system.

7   Refill the master cylinder with fluid and check the operation of the brakes. The pedal should feel solid when depressed, with no sponginess. **Warning:** *Do not operate the vehicle if you are in doubt about the effectiveness of the brake system.*

24   Steering and suspension check (every 30,000 miles or 24 months)

Refer to illustrations 24.6, 24.9a, 24.9b, 24.9c, 24.11 and 24.14

Note: *The steering linkage and suspension components should be checked periodically. Worn or damaged suspension and steering linkage components can result in excessive and abnormal tire wear, poor ride quality and vehicle handling and reduced fuel economy. For detailed illustrations of the steering and suspension components, refer to Chapter 10.*

Shock absorber check

1   Park the vehicle on level ground, turn the engine off and set the parking brake. Check the tire pressures.

2   Push down at one corner of the vehicle, then release it while noting the movement of the body. It should stop moving and come to rest in a level position within one or two bounces.

3   If the vehicle continues to move up-and-down or if it fails to return to its original position, a worn or weak shock absorber (which is part of the strut assembly) is probably the reason.

4   Repeat the above check at each of the three remaining corners of the vehicle.

5   Raise the vehicle and support it securely on jackstands.

6   Check the shock absorbers for evidence of fluid leakage **(see illustration)**. A light film of fluid is no cause for concern. Make sure that any fluid noted is from the shocks and not from some other source. If leakage is noted, replace the shocks as a set.

7   Check the shocks to be sure that they are securely mounted and undamaged. Check the upper mounts for damage and wear. If damage or wear is noted, replace the shocks as a set (front or rear).

8   If the shocks must be replaced, refer to Chapter 10 for the procedure.

9   Visually inspect the steering and suspension components (front and rear) for damage and distortion. Look for damaged seals, boots and bushings and leaks of any kind. Examine the bushings where the lower control arm meets the chassis and on the stabilizer bar connections **(see illustrations)**.

24.9c Check the stabilizer bar links (arrows) for looseness at the front and rear of the vehicle; also check the stabilizer bar bushings

10   Clean the lower end of the steering knuckle. Have an assistant grasp the lower edge of the tire and move the wheel in-and-out while you look for movement at the steering knuckle-to-control arm balljoint. If there is any movement, the suspension balljoint(s) must be replaced.

11   Grasp each front tire at the front and rear edges, push in at the front, pull out at the rear and feel for play in the steering system components. If any freeplay is noted, check the idler arm and the tie-rod ends for looseness **(see illustration)**.

12   Additional steering and suspension system information and illustrations can be found in Chapter 10.

Driveaxle boot check

13   The driveaxle boots are very important because they prevent dirt, water and foreign material from entering and damaging the constant velocity (CV) joints. Oil and grease can cause the boot material to deteriorate prematurely, so it's a good idea to wash the

24.11 With the steering wheel in the lock position and the vehicle raised, grasp the front tire as shown and try to move it back-and-forth - if any play is noted, check the steering gear mounts and tie-rod ends for looseness

24.14 Flex the inner and outer driveaxle boots by hand to check for cracks and/or tears

25.7a Remove the automatic transaxle drain plug (arrow) (earlier model)

boots with soap and water. Because it constantly pivots back and forth following the steering action of the front hub, the outer CV boot wears out sooner and should be inspected regularly.

14   Inspect the boots for tears and cracks as well as loose clamps **(see illustration)**. If there is any evidence of cracks or leaking lubricant, they must be replaced as described in Chapter 8.

---

25 Automatic transaxle fluid change (every 30,000 miles or 24 months)

Refer to illustrations 25.7a and 25.7b

1   At the specified time intervals, the automatic transaxle fluid should be drained and replaced.

2   Before beginning work, purchase the specified transmission fluid (*see Recommended lubricants and fluids* at the front of this Chapter).

3   Other tools necessary for this job include jackstands to support the vehicle in a raised position, 3/8-inch drive ratchet, a drain pan capable of holding least six quarts, newspapers and clean rags.

4   The fluid should be drained immediately after the vehicle has been driven. Hot fluid is more effective than cold fluid at removing built-up sediment. **Warning:** *Fluid temperature can exceed 350-degrees F in a hot transaxle. Wear protective gloves.*

5   After the vehicle has been driven to warm up the fluid, raise it and place it on jackstands for access to the transaxle drain plug.

6   Move the necessary equipment under the vehicle, being careful not to touch any of the hot exhaust components.

7   Place the drain pan under the transaxle and remove the drain plug **(see illustrations)**. Be sure the drain pan is in position, as fluid will come out with some force. Once the fluid has drained, clean the drain plug and reinstall it securely.

2000 and earlier models

8   Remove the transaxle pan bolts.

9   Carefully pry the transaxle pan loose with a screwdriver. Don't damage the pan or transaxle gasket surface or leaks could develop.

10   Remove the pan and gasket. Carefully clean the gasket surface of the transaxle to remove all traces of the old gasket and sealant.

11   Drain any remaining fluid from the transaxle pan, clean it with solvent and dry it thoroughly. Make sure to install magnets in their original positions (indentations) in the pan.

12   Remove the retaining bolts and detach the old filter from the transaxle.

13   Install the new filter and tighten the bolts.

14   Make sure the gasket surface on the transaxle pan is clean, then install a new gasket. Put the pan in place against the transaxle and install the bolts. Working around the pan, tighten each bolt a little at a time until the final torque figure listed in this Chapter's Specifications is reached. Don't overtighten the bolts!

Later models

15   Some later models may have a spin-on canister-type transmission filter that resembles the engine oil filter, located on top of the transaxle. Replace this filter with a new one in the same manner as an engine oil filter (see Section 8).

All models

16   Lower the vehicle.

17   Pull out the dipstick and add new fluid to the transaxle through the dipstick tube (see *Recommended lubricants and fluids* for the recommended fluid type and capacity). Use a funnel to prevent spills. It is best to add a little fluid at a time, continually checking the level with the dipstick (see Section 7). Allow the fluid time to drain into the pan.

25.7b Later model automatic transaxle drain plug location (arrow)

18   Install the dipstick.

19   Start the engine and shift the selector into all positions from P through 2, then shift into P and apply the parking brake.

20   Turn off the engine and check the fluid level. Add fluid to bring the level into the notched area on the dipstick.

---

26 Manual transaxle lubricant change - (every 30,000 miles or 24 months)

1   At the specified time intervals, the manual transaxle lubricant should be drained and replaced.

2   Before beginning work, purchase the specified transaxle lubricant (see *Recommended lubricants and fluids* and *Capacities* at the beginning of this Chapter).

3   Other tools necessary for this job include jackstands to support the vehicle in a raised position, 3/8-inch drive ratchet, a drain pan capable of holding at least four quarts, newspapers and clean rags.

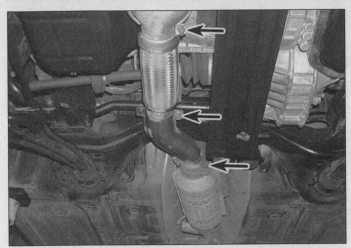

27.2a Check all of the flanged and slip-jointed exhaust connections (arrows) - look for stains that indicate exhaust leakage

27.2b Check each exhaust system hanger (arrow) for damage and cracks

4   After the vehicle has been driven to warm up the fluid, raise it and place it on jackstands for access to the transaxle drain plug. Place the drain pan under the transaxle, remove the drain plug and allow the old oil to drain into the pan (see Section 17).

5   Reinstall the drain plug securely.

6   Add new fluid through the filler hole until it begins to run out of the filler hole (see Section 17). Install the check/fill plug and tighten it securely.

27 Exhaust system check (every 30,000 miles or 24 months)

Refer to illustrations 27.2a and 27.2b

1   With the engine cold (at least three hours after the vehicle has been driven), check the complete exhaust system from the engine to the end of the tailpipe. Ideally, the inspection should be done with the vehicle on a hoist to permit unrestricted access. If a hoist isn't available, raise the vehicle and support it securely on jackstands.

2   Check the exhaust pipes and connections for evidence of leaks, severe corrosion and damage. Make sure that all brackets and hangers are in good condition and tight **(see illustrations)**.

3   At the same time, inspect the underside of the body for holes, corrosion, open seams, etc. which may allow exhaust gases to enter the passenger compartment. Seal all body openings with silicone or body putty.

4   Rattles and other noises can often be traced to the exhaust system, especially the mounts and hangers. Try to move the pipes, muffler and catalytic converter. If the components can come in contact with the body or suspension parts, secure the exhaust system with new mounts.

5   Check the running condition of the engine by inspecting inside the end of the tailpipe. The exhaust deposits here are an indication of engine state-of-tune. If the pipe

is black and sooty or coated with white deposits, the engine may need a tune-up, including a thorough fuel system inspection and adjustment.

28 Fuel system check (every 30,000 miles or 24 months)

Warning: *Gasoline is extremely flammable, so take extra precautions when you work on any part of the fuel system. Don't smoke or allow open flames or bare light bulbs near the work area, and don't work in a garage where a gas-type appliance (such as a water heater or clothes dryer) is present. Since gasoline is carcinogenic, wear latex gloves when there's a possibility of being exposed to fuel, and, if you spill any fuel on your skin, rinse it off immediately with soap and water. Mop up any spills immediately and do not store fuel-soaked rags where they could ignite. When you perform any kind of work on the fuel system, wear safety glasses and have a Class B type fire extinguisher on hand. The fuel system is under constant pressure, so, before any lines are disconnected, the fuel system pressure must be relieved (see Chapter 4).*

1   If you smell gasoline while driving or after the vehicle has been sitting in the sun, inspect the fuel system immediately.

2   Remove the gas filler cap and inspect it for damage and corrosion. The gasket should have an unbroken sealing imprint. If the gasket is damaged or corroded, install a new cap.

3   Inspect the fuel feed and return lines for cracks. Make sure that the connections between the fuel lines and the fuel injection system and between the fuel lines and the in-line fuel filter are tight. **Warning:** *Your vehicle is fuel injected, so you must relieve the fuel system pressure before servicing fuel system components. The fuel system pressure relief procedure is outlined in Chapter 4.*

4   If the fuel injectors are visible, look for

signs of fuel leakage (wet spots) around any of the injectors, they may need new O-rings (see Chapter 4).

5   Since some components of the fuel system - the fuel tank and part of the fuel feed and return lines, for example - are underneath the vehicle, they can be inspected more easily with the vehicle raised on a hoist. If that's not possible, raise the vehicle and support it on jackstands.

6   With the vehicle raised and safely supported, inspect the gas tank and filler neck for punctures, cracks and other damage. The connection between the filler neck and the tank is particularly critical. Sometimes a rubber filler neck will leak because of loose clamps or deteriorated rubber. Inspect all fuel tank mounting brackets and straps to be sure that the tank is securely attached to the vehicle. **Warning:** *Do not, under any circumstances, try to repair a fuel tank (except rubber components). A welding torch or any open flame can easily cause fuel vapors inside the tank to explode.*

7   Carefully check all rubber hoses and metal lines leading away from the fuel tank. Check for loose connections, deteriorated hoses, crimped lines and other damage. Repair or replace damaged sections as necessary (see Chapter 4).

8   The evaporative emissions control system can also be a source of fuel odors. The function of the system is to store fuel vapors from the fuel tank in a charcoal canister until they can be routed to the intake manifold where they mix with incoming air before being burned in the combustion chambers.

9   The most common symptom of a faulty evaporative emissions system is a strong odor of fuel in the engine compartment. If a fuel odor has been detected, and you have already checked the areas described above, check the charcoal canister, located behind the left front suspension tower on earlier models or under the rear of the vehicle on 1998 and later models, and the hoses connected to it.

29   Fuel filter replacement (every 60,000 miles or 48 months)

Warning: *Gasoline is extremely flammable, so take extra precautions when you work on any part of the fuel system. Don't smoke or allow open flames or bare light bulbs near the work area, and don't work in a garage where a gas-type appliance (such as a water heater or clothes dryer) is present. Since gasoline is carcinogenic, wear latex gloves when there's a possibility of being exposed to fuel, and, if you spill any fuel on your skin, rinse it off immediately with soap and water. Mop up any spills immediately and do not store fuel-soaked rags where they could ignite. When you perform any kind of work on the fuel system, wear safety glasses and have a Class B type fire extinguisher on hand. The fuel system is under constant pressure, so, before any lines are disconnected, the fuel system pressure must be relieved (see Chapter 4).*

Caution: *Some models are equipped with an anti-theft radio. Before performing a procedure that requires disconnecting the battery, make sure you have the activation code.*

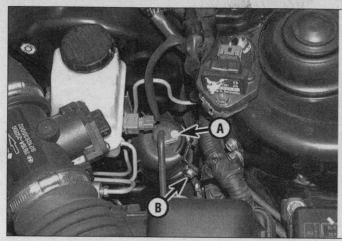

29.4 Remove the bolt (A) and detach the fuel lines, then remove the bracket nut (B) so the filter can be detached from the bracket assembly and removed

Refer to illustration 29.4

1   Refer to Chapter 4 and relieve the fuel system pressure.

2   Disconnect the negative battery cable.

3   If necessary for access, remove the air cleaner assembly (see Chapter 4).

4   Remove the clips and detach the hoses from the fuel filter, then remove the filter bracket nuts and lift the assembly out of the engine compartment **(see illustration)**.

5   Note the direction that the inlet and outlet pipes are facing. Make sure the new filter is installed so that it's facing the proper direction as noted above. Install the inlet and outlet hoses and secure them with clamps.

6   The remainder of installation is the reverse of the removal procedure.

Chapter 2 Part A
Engines

Contents

Specifications

Flywheel
Maximum allowable warpage... 0.004 inch

Oil pump
Body clearance (between outer circumference of outer rotor and case)..	0.005 to 0.007 inch (0.12 to 0.18 mm)
Inner pump rotor axial (side) clearance	
2000 and earlier...	0.0008 to 0.0025 inch (0.02 to 0.065 mm)
2001	0.0016 to 0.0033 inch (0.04 to 0.085 mm)
Outer pump rotor axial (side) clearance	
2000 and earlier...	0.0008 to 0.0027 inch (0.02 to 0.07 mm)
2001	0.0016 to 0.0035 inch (0.04 to 0.09 mm)
Rotor tip clearance	0.001 to 0.003 inch (0.025 to 0.069 mm)
Relief valve spring free length...	1.724 inches (43.8 mm)

Torque specifications

	Ft-lbs (unless otherwise indicated)	Nm
Camshaft bearing cap bolts	120 to 132 in-lbs	14 to 15
Camshaft sprocket retaining bolt	74 to 89	100 to 120
Crankshaft sprocket bolt	125 to 133	170 to 180
Cylinder head bolts		
First step		
2000 and earlier		
10mm bolts	22	30
12mm bolts	26	35
2001		
10mm bolts	18	25
12mm bolts	22	30
Second step	60 to 65-degrees	
Third step	60 to 65-degrees	
Exhaust manifold heat shield bolts	132 to 180 in-lbs	15 to 20
Exhaust manifold bolts/nuts	32 to 37	43 to 55
Flywheel/driveplate bolts	90 to 96	120 to 130
Intake manifold nuts/bolts		
2000 and earlier	144 to 204 in-lbs	16 to 23
2001	132 to 168 in-lbs	15 to 20
Oil pan bolts		
2000 and earlier	48 to 72 in-lbs	6 to 8
2001	84 to 108 in-lbs	10 to 12
Oil pump		
Oil pump-to-block bolts	15 to 20	20 to 27
Oil pump cover bolts	48 to 84 in-lbs	6 to 9
Relief valve plug	30 to 36	41 to 49
Timing belt		
Tensioner pulley bolt	31 to 40	43 to 55
Idler pulley bolt	31 to 40	43 to 55
Timing belt cover bolts	72 to 84 in-lbs	8 to 10
Valve cover bolts	72 to 84 in-lbs	8 to 10

1 General information

This Part of Chapter 2 is devoted to in-vehicle repair procedures for the engine. The engine has a cast-iron engine block an aluminum cylinder head. The cylinder head is equipped with dual overhead camshafts. Hydraulic lifters are used to actuate the valves on 1996 through 2000 engines; these models require no periodic valve clearance adjustments. On 2001 engines, which use "shim-and-bucket" style lifters, the valve clearances may occasionally need to be checked and, if necessary, adjusted (see Section 12 in Chapter 2B). The aluminum cylinder head on all models is equipped with pressed-in valve guides and hardened valve seats. The gear-type oil pump is mounted on the front of the engine block and is driven by the crankshaft.

The following repair procedures are based on the assumption that the engine is installed in the vehicle. If the engine has been removed from the vehicle and mounted on a stand, many of the steps outlined in this Part of Chapter 2 will not apply.

The Specifications included in this Part of Chapter 2 apply only to the procedures contained in this Part. All information concerning engine removal and installation, engine block and cylinder head overhaul and the Specifications necessary for cylinder head and engine block rebuilding, is in Part B of Chapter 2.

2 Repair operations possible with the engine in the vehicle

Many major repair operations can be accomplished without removing the engine from the vehicle.

Clean the engine compartment and the exterior of the engine with some type of degreaser before any work is done. It will make the job easier and help keep dirt out of the internal areas of the engine.

Depending on the components involved, it may be helpful to remove the hood to improve access to the engine as repairs are performed (refer to Chapter 11 if necessary). Cover the fenders to prevent damage to the paint. Special pads are available, but an old bedspread or blanket will also work.

If vacuum, exhaust, oil or coolant leaks develop, indicating a need for gasket or seal replacement, the repairs can generally be made with the engine in the vehicle. The intake and exhaust manifold gaskets, oil pan gasket, crankshaft oil seals and cylinder head gasket are all accessible with the engine in place.

Exterior engine components, such as the intake and exhaust manifolds, the oil pan, the oil pump, the water pump, the starter motor, the alternator and the fuel system components can be removed for repair with the engine in the vehicle.

Since the cylinder head can be removed without pulling the engine, camshaft and valve component servicing can also be accomplished with the engine in the vehicle. Replacement of the timing belt and pulleys is also possible with the engine in the vehicle.

In extreme cases caused by a lack of necessary equipment, repair or replacement of piston rings, pistons, connecting rods and rod bearings is possible with the engine in the vehicle. However, this practice is not recommended because of the cleaning and preparation work that must be done to the components involved.

3.5 Use a compression gauge in the number one spark plug hole to assist in finding TDC

3.6 Align the notch (arrow) on the crankshaft drivebelt pulley with the mark on the timing belt cover

3   Top Dead Center (TDC) for number one piston - locating

Refer to illustrations 3.5 and 3.6

1   Top Dead Center (TDC) is the highest point in the cylinder that each piston reaches as it travels up-and-down when the crankshaft turns. Each piston reaches TDC on the compression stroke and again on the exhaust stroke, but TDC generally refers to piston position on the compression stroke. The timing marks on the vibration damper/crankshaft pulley installed on the front of the crankshaft are referenced to the number one piston at TDC.

2   Positioning the piston(s) at TDC is an essential part of procedures such as timing belt and sprocket replacement.

3   In order to bring any piston to TDC, the crankshaft must be turned using one of the methods outlined below. When looking at the timing belt end of the engine, normal crankshaft rotation is clockwise. **Warning:** *Before beginning this procedure, be sure to place the transmission in Park or Neutral, set the parking brake and remove the ignition key.*

   a) *The preferred method is to turn the crankshaft with a large socket and breaker bar attached to the large bolt threaded into the center of the crankshaft pulley.*

   b) *A remote starter switch, which may save some time, can also be used. Attach the switch leads to the S (switch) and B (battery) terminals on the starter motor. Once the piston is close to TDC, use a socket and breaker bar as described in the previous paragraph.*

   c) *If an assistant is available to turn the ignition switch to the Start position in short bursts, you can get the piston close to TDC without a remote starter switch. Use a socket and breaker bar as described in Paragraph a) to complete the procedure.*

4   Disable the ignition system by disconnecting the primary electrical connectors at the ignition coil pack/modules (see Chapter 5).

5   Remove the spark plugs (see Chapter 1) and install a compression gauge in the number one cylinder **(see illustration)**. Turn the crankshaft clockwise with a socket and breaker bar as described above.

6   When the piston approaches TDC, compression will be noted on the compression gauge. Continue turning the crankshaft until the notch in the crankshaft damper is aligned with the TDC mark on the front cover **(see illustration)**. At this point number one cylinder is at TDC on the compression stroke. If the marks aligned but there was no compression, the piston was on the exhaust stroke; continue rotating the crankshaft 360-degrees (1-turn) and line-up the marks. **Note:** *If a compression gauge is not available, TDC for the No.1 piston can be obtained by simultaneously aligning the marks on the camshaft timing belt sprocket with the top of the cylinder head (see illustration 5.7) and the marks on the crankshaft damper with the TDC mark on the front cover.*

7   After the number one piston has been positioned at TDC on the compression stroke, TDC for any of the remaining cylinders can be located by turning the crankshaft 180 degrees and following the firing order (refer to the Specifications). Rotating the engine 180 degrees past TDC #1 will put the engine at TDC compression for cylinder #3.

4   Valve cover - removal and installation

Removal

Caution: *Some models are equipped with an anti-theft radio. Before performing a procedure that requires disconnecting the battery, make sure you have the activation code.*

Refer to illustrations 4.2, 4.5, 4.6 and 4.7

1   Disconnect the negative battery cable.

2   Detach the accelerator cable from the cable guides on the valve cover **(see illustration)**. (It's not necessary to remove the cable guides themselves unless you're planning to replace the valve cover.)

3   Disconnect the PCV and breather hoses from the valve cover **(see illustration 4.2)**.

4   Remove the spark plug wire cover bolts **(see illustration 4.2)**, remove the cover and then remove the spark plug wires (see Chapter 1).

5   Remove the bolts that attach the upper timing belt cover to the valve cover **(see illustration)**.

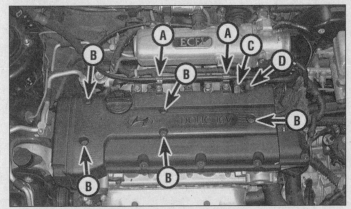

4.2 Detach the accelerator cable from the cable guides (A) on the valve cover, remove the spark plug cover bolts (B), remove the spark plug cover and then disconnect the PCV hose (C) and the breather hose (D)

4.5 Remove the bolts (upper arrows) that attach the upper timing belt cover to the valve cover; to remove the upper timing belt cover, remove the two lower bolts (lower arrows) as well

4.6 Remove the valve cover bolts (arrows) and then remove the valve cover (if the cover is stuck, bump the end with a block of wood and a hammer to jar it loose, or slip a flexible putty knife between the head and cover to break the seal

4.7 Remove the valve cover gasket from the valve cover

6   Remove the valve cover bolts **(see illustration)**.and then remove the valve cover. If the cover is stuck to the head, bump the end with a block of wood and a hammer to jar it loose. If that doesn't work, try to slip a flexible putty knife between the head and cover to break the seal. **Caution:** *Don't pry at the cover-to-head joint or damage to the sealing surfaces may occur, leading to oil leaks after the cover is reinstalled.*
7   Remove the valve cover gasket from the valve cover **(see illustration)**.

Installation

8   The mating surfaces of the cylinder head and the valve cover must be clean when the cover is installed. Use a gasket scraper to remove all traces of sealant and old gasket material, then clean the mating surfaces with lacquer thinner or acetone. If there's residue or oil on the mating surfaces when the cover is installed, oil leaks may develop.
9   Inspect the old valve cover gasket for cracks, tears and deterioration. If it's damaged, replace it.
10   Position the valve cover gasket over the studs on the cylinder head.
11   Install the valve cover and then, working from the center of the valve cover out toward the ends, tighten the valve cover bolts gradually and evenly, in a criss-cross fashion, to the torque listed in this Chapter's Specifications. Don't forget to install the timing cover-to-valve cover bolts and tighten them to the torque listed in this Chapter's Specifications.
12   Install the spark plug wires and the spark plug wire cover (see Chapter 1).
13   Reconnect the breather hose and the PCV hose.
14   Reattach the accelerator cable guides, if they were removed, to the valve cover, and then reattach the accelerator cable to the guides.
15   Reconnect the negative battery cable.
16   Start the engine and check the valve cover for oil leaks.

5   Timing belt and sprockets - removal, inspection and installation

Warning: *Wait until the engine is completely cool before beginning this procedure.*
Caution: *Do not rotate the crankshaft or the camshaft separately during this procedure with the timing belt removed as damage to valves may occur. Only rotate the camshaft a few degrees as necessary to align the camshaft sprocket marks with the marks on the rear timing cover.*

Removal

Caution: *Some models are equipped with an anti-theft radio. Before performing a procedure that requires disconnecting the battery, make sure you have the activation code.*
Refer to illustrations 5.5a, 5.5b, 5.6, 5.7, 5.8, 5.9, 5.11 and 5.12
1   Disconnect the negative battery cable.
2   Rotate the engine in the normal direction

of rotation (clockwise) until the No.1 cylinder is located at TDC (see Section 3).
3   Remove the accessory drivebelts (see Chapter 1).
4   Loosen the water pump pulley bolts and then remove the water pump pulley. (see Chapter 3).
5   Using a chain wrench or a strap wrench to hold the crankshaft pulley, loosen the crank pulley bolt **(see illustration)** and then remove the pulley bolt and the crank pulley. Make sure that you don't move the No. 1 cylinder from TDC while loosening the crank pulley bolt. After removing the crankshaft pulley, remove the timing belt retainer/guide flange **(see illustration)**.
6   Remove the four upper timing belt cover bolts **(see illustration 4.5)** and then remove the upper timing belt cover. Remove the lower timing belt cover bolts **(see illustration)**.
7   Make sure that the timing belt camshaft sprocket timing marks are aligned with the top of the cylinder head **(see illustration)**.
8   If you're planning to re-use the timing

5.5a Using a chain wrench or a strap wrench to hold the crankshaft pulley, loosen the crank pulley bolt and then remove the pulley bolt and the crank pulley

5.5b After removing the crankshaft pulley, remove the timing belt retainer/guide flange

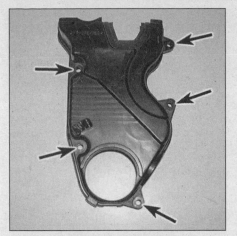

5.7 Make sure that the camshaft sprocket timing marks (arrows) are aligned with the top of the cylinder head

5.6 To detach the lower timing belt cover from the engine, remove the bolts (arrows) (cover removed for clarity)

belt, put a directional arrow, indicating the normal (clockwise) direction of rotation, on the belt **(see illustration)**.

9 Remove the timing belt tensioner pulley bolt **(see illustration)** and then remove the tensioner pulley.

10 Remove the timing belt.

11 Remove the timing belt idler pulley bolt **(see illustration)** and then remove the idler pulley.

12 If the camshaft sprocket is damaged or must be removed to replace the camshaft seal or to strip the cylinder head for overhaul, use a wrench to hold the camshaft in place, and then remove the sprocket retaining bolt **(see illustration)**. Then remove the camshaft sprocket from the end of the camshaft.

13 Remove the crankshaft timing belt sprocket.

Inspection

Refer to illustration 5.15

Caution: *Do not bend, twist or turn the timing belt inside out. Do not allow it to come in*

5.8 If you're planning to re-use the timing belt, put a directional arrow, indicating the normal (clockwise) direction of rotation, on the belt

5.9 Remove the timing belt tensioner pulley bolt (arrow) and then remove the tensioner pulley

contact with oil, coolant or fuel. Do not turn the crankshaft or camshaft more than a few degrees (if necessary for tooth alignment) while the timing belt is removed.

14 Spin the idler pulley and the timing belt tensioner and check their bearings for

smooth operation and excessive play. Inspect the timing belt sprocket teeth for any obvious damage. Replace all worn parts as necessary.

15 Examine the belt for evidence of contamination by coolant or lubricant. If this is

5.11 Remove the timing belt idler pulley bolt (arrow) and then remove the idler pulley

5.12 To remove the camshaft sprocket, use a wrench to hold the camshaft in place while you loosen the camshaft sprocket retaining bolt, and then remove the sprocket bolt and the cam sprocket

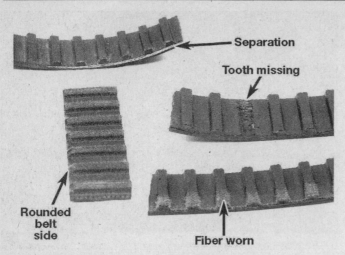

5.15 Inspect the timing belt for cracked and missing teeth; wear on one side of the belt indicates an alignment problem between the belt and the sprocket(s)

5.22 After rotating the crankshaft at least twice, verify that the mark (arrow) on the crankshaft timing belt sprocket is aligned with the stationary index mark (arrow) on the oil pump housing

the case, find the source of the contamination before progressing any further. Check the belt for signs of wear or damage, particularly around the leading edges of the belt teeth **(see illustration). Caution:** *If the belt appears to be in good condition and can be re-used, it is essential that it is reinstalled the same way around, otherwise accelerated wear will result, leading to premature failure.*

16   Replace the belt if its condition is in doubt; the cost of belt replacement is negligible compared with potential cost of the engine repairs, should the belt fail in service. Similarly, if the belt is known to have covered more than 80,000 miles, it is prudent to replace it regardless of condition, as a precautionary measure.

Installation

Refer to illustration 5.22

17   Verify that the No. 1 piston is still at TDC (see Section 3) and that the camshaft timing sprocket is still correctly aligned **(see illustration 5.7)**. If the cam sprocket, idler pulley and/or crankshaft sprocket was removed for inspection or replacement, install it now. Be sure to tighten the camshaft sprocket retaining bolt and/or the idler pulley bolt to the torque listed in this Chapter's Specifications.

18   Loop the timing belt loosely under the crankshaft sprocket. If you're installing the old belt, don't forget to install it with the directional arrow facing in the correct direction.

19   Engage the timing belt teeth with the crankshaft sprocket, then maneuver it into position over the idler pulley and the camshaft sprocket. Make sure that the belt teeth are correctly seated on the sprockets, then install the belt around the timing belt tensioner. **Note:** *Very slight adjustment of the position of the camshaft sprocket is permissible, if necessary, to get the belt teeth to "lock into" the teeth on the sprocket.*

20   Make sure that the "front run" of the belt (the side nearer the front of the vehicle) is taut, and that all belt slack is in the "rear run," (the part of the belt that is going to be tensioned by the tensioner pulley).

21   Tension the belt by turning the eccentrically-mounted tensioner counterclockwise, toward the water pump, and then tighten the tensioner bolt to the torque listed in this Chapter's Specifications. The belt tension is correct if the belt can be deflected about 1/4-inch when pushed with about five pounds of pressure.

22   At this point, double check to make sure that the crankshaft is still set to TDC for the No. 1 cylinder (see Section 3) and the camshaft sprocket marks are aligned with the top of the cylinder head **(see illustration 5.7)**. Also, make sure that the mark on the crankshaft timing belt sprocket is aligned with the stationary index mark on the oil pump housing **(see illustration)**.

23   Rotate the crankshaft through two complete revolutions. Reset the engine to TDC on No. 1 cylinder, with reference to Section 3 and check the alignment marks again. Also re-check the timing belt tension and adjust it, if necessary (see Step 21).

24   Install the upper and lower timing belt covers and then tighten the timing belt cover bolts to the torque listed in this Chapter's Specifications.

25   Install the crankshaft pulley and, using a strap wrench or chain wrench to hold the pulley, tighten the crankshaft pulley bolt to the torque listed in this Chapter's Specifications.

26   Install the water pump pulley and tighten the pulley bolts as tightly as possible.

27   Install the accessory drivebelt (see Chapter 1).

28   Tighten the water pump pulley bolts to the torque listed in this Chapter's Specifications.

29   Reconnect the negative battery cable.

6   Camshafts and lifters - removal and installation

Note: *The camshaft and lifters should always be thoroughly inspected before installation and camshaft endplay should always be checked prior to camshaft removal. Although the hydraulic lifters on 1996 through 2000 models are self-adjusting and require no periodic service, there is an in-vehicle procedure for checking excessively noisy hydraulic lifters. Refer to Chapter 2B for the camshaft and lifter inspection procedures.*

Removal

Refer to illustrations 6.3a, 6.3b, 6.5, 6.6, 6.7, 6.9a and 6.9b

1   Remove the valve cover (see Section 4).

2   Remove the timing cover, the timing belt and the camshaft timing belt sprocket (see Section 5).

3   Starting in the middle of the cylinder head, at bearing cap No. 3 on the intake camshaft or at cap No. 4 on the exhaust cam, loosen the camshaft bearing caps, working your way out toward the ends of the head in a criss-cross fashion **(see illustration)**. Don't loosen two cap bolts completely and then proceed to the next cap; this puts unnecessary stress on the camshafts. Instead, loosen the cap bolts gradually and evenly, in two or three passes. After removing the two inner bolts for the two rear caps, remove the upper chain guide **(see illustration)**.

4   Remove the bearing caps. Keep the intake and exhaust cam caps separated. They must be installed at the same location from which they were removed. If you get them mixed up, the caps are marked "I" (intake) or "E" (exhaust) and are numbered (1, 2, 3, etc.).

5   Remove the intake and exhaust camshafts and the camshaft timing chain as a single assembly **(see illustration)**. Remove.

6.3a Starting at the center of the cylinder head and then working your way toward the ends of the head, gradually and evenly loosen the camshaft bearing cap bolts (arrows) in a criss-cross fashion

6.3b When you get to these two bolts for the last two caps, remove the upper chain guide (arrow)

2A

6.5 Remove the camshafts and the timing chain as a single assembly

6.6 To detach the lower timing chain guide, remove these two bolts

6.7 Wipe off the tops of the hydraulic lifters (1996 through 2000 models) or the shims (2001 models) and then mark them with a laundry marker (I-1, I-2, E-1, E-2, etc.) or, as shown, mark pieces of tape and then affix them to the tops of the lifters

the old camshaft seal from the exhaust cam and discard it.

6   Remove the lower chain guide **(see illustration)**.

7   Wipe off the tops of the hydraulic lifters (1996 through 2000 models) or the shims (2001 models) and then mark them with a laundry marker (I-1, I-2, E-1, E-2, etc.), or mark strips of tape and then affix them to the top of each lifter **(see illustration)**.

8   Remove the lifters from the cylinder head. Keep the intake and exhaust lifters separated, and keep them in order.

9   Thoroughly clean the cam timing chain and the timing chain sprockets on the camshafts with fresh solvent and a stiff brush and then inspect the timing chain and the sprockets **(see illustration)**. Make sure that the bearing surfaces (the shiny parts) of the chain rollers are in good condition and that the chain isn't stiff. If the chain is excessively worn or damaged, replace it. Make sure that the teeth on the camshaft timing chain sprockets are in good condition. If any of the teeth are broken or excessively worn, replace the camshaft(s). Also inspect the timing chain

guides **(see illustration)**. Make sure that the friction surfaces of the guides are still in good condition. If either guide is excessively worn, replace it.

10   Inspect the camshafts and the lifters (see Chapter 2B).

6.9a Inspect the bearing surfaces (the shiny parts) of the chain rollers and the teeth on the camshaft timing chain sprockets

6.9b Also inspect the friction surfaces of the timing chain guides

6.13 Slide the new cam seal over the nose of the cam, place the cam in position in the head and then gently push the seal onto the nose of the cam until the chamfered edge around the face of the seal bore is exposed

6.14 When installing the camshaft timing chain on the camshaft sprockets, make sure that the timing marks on the cam chain sprockets are aligned with the centers of the two dark side plates, with four links in between

Installation

Refer to illustrations 6.13 and 6.14

11 Apply clean engine oil to the walls of the lifters and then insert the lifters into their respective bores in the cylinder head. Push down the lifters until they contact the valves, then lubricate the camshaft lobe contact surfaces (1996 through 2000 models) or the shims (2001 models).

12 Lubricate the camshaft and cylinder head bearing journals with clean engine oil.

13 Clean the oil seal bore and the sealing surface of the "nose" (forward end) of the camshaft, lubricate the lip of the new camshaft oil seal with clean engine oil and slide it over the nose. Place the camshaft in position in the cylinder head and then gently push the seal onto the nose of the cam until the chamfered edge around the face of the cam seal bore is visible **(see illustration)**.

14 Install the camshaft timing chain on the camshaft sprockets. Make sure that the timing marks on the cam chain sprockets are aligned with the centers of the two dark side plates, with four links in between **(see illustration)**.

15 Carefully lower the camshafts and timing chain into position on the cylinder head with the camshaft lobes for the No. 1 cylinder facing up (180 degrees from the cylinder head mating surface).Oil the upper surfaces of the camshaft bearing journals, then install the bearing caps over the camshafts and then, working in a criss-cross fashion from the ends of the head toward the center, gradually and evenly tighten the cap retaining bolts to the torque listed in this Chapter's Specifications.

16 Install the timing belt sprocket on the exhaust camshaft (see Section 5).

17 Install the timing belt (see Section 5). When installing the timing belt, make sure the crankshaft is at TDC for the No. 1 cylinder (see Section 3), the camshaft sprocket marks are aligned with the upper edge of the cylinder head **(see illustration 5.7)**. and the crankshaft sprocket mark is aligned with the

stationary index mark on the oil pump housing **(see illustration 5.22)**.

18 The remainder of installation is the reverse of removal.

7   Camshaft oil seal - replacement

Refer to illustrations 7.2 and 7.3

1 Remove the timing cover, the timing belt and the camshaft timing belt sprocket (see Section 5).

2 Using a seal removal tool, carefully dig out the old cam seal **(see illustration)**.

3 Clean the oil seal bore, lubricate the lip of the new camshaft oil seal with clean engine oil and slide it over the end of the camshaft. Gently push the seal onto the nose of the camshaft until it's positioned square to the seal bore. Using a socket with an outside diameter slightly smaller than the outside diameter of the seal, carefully drive the new seal into place with a hammer **(see illustration)**. Make sure it's installed squarely and driven in to the same depth as the original. If a socket isn't available, a short section of

pipe will also work.

4 Install the camshaft timing belt sprocket, the timing belt and the timing cover (see Section 5).

8   Intake manifold - removal and installation

Refer to illustrations 8.5, 8.6, 8.8, 8.10 and 8.11

Warning: *Wait until the engine is completely cool before beginning this procedure.*

1 Remove the idle speed actuator (see Chapter 6).

2 Remove the air intake duct that connects the MAF sensor to the throttle body (see Chapter 4).

3 Disconnect the accelerator cable from the throttle body linkage and from the cable brackets (see Chapter 4) and set it aside. Also remove the cruise control cable (see Chapter 12), if equipped.

4 If you're planning to replace the intake manifold, remove the throttle body now (see Chapter 4). If you're only removing the intake

7.2 Using a seal removal tool, carefully dig out the old cam seal

7.3 Using a socket with an outside diameter slightly smaller than the outside diameter of the seal, carefully drive the new seal into place with a hammer

8.5 Disconnect the PCV hose (arrow) from the intake manifold

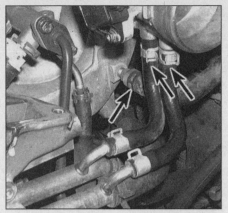

8.6 Disconnect the two coolant hoses from the underside of the throttle body and disconnect the power brake booster vacuum hose (arrow) from the air intake plenum

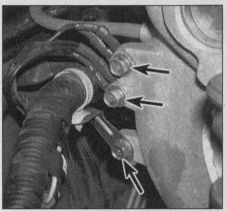

8.8 Label and then disconnect the electrical grounds (upper arrows) from the right end of the intake manifold and then remove the bracket bolt (lower arrow) and detach the wiring harness bracket from the manifold

manifold in order to replace a manifold gasket or to service the cylinder head, it's not necessary to remove the throttle body. Just unplug the electrical connector from the Throttle Position Sensor (TPS) and detach the coolant hoses from the underside of the throttle body (see Chapter 4).

5   Disconnect the PCV hose **(see illustration)** from the intake manifold.

6   Disconnect the power brake booster vacuum hose from the air intake plenum **(see illustration)**.

7   Label and then disconnect all vacuum hoses from the air intake plenum and from the throttle body.

8   Label and then disconnect the electrical grounds **(see illustration)** from the right end of the intake manifold and then detach the wiring harness bracket from the manifold.

9   Remove the fuel rail and the injectors (see Chapter 4).

10   Remove the intake manifold support bracket **(see illustration)**.

11   Working from the center of the intake manifold, remove the manifold retaining nuts (1996 through 2000 models) **(see illustration)** or bolts (2001 models) gradually and evenly until all nuts or bolts are loose. Remove the nuts/bolts by hand and remove

the intake manifold. Remove and discard the old intake manifold gasket.

12   Before installing the intake manifold, clean the mounting surfaces of the manifold and the cylinder head with lacquer thinner and remove all traces of the old gasket material or sealant.

13   Install the new gasket over the intake manifold studs, then install the intake manifold and tighten the nuts or bolts in a criss cross pattern to the torque listed in this Chapter's Specifications.

14   The remainder of installation is the reverse of removal.

15   When you're done, check the coolant level (see Chapter 1) and top up the coolant system if necessary.

---

9   Exhaust manifold - removal and installation

Refer to illustrations 9.2a 9.2b, 9.4 and 9.5
Warning: *The engine must be completely cool before beginning this procedure.*
1   On 2001 models, unplug the electrical

8.10 Remove the intake manifold support bracket bolts (arrows) and then remove the bracket

connector for the upstream Heated Oxygen Sensor (HO2S) (see Chapter 6).

2   Remove the exhaust manifold heat shield bolts **(see illustrations)** and then

8.11 To detach the intake manifold, remove these retaining nuts (arrows)

9.2a To detach the exhaust manifold heat shield from the exhaust manifold on 1996 through 2000 models, remove these seven bolts (arrows) (two bolts, on right side of shield, not visible in this photo)

remove the exhaust heat shield. Inspect the heat shield bolts for damage and corrosion. If they're rusted or damaged, replace them.

3   Raise the front of the vehicle and place it securely on jackstands.

4   Working from under the vehicle, apply penetrating oil to the exhaust manifold-to-exhaust pipe flange studs and nuts. Wait a while for the penetrant to loosen up the fasteners, and then remove the exhaust manifold-to-exhaust pipe flange nuts **(see illustration)** and disconnect the exhaust pipe from the exhaust manifold.

5   Working from above, apply penetrating oil to the exhaust manifold mounting nuts and studs. Wait a while for the penetrant to loosen up the fasteners, and then remove the exhaust manifold nuts **(see illustration)** and remove the exhaust manifold. Discard the old exhaust manifold retaining nuts. Do NOT reuse the old manifold nuts.

6   Remove and discard the old exhaust manifold gasket.

7   Use a scraper to remove all traces of old gasket material and carbon deposits from the manifold and cylinder head mating surfaces. If the gasket was leaking, have the manifold checked for warpage at an automotive machine shop and resurfaced if necessary.

8   Position a new gasket over the cylinder head studs.

9   Install the exhaust manifold and thread the new mounting nuts into place. Make sure to use high-temperature anti-seize compound on the threads of the exhaust manifold studs. Working from the center out, tighten the exhaust manifold nuts to the torque listed in this Chapter's Specifications.

10   Working from under the vehicle, reattach the exhaust pipe to the exhaust manifold with new nuts. Be sure to use high-temperature anti-seize compound on the threads of the studs, then tighten the new nuts securely.

11   Install the heat shield, coat the heat shield bolts with high-temperature anti-seize compound and then tighten them to the torque listed in this Chapter's Specifications.

12   On 2001 models, plug in the electrical

9.2b To detach the exhaust manifold heat shield on 2001 models, remove these three bolts (arrows)

connector for the upstream HO2S.

13   Run the engine and check for exhaust leaks.

---

10   Cylinder head - removal and installation

Removal

Refer to illustrations 10.10 and 10.11

Note: *If you're only removing the cylinder head to replace the head gasket, or to service the cylinder block, the cylinder head can be removed with the intake and exhaust manifold attached. In this case, simply disregard any of the following steps that don't apply. However, if you're removing the head in order to overhaul it, or to have it overhauled, follow all of the steps below.*

1   Drain the engine coolant (See Chapter 1). Then disconnect the upper radiator hose and the other two coolant hoses from the thermostat housing (see Chapter 3).

2   Remove the spark plugs and the spark plug wires (see Chapter 1).

3   If you're going to disassemble the cylin-

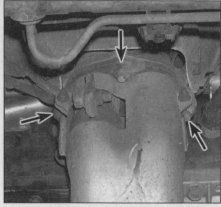

9.4 To detach the exhaust pipe from the exhaust manifold flange on 1996 through 2000 models, remove these nuts (arrows) (on 2001 models, the upstream catalytic converter is an integral part of the exhaust manifold, so this flange is below the converter)

der head, remove the ignition coil assembly (see Chapter 5).

4   Disconnect the valve cover (see Section 4).

5   Remove the timing belt cover and the timing belt (see Section 5).

6   Remove the camshafts and the lifters (see Section 6).

7   If you're going to disassemble the cylinder head, remove the fuel rail and the fuel injectors (see Chapter 4). If you're not going to disassemble the head, it's not necessary to remove the fuel rail and injectors; just unplug the electrical connectors, set the injector harness aside, disconnect the vacuum hose from the fuel pressure regulator and disconnect the fuel pressure and return lines (see Chapter 4).

8   Remove the power steering pump and then remove the pump bracket (see Chapter 10).

9   If you're going to disassemble the cylinder head for service, the intake manifold (see Section 8) and the exhaust manifold (see

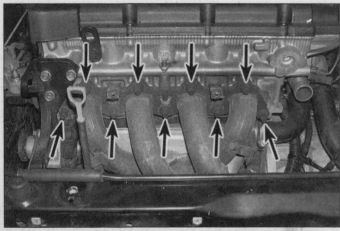

9.5 To detach the exhaust manifold from the cylinder head, remove these nuts (arrows) (1996 through 2000 model shown, 2001 models similar)

10.10 Cylinder head bolt loosening sequence

10.11 If the cylinder head is stuck to the block, carefully pry it loose at a casting protrusion

Section 9) will have to be removed, either now, or after the head is removed. If you're *not* going to disassemble the head, it's not necessary to remove the intake manifold or the exhaust manifold. In either case, it's not absolutely necessary that the manifolds be removed while the cylinder head is still installed on the block, but if you're going to lift off the head *by yourself*, removing the manifolds now will *lighten* the head considerably. On the other hand, if you have help, it's easier to remove the fasteners that secure the manifolds *after* the head has been removed.

10   Remove the cylinder head bolts in the sequence shown **(see illustration)**. Progressively loosen the cylinder head bolts, by half a turn at a time, until all bolts can be unscrewed by hand. Discard the old head bolts; the head must be reinstalled with new bolts.

11   Verify that nothing is still connected to the cylinder head, then lift the head off the block. Get help if possible; the head is quite heavy, particularly if it's being removed with the manifolds still attached. If the head is stuck to the block, carefully pry it loose at a casting protrusion **(see illustration)**. **Caution:** *Do NOT rotate the engine while the*

cylinder head is removed, unless absolutely necessary. If you do rotate the crankshaft, make sure that you put the piston in the No. 1 cylinder back to TDC before installing the cylinder head (see Section 3).

12   Remove the gasket from the top of the block, but don't discard it yet; you'll need to compare the new head gasket to the old one to make sure that you've got the right gasket. Remove the dowel pins and put them in a plastic bag.

13   If the cylinder head is going to be serviced, separate the manifolds, if you haven't already done so (see Sections 8 and 9, but disregard the steps that don't apply). Then proceed to Chapter 2B for the cylinder head disassembly and overhaul procedures.

Installation

Refer to illustrations 10.23a and 10.23b

14   The mating faces of the cylinder head and cylinder block must be perfectly clean before installing the head. Use a hard plastic or wood scraper to remove all traces of old gasket, sealing compound, scale and carbon deposits. Also clean the piston crowns. Use particular care when cleaning the head and the pistons; aluminum alloy is easily damaged. And make sure that no carbon or gasket material enters the oil or coolant passages; a chunk of carbon or gasket could block an oil or coolant passage, which would seriously damage the engine. To prevent debris from entering lubrication or coolant passages, use adhesive tape and paper to seal off all lubrication, coolant and cylinder-head-bolt holes in the block.

15   Inspect the mating surfaces of the cylinder block and the cylinder head for nicks, deep scratches and other damage. If they're slight, they may be removed carefully with abrasive paper.

16   If the cylinder head gasket surface is warped, or might be warped, use a straightedge to check it for distortion (see Chapter 2B).

17   Install the intake and exhaust manifolds, if they were removed. You could also elect to install the manifolds later, after the head has been bolted to the block, but it's much easier

to install the manifolds now, with the head removed, even though you'll probably need help when setting the head on the block.

18   To ensure that the cylinder head bolt holes are clean and dry before installing the head bolts, clean out the cylinder head bolt holes with a suitable tap and then blow them out with compressed air.

19   Make sure that the piston in the No. 1 cylinder is still at TDC (see Section 3).

20   Install the dowel pins in the cylinder block and then position the new head gasket on the block. Make sure that the manufacturer's markings are facing up.

21   With the help of an assistant, place the cylinder head and manifolds on the cylinder block. Verify that the head gasket is still flat and correctly seated before allowing the full weight of the cylinder head to rest upon it. Make sure that the head is seated on the dowel pins. **Note:** *If the cylinder head was disassembled for service, make sure that the camshaft lobes for the No. 1 cylinder are pointing upward.*

22   Oil the threads and the underside of the bolt heads, then carefully enter each bolt into its relevant hole and screw them in hand tight. Be sure to use NEW cylinder head bolts; the old bolts, which have already been stretched, cannot be correctly torqued.

23   Working progressively and in the sequence shown **(see illustration)**, tighten the cylinder head bolts in three steps, first to the torque, and then to the angle, listed in this Chapter's Specifications. **Note:** *It is recommended that an angle-measuring gauge be used during the final stages of the tightening, to ensure accuracy* **(see illustration)**. *If a gauge is not available, use white paint to make alignment marks between the bolt head and cylinder head prior to tightening; the marks can then be used to check the bolt has been rotated through the correct angle during tightening.*

24   Install the intake manifold (see Section 8) and the exhaust manifold (see Section 9), if they haven't already been installed.

25   Install the power steering pump bracket and the power steering pump (see Chapter 10).

2A

10.23a Cylinder head bolt tightening sequence

10.23b Use an angle-measuring gauge to angle-torque the cylinder head bolts

11.2 To detach the splash shield on 2001 models, remove these bolts (arrows)

11.4 To disconnect the exhaust pipe underneath the oil pan on 2001 models, remove the catalyst-to-exhaust pipe flange bolts and nuts (A) and then remove the exhaust pipe bracket bolt (B); to detach the oil pan on 2001 models, remove these bolts (arrows) (not all bolts visible in this photo)

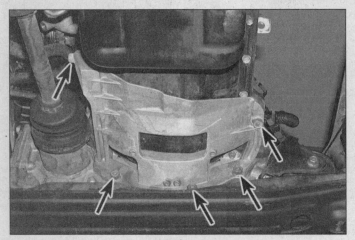

11.5 To detach the engine block-to-transaxle reinforcement bracket on 1996 through 2000 models, remove these bolts (arrows)

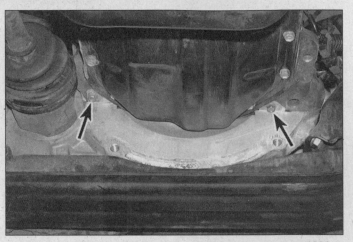

11.6 To detach the flywheel/driveplate access cover on 1996 through 2000 models, remove these two bolts (arrows)

26   Install the fuel rail and the fuel injectors (see Chapter 4), if they were removed.
27   Reconnect the fuel pressure line to the fuel rail and the fuel return line to the fuel pressure regulator; reconnect the vacuum hose to the pressure regulator and then plug in the injector harness electrical connectors (see Chapter 4).
28   Install the camshafts and the lifters (see

11.7 Oil pan bolts (arrows) (1996 through 2000 models)

Section 6).
29   Install the timing belt and the timing belt cover (see Section 5).
30   Install the valve cover (see Section 4).
31   Install the ignition coil assembly, if it was removed (see Chapter 5).
32   Install the spark plugs, the spark plug wires and the spark plug wire cover (see Chapter 1).
33   Reconnect the upper radiator hose and the other two coolant hoses to the thermostat housing (see Chapter 3). Fill the engine cooling system with coolant (See Chapter 1).
34   Change the engine oil (see Chapter 1).
35   Run the engine and check for leaks.

11   Oil pan - removal and installation

Removal

Refer to illustrations 11.2, 11.4, 11.5, 11.6 and 11.7

1   Set the parking brake and block the rear wheels. Raise the front of the vehicle and support it securely on jackstands.
2   On 2001 models, remove the splash

shield below the oil filter **(see illustration)**.
3   Drain the engine oil (see Chapter 1). Remove the oil dipstick.
4   On most models, it will be necessary to remove the section of the exhaust system that's under the engine **(see illustration)**.
5   On 1996 through 2000 models, remove the engine block-to-transaxle reinforcement bracket **(see illustration)**.
6   On 1996 through 2000 models, remove the flywheel/driveplate access cover **(see illustration)**.
7   Remove the oil pan bolts **(1996 through 2000 models, see illustration; 2001 models, see illustration 11.4)** and then detach the oil pan. If it's stuck, pry it loose very carefully with a small screwdriver or putty knife. Don't damage the mating surfaces of the pan and block or oil leaks could develop.

Installation

Refer to illustration 11.11

8   Use a scraper to remove all traces of old sealant from the block and oil pan. Clean the mating surfaces with lacquer thinner or acetone. Make sure the threaded bolt holes in the block are clean.

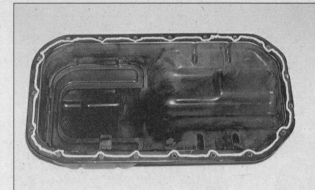

11.11 Apply a 3/16-inch (5 mm) bead of RTV sealant to the oil pan flange

12.3 To detach the oil pump pick-up tube, remove these bolts (arrows)

9   Inspect the oil pan flange for distortion, particularly around the bolt holes. Remove any nicks or burrs as necessary.

10   Inspect the oil pump pick-up tube assembly for cracks and a blocked strainer. If the pick-up was removed, clean it thoroughly and install it now, using a new O-ring or gasket. Tighten the nuts/bolts to the torque listed in this Chapter's Specifications.

11   Apply a 3/16-inch (5 mm) bead of RTV sealant to the oil pan flange **(see illustration)**. **Note:** *The oil pan must be installed within 5 minutes after the sealant has been applied.*

12   Carefully position the oil pan on the engine block, install the oil pan-to-engine block bolts by hand and lightly tighten, but don't torque, the bolts.

13   Working from the center out, tighten the oil pan-to-engine block bolts to the torque listed in this Chapter's Specifications in three or four steps.

14   Install the flywheel/driveplate access cover and then tighten the access cover bolts securely.

15   Install the engine block-to-transaxle reinforcement bracket and then tighten the bracket bolts securely.

16   The remainder of installation is the reverse of removal. Be sure to wait one hour before adding oil to allow the sealant to properly cure.

17   Run the engine and check for oil pressure and leaks.

12   Oil pump - removal, inspection and installation

Removal

Refer to illustrations 12.3 and 12.5

1   Remove the timing belt cover, the timing belt and the crankshaft drive sprocket (see Section 5).

2   Remove the oil pan (see Section 11).

3   Remove the oil pump pick-up tube bolts **(see illustration)** and then remove the oil pump pick-up tube.

4   Inspect the crankshaft front oil seal. If it's leaking, replace it while the pump is removed (see below).

5   Remove the oil pump-to-block bolts **(see illustration)** and then remove the oil pump assembly.

6   Remove the oil pump gasket.

Inspection

Disassembly

Refer to illustrations 12.7, 12.8, 12.9a, 12.9b and 12.10

7   Clean off the pump assembly with solvent, remove the cover bolts **(see illustra-**

12.5 Remove the oil pump-to-block bolts (arrows) and then remove the oil pump assembly

tion) and then remove the cover from the oil pump case.

8   Note the mating marks on the inner and outer rotors **(see illustration)**, and then remove the inner and outer rotors from the pump case.

9   Remove the plug and then remove the relief spring and the relief plunger from the pump case **(see illustrations)**.

12.7 Remove the cover bolts (arrows) and then remove the cover from the oil pump case

12.8 Note the mating marks on the inner and outer rotors (arrows) and then remove the inner and outer gears from the pump case

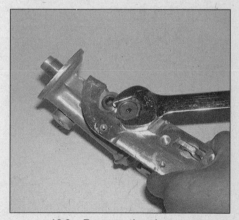

12.9a Remove the plug . . .

12.9b . . . and then remove the relief spring and the relief plunger from the pump case

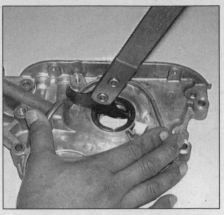

12.10 Remove the old crankshaft front seal from the oil pump housing with a seal removal tool

12.14 Measure the clearance between the outer circumference of the outer rotor and the front case with a feeler gauge and then compare your measurement to the clearance listed in this Chapter's Specifications

10   If you're going to replace the crankshaft front oil seal, carefully pry out the old seal with a seal removal tool or with a screwdriver **(see illustration)**. Don't scratch or gouge the seal bore.

11   Clean all the parts in solvent and then wipe them off with a clean shop rag.

Pick-up tube

12   Inspect the pick-up tube filter screen. Make sure that it's not clogged or damaged. If it's clogged, clean it with a wire brush. If it's damaged, replace the pick-up tube.

Pump case

13   Inspect the front case for cracks. If any damage is evident, replace the pump.

Oil pump rotors

Refer to illustrations 12.14, 12.15, 12.16 and 12.17

14   Measure the clearance between the outer circumference of the outer rotor and the front case **(see illustration)** and then compare your measurement to the clearance listed in this Chapter's Specifications.

15   Measure the clearance between the tip of the inner rotor and the inner circumference of the outer rotor **(see illustration)** and then compare your measurement to the clearance listed in this Chapter's Specifications.

16   Measure the axial (side) clearance between the outer pump rotor and a straight edge **(see illustration)** and then compare your measurement to the clearance listed in this Chapter's Specifications.

17   Measure the axial (side) clearance between the inner pump rotor and a straight edge **(see illustration)** and then compare your measurement to the clearance listed in this Chapter's Specifications.

18   If any of the above clearances are excessive, replace the pump.

Pressure relief spring and plunger

Refer to illustrations 12.19

19   Measure the free height of the pressure relief spring **(see illustration)**. If the spring height is incorrect, replace the spring. Verify that the relief spring plunger moves freely in its bore. If it doesn't, inspect the walls of the bore and the plunger. If the plunger is damaged, replace it. If the bore is damaged, replace the pump.

12.15 Measure the clearance between the tip of the inner rotor and the inner circumference of the outer rotor and then compare your measurement to the clearance listed in this Chapter's Specifications

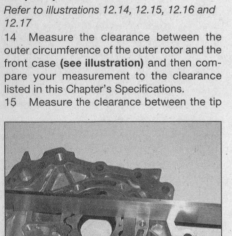

12.16 Measure the axial (side) clearance between the outer pump rotor and a straight edge and then compare your measurement to the clearance listed in this Chapter's Specifications

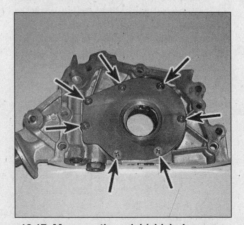

12.17 Measure the axial (side) clearance between the inner pump rotor and a straight edge and then compare your measurement to the clearance listed in this Chapter's Specifications

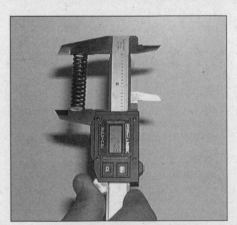

12.19 Measure the free height of the pressure relief spring and then compare your measurement to the spring free height listed in this Chapter's Specifications

Reassembly

Refer to illustration 12.21

20   Make sure that the pump case is clean.

21   If you removed the old crankshaft front oil seal during disassembly, install a new seal now. Use a large socket with an outer circumference slightly smaller than the circumference of the new seal. Make sure that the seal bore is clean, place the new seal in position over the seal bore and then carefully tap it into the bore until it's correctly seated **(see illustration)**.

22   Install the relief valve plunger and the pressure relief spring and then screw in the plug. Tighten the plug to the torque listed in this Chapter's Specifications.

23   Coat the inner and outer rotors with clean engine oil and then install them in the case. Make sure that the mating marks are facing out (toward you) and that they're aligned **(see illustration 12.8)**.

24   Install the cover, install the cover bolts and then tighten the bolts to the torque listed in this Chapter's Specifications.

Installation

Refer to illustration 12.26

25   Make sure that the gasket mating surface of the block is clean. Use a scraper to remove all traces of old gasket material from the engine block, then clean the mating surface with lacquer thinner or acetone.

26   Install a new pump gasket **(see illustration)**.

27   Install the pump assembly, install the pump retaining bolts and then tighten them to the torque listed in this Chapter's Specifications.

28   Install the oil pump pick-up tube assembly. Tighten the pick-up tube bolts to the torque listed in this Chapter's Specifications.

29   Install the oil pan (see Section 11).

30   Install the crankshaft timing belt sprocket, the timing belt and the timing belt cover (see Section 5).

31   Add oil, start the engine and check for oil pressure and leaks.

32   Turn off the engine and then recheck the engine oil level.

13   Flywheel/driveplate - removal, inspection and installation

Caution: *The manufacturer recommends replacing the flywheel/driveplate bolts with new ones whenever they are removed.*

Removal

Refer to illustrations 13.4a and 13.4b

1   Raise the vehicle and support it securely on jackstands and then remove the transaxle (see Chapter 7).

2   On vehicles with a manual transaxle, remove the pressure plate and clutch disc (see Chapter 8). While the clutch components are removed, be sure inspect them.

3   Use a center punch or paint to make

12.21 Using a socket with an outside diameter slightly smaller than the outside diameter of the seal, install a new seal in the seal bore of the oil pump housing

alignment marks on the flywheel/driveplate and crankshaft to ensure correct alignment during reinstallation.

4   Remove the bolts that secure the flywheel/driveplate to the crankshaft **(see illustrations)**. If the crankshaft turns, jam the flywheel/driveplate by wedging a screwdriver in the ring gear teeth.

5   Remove the flywheel/driveplate from the crankshaft. Since the flywheel is fairly heavy, be sure to support it while removing the last bolt. Automatic transaxle equipped vehicles have spacers on both sides of the driveplate. Keep them with the driveplate.

6   Inspect the crankshaft rear seal. If it's leaking, replace it before reinstalling the flywheel/driveplate (see Section 14).

Inspection

7   Clean the flywheel to remove grease and oil. Inspect the surface for cracks, rivet grooves, burned areas and score marks. Light scoring can be removed with emery cloth. Check the ring gear for cracked and

13.4a Remove the bolts that secure the flywheel (models with a manual transaxle) to the crankshaft; if the crankshaft turns, jam the flywheel/driveplate by wedging a screwdriver in the ring gear teeth - the holding tool shown (arrow) is helpful but not commonly available

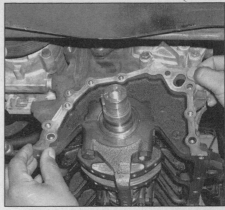

12.26 Install a new oil pump gasket

broken teeth. If the ring gear teeth are damaged, replace the flywheel, or have a new ring gear pressed onto the flywheel.

8   Lay the flywheel on a flat surface and use a straightedge to check for warpage and then compare your measurement to the allowable warpage listed in this Chapter's Specifications. If the flywheel warpage is excessive, you might able to have the flywheel resurfaced by an automotive machine shop, or you might have to replace the flywheel. Have the flywheel examined by an automotive machine shop. **Note:** *It's a good idea to have the flywheel inspected by a competent automotive machine shop even if the flywheel does not appear to be warped.*

9   Clean and inspect the mating surfaces of the flywheel/driveplate and the crankshaft.

Installation

10   Position the flywheel, or driveplate and spacers, against the crankshaft. Be sure to align the marks made during removal. Note that some engines have an alignment dowel or staggered bolt holes to ensure correct installation. Before installing the bolts, apply thread-locking compound to the threads.

11   Wedge a screwdriver in the ring gear

13.4b To detach the driveplate (models with an automatic transaxle) from the crankshaft, remove these bolts (driveplates have spacers on both sides of the driveplate - mark the spacers to ensure that they're installed correctly

2A

14.2a Carefully pry the crankshaft front oil seal out of the oil pump housing with a screwdriver or seal removal tool; be careful not to scratch, nick or gouge the crankshaft or the seal bore in the oil pump housing

14.2b If a seal removal tool isn't available, remove the front seal by installing a pair of self-tapping screws and then, using the nose of the crank as a fulcrum, lever out the old seal with needle nose pliers as shown

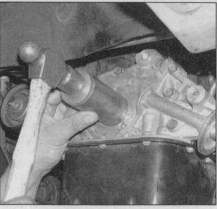

14.4 Using a socket with an outside diameter slightly smaller than the outside diameter of the seal, carefully drive the new seal into place with a hammer

teeth to keep the flywheel/driveplate from turning and tighten the bolts to the torque listed in this Chapter's Specifications. Follow a criss-cross pattern and work up to the final torque in three or four steps.
12   Install the transaxle (see Chapter 7).
13   Lower the vehicle.

14   Crankshaft oil seals - replacement

Crankshaft front oil seal

Refer to illustrations 14.2a, 14.2b and 14.4
Note: *The following procedure explains how to replace the front crank seal with the oil pump installed. If you're planning to remove the oil pump for inspection (see Section 12), the front crank seal is easier to replace with the pump removed.*
1   Remove the timing belt cover, the timing belt and the crankshaft sprocket (see Section 5).
2   Note how far the seal is recessed in the bore, then carefully pry it out of the oil pump housing with a screwdriver or seal removal tool **(see illustration)**. Don't scratch the housing bore or damage the crankshaft in the process (if the crankshaft is damaged, the new seal will end up leaking). **Note:** *If a seal removal tool is unavailable, you can thread two self tapping screws (180 degrees apart from one another) into the front seal to pry out the seal **(see illustration)**.*
3   Clean the bore in the housing and coat the outer edge of the new seal with engine oil or multi-purpose grease. Apply multi-purpose grease to the seal lip.
4   Using a socket with an outside diameter slightly smaller than the outside diameter of the seal, carefully drive the new seal into place with a hammer **(see illustration)**. Make sure it's installed squarely and driven in to the same depth as the original. If a socket isn't available, a short section of large diameter

pipe will also work. Check the seal after installation to make sure the spring didn't pop out of place.
5   Reinstall the crankshaft sprocket and timing belt (see Section 5).
6   Run the engine and check for oil leaks at the front seal.

Crankshaft rear oil seal

Refer to illustrations 14.10 and 14.12
7   Remove the transaxle (see Chapter 7).
8   On models with a manual transaxle, remove the pressure plate and the clutch disc (see Chapter 8).
9   Remove the flywheel (manual transaxle) or the driveplate (automatic transaxle) (see Section 13).
10   Pry out the old seal out of the housing with a seal removal tool **(see illustration)**.
11   Coat the lip of the new seal with clean engine oil.
12   Using a large socket with an outside diameter slightly smaller than the outside

diameter of the new seal, place the seal in position and carefully tap it into the seal housing **(see illustration)** until it's fully seated.
13   Install the flywheel (manual transaxle) or the driveplate (automatic transaxle) (see Section 13).
14   On models with a manual transaxle, install the clutch disc and the pressure plate (see Chapter 8).
15   Install the transaxle (see Chapter 7).

15   Engine/transaxle mounts - check and replacement

Check

Refer to illustrations 15.4a, 15.4b, 15.4c, 15.4d and 15.5
1   Engine mounts seldom require attention, but broken or deteriorated mounts should be replaced immediately, because the added strain placed on the driveline components may cause damage or wear.

14.10 Pry the old seal out of the seal housing with a seal removal tool

14.12 Using a large socket with an outside diameter slightly smaller than the outside diameter of the new seal, place the seal in position and carefully tap it into the seal housing until it's fully seated.

15.4a Engine mount and bracket nuts and bolts (arrows)

15.4b Transaxle mount and bracket nuts and bolts (arrows)

2   Raise the front of the vehicle and support it securely on jackstands.

3   To inspect the mounts properly, the engine must be raised slightly to remove the weight from the mounts. Position a jack under the engine oil pan. Place a large block of wood between the jack head and the oil pan, then carefully raise the engine just enough to take the weight off the mounts. Do not position the wood block under the drain plug. **Warning:** *DO NOT place any part of your body under the engine when it's supported only by a jack!*

4   Using a drop light or a flashlight, inspect each mount **(see illustrations)**. Note whether the rubber is cracked, hardened or separated from the metal plates. Sometimes the rubber will split right down the center. If any damage is obvious replace the mount(s).

5   Check for movement between the insulator and the metal bracket(s) of each mount as follows: Insert a large pry bar or screwdriver between the rubber insulator of the mount and its bracket **(see illustration)** and then try to pry them apart. If the rubber insulator is cracked, torn or deteriorated, it will be relatively easy to move the bracket in relation to the insulator (or vice versa). This kind of excessive play between the insulator and the bracket translates into excessive movement of the engine and/or the transaxle under acceleration and deceleration, when shifting gears, and when traveling over a rough road. Loose mounts the rubber portion of that mount has deteriorated (even if it still looks okay). Lower the engine and tighten the mount fasteners until you can obtain new mounts.

6   Apply rubber preservative to the mounts to slow deterioration.

Replacement

Refer to illustrations 15.8a, 15.8b and 15.8c

7   Raise the vehicle and support it securely on jackstands (if not already done). Support the engine (see Step 3).

15.4c Front roller stopper nuts and bolts (arrows) (other bracket to transaxle bolt not visible in this photo)

2A

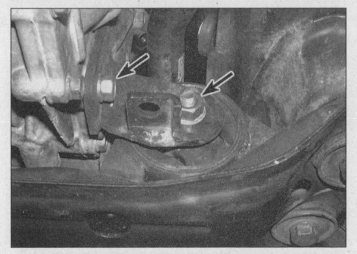

15.4d Rear roller stopper nuts and bolts (arrows) (other bracket to transaxle bolt not visible in this photo)

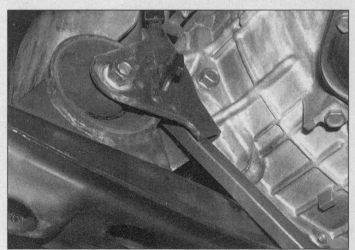

15.5 To check a rubber insulator for wear or damage, insert a large prybar or screwdriver between the rubber insulator and the mount bracket and then try to lever them apart; if the metal bracket moves away from the rubber insulator relatively easily, the insulator should be replaced

15.8a To access the transaxle mount bracket bolts, remove these plugs (arrows) (lower right plug already removed)

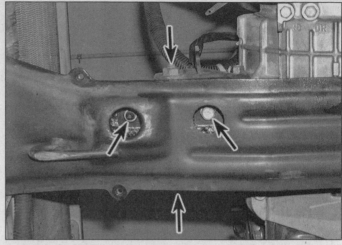

15.8b Front roll stopper nuts and bolts (arrows) (as seen from underneath vehicle, actual mount not visible in this photo)

8   Remove the mount and bracket bolts and detach the mount and bracket **(see illustrations 15.4a, 15.4b, 15.4c and/or 15.4d)**. The body-to-bracket bolts for the transaxle mount are accessed inside the left front wheel well; remove the four protective caps **(see illustration)** to access the bolts. The crossmember-to-bracket bolts for the front and rear roll stoppers are accessed through holes in the underside of the crossmember **(see illustrations)**.

9   Installation is the reverse of removal. Always install NEW mounting bolts and be sure to tighten them securely.

15.8c Rear roll stopper nuts and bolts (arrows) (as seen from underneath vehicle, actual mount not visible in this photo)

Chapter 2 Part B
General engine overhaul procedures

Contents

2B

Specifications

General

Engine designation
  1996 through 1998 (1.8L) G4GM
  1999 and 2000 (2.0L) G4GF
  2001 and later (2.0L) .... G4GC (also referred to as the "Beta" engine)
Displacement
  1.8L (G4GM) .... 109.54 cubic inches (1795 cc)
  2.0L (G4GF and G4GC) .... 120.52 cubic inches (1975 cc)
Bore and stroke
  1.8 L (G4GM) .... 3.228 x 3.346 inches (82 x 85 mm)
  2.0 L (G4GF and G4GC) .... 3.228 x 3.681 inches (82 x 93.5 mm)
Cylinder numbers (drivebelt end-to-transaxle end) 1-2-3-4
Firing order 1-3-4-2
Cylinder compression pressure (cranking, at 250 to 400 rpm)
  1996 through 2000
    Standard .... 213 psi (14.5 kg/cm2)
    Limit .... 199 psi (13 kg/cm2)
  2001 and later
    Standard .... 218 psi (15 kg/cm2)
    Limit .... 203 psi (14 kg/cm2)
  Variation between cylinders (all models) .... No more than 14 psi (1.0 kg/cm2)
Oil pressure (at idle) .... 24.2 psi (1.7 kg/cm2) minimum

Cylinder head

Flatness
  1996 through 2000
    Standard .... Less than 0.002 inch (0.05 mm)
    Limit .... 0.004 inch (0.10 mm)
  2001 and later
    Standard .... Less than 0.0012 inch (0.03 mm)
    Limit .... 0.0024 inch (0.06 mm)

Camshaft

Camshaft endplay.. 0.004 to 0.008 inch (0.01 to 0.2 mm)
Camshaft bearing oil clearance
  1996 and 1997 .... 0.0008 to 0.0024 inch (0.02 to 0.061 mm)
  1998 through 2000 .... 0 to 0.0009 inch (0 to 0.025 mm)
  2001 and later
    Standard .... 0.0008 to 0.0024 inch (0.02 to 0.061 mm)
    Limit .... 0.0039 inch (0.1 mm)
Camshaft journal outside diameter................................. 1.1023 inch (28 mm)
Camshaft lobe height
  1996 and 1997
    Intake
      Standard .... 1.7499 inch (44.449 mm)
      Limit .... 1.7302 inch (43.939 mm)
    Exhaust
      Standard .... 1.7736 inch (45.049 mm)
      Limit .... 1.7538 inch (44.549 mm)
  1998
    Intake
      Standard .... 1.7499 inch (44.449 mm)
      Limit .... 1.7460 inch (44.349 mm)
    Exhaust
      Standard .... 1.7736 inch (45.049 mm)
      Limit .... 1.7696 inch (44.949 mm)
  1999 and 2000
    Intake
      Standard .... 1.7342 inch (44.049 mm)
      Limit .... 1.7302 inch (43.949 mm)
    Exhaust
      Standard .... 1.7736 inch (45.049 mm)
      Limit .... 1.7696 inch (44.949 mm)
  2001 and later
    Intake
      Standard .... 1.7646 inch (44.820 mm)
      Limit .... 1.7606 inch (44.720 mm)
    Exhaust
      Standard .... 1.7606 inch (44.720 mm)
      Limit .... 1.7567 inch (44.620 mm)

Valves and related components

Valve stem diameter
  Intake.. 0.2348 to 0.2354 inch (5.965 to 5.98 mm)
  Exhaust.. 0.2334 to 0.2342 inch (5.965 to 5.98 mm)
Valve stem-to-guide clearance
  Intake
    Standard .... 0.0008 to 0.0019 inch (0.02 to 0.05 mm)
    Limit .... 0.0039 inch (0.10 mm)
  Exhaust..
    1996 through 2000
      Standard .... 0.0019 to 0.0033 inch (0.05 to 0.085 mm)
      Limit .... 0.0059 inch (0.15 mm)
    2001 and later
      Standard .... 0.0014 to 0.0026 inch (0.035 to 0.065 mm)
      Limit .... 0.0051 inch (0.13 mm)
Valve spring
  1996 and 1997
    Free length .... 1.8137 inches (46.07 mm)
    Installed height.. 1.358 inches (34.5 mm)
  1998 through 2000
    Free length .... 1.8137 inches (46.07 mm)
    Installed height.. 1.456 inches (37 mm)

2001 and later
  Free length .... 1.9236 inches (48.86 mm)
  Installed height .... 1.5354 inches (39 mm)
Valve clearance (2001 and later)
  Intake
    Standard .... 0.0079 inch (0.20 mm)
    Limit .... 0.0047 to 0.0110 inch (0.12 to 0.28 mm)
  Exhaust
    Standard .... 0.0110 inch (0.28 mm)
    Limit .... 0.0079 to 0.0142 inch (0.20 to 0.36 mm)

Crankshaft

Endplay
  Standard .... 0.0023 to 0.010 inch (0.06 to 0.26 mm)
  Service limit .... 0.0118 inch (0.30 mm)
Runout .... N/A
Main bearing journal diameter
  Standard .... 2.244 inches (57 mm)
    1st undersize .... 2.2333 to 2.2339 inches (56.727 to 56.742 mm)
    2nd undersize .... 2.2235 to 2.2240 inches (56.477 to 56.492 mm)
    3rd undersize .... 2.2136 to 2.2142 inches (56.227 to 56.242 mm)
  Out-of-round limit .... 0.0004 inch (0.01 mm)
  Taper limit .... 0.0004 inch (0.01 mm)
Main bearing oil clearance
  Standard .... 0.0011 to 0.0018 inch (0.028 to 0.048 mm)
  Service limit .... 0.0039 inch (0.1 mm)
Clearance between sensor wheel and Crankshaft Position (CKP) sensor
  1996 through 2000 .... 0.020 to 0.059 inch (0.5 to 1.5 mm)
  2001 and later .... 0.020 to 0.043 inch (0.5 to 1.1 mm)

Connecting rods

Connecting rod bearing journal diameters
  Standard .... 1.77 inches (45 mm)
    1st undersize .... 1.7608 to 1.7614 inches (44.725 to 44.740 mm)
    2nd undersize .... 1.7509 to 1.7516 inches (44.475 to 44.490 mm)
    3rd undersize .... 1.7411 to 1.7417 inches (44.225 to 44.240 mm)
Out-of-round limit .... 0.0004 inch (0.01 mm)
Taper limit .... 0.0004 inch (0.01 mm)
Connecting rod bearing oil clearance .... 0.0009 to 0.0017 inch (0.024 to 0.044 mm)
Connecting rod side clearance (endplay)
  Standard .... 0.0039 to 0.0098 inch (0.100 to 0.250 mm)
  Service limit .... 0.0157 inch (0.4 mm)

Engine block

Cylinder bore diameter .... 3.2283 to 3.2295 inches (82.00 to 82.03 mm)
Out-of-round limit .... 0.0004 inch (0.01 mm)
Taper limit .... 0.0004 inch (0.01 mm)
Block deck warpage
  1996 through 2000 .... 0.0020 inch (0.05 mm)
  2001 and later .... 0.0012 inch (0.03 mm)
  Service limit (all models) .... 0.0039 inch (0.10 mm)

Pistons and rings

Piston diameter
  Standard .... 3.2271 to 3.2283 inches (81.97 to 82.00 mm)
    1st oversize .... 0.010 inch (0.25 mm)
    2nd oversize .... 0.020 inch (0.50 mm)
    3rd oversize .... 0.030 inch (0.75 mm)
    4th oversize .... 0.039 inch (1.00 mm)
Piston ring end gap
  1996 through 2000
    Top compression ring .... 0.0059 to 0.0118 inch (0.15 to 0.30 mm
    Second compression ring .... 0.008 to 0.014 inch (0.25 to 0.40 mm
    Oil control ring .... 0.078 to 0.0275 inch (0.20 to 0.70 mm)
    Limit (all three rings) .... 0.039 inch (1.0 mm)
  2001 and later
    Top compression ring .... 0.0091 to 0.0150 inch (0.23 to 0.38 mm)
    Second compression ring .... 0.0139 to 0.0189 inch (0.33 to 0.48 mm)
    Oil control ring .... 0.0079 to 0.0236 inch (0.20 to 0.60 mm)
    Limit (all three rings) .... 0.039 inch (1.0 mm)

Pistons and rings (continued)

Piston ring side clearance

1996 through 2000

Top compression ring.. 0.0016 to 0.0031 inch (0.04 to 0.085 mm)

Second compression ring.. 0.0016 to 0.0031 inch (0.04 to 0.085mm)

Limit (both rings) .... 0.004 inch (0.1 mm)

2001 and later

Top compression ring.. 0.0016 to 0.0031 inch (0.04 to 0.085 mm)

Second compression ring.. 0.0012 to 0.0028 inch (0.03 to 0.07mm)

Limit (both rings) .... 0.004 inch (0.1 mm)

Torque specifications*

	Ft-lbs (unless otherwise indicated)	Nm
Main bearing cap bolts (always replace)		
1996 through 2000	40 to 43.4	55 to 60
2001 and later		
First step	20 to 24	27 to 33
Second step	60 to 65 degrees rotation	
Connecting rod cap bolts (always replace)	37 to 39	50 to 53
Crankshaft sensor wheel retaining screws	45 to 52 in-lbs	5 to 6
Oil pressure switch	120 to 132 in-lbs	13 to 15

*Note: *Refer to Chapter 2A for additional torque specifications.*

1   General information - engine overhaul

Included in this portion of Chapter 2 are the general overhaul procedures for the cylinder head and internal engine components.

The information ranges from advice concerning preparation for an overhaul and the purchase of replacement parts to detailed, step-by-step procedures covering removal and installation of internal engine components and the inspection of parts.

The following Sections have been written based on the assumption that the engine has been removed from the vehicle. For information concerning in-vehicle engine repair, as well as removal and installation of the external components necessary for the overhaul, see Chapter 2A, and Section 8 of this Chapter.

The Specifications included in this Part are only those necessary for the inspection and overhaul procedures which follow. Refer to Chapter 2A for additional Specifications.

It's not always easy to determine when, or if, an engine should be completely overhauled, as a number of factors must be considered.

High mileage is not necessarily an indication that an overhaul is needed, while low mileage doesn't preclude the need for an overhaul. Frequency of servicing is probably the most important consideration. An engine that's had regular and frequent oil and filter changes, as well as other required maintenance, will most likely give many thousands of miles of reliable service. Conversely, a neglected engine may require an overhaul very early in its life.

Excessive oil consumption is an indication that piston rings, valve seals and/or valve guides are in need of attention. Make sure that oil leaks aren't responsible before deciding that the rings and/or guides are bad. Perform a cylinder compression check to determine the extent of the work required (see Section 3). Also check the vacuum readings under various conditions (see Section 4).

Loss of power, rough running, knocking or metallic engine noises, excessive valve train noise and high fuel consumption rates may also point to the need for an overhaul, especially if they're all present at the same time. If a complete tune-up doesn't remedy the situation, major mechanical work is the only solution.

An engine overhaul involves restoring the internal parts to the specifications of a new engine. During an overhaul, the piston rings are replaced and the cylinder walls are reconditioned (re-bored and/or honed). If a re-bore is done by an automotive machine shop, new oversize pistons will also be installed. The main bearings and connecting rod bearings are generally replaced with new ones and, if necessary, the crankshaft may be reground to restore the journals. Generally, the valves are serviced as well, since they're usually in less-than-perfect condition at this point. While the engine is being overhauled, other components, such as the starter and alternator, can be rebuilt as well. The end result should be a like new engine that will give many trouble free miles. **Note:** *Critical cooling system components such as the hoses, drivebelts, thermostat and water pump should be replaced with new parts when an engine is overhauled. The radiator should be checked carefully to ensure that it isn't clogged or leaking (see Chapter 3). If you purchase a rebuilt engine or short block, some rebuilders will not warranty their engines unless the radiator has been professionally flushed. Also, we don't recommend overhauling the oil pump - always install a new one when an engine is rebuilt.*

Before beginning the engine overhaul, read through the entire procedure to familiarize yourself with the scope and requirements of the job. Overhauling an engine isn't difficult, but it is time-consuming. Plan on the vehicle being tied up for a minimum of two weeks, especially if parts must be taken to an automotive machine shop for repair or reconditioning. Check on availability of parts and make sure that any necessary special tools and equipment are obtained in advance. Most work can be done with typical hand tools, although a number of precision measuring tools are required for inspecting parts to determine if they must be replaced. Often an automotive machine shop will handle the inspection of parts and offer advice concerning reconditioning and replacement. **Note:** *Always wait until the engine has been completely disassembled and all components, especially the engine block, have been inspected before deciding what service and repair operations must be performed by an automotive machine shop. Since the block's condition will be the major factor to consider*

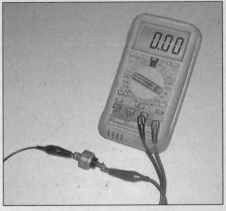

2.2 The oil pressure sending unit (arrow) is mounted on the front of the block, below the exhaust manifold, near the left (transaxle) end of the block

2.3 Remove the oil pressure sending unit and then screw an oil pressure gauge in its place; use Teflon tape or sealant to seal the threads of the fitting on the end of the gauge hose

2.7 Using an ohmmeter, check continuity between the sending unit terminal and the body; if there is no continuity, replace the sending unit

when determining whether to overhaul the original engine or buy a rebuilt one, never purchase parts or have machine work done on other components until the block has been thoroughly inspected. As a general rule, time is the primary cost of an overhaul, so it doesn't pay to install worn or substandard parts.

As a final note, to ensure maximum life and minimum trouble from a rebuilt engine, everything must be assembled with care in a spotlessly-clean environment.

2   Oil pressure check

Refer to illustrations 2.2, 2.3, 2.7 and 2.8

1   Low engine oil pressure can be a sign of an engine in need of rebuilding. A "low oil pressure" indicator (often called an "idiot light") is not a test of the oiling system. Such indicators only come on when the oil pressure is dangerously low. Even a factory oil pressure gauge in the instrument panel is only a relative indication, although much better for driver information than a warning light. A better test is with a mechanical (not electrical) oil pressure gauge. When used in conjunction with an accurate tachometer, an engine's oil pressure performance can be compared to the manufacturers Specifications.

2   Find the oil pressure sending unit **(see illustration)** on the front side of the engine block, below the exhaust manifold, near the left (transaxle) end of the block.

3   Remove the oil pressure sending unit **(see illustration)** and then screw in an oil pressure gauge in its place. Use Teflon tape or sealant on the threads of the fitting on the end of your gauge's hose.

4   Connect an accurate tachometer to the engine, according to the tachometer manufacturer's instructions.

5   Check the oil pressure with the engine fully warmed up and running at idle, and then compare it to oil pressure listed in this Chap-

ter's Specifications. If it's extremely low, the crankshaft main bearings and/or the oil pump are probably worn out.

6   If the oil pressure is correct, but the oil pressure indicator light has been indicating low oil pressure, the oil pressure sending unit might be defective. Test it as follows.

7   Using an ohmmeter, check continuity between the sending unit terminal and the body **(see illustration)**. If there is no continuity, replace the sending unit.

8   Using a short section of wire or a T-pin, push in the sending unit plunger and check continuity between the sending unit terminal and the body again **(see illustration)**. If there is continuity, replace the sending unit.

3   Cylinder compression check

Refer to illustration 3.6

1   A compression check will tell you what mechanical condition the upper end (pistons,

rings, valves, head gaskets) of the engine is in. Specifically, it can tell you if the compression is down due to leakage caused by worn piston rings, defective valves and seats or a blown head gasket. **Note:** *The engine must be at normal operating temperature and the battery must be fully charged for this check.*

2   Begin by cleaning the area around the spark plugs before you remove them. Compressed air should be used, if available, otherwise a small brush will work. The idea is to prevent dirt from getting into the cylinders as the compression check is being done.

3   Remove all of the spark plugs (see Chapter 1).

4   Block the throttle wide open.

5   Disable the fuel and ignition systems by disconnecting the primary electrical connectors at the ignition coil pack/modules (see Chapter 5) and the electrical connectors at the fuel injectors (see Chapter 4).

6   Install the compression gauge in the number one spark plug hole **(see illustration)**.

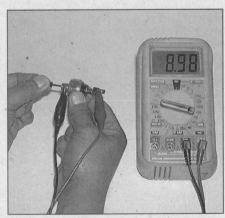

2.8 Using a short section of wire or a T-pin, push in the sending unit plunger and check continuity between the sending unit terminal and the body again; if there is continuity, replace the sending unit

3.6 A compression gauge with a threaded fitting for the spark plug hole is preferred over the type that requires hand pressure to maintain the seal - be sure to open the throttle valve as far as possible during the compression check

2B

7   Crank the engine over at least seven compression strokes and watch the gauge. The compression should build up quickly in a healthy engine. Low compression on the first stroke, followed by gradually increasing pressure on successive strokes, indicates worn piston rings. A low compression reading on the first stroke, which doesn't build up during successive strokes, indicates leaking valves or a blown head gasket (a cracked head could also be the cause). Deposits on the undersides of the valve heads can also cause low compression. Record the highest gauge reading obtained.

8   Repeat the procedure for the remaining cylinders, turning the engine over for the same length of time for each cylinder, and compare the results to this Chapter's Specifications.

9   If the readings are below normal, add some engine oil (about three squirts from a plunger-type oil can) to each cylinder, through the spark plug hole, and then repeat the test.

10   If the compression increases after the oil is added, the piston rings are definitely worn. If the compression doesn't increase significantly, the leakage is occurring at the valves or head gasket. Leakage past the valves may be caused by burned valve seats and/or faces or warped, cracked or bent valves.

11   If two adjacent cylinders have equally low compression, there's a strong possibility that the head gasket between them is blown. The appearance of coolant in the combustion chambers or the crankcase would verify this condition.

12   If one cylinder is about 20-percent lower than the others, and the engine has a slightly rough idle, a worn exhaust lobe on the camshaft could be the cause.

13   If the compression is unusually high, the combustion chambers are probably coated with carbon deposits. If that's the case, the cylinder heads should be removed and decarbonized.

14   If compression is way down or varies greatly between cylinders, it would be a good idea to have a leak-down test performed by an automotive repair shop. This test will pinpoint exactly where the leakage is occurring and how severe it is.

15   Installation of the remaining components is the reverse of removal.

4   Vacuum gauge diagnostic checks

Refer to illustrations 4.4 and 4.6

1   A vacuum gauge provides valuable information about what is going on in the engine at a low cost. You can check for worn rings or cylinder walls, leaking head or intake manifold gaskets, incorrect carburetor adjustments, restricted exhaust, stuck or burned valves, weak valve springs, improper ignition or valve timing and ignition problems.

2   Unfortunately, vacuum gauge readings are easy to misinterpret, so they should be used in conjunction with other tests to confirm the diagnosis.

3   Both the gauge readings and the rate of needle movement are important for accurate interpretation. Most gauges measure vacuum in inches of mercury (in-Hg). As vacuum increases (or atmospheric pressure decreases), the reading will increase. Also, for every 1,000-foot increase in elevation above sea level, the gauge readings will decrease about one inch of mercury.

4   Connect the vacuum gauge directly to intake manifold vacuum, not to ported vacuum **(see illustration)**. Be sure no hoses are left disconnected during the test or false readings will result.

5   Before you begin the test, allow the engine to warm up completely. Block the wheels and set the parking brake. With the transmission in Park, start the engine and allow it to run at normal idle speed.

6   Read the vacuum gauge; an average, healthy engine should normally produce about 17 to 22 inches of vacuum with a fairly steady needle. Refer to the following vacuum gauge readings and what they indicate about the engine's condition **(see illustration)**.

7   A low, steady reading usually indicates a leaking gasket between the intake manifold and carburetor or throttle body, a leaky vac-

4.4 A simple vacuum gauge can be very handy in diagnosing engine condition and performance

uum hose, late ignition timing or incorrect camshaft timing. Eliminate all other possible causes, utilizing the tests provided in this Chapter before you remove the timing belt cover to check the timing marks.

8   If the reading is three to eight inches below normal and it fluctuates at that low reading, suspect an intake manifold gasket leak at an intake port.

9   If the needle has regular drops of about

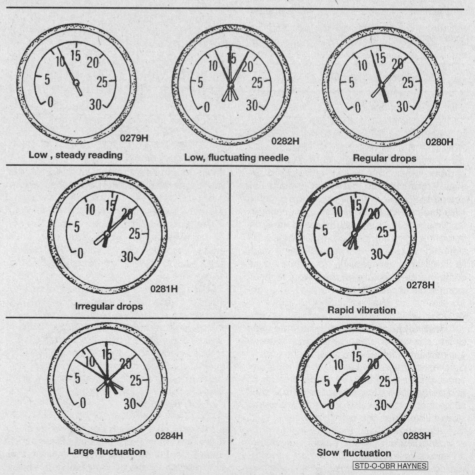

Low, steady reading	Low, fluctuating needle	Regular drops
0279H	0282H	0280H

Irregular drops	Rapid vibration
0281H	0278H

Large fluctuation	Slow fluctuation
0284H	0283H

STD-O-OBR HAYNES

4.6 Typical vacuum gauge diagnostic readings

two to four inches at a steady rate, the valves are probably leaking. Perform a compression or leak-down test to confirm this.

10 An irregular drop or down-flick of the needle can be caused by a sticking valve or an ignition misfire. Perform a compression or leak-down test and read the spark plugs.

11 A rapid vibration of about four inches-Hg vibration at idle combined with exhaust smoke indicates worn valve guides. Perform a leak-down test to confirm this. If the rapid vibration occurs with an increase in engine speed, check for a leaking intake manifold gasket or head gasket, weak valve springs, burned valves or ignition misfire.

12 A slight fluctuation, say one inch up and down, may mean ignition problems. Check all the usual tune-up items and, if necessary, run the engine on an ignition analyzer.

13 If there is a large fluctuation, perform a compression or leak-down test to look for a weak or dead cylinder or a blown head gasket.

14 If the needle moves slowly through a wide range, check for a clogged PCV system, throttle body or intake manifold gasket leaks.

15 Snap the throttle open until the engine reaches about 2,500 rpm and then abruptly snap it closed. Normally the reading should drop to near zero, rise above the normal idle reading (about 5 in-Hg over) and then return to the previous idle reading. If the vacuum returns slowly and doesn't peak when the throttle is snapped shut, the rings may be worn. If there is a long delay, look for a restricted exhaust system (usually either the muffler or the catalytic converter). A good way to verify this is to disconnect the exhaust ahead of the suspected part and then re-test.

5 Engine rebuilding alternatives

The home mechanic is faced with a number of options when performing an engine overhaul. The decision to replace the engine block, piston/connecting rod assemblies and crankshaft depends on a number of factors, with the number one consideration being the condition of the block. Other considerations are cost, access to machine shop facilities, parts availability, time required to complete the project and the extent of prior mechanical experience.

Some of the rebuilding alternatives include:

Individual parts - If the inspection procedures reveal the engine block and most engine components are in reusable condition, purchasing individual parts may be the most economical alternative. The block, crankshaft and piston/connecting rod assemblies should all be inspected carefully. Even if the block shows little wear, the cylinder bores should be surface-honed.

Short-block - A short-block consists of an engine block with a crankshaft and piston/connecting rod assemblies already installed. All new bearings are incorporated and all clearances will be correct. The exist-ing camshaft, valve train components, cylinder head and external parts can be bolted to the short block with little or no machine shop work necessary.

Long-block - A long-block consists of a short block plus an oil pump, oil pan, cylinder head, valve cover, camshaft and valve train components, timing sprockets and a timing belt. All components are installed with new bearings, seals and gaskets incorporated throughout. The installation of manifolds and external parts is all that's necessary. Give careful thought to which alternative is best for you and discuss the situation with local automotive machine shops, auto parts dealers and experienced rebuilders before ordering or purchasing replacement parts.

6 Engine removal - methods and precautions

If you've decided the engine must be removed for overhaul or major repair work, several preliminary steps should be taken. Locating a suitable place to work is extremely important. Adequate workspace, along with storage space for the vehicle, will be needed.

Cleaning the engine compartment and engine before beginning the removal procedure will help keep tools clean and organized. An engine hoist will also be necessary. Safety is of primary importance, considering the potential hazards involved in removing the engine from this vehicle.

If you're a novice at engine removal, make sure that you have a helper. Advice and aid from someone more experienced is also helpful. Sometimes one person simply can't do everything necessary, all at the same time, when lifting or lowering the engine out of the vehicle.

Plan the operation ahead of time. Arrange for or obtain all of the tools and equipment you'll need prior to beginning the job. Some of the equipment necessary to easily and safely remove and install an engine are a hydraulic jack, jack stands and an engine hoist. Also handy are a complete set of wrenches and sockets (see the front of this manual), wooden blocks, and plenty of rags and cleaning solvent for mopping up spilled oil, coolant and gasoline.

Plan for the vehicle to be out of use for quite a while. A machine shop will be required to perform some of the work which the do-it-yourselfer can't accomplish without special equipment. These shops often have a busy schedule, so it would be a good idea to consult them before removing the engine in order to accurately estimate the amount of time required to rebuild or repair components that may need work.

Always be extremely careful when removing and installing the engine. Serious injury can result from careless actions. Plan ahead, take your time and a job of this nature, although major, can be accomplished successfully. **Note:** *Because it may be some time before you reinstall the engine, it is very* helpful to make sketches or take photos of various accessory mountings and wiring hookups before removing the engine.

7 Engine - removal and installation

Warning 1: *The models covered by this manual are equipped with airbags. Always disable the airbag system before working in the vicinity of any airbag system component to avoid the possibility of accidental deployment of the airbag(s), which could cause personal injury (see Chapter 12).*

Warning 2: *Gasoline is extremely flammable, so take extra precautions when you work on any part of the fuel system. Don't smoke or allow open flames or bare light bulbs near the work area, and don't work in a garage where a gas-type appliance (such as a water heater or a clothes dryer) is present. Since gasoline is carcinogenic, wear latex gloves when there's a possibility of being exposed to fuel, and, if you spill any fuel on your skin, rinse it off immediately with soap and water. Mop up any spills immediately and do not store fuel-soaked rags where they could ignite. The fuel system is under constant pressure, so, if any fuel lines are to be disconnected, the fuel pressure in the system must be relieved first (see Chapter 4). When you perform any kind of work on the fuel system, wear safety glasses and have a Class B type fire extinguisher on hand.*

Warning 3: *The air conditioning system is under high pressure - have a dealer service department or an automotive air conditioning shop evacuate the system and recover the refrigerant before disconnecting any of the hoses or fittings.*

Caution: *Some models are equipped with an anti-theft radio. Before performing a procedure that requires disconnecting the battery, make sure you have the activation code.*

Removal

Refer to illustrations 7.6, 7.18a, 7.18b and 7.20

Note: *Read through the entire Section before beginning this procedure. The engine and transaxle are removed as a unit from below and then separated outside the vehicle.*

1 Relieve the fuel system pressure (see Chapter 4).

2 Disconnect the cables from the negative terminal of the battery and then from the positive terminal. Remove the battery (see Chapter 5).

3 Place protective covers on the fenders and cowl and remove the hood (see Chapter 11).

4 Remove the air cleaner assembly (see Chapter 4).

5 Disconnect the throttle cable (see Chapter 4) and the cruise control cable (see Chapter 12), if equipped, from the throttle linkage. Unplug the electrical connectors from the fuel injectors (see Chapter 4) and then set the fuel injector harness aside. Disconnect the fuel

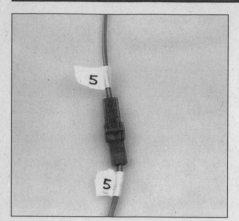

7.6 Label each wire before unplugging the connector

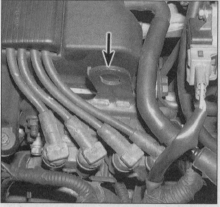

7.18a Attach the chain or sling to this lifting eye (arrow) . . .

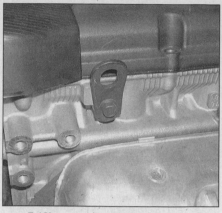

7.18b . . . and to this one

pressure line from the fuel rail and then disconnect the fuel return line from the fuel pressure regulator (see Chapter 4). Plug or cap all open fittings.

6   Clearly label, and then disconnect, all wiring harness connectors and ground straps (see Chapters 4, 5 and 6). Masking tape and/or a touch up paint applicator work well for marking items **(see illustration)**. If you have a digital, a disposable or an instant camera, take photos of, or sketch, the locations of brackets, connectors, components, etc.

7   Clearly label, and then disconnect, all vacuum lines and emissions hoses (see Chapters 4 and 6.)

8   Remove the accessory drivebelt(s) (see Chapter 1).

9   Raise the vehicle and support it securely on jackstands.

10   Label and disconnect the main engine electrical harnesses from the starter and the engine, and then remove the alternator (see Chapter 5).

11   Drain the engine oil (see Chapter 1).

12   Drain the transaxle gear oil or ATF (see Chapter 7A or 7B, respectively). Clearly label, and then disconnect, all electrical connectors on the transaxle, and then set the harness aside. Disconnect the shift linkage from the transaxle (see Chapter 7A or 7B). On vehicles with an automatic transaxle, disconnect the oil cooler hoses (see Chapter 7B).

13   Drain the cooling system (see Chapter 1). Disconnect all coolant hoses between the engine, the radiator, the water pump, the thermostat and the heater core, and then remove the cooling fan assembly and the radiator (see Chapter 3).

14   Unbolt, and then push back, the air conditioning compressor, but don't disconnect the refrigerant lines (see Chapter 3).

15   Unbolt the power steering pump. Tie the pump aside without disconnecting the hoses (see Chapter 10).

16   Remove the front section of the exhaust system (see Chapter 4).

17   Remove the driveaxles (see Chapter 8).

18   Attach a lifting chain to the lifting eyes on the engine **(see illustrations)**. (If two lifting eyes are not provided, attach the lifting

sling or chain to a safe place such as a bracket on the cylinder head.) Roll an engine hoist into position adjacent to the engine compartment and connect the lifting chain to it. Take up the slack until there is slight tension on the hoist.

19   Thoroughly recheck the engine and transaxle to be sure that nothing except the engine/transaxle mounts is still connected to the engine or to the transaxle. Disconnect all remaining connectors, hoses, lines, fasteners, components, etc.

20   Raise the engine just enough to take the weight off the engine mounts **(see illustration)**. **Warning:** *Do not place any part of your body under the engine/transaxle when it's supported only by a hoist or other lifting device.*

21   Remove the engine mounts (see Chapter 2A).

22   Slowly lift the engine/transaxle assembly out of the engine compartment.

23   Set the engine/transaxle assembly on the floor and then disconnect the engine lifting hoist. **Note:** *A sheet of old hardboard or paneling between the engine/transaxle assembly and the floor makes it easier to move the assembly around. Get help before trying to move the engine/transaxle assembly.*

24   Separate the transaxle from the engine (see Chapter 7A or 7B).

25   If the vehicle is equipped with a manual

transaxle, remove the pressure plate and the clutch disc (see Chapter 8).

26   Remove the flywheel/driveplate (see Chapter 2A).

27   Hoist the engine off the floor and attach it to an engine stand.

Installation

28   Inspect the engine and transaxle mounts (see Chapter 2A). If any of them are worn or damaged, replace them.

29   If the vehicle is equipped with a manual transaxle, inspect the clutch components (see Chapter 8).

30   If the vehicle is equipped with an automatic transaxle, inspect the converter seal and bushing (see Chapter 7B), and then apply a dab of grease to the nose of the converter and to the seal lips.

31   Reattach the transaxle to the engine (see Chapter 7A or 7B).

32   Lift the engine with the engine hoist and then carefully lower the engine/transaxle assembly into position in the engine compartment.

33   Install the engine and transaxle mounts (see Chapter 2A) and then reattach the engine and transaxle to the mounts.

34   Disconnect the engine hoist from the engine/transaxle assembly.

35   Installation is otherwise the reverse of removal.

7.20 Raise the engine enough to remove the engine mounts, and then lift the engine/transaxle assembly out of the engine compartment and lower it to the floor

36   After everything has been reassembled, add coolant, oil, power steering and transmission fluids as needed (see Chapter 1).

37   Run the engine and check for proper operation and leaks. Shut off the engine and recheck the fluid levels.

8   Engine overhaul - disassembly sequence

1   It's much easier to disassemble and work on the engine if it's mounted on a portable engine stand. A stand can often be rented quite cheaply from an equipment rental yard. Before it's mounted on a stand, the flywheel/driveplate should be removed from the engine.

2   If a stand isn't available, it's possible to disassemble the engine with it blocked up on the floor. Be extra careful not to tip or drop the engine when working without a stand.

3   If you're going to obtain a rebuilt engine, all external components must come off first, to be transferred to the replacement engine, just as they will if you're doing a complete engine overhaul yourself. These include:

*Ignition coil, ignition coil mounting
    bracket, spark plug wires and spark
    plugs*
*Air conditioning, alternator and power
    steering pump mounting brackets*
Valve cover (see Chapter 2A)
*Timing belt covers, timing belt and timing
    belt sprockets (see Chapter 2A)*
*Any emissions control components not
    already removed (see Chapter 6)*
Water pump (see Chapter 3)
*Thermostat and housing cover and
    coolant supply tubes (see Chapter 3)*
Fuel system components (see Chapter 4)
*Intake and exhaust manifolds (see
    Chapter 2A)*
*Camshaft and crankshaft position sensors
    (see Chapter 6)*
*Oil filter (see Chapter 1) and adapter
    housing*
Oil dipstick and dipstick tube
Flywheel/driveplate (see Chapter 2A)

Note: *When removing external components from the engine, pay close attention to details that may be helpful or important during installation. Note the installed position of gaskets, seals, spacers, pins, brackets, washers, bolts and other small items.*

4   If you're obtaining a short-block, then the cylinder heads, oil pan and oil pump will have to be removed as well. See *Engine rebuilding alternatives* for additional information regarding the different possibilities to be considered.

5   If you're planning a complete overhaul, the engine must be disassembled and the internal components removed in the following general order:

Camshafts and lifters (see Chapter 2A)
Cylinder head (see Chapter 2A)
Oil pan (see Chapter 2A)

9.2 A small plastic bag, with an appropriate label, can be used to store the valve train components so they can be kept together and reinstalled in the original positions

*Oil pump and pick-up tube (see
    Chapter 2A)*
*Piston/connecting rod assemblies (see
    Section 13)*
*Rear main oil seal housing (see
    Chapter 2A)*

Crankshaft and main bearings

6   Before beginning the disassembly and overhaul procedures, make sure the following items are available. Also, refer to *Engine overhaul - reassembly sequence* for a list of tools and materials needed for engine reassembly.

Common hand tools
*Small cardboard boxes or plastic bags for
    storing parts*
Gasket scraper
Ridge reamer
Engine balancer puller
Micrometers
Telescoping gauges
Dial indicator set
Valve spring compressor
Cylinder surfacing hone
Piston ring groove-cleaning tool
Electric drill motor
Tap and die set
Wire brushes
Oil gallery brushes
Cleaning solvent

9   Cylinder head - disassembly

Refer to illustrations 9.2 and 9.3
Note: *New and rebuilt cylinder heads are commonly available for most engines at dealerships and auto parts stores. Due to the fact that some specialized tools are necessary for the disassembly and inspection procedures, and replacement parts aren't always readily available, it may be more practical and economical for the home mechanic to purchase a replacement head rather than taking the time*

9.3 You'll need a valve spring compressor with a special adapter to compress the spring and allow removal of the keepers from the valve stem

to disassemble, inspect and recondition the original.

1   Cylinder head disassembly involves removal of the intake and exhaust valves and related parts. If you have not yet removed the camshafts and lifters, do so now (see Chapter 2A).

2   Before the valves are removed, arrange to label and store them, along with their related components, so they can be kept separate and reinstalled in their original locations **(see illustration)**.

3   Compress the springs on the first valve with a spring compressor and remove the keepers **(see illustration)**. Carefully release the valve spring compressor and remove the retainer, the spring and the spring seat (if used).

4   Pull the valve out of the head, then remove the oil seal from the guide. If the valve binds in the guide (won't pull through), push it back into the head and deburr the area around the keeper groove with a fine file or whetstone.

5   Repeat the procedure for the remaining valves. Remember to keep all the parts for each valve together so they can be reinstalled in the same locations.

6   Once the valves and related components have been removed and stored in an organized manner, the heads should be thoroughly cleaned and inspected. If a complete engine overhaul is being done, finish the engine disassembly procedures before beginning the cylinder head cleaning and inspection process.

10   Cylinder head - cleaning and inspection

1   Thorough cleaning of the cylinder head and related valve train components, followed by a detailed inspection, will enable you to decide how much valve service work must be done during the engine overhaul. **Note:** *If the engine was severely overheated, the cylinder head is probably warped (see Step 12).*

2B

Cleaning

2   Scrape all traces of old gasket material and sealant off the head gasket, intake manifold and exhaust manifold mating surfaces. Be very careful not to gouge the cylinder head. Special gasket-removal solvents that soften gaskets and make removal much easier are available at auto parts stores.

3   Remove all built-up scale from the coolant passages.

4   Run a stiff wire brush through the various holes to remove deposits that may have formed in them.

5   Run an appropriate-size tap into each of the threaded holes to remove corrosion and thread sealant that may be present. If compressed air is available, use it to clear the holes of debris produced by this operation. **Warning:** *Wear eye protection when using compressed air!*

6   Clean the exhaust manifold and intake manifold stud threads with a wire brush.

7   Clean the cylinder head with solvent and dry it thoroughly.

8   Compressed air will speed the drying process and ensure that all holes and oil passages are clean. **Note:** *Decarbonizing chemicals are available and may prove very useful when cleaning cylinder heads and valve train components. They're very caustic and should be used with caution. Be sure to follow the instructions on the container.*

9   Clean all the valve springs, keepers and retainers with solvent and dry them thoroughly. Do the components from one valve at a time to avoid mixing up the parts.

10   Scrape off any heavy deposits that may have formed on the valves, then use a motorized wire brush to remove deposits from the valve heads and stems. Again, make sure the valves don't get mixed up.

Inspection

Note: *Be sure to perform all of the following inspection procedures before concluding* machine shop work is required. Make a list of the items that need attention.

Cylinder head

Refer to illustrations 10.11, 10.12 and 10.14

11   Inspect the head very carefully for cracks, evidence of coolant leakage and other damage. If cracks are found, check with an automotive machine shop concerning repair. If repair isn't possible, a new cylinder head must be obtained **(see illustration)**.

12   Using a straightedge and feeler gauge, check the head gasket mating surface for warpage, then compare the measurement against this Chapter's Specifications **(see illustration)**. If the warpage exceeds the limit, it can be resurfaced at an automotive machine shop.

13   Examine the valve seats in each of the combustion chambers. If they're pitted, cracked or burned, the head will require valve service that's beyond the scope of the home mechanic.

14   Check the valve stem-to-guide clearance by measuring the lateral movement of the valve stem with a dial indicator attached securely to the head **(see illustration)**. Install the valve into the guide until the stem is flush with the top of the guide. Compare the total valve stem movement indicated by the gauge needle to the stem-to-guide clearance listed in this Chapter's Specifications. If the stem-to-guide clearance is excessive, have the valve guides checked, and if necessary, knurled or replaced by an automotive machine shop.

Valves

Refer to illustrations 10.15 and 10.16

15   Carefully inspect each valve face for uneven wear, deformation, cracks, pits and burned areas. Check the valve stem for scuffing and galling and the neck for cracks. Rotate the valve and check for any obvious indication that it's bent. Look for pits and excessive wear on the end of the stem. The

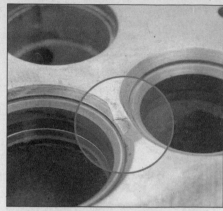

10.11 Check for cracks between the valve seats

presence of any of these conditions **(see illustration)** indicates the need to consult an automotive machine shop. **Note:** *The manufacturer recommends the valves be replaced, if refacing is necessary.*

16   Also measure the stem diameter at several points along their lengths **(see illustration)**. Taper should not exceed the limit listed in this Chapter's Specifications.

Valve components

Refer to illustrations 10.17 and 10.18

17   Check each valve spring for wear (on the ends) and pits. Measure the free length of each intake valve spring and compare them with one another **(see illustration)**. Any springs that are shorter have sagged and shouldn't be re-used. Now repeat this check on the exhaust valve springs. If, in either check, any of the springs measures shorter than another (intake-to-intake, exhaust-to-exhaust) replace all of the springs as a set. The tension of all springs should be checked with a special fixture before deciding they're suitable for use in a rebuilt engine (take the springs to an automotive machine shop for

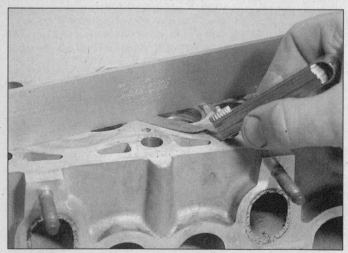

10.12 Check the cylinder head gasket surface for warpage by trying to slip a feeler gauge under the straightedge (see this Chapter's Specifications for the maximum warpage allowed and use a feeler gauge of that thickness)

10.14 A dial indicator can be used to determine the valve stem-to-guide clearance - measure the maximum deflection of the valve in its guide

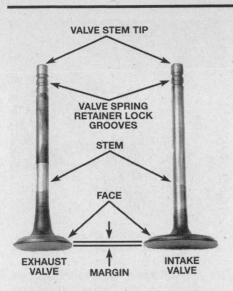

10.15 Check for valve wear at the points shown here

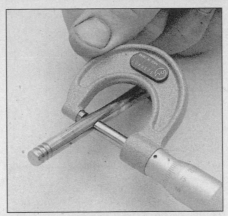

10.16 Measure the diameter of the valve stems at several points

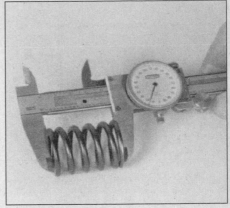

10.17 Measure the free length of each valve spring with a dial or vernier caliper

this check). **Note:** *If the engine has accumulated many miles, it's a good idea to replace all of the springs as a matter of course.*

18   Stand each spring on a flat surface and check it for squareness **(see illustration)**. If any of the springs are distorted or sagged, replace all of them with new parts.

19   Check the spring retainers, spring seats and the keepers for obvious wear and cracks. Any questionable parts should be replaced with new ones, as extensive damage will occur if they fail during engine operation.

Camshafts and lifters

20   Refer to Section 21 of this Chapter for the camshaft and lifter inspection procedures. Be sure to inspect the camshaft bearing journals on the cylinder head before the head is sent to a machine shop to have the valves serviced. If the journals are gouged or scored the cylinder head will have to be replaced regardless of the condition of the valves and related components.

All components

21   If the inspection process indicates the valve components are in generally poor condition and worn beyond the limits specified, which is usually the case in an engine that's being overhauled, reassemble the valves in the cylinder head (see Section 11 for valve servicing recommendations).

11   Valves - servicing

1   Because of the complex nature of the job and the special tools and equipment needed, servicing of the valve seats and the valve guides, commonly known as a valve job, should be done by a professional (the valves themselves aren't serviceable).

2   The home mechanic can remove and disassemble the head, do the initial cleaning and inspection, then reassemble and deliver

it to an automotive machine shop for the actual service work. Doing the inspection will enable you to see what condition the head and valvetrain components are in and will ensure that you know what work and new parts are required when dealing with an automotive machine shop. **Note:** *Be aware that Volkswagen cylinder heads have a maximum valve seat refacing dimension. This is the maximum amount of material that can be removed from the valve seats before cylinder head replacement is required. This measurement will be taken by the automotive machine shop.*

3   The automotive machine shop, will remove the valves and springs, recondition the seats, recondition the valve guides, check and replace the valves, valve springs, spring retainers and keepers (as necessary), replace the valve seals with new ones, reassemble the valve components and make sure the valve stem height is correct. If warped, the cylinder head gasket surface will also be resurfaced as long as the cylinder head is within the specified minimum height listed in this Chapter's Specifications.

4   After the valve job has been performed by a professional, the head will be in like new condition. When the head is returned, be sure to clean it again before installation on the engine to remove any metal particles and

abrasive grit that may still be present from the valve service or head resurfacing operations. Use compressed air, if available, to blow out all the oil holes and passages.

12   Cylinder head - reassembly

Refer to illustrations 12.3, 12.6 and 12.7

1   Regardless of whether or not the head was sent to an automotive repair shop for valve servicing, make sure it's clean before beginning reassembly.

2   If the head was not sent out for service, proceed to the next step. If the head was sent out for valve servicing, the valves and related components will already be in place; begin the reassembly procedure with Step 8.

3   Beginning at one end of the head, lubricate and install the first valve. Apply moly-base grease or clean engine oil to the valve stem **(see illustration)**.

4   Install the spring seat and shims, if originally installed, before the valve seals.

5   Install new seals on each of the valve guides. Gently tap each seal into place until it's completely seated on the guide. Many seal sets come with a plastic installer, but use hand pressure. Do not hammer on the seals or they could be driven down too far and subsequently leak. Don't twist or cock the seals

10.18 Check each valve spring for squareness

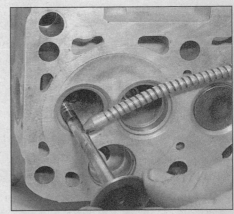

12.3 Lubricate the valve stem with clean engine oil before installing it into the guide

2B

12.6 Typical valve components

1   *Keepers*
2   *Retainer*
3   *Oil seal*
4   *Spring*
5   *Valve*
6   *Valve spring seat*

24053-2C-12.6 HAYNES

12.7 Apply a small dab of grease to each keeper as shown here before installation - it'll hold them in place on the valve stem as the spring is released

during installation or they won't seal properly on the valve stems.

6   The valve components **(see illustration)** may be installed in the following order:

    Valves
    Valve spring seat
    Valve stem seals
    Valve spring shims (if any)
    Valve springs
    Retainers
    Keepers

7   Compress the springs with a valve spring compressor and carefully install the keepers in the groove, then slowly release the compressor and make sure the keepers seat properly. Apply a small dab of grease to each keeper to hold it in place if necessary **(see illustration)**. Tap the valve stem tips with a plastic hammer to seat the keepers, if necessary.

8   Repeat the procedure for the remaining valves. Be sure to return the components to their original locations - don't mix them up!

9   Check the installed valve height with a straightedge and a dial or vernier caliper. If the head was sent out for service work, the installed height should be correct (but don't automatically assume it is). Measure valve spring height from the top of the valve spring seat to the underside of the valve spring retainer. If the height is less than the valve spring height listed in this Chapter's Specifications, the valve seats have been reworked

past their limits. On 1996 through 2000 models, insufficient valve spring height will prevent the hydraulic valve lifters from operating correctly, i.e. the valves might not close fully. On 2001 models, insufficient valve spring height will require that thinner shims be installed to restore the correct valve clearance and, in some cases, might make it impossible to install shims thin enough to restore the correct valve clearance. Valve seats that have been reworked past their limits must be replaced, or the cylinder head will have to be replaced.

10   On 2001 models, after installing the cylinder head (see Chapter 2A), check and, if necessary, adjust the valve clearances as follows.

Valve clearance check and adjustment (2001 models)

Refer to illustrations 12.16a, 12.16b, 12.17, 12.19a, 12.19b, 12.19c and 12.20

Note: *The following procedure requires the use of a special lifter tool. It is impossible to perform this task without it.*

11   Disconnect the negative cable from the battery.

12   Disconnect the spark plug wires (Section 20) and remove any other components that will interfere with valve cover removal.

13   Blow out the spark plug recess with compressed air, if available, to remove any

debris that might fall into the cylinders, then remove the spark plugs (see Section 19). **Warning:** *Always wear eye protection when using compressed air!*

14   Remove the valve cover (refer to Chapter 2A).

15   Refer to Chapter 2 and position the number 1 piston at TDC on the compression stroke.

16   Measure the clearance of the indicated valves with a feeler gauge of the specified thickness **(see illustrations)**. Record the clearance of each valve, noting which are out of specification. This information will be used later to determine the required replacement shims.

17   Turn the crankshaft one complete revolution and realign the timing marks. Measure the remaining valves **(see illustration)**.

18   After the measuring and recording the clearance of each valve, turn the crankshaft pulley until the camshaft lobe above the first valve which you intend to adjust is pointing upward, away from the shim.

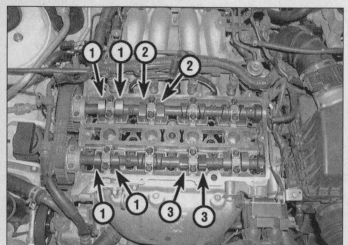

12.16a When the no. 1 piston is at TDC, measure the clearance on the indicated valves

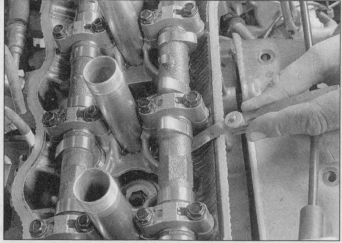

12.16b Measure the lifter-to-cam lobe clearance for each valve with a feeler gauge of the specified thickness - if the clearance is correct, you should feel a slight drag on the gauge as you pull it out

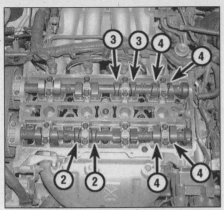

12.17 When the no. 4 piston is at TDC on the compression stroke, the valve clearance for the no. 2 and no. 4 exhaust valves and the no. 3 and no. 4 intake valves can be measured

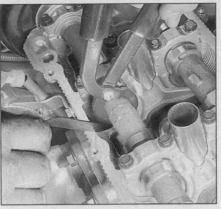

12.19a Install the special lifter tool as shown, squeeze the handles together to depress the lifter and then hold the lifter down with the smaller tool so that the shim can be removed

12.19b Keep pressure on the lifter with the smaller tool and then remove the shim with a small screwdriver . . .

19   Position the notch in the lifter toward the spark plug. Then depress the lifter with the special lifter tool **(see illustration)**. Place the special lifter tool in position as shown, with the longer jaw of the tool gripping the lower edge of the cast lifter boss and the upper, shorter jaw gripping the upper edge of the lifter itself. Depress the lifter by squeezing the handles of the lifter tool together, then hold the lifter down with the smaller tool and remove the larger one. Remove the adjusting shim with a small screwdriver or a pair of tweezers **(see illustrations)**. Note that the wire hook on the end of some lifter tool handles can be used to clamp both handles together to keep the lifter depressed while the shim is removed.

20   Measure the thickness of the shim with a micrometer **(see illustration)**. To calculate the correct thickness of a replacement shim that will place the valve clearance within the specified value, use the following formula:

$N = T + (A - V)$

T = thickness of the old shim
A = valve clearance measured
N = thickness of the new shim
V = desired valve clearance (see this Chapter's Specifications)

21   Select a shim with a thickness as close as possible to the valve clearance calculated. Shims, which are available in 20 sizes in increments of 0.0016-inch (0.040 mm), range in size from 0.079-inch (2.00 mm) to 0.1087-inch (2.76 mm). **Note:** *Through careful analysis of the shim sizes needed to bring the out-of-specification valve clearance within specification, it is often possible to simply move a shim that has to come out anyway to another lifter requiring a shim of that particular size, thereby reducing the number of new shims that must be purchased.*

22   Place the special lifter tool in position as shown in **illustration 12.19a**, with the longer jaw of the tool gripping the lower edge of the cast lifter boss and the upper, shorter jaw gripping the upper edge of the lifter itself, press down the lifter by squeezing the handles of the lifter tool together and install the new adjusting shim (note that the wire hook on the end of one lifter tool handle can be used to clamp the handles together to keep the lifter depressed while the shim is inserted). Measure the clearance with a feeler gauge to make sure that your calculations are correct.

23   Repeat this procedure until all the valves

which are out of clearance have been corrected.

24   Installation of the spark plugs, valve cover, spark plug wires and boots, accelerator cable bracket, etc. is the reverse of removal.

13 Pistons and connecting rods - removal

Refer to illustrations 13.1, 13.3, 13.4 and 13.6
Note: *Prior to removing the piston/connecting rod assemblies, remove the cylinder head, the oil pan, the oil pump drive chain, the oil pump and baffle by referring to the appropriate Sections in chapter 2 Part A or B.*

1   Use your fingernail to feel if a ridge has formed at the upper limit of ring travel (about 1/4-inch down from the top of each cylinder). If carbon deposits or cylinder wear have produced ridges, they must be completely removed with a special tool **(see illustration)**. Follow the manufacturer's instructions provided with the tool. Failure to remove the ridges before attempting to remove the piston/connecting rod assemblies may result in piston breakage.

12.19c . . . or with a pair of tweezers or a magnet, as shown here

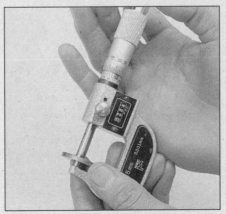

12.20 Measure the shim thickness with a micrometer or dial caliper

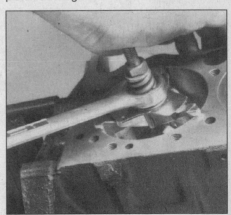

13.1 Before removing the pistons, remove the ridge from the top of each cylinder with a ridge reamer

2B

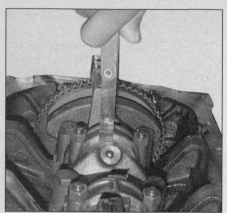

13.3 Check the connecting rod side clearance with a feeler gauge as shown

13.4 The rods and the rod bearing caps should be marked in the order in which they're installed, from the front of the engine to the rear ("1 for the first cap, "2" for the second cap, etc.)

13.6 To prevent damage to the crankshaft journals and cylinder walls, slip sections of rubber or plastic hose over the rod bolts before removing the pistons/rods

2   After the cylinder ridges have been removed, turn the engine upside-down so the crankshaft is facing up.

3   Before the connecting rods are removed, check the endplay (side clearance) with feeler gauges **(see illustration)**. Slide them between the first connecting rod and the crankshaft throw until the play is removed. The endplay is equal to the thickness of the feeler gauge(s). If the endplay exceeds the service limit, new connecting rods will be required. If new rods (or a new crankshaft) are installed, the endplay may fall under the minimum specified in this Chapter (if it does, the rods will have to be machined to restore it - consult an automotive machine shop for advice if necessary). Repeat the procedure for the remaining connecting rods.

4   Check the connecting rods and caps for identification marks **(see illustration)**. If they aren't plainly marked, use a small center-punch to make the appropriate number of indentations on each rod and cap (1, 2, 3, etc., depending on the cylinder they're associated with).

5   Loosen each of the connecting rod cap nuts 1/2-turn at a time until they can be removed by hand. Remove the number one

connecting rod cap and bearing insert. Don't drop the bearing insert out of the cap.

6   Slip a short length of plastic or rubber hose over each connecting rod cap bolt to protect the crankshaft journal and cylinder wall as the piston is removed **(see illustration)**.

7   Remove the bearing insert and push the connecting rod/piston assembly out through the top of the engine. Use a wooden or plastic hammer handle to push on the upper bearing surface in the connecting rod. If resistance is felt, double-check to make sure all of the ridge was removed from the cylinder.

8   Repeat the procedure for the remaining cylinders.

9   After removal, reassemble the connecting rod caps and bearing inserts in their respective connecting rods and install the cap nuts finger tight. Leaving the old bearing inserts in place until reassembly will help prevent the connecting rod bearing surfaces from being accidentally nicked or gouged.

10   Don't separate the pistons from the connecting rods.

14 Crankshaft - removal

Refer to illustrations 14.1, 14.2, 14.3 and 14.4
Note: *The crankshaft can be removed only after the engine has been removed from the vehicle. It's assumed the flywheel/driveplate, timing belt, oil pan, oil pump, the front and rear oil seal housings and the piston/connecting rod assemblies have already been removed.*

1   Before the crankshaft is removed, check the endplay. Mount a dial indicator with the stem in line with the crankshaft and touching the snout of the crank **(see illustration)**. Push the crankshaft all the way to the rear and zero the dial indicator. Next, pry the crankshaft to the front as far as possible and check the reading on the dial indicator. The distance it moves is the endplay. If it's greater than listed in this Chapter's Specifications, check the crankshaft thrust surfaces for wear. If no wear is evident, new main bearings should correct the endplay.

2   If a dial indicator isn't available, feeler gauges can be used. Gently pry or push the crankshaft all the way to the front of the engine. Slip feeler gauges between the crankshaft and the front face of the thrust

14.1 Measuring crankshaft endplay using a dial indicator

14.2 Checking crankshaft endplay with a feeler gauge

14.3 Using an appropriate feeler gauge, measure the clearance (arrow) between the sensor wheel on the crankshaft and the Crankshaft Position (CKP) sensor, which is bolted to the block

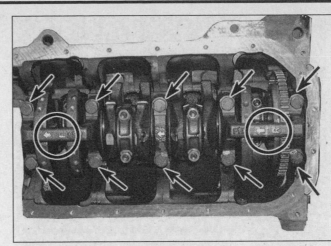

14.4 The manufacturer's identification markings on the main bearing caps (circled) indicate the direction in which they must be installed (directional arrows on caps face to the front) and indicate which cap is the front ("F") and which is the rear ("R") cap; to detach the caps, remove these bolts (arrows)

main bearing to determine the clearance **(see illustration)**. **Note:** *The thrust bearing is located at the number three main bearing cap on all engines.*

3   Measure the clearance between the crankshaft sensor wheel and the Crankshaft Position (CKP) sensor **(see illustration)**, and then compare your measurement to the clearance listed in this Chapter's Specifications. If the clearance is excessive, the CKP sensor might be loose. Make sure that the CKP sensor bolt is tightened to the torque listed in the Chapter 6 Specifications.

4   Check the main bearing caps to see if they're marked to indicate their locations. They should be numbered consecutively from the front of the engine to the rear **(see illustration)**. If they aren't, mark them with number stamping dies or a center-punch. Main bearing caps generally have a cast-in arrow, which points to the front of the engine. Loosen the main bearing cap bolts 1/4-turn at a time each, until they can be removed by hand. Note if any stud bolts are used and make sure they're returned to their original

15.7 All bolt holes in the block - particularly the main bearing cap and head bolt holes - should be cleaned and restored with a tap (be sure to remove debris from the holes after this is done)

locations when the crankshaft is reinstalled.

5   Gently tap the caps with a soft-face hammer, then separate them from the engine block. If necessary, use the bolts as levers to remove the caps. Try not to drop the bearing inserts if they come out with the caps.

6   Carefully lift the crankshaft straight out of the engine. It may be a good idea to have an assistant available, since the crankshaft is quite heavy. Be careful not to damage the reluctor ring for the crankshaft position sensor. With the bearing inserts in place in the engine block and main bearing caps, return the caps to their respective locations on the engine block and tighten the bolts finger tight.

15   Engine block - cleaning

Refer to illustration 15.7

1   Remove the main bearing caps and separate the bearing inserts from the caps and the engine block. Tag the bearings, indicating which cylinder they were removed from and whether they were in the cap or the block, then set them aside.

2   Using a gasket scraper, remove all traces of gasket material from the engine block. Be very careful not to nick or gouge the gasket sealing surfaces.

3   Remove all of the covers and threaded oil gallery plugs from the block. The plugs are usually very tight - they may have to be drilled out and the holes retapped. Use new plugs when the engine is reassembled.

4   If the engine is extremely dirty, it should be taken to an automotive machine shop to be cleaned.

5   After the block is returned, clean all oil holes and oil galleries one more time. Brushes specifically designed for this purpose are available at most auto parts stores. Flush the passages with warm water until the water runs clear, dry the block thoroughly and wipe all machined surfaces with a light, rust preventive oil. If you have access to compressed air, use it to speed the drying process and blow out all the oil holes and galleries. **Warning:** *Wear eye protection*

when using compressed air!

6   If the block isn't extremely dirty or sludged up, you can do an adequate cleaning job with hot soapy water and a stiff brush. Take plenty of time and do a thorough job. Regardless of the cleaning method used, be sure to clean all oil holes and galleries very thoroughly, dry the block completely and coat all machined surfaces with light oil.

7   The threaded holes in the block must be clean to ensure accurate torque readings during reassembly. Run the proper size tap into each of the holes to remove rust, corrosion, thread sealant or sludge and restore damaged threads **(see illustration)**. If possible, use compressed air to clear the holes of debris produced by this operation. Now is a good time to clean the threads on the head bolts and the main bearing cap bolts as well.

8   Reinstall the main bearing caps and tighten the bolts finger tight.

9   Apply non-hardening sealant (such as Permatex no. 2 or Teflon pipe sealant) to the new oil gallery plugs and thread them into the holes in the block. Make sure they're tightened securely.

10   If the engine isn't going to be reassembled right away, cover it with a large plastic trash bag to keep it clean.

16   Engine block - inspection

Refer to illustrations 16.4a, 16.4b and 16.4c
Note: *The manufacturer recommends checking the block deck for warpage and the main bearing bore concentricity and alignment. Since special measuring tools are needed, the checks should be done by an automotive machine shop.*

1   Before the block is inspected, it should be cleaned as described in Section 15.

2   Visually check the block for cracks, rust and corrosion. Look for stripped threads in the threaded holes. It's also a good idea to have the block checked for hidden cracks by an automotive machine shop that has the special equipment to do this type of work. If defects are found, have the block repaired, if possible, or replaced.

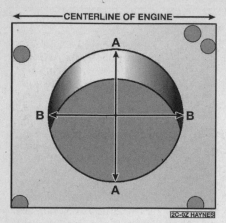

16.4a Measure the diameter of each cylinder at a right angle to the engine centerline (A), and parallel to the engine centerline (B) - out-of-round is the difference between A and B; taper is the difference between the diameter at the top of the cylinder and the diameter at the bottom of the cylinder

3   Check the cylinder bores for scuffing and scoring.

4   **Note:** *The following checks should not be made with the engine block mounted on a stand - the cylinders will be distorted and the measurements will be inaccurate.* Check the cylinders for taper and out-of-round conditions as follows **(see illustrations):**

5   Measure the diameter of each cylinder at the top (just under the ridge area), center and bottom of the cylinder bore, parallel to the crankshaft axis.

6   Next, measure each cylinder's diameter at the same three locations perpendicular to the crankshaft axis.

7   The taper of each cylinder is the difference between the bore diameter at the top of the cylinder and the diameter at the bottom. The out-of-round specification of the cylinder bore is the difference between the parallel and perpendicular readings. Compare your results to this Chapter's Specifications.

8   If the cylinder walls are badly scuffed or scored, or if they're out-of-round or tapered beyond the limits given in this Chapter's Specifications, have the engine block rebored and honed at an automotive machine shop.

9   If a rebore is done, oversize pistons and rings will be required.

10   Using a precision straightedge and feeler gauge, check the block deck (the surface the cylinder heads mate with) for distortion as you did with the cylinder heads (see Section 10). If it's distorted beyond the specified limit, the block decks can be resurfaced by an automotive machine shop, but is not recommended on these engines.

11   If the cylinders are in reasonably good condition and not worn to the outside of the limits, and if the piston-to-cylinder clearances can be maintained properly, they don't have to be rebored. Honing is all that's necessary (see Section 17).

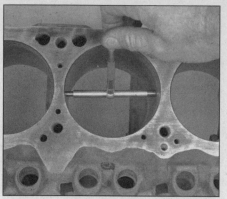

16.4b The ability to "feel" when the telescoping gauge is at the correct point will be developed over time, so work slowly and repeat the check until you're satisfied the bore measurement is accurate

17 Cylinder honing

Refer to illustrations 17.3a and 17.3b

1   Prior to engine reassembly, the cylinder bores must be honed so the new piston rings will seat correctly and provide the best possible combustion chamber seal. **Note:** *If you don't have the tools or don't want to tackle the honing operation, most automotive machine shops will do it for a reasonable fee.*

2   Before honing the cylinders, install the main bearing caps and tighten the bolts to the torque listed in this Chapter's Specifications.

3   Two types of cylinder hones are commonly available - the flex hone or "bottle brush" type and the more traditional surfacing hone with spring-loaded stones. Both will do the job, but for the less experienced mechanic the "bottle brush" hone will probably be easier to use. You'll also need some honing oil (kerosene will work if honing oil isn't available), rags and an electric drill motor. Proceed as follows:

a) *Mount the hone in the drill motor, compress the stones and slip it into the first cylinder* **(see illustration)**. *Be sure to wear safety goggles or a face shield!*

17.3a A "bottle brush" hone will produce a better cross hatch pattern when using a drill motor to hone the cylinders

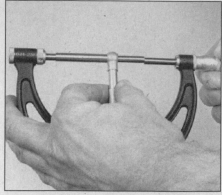

16.4c The gauge is then measured with a micrometer to determine the bore size

b) *Lubricate the cylinder with plenty of honing oil, turn on the drill and move the hone up-and-down in the cylinder at a pace that will produce a fine crosshatch pattern on the cylinder walls, and with the drill square and centered with the bore. Ideally, the crosshatch lines should intersect at approximately a 45-60-degree angle* **(see illustration)**. *Be sure to use plenty of lubricant and don't take off any more material than is absolutely necessary to produce the desired finish.* **Note:** *Piston ring manufacturers may specify a different crosshatch angle - read and follow any instructions included with the new rings.*

c) *Don't withdraw the hone from the cylinder while it's running. Instead, shut off the drill and continue moving the hone up-and-down in the cylinder until it comes to a complete stop, then compress the stones and withdraw the hone. If you're using a "bottle brush" type hone, stop the drill motor, then turn the chuck in the normal direction of rotation while withdrawing the hone from the cylinder.*

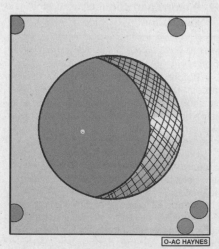

17.3b The cylinder hone should leave a smooth, crosshatch pattern with the lines intersecting at approximately a 60-degree angle

18.4a The piston ring grooves can be cleaned with a special tool, as shown here . . .

18.4b . . . or a section of broken ring

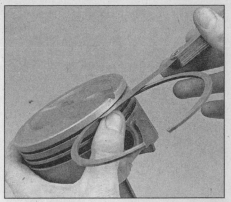

18.10 Check the ring side clearance with a feeler gauge at several points around the groove

d) Wipe the oil out of the cylinder and repeat the procedure for the remaining cylinders.

4   After the honing job is complete, chamfer the top edges of the cylinder bores with a small file so the rings won't catch when the pistons are installed. Be very careful not to nick the cylinder walls with the end of the file.

5   The entire engine block must be washed again very thoroughly with warm, soapy water to remove all traces of the abrasive grit produced during the honing operation. **Note:** *The bores can be considered clean when a lint-free white cloth - dampened with clean engine oil - used to wipe them out doesn't pick up any more honing residue, which will show up as gray areas on the cloth. Be sure to run a brush through all oil holes and galleries and flush them with running water.*

6   After rinsing, dry the block and apply a coat of light rust preventive oil to all machined surfaces. Wrap the block in a plastic trash bag to keep it clean and set it aside until reassembly.

18 Pistons and connecting rods - inspection

Refer to illustrations 18.4a, 18.4b, 18.10 and 18.11

1   Before the inspection process can be carried out, the piston/connecting rod assemblies must be cleaned and the original piston rings removed from the pistons. **Note:** *Always use new piston rings when the engine is reassembled.*

2   Using a piston ring installation tool, carefully remove the rings from the pistons. Be careful not to nick or gouge the pistons in the process.

3   Scrape all traces of carbon from the top of the piston. A hand-held wire brush or a piece of fine emery cloth can be used once the majority of the deposits have been scraped away. Do not, under any circumstances, use a wire brush mounted in a drill motor to remove deposits from the pistons. The piston material is soft and may be eroded away by the wire brush.

4   Use a piston ring groove-cleaning tool to remove carbon deposits from the ring grooves. If a tool isn't available, a piece broken off the old ring will do the job. Be very careful to remove only the carbon deposits - don't remove any metal and do not nick or scratch the sides of the ring grooves **(see illustrations).**

5   Once the deposits have been removed, clean the piston/rod assemblies with solvent and dry them with compressed air (if available). **Warning:** *Wear eye protection. Make sure the oil return holes in the back sides of the ring grooves are clear.*

6   If the pistons and cylinder walls aren't damaged or worn excessively, and if the engine block isn't rebored, new pistons won't be necessary. Normal piston wear appears as even vertical wear on the piston thrust surfaces and slight looseness of the top ring in its groove. New piston rings, however, should always be used when an engine is rebuilt.

7   Carefully inspect each piston for cracks around the skirt, at the pin bosses and at the ring lands.

8   Look for scoring and scuffing on the thrust faces of the skirt, holes in the piston crown and burned areas at the edge of the crown. If the skirt is scored or scuffed, the engine may have been suffering from overheating and/or abnormal combustion, which caused excessively high operating tempera-

tures. The cooling and lubrication systems should be checked thoroughly. A hole in the piston crown is an indication that abnormal combustion (preignition) was occurring. Burned areas at the edge of the piston crown are usually evidence of spark knock (detonation). If any of the above problems exist, the causes must be corrected or the damage will occur again. The causes may include intake air leaks, incorrect fuel/air mixture, low octane fuel, ignition timing and EGR system malfunctions.

9   Corrosion of the piston, in the form of small pits, indicates coolant is leaking into the combustion chamber and/or the crankcase. Again, the cause must be corrected or the problem may persist in the rebuilt engine.

10   Measure the piston ring side clearance by laying a new piston ring in each ring groove and slipping a feeler gauge in beside it **(see illustration).** Check the clearance at three or four locations around each groove. Be sure to use the correct ring for each groove - they are different. If the side clearance is greater than specified in this Chapter, new pistons will have to be used.

11   Check the piston-to-bore clearance by measuring the bore (see Section 16) and the piston diameter. Make sure the pistons and bores are correctly matched. Measure the piston across the skirt, at a 90-degree angle to the piston pin **(see illustration).** The mea-

2B

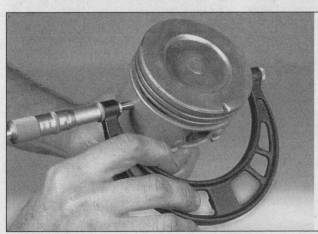

18.11 Measure the piston diameter at a 90-degree angle to the piston pin and at the specified distance from the bottom of the piston skirt

19.1 The oil holes should be chamfered so sharp edges don't gouge or scratch the new bearings

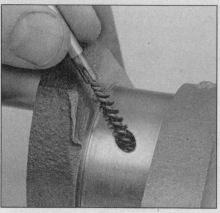

19.2 Use a wire or stiff plastic bristle brush to clean the oil passages in the crankshaft

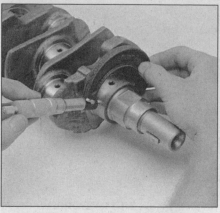

19.5 Measure the diameter of each crankshaft journal at several points to detect taper and out-of-round conditions

surement must be taken at a specific point to be accurate: The pistons should be measured about 1/4-inch (6.3 mm) from the bottom of the skirt, at right angles to the piston pin. Measure the cylinder bore at three equal places-in the bore (top, middle and bottom) and use the average dimension for comparison with the piston measurement.

12   Subtract the piston diameter from the bore diameter to obtain the clearance. If it's greater than specified, the block will have to be rebored and new pistons and rings installed.

13   Check the piston pin-to-rod and piston clearances by twisting the piston and rod in opposite directions. Any noticeable play indicates excessive wear, which must be corrected. If the piston pin, or the pin bore in the piston, is worn excessively, take the piston/connecting rod assemblies to an automotive machine shop and have the pistons and rods re-sized and new pins installed.

14   If the pistons must be separated from the connecting rods in order to replace the pistons or the rods, take them to an automotive machine shop to have them pressed apart. While the connecting rods are removed, have them checked for "bend" and "twist."

19.7 If the seals have worn grooves in the crankshaft journals, or if the seal contact surfaces are nicked or scratched, the new seals will leak

15   Inspect the connecting rods for cracks and other damage. Temporarily remove the rod caps, lift out the old bearing inserts, wipe the rod and cap bearing surfaces clean and inspect them for nicks, gouges and scratches. After inspecting the rods, replace the old bearings, slip the caps into place and tighten the nuts finger tight. **Note:** *If the engine is being rebuilt because of a connecting rod knock, be sure to install new or remanufactured connecting rods.*

19   Crankshaft - inspection

Refer to illustrations 19.1, 19.2, 19.5 and 19.7

1   Remove all burrs from the crankshaft oil holes with a stone, file or scraper **(see illustration)**.

2   Clean the crankshaft with solvent and dry it with compressed air (if available). **Warning:** *Wear eye protection when using compressed air.* Be sure to clean the oil holes with a stiff brush **(see illustration)** and flush them with solvent.

3   Check the main and connecting rod bearing journals for uneven wear, scoring, pits and cracks.

4   Check the rest of the crankshaft for cracks and other damage. It should be Magnafluxed to reveal hidden cracks - an automotive machine shop will handle the procedure.

5   Using a micrometer, measure the diameter of the main and connecting rod journals and compare the results to this Chapter's Specifications **(see illustration)**. By measuring the diameter at a number of points around each journal's circumference, you'll be able to determine whether or not the journal is out-of-round. Take the measurement at each end of the journal, near the crank throws, to determine if the journal is tapered.

6   If the crankshaft journals are damaged, tapered, out-of-round or worn beyond the limits given in the Specifications, have the crankshaft reground by an automotive machine shop. Be sure to use the correct-

size bearing inserts if the crankshaft is reconditioned.

7   Check the oil seal journals at each end of the crankshaft for wear and damage. If the seal has worn a groove in the journal, or if it's nicked or scratched **(see illustration)**, the new seal may leak when the engine is reassembled. In some cases, an automotive machine shop may be able to repair the journal by pressing on a thin sleeve. If repair isn't feasible, a new or different crankshaft should be installed.

8   Examine the main and rod bearing inserts (see Section 20).

9   Inspect the crankshaft sensor wheel at the rear of the crankshaft for cracks, wear and any other damage. If the sensor wheel is damaged, replace it. Damage to this component can result in severe driveability problems. To remove the sensor wheel from the crankshaft, remove the three retaining screws. When installing the sensor wheel, be sure to tighten the retaining screws to the torque listed in this Chapter's Specifications.

20   Main and connecting rod bearings - inspection and selection

Refer to illustration 20.1

1   Even though the main and connecting rod bearings should be replaced with new ones during the engine overhaul, the old bearings should be retained for close examination, as they may reveal valuable information about the condition of the engine **(see illustration)**.

2   Bearing failure occurs because of lack of lubrication, the presence of dirt or other foreign particles, overloading the engine and corrosion. Regardless of the cause of bearing failure, it must be corrected before the engine is reassembled to prevent it from happening again.

3   When examining the bearings, remove them from the engine block, the main bearing caps, the connecting rods and the rod caps

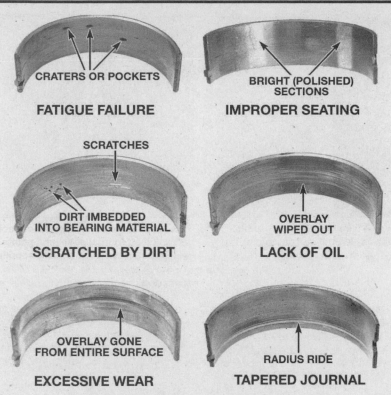

FATIGUE FAILURE
CRATERS OR POCKETS

IMPROPER SEATING
BRIGHT (POLISHED) SECTIONS

SCRATCHED BY DIRT
SCRATCHES
DIRT IMBEDDED INTO BEARING MATERIAL

LACK OF OIL
OVERLAY WIPED OUT

EXCESSIVE WEAR
OVERLAY GONE FROM ENTIRE SURFACE

TAPERED JOURNAL
RADIUS RIDE

20.1 Typical bearing failures

and lay them out on a clean surface in the same general position as their location in the engine. This will enable you to match any bearing problems with the corresponding crankshaft journal.

4   Dirt and other foreign particles get into the engine in a variety of ways. It may be left in the engine during assembly, or it may pass through filters or the PCV system. It may get into the oil, and from there into the bearings. Metal chips from machining operations and normal engine wear are often present. Abrasives are sometimes left in engine components after reconditioning, especially when parts aren't thoroughly cleaned using the proper cleaning methods. Whatever the source, these foreign objects often end up embedded in the soft bearing material and are easily recognized. Large particles won't embed in the bearing and will score or gouge the bearing and journal. The best prevention for this cause of bearing failure is to clean all parts thoroughly and keep everything spotlessly clean during engine assembly. Frequent and regular engine oil and filter changes are also recommended.

5   Lack of lubrication (or lubrication breakdown) has a number of interrelated causes. Excessive heat (which thins the oil), overloading (which squeezes the oil from the bearing face) and oil leakage or throw off (from excessive bearing clearances, worn oil pump or high engine speeds) all contribute to lubrication breakdown. Blocked oil passages, which usually are the result of misaligned oil holes in a bearing shell, will also oil starve a bearing and destroy it. When lack of lubrication is the cause of bearing failure, the bearing material is wiped or extruded from the steel backing of the bearing. Temperatures may increase to the point where the steel backing turns blue from overheating.

6   Driving habits can have a definite effect on bearing life. Low speed operation in too high a gear (lugging the engine) puts very high loads on bearings, which tends to squeeze out the oil film. These loads cause the bearings to flex, which produces fine cracks in the bearing face (fatigue failure). Eventually the bearing material will loosen in pieces and tear away from the steel backing. Short trip driving leads to corrosion of bearings because insufficient engine heat is produced to drive off the condensed water and corrosive gases. These products collect in the engine oil, forming acid and sludge. As the oil is carried to the engine bearings, the acid attacks and corrodes the bearing material.

7   Incorrect bearing installation during engine assembly will lead to bearing failure as well. Tight-fitting bearings leave insufficient oil clearance and will result in oil starvation. Dirt or foreign particles trapped behind a bearing insert result in high spots on the bearing which lead to failure.

2B

21   Camshaft, lifters and bearings - inspection

Refer to illustrations 21.1, 21.2, 21.4, 21.5, 21.6a and 21.6b

1   Visually check the camshaft bearing surfaces for pitting, score marks, galling and abnormal wear. If the bearing surfaces are damaged, the cylinder head will have to be replaced **(see illustration)**.

21.1 Inspect the camshaft bearing surfaces in the cylinder head for pits, score marks and abnormal wear - if damage is noted, the cylinder head must be replaced

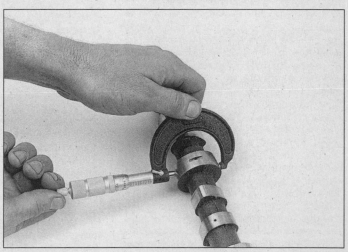

21.2 Measure the outside diameter of each camshaft journal and the inside diameter of each bearing surface on the cylinder head to determine the oil clearance measurement

21.4 Checking camshaft endplay with a dial indicator

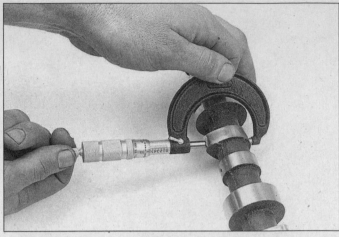

21.5 Measuring the camshaft lobe height with a micrometer - make sure you move the micrometer to get the highest reading (top of cam lobe)

2   Measure the outside diameter of each camshaft bearing journal and record your measurements **(see illustration)**. Compare them to the journal outside diameter specified in this Chapter, then measure the inside diameter of each corresponding camshaft bearing and record the measurements. Subtract each cam journal outside diameter from its respective cam bearing bore inside diameter to determine the oil clearance for each bearing. Compare the results to the specified journal-to-bearing clearance. If any of the measurements fall outside the standard specified wear limits in this Chapter, either the camshaft or the cylinder head, or both, must be replaced.

3   Measure camshaft runout by placing the camshaft back into the cylinder head and set up a dial indicator on the center journal. Zero the dial indicator. Turn the camshaft slowly and note the dial indicator readings. Record your readings and compare them with the specified runout in this Chapter. If the measured runout exceeds the runout specified in this Chapter, replace the camshaft.

4   Measure the camshaft endplay by placing a dial indicator with the stem in line with the camshaft and touching the snout **(see illustration)**. Push the camshaft all the way to the rear and zero the dial indicator. Next, pry the camshaft to the front as far as possible and check the reading on the dial indicator. The distance it moves is the endplay. If it's greater than the Specifications listed in Chapter 2A or 2B, check the bearing caps for wear. If the bearing caps are worn the cylinder head must be replaced.

5   Compare the camshaft lobe height by measuring each lobe with a micrometer **(see illustration)**. Measure each of the intake lobes and write the measurements and relative positions down on a piece of paper. Then measure each of the exhaust lobes and record the measurements and relative positions also. This will let you compare all of the intake lobes to one another and all of the exhaust lobes to one another. If the differ-

ence between the lobes exceeds 0.005 inch the camshaft should be replaced. Do not compare intake lobe heights to exhaust lobe heights as lobe lift may be different. Only compare intake lobes-to-intake lobes and exhaust lobes-to exhaust lobes for this comparison.

6   Inspect the contact and sliding surfaces of each lifter for wear and scratches **(see illustrations)**. **Note:** *If the lifter pad is worn, it's a good idea to check the corresponding camshaft. Do not lay the lifters on their side or upside down, or air can become trapped inside and the lifter will have to be bled. The lifters can be laid on their side only if they are submerged in a pan of clean engine oil until reassembly.*

7   Verify that each lifter moves up and down freely in its bore on the cylinder head. If it doesn't the valve may stick open and cause internal engine damage.

8   In any case make sure all the parts, new or old, have been thoroughly inspected before reassembly.

Hydraulic lifters - in vehicle check

9   Noisy valve lifters can be checked for

wear without disassembling the engine by following the procedure outlined below:

a) *Run the engine until reaches normal operating temperature.*

b   *Remove the valve cover (see Chapter 2A).*

c) *Rotate the engine by hand until the No.1 piston is located at TDC (see Chapter 2A).*

d) *Insert a feeler gauge between the camshaft lobe and the lifter to measure the clearance. If the clearance exceeds 0.008 inch (0.2 mm), the lifter and/or the camshaft lobe has worn beyond it limits.*

e) *If no clearance exists, depress the lifter to force it to bleed down and then check the clearance again.*

f) *Lifter clearance on the remaining cylinders can be checked by following the firing order sequence and positioning each of the remaining pistons at TDC. **Note:** Lifter clearance can also be checked on any lifter whose cam lobe is pointing upward.*

g) *If the clearance is beyond the maximum allowed, inspect the camshaft as described in Step 5.*

h) *If the camshaft is OK, the lifters are faulty and must be replaced.*

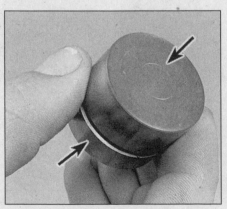

21.6a Inspect the valve lifters at the areas shown (arrows)

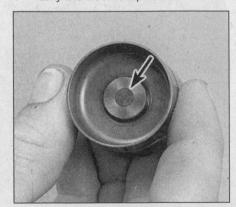

21.6b Also check the valve stem contact area of the lifter

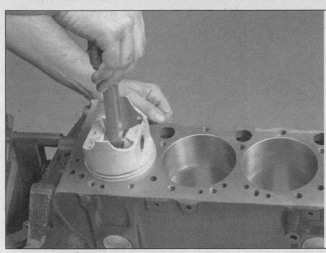

23.3 When checking piston ring end gap, the ring must be square in the cylinder bore (this is done by pushing the ring down with the top of a piston as shown)

and cylinder during the end gap measurement and engine assembly.

3   Insert the top (number one) ring into the first cylinder and square it up with the cylinder walls by pushing it in with the top of the piston **(see illustration)**. The ring should be near the bottom of the cylinder, at the lower limit of ring travel.

4   To measure the end gap, slip feeler gauges between the ends of the ring until a gauge equal to the gap width is found **(see illustration)**. The feeler gauge should slide between the ring ends with a slight amount of drag. Compare the measurement to this Chapter's Specifications. If the gap is larger or smaller than specified, double-check to make sure you have the correct rings before proceeding.

5   If the gap is too small, it must be enlarged or the ring ends may come in contact with each other during engine operation, which can cause serious engine damage. The end gap can be increased by filing the ring ends very carefully with a fine file. Mount the file in a vise equipped with soft jaws, slip the ring over the file with the ends contacting the file teeth and slowly move the ring to remove material from the ends. When performing this operation, file only from the outside in **(see illustration)**. **Note:** *When you have the end gap correct, remove any burrs from the filed ends of the rings with a whetstone.*

6   Excess end gap isn't critical unless it's greater than 0.040-inch (1.0 mm). Again, double-check to make sure you have the correct rings for the engine. If the engine block has been bored oversize, necessitating oversize pistons, matching oversize rings are required.

7   Repeat the procedure for each ring that will be installed in the first cylinder and for each ring in the remaining cylinders. Remember to keep rings, pistons and cylinders matched up.

8   Once the ring end gaps have been checked/corrected, the rings can be installed on the pistons.

9   The oil control ring (lowest one on the

22 Engine overhaul - reassembly sequence

1   Before beginning engine reassembly, make sure you have all the necessary new parts, gaskets and seals as well as the following items on hand:

   Common hand tools
   Torque wrench (1/2-inch drive) with
      angle-torque gauge
   Piston ring Installation tool
   Piston ring compressor
   Crankshaft balancer installation tool
   Short lengths of rubber or plastic hose to
      fit over connecting rod bolts
   Plastigage
   Feeler gauges
   Fine-tooth file
   New engine oil
   Engine assembly lube or moly-base
      grease
   Gasket sealant
   Thread locking compound

2   In order to save time and avoid problems, engine reassembly must be done in the following general order:

   Crankshaft and main bearings
   Piston/connecting rod assemblies
   Crankshaft front oil seal and oil pump
   Oil pump pick-up tube
   Crankshaft rear oil seal and seal housing
   Oil pan
   Flywheel/driveplate
   Cylinder head (with valve components
      installed)
   Lifters and camshafts
   Timing belt sprockets, timing belt and
      timing belt cover
   Valve cover
   Intake and exhaust manifolds

23 Piston rings - installation

Refer to illustrations 23.3, 23.4, 23.5, 23.9a, 23.9b and 23.12

1   Before installing the new piston rings, the ring end gaps must be checked. It's assumed the piston ring side clearance has been checked and verified correct (see Section 18).

2   Lay out the piston/connecting rod assemblies and the new ring sets so the ring sets will be matched with the same piston

2B

23.4 With the ring square in the cylinder, measure the end gap with a feeler gauge

23.5 If the end gap is too small, clamp a file in a vise and file the ring ends (from the outside in only) to enlarge the gap slightly

23.9a Installing the spacer/expander in the oil control ring groove

23.9b DO NOT use a piston ring installation tool when installing the oil ring side rails

23.12 Installing the compression rings with a ring expander - the "TOP" mark (arrow) must face up

piston) is usually installed first. Some piston ring manufactures supply one-piece oil rings - others may supply three-piece oil rings. One-piece rings can be installed as shown in **illustration 23.12**. If you're installing three-piece oil rings, slip the spacer/expander into the groove **(see illustration)**. If an anti-rotation tang is used, make sure it's inserted into the drilled hole in the ring groove. Next, install the lower side rail. Don't use a piston ring installation tool on the oil ring side rails, as they may be damaged. Instead, place one end of the side rail into the groove between the spacer/expander and the ring land, hold it firmly in place and slide a finger around the piston while pushing the rail into the groove **(see illustration)**. Next, install the upper side rail in the same manner. **Note:** *Some engines may have a two piece oil ring. If so, follow the installation instructions that come with the piston rings if they differ from the instructions outlined here.*

10   After the three oil ring components have been installed, check to make sure both the upper and lower side rails can be turned smoothly in the ring groove.

11   The number two (middle) ring is installed next. It's usually stamped with a mark, which must face up, toward the top of the piston. **Note:** *Always follow the instructions printed on the ring package or box - different manu-*

facturers may require different approaches. Don't mix up the top and middle rings, as they have different cross-sections.

12   Use a piston ring installation tool and make sure the identification mark is facing the top of the piston, then slip the ring into the middle groove on the piston **(see illustration)**. Don't expand the ring any more than necessary to slide it over the piston.

13   Install the number one (top) ring in the same manner. Make sure the mark is facing up. Be careful not to confuse the number one and number two rings.

14   Repeat the procedure for the remaining pistons and rings.

24   Crankshaft - installation and main bearing oil clearance check

1   Crankshaft installation is the first step in engine reassembly. It's assumed at this point that the engine block and crankshaft have been cleaned, inspected and repaired or reconditioned.

2   Position the engine with the bottom facing up.

3   Remove the main bearing cap bolts and lift out the caps. Lay them out in the proper order to ensure correct installation.

4   If they're still in place, remove the original bearing inserts from the block and the main bearing caps. Wipe the bearing surfaces of the block and caps with a clean, lint-free cloth. They must be kept spotlessly clean.

Main bearing oil clearance check

Refer to illustrations 24.5, 24.6, 24.11 and 24.15

Note: *Don't touch the faces of the new bearing inserts with your fingers. Oil and acids from your skin can etch the bearings.*

5   Clean the back sides of the new main bearing inserts and lay one in each main bearing saddle in the block. If one of the bearing inserts from each set has a large groove in it, make sure the grooved insert is installed in the block **(see illustration)**. Lay the other bearing from each set in the corresponding main bearing cap. Make sure the tab on the bearing insert fits into the recess in the block or cap, neither higher than the cap's edge nor lower. **Caution:** *The oil holes in the block must line up with the oil holes in the bearing inserts. Do not hammer the bearing into place and don't nick or gouge the bearing faces. No lubrication should be used at this time.*

6   The thrust washers must be installed on each side of the number three main journal and the main cap **(see illustration)**.

7   Clean the faces of the bearings in the block and the crankshaft main bearing journals with a clean, lint-free cloth.

8   Check or clean the oil holes in the crankshaft, as any dirt here can go only one way - straight through the new bearings.

9   Once you're certain the crankshaft is clean, carefully lay it in position in the main bearings.

10   Before the crankshaft can be permanently installed, the main bearing oil clearance must be checked.

11   Cut several pieces of the appropriate size Plastigage (they should be slightly shorter than the width of the main bearings) and place one piece on each crankshaft main

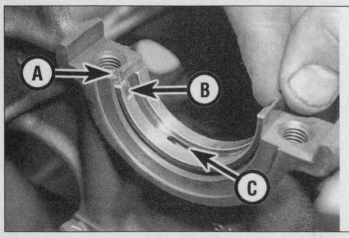

24.5 Bearing shell correctly installed

A   *Recess in bearing saddle*
B   *Lug on bearing shell*
C   *Oil hole*

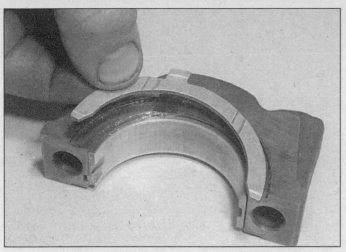

24.6 Installing the thrust washers on the No. 3 main bearing cap

24.11 Lay the Plastigage strips (arrow) on the main bearing journals, parallel to the crankshaft centerline

bearing journal, parallel with the journal axis **(see illustration)**.

12   Clean the faces of the bearings in the caps and install the caps in their original locations (don't mix them up) with the arrows pointing toward the front of the engine. Don't disturb the Plastigage.

13   Starting with the center main and working out toward the ends, tighten the main bearing cap bolts to the torque listed in this Chapter's Specifications in three steps. Don't rotate the crankshaft at any time during this operation, and do not tighten one cap completely - tighten all caps equally. Before tightening, the main caps should be seated using light taps with a brass or plastic mallet.

14   Remove the bolts/studs and carefully lift off the main bearing caps. Keep them in order. Don't disturb the Plastigage or rotate the crankshaft. If any of the main bearing caps are difficult to remove, tap them gently from side-to-side with a soft-face hammer to loosen them.

15   Compare the width of the crushed Plastigage on each journal to the scale printed on the Plastigage envelope to obtain the main bearing oil clearance **(see illustration)**. Check the Specifications to make sure it's correct.

16   If the clearance is not as specified, the bearing inserts may be the wrong size (which means different ones will be required). Before deciding different inserts are needed, make sure no dirt or oil was between the bearing inserts and the caps or block when the clearance was measured. If the Plastigage was wider at one end than the other, the journal may be tapered (see Section 19).

17   Carefully scrape all traces of the Plastigage material off the main bearing journals and/or the bearing faces. Use your fingernail or the edge of a credit card - don't nick or scratch the bearing faces.

Final crankshaft installation

18   Carefully lift the crankshaft out of the engine.

19   Clean the bearing faces in the block, then apply a thin, uniform layer of moly-base grease or engine assembly lube to each of the bearing surfaces. Be sure to coat the thrust faces as well as the journal face of the thrust bearing.

20   Make sure the crankshaft journals are clean, then lay the crankshaft back in place in the block.

21   Clean the faces of the bearings in the caps, then apply lubricant to them.

22   Install the caps in their original locations with the arrows (made earlier) pointing toward the front of the engine.

23   With all caps in place and bolts just started, tap the ends of the crankshaft forward and backward with a lead or brass hammer to line up the main bearing and crankshaft thrust surfaces.

24   Following the procedures outlined in Step 13, retighten all main bearing cap bolts to the torque listed in this Chapter's Specifications, starting with the center main and working out toward the ends.

25   Rotate the crankshaft a number of times by hand to check for any obvious binding.

26   The final step is to check the crankshaft endplay with feeler gauges or a dial indicator as described in Section 14. The endplay should be correct if the crankshaft thrust faces aren't worn or damaged and new bearings have been installed.

25   Rear main oil seal - replacement

All models are equipped with a one piece rear main oil seal and housing. The crankshaft must be installed first and the main bearing caps bolted in place before the seal and housing can be installed on the engine block. Refer to Chapter 2A for the rear main seal replacement procedure. Disregard the Steps that do not apply since the engine is out of the vehicle and the oil pan is not installed.

26   Pistons and connecting rods - installation and rod bearing oil clearance check

1   Before installing the piston/connecting rod assemblies, the cylinder walls must be perfectly clean, the top edge of each cylinder must be chamfered, and the crankshaft must be in place.

2   Remove the cap from the end of the number one connecting rod (check the marks made during removal). Remove the original bearing inserts and wipe the bearing surfaces of the connecting rod and cap with a clean, lint-free cloth. They must be kept spotlessly clean.

Piston installation and rod bearing oil clearance check

Refer to illustrations 26.5a, 26.5b, 26.11, 26.13 and 26.17

3   Clean the back side of the new upper bearing insert, then lay it in place in the connecting rod. Make sure the tab on the bearing

2B

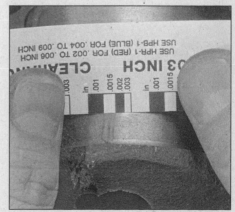

24.15 Measuring the width of the crushed Plastigage to determine the main bearing oil clearance (be sure to use the correct scale - standard and metric ones are included)

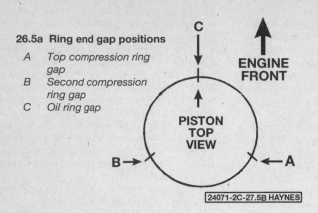

26.5a Ring end gap positions

A   Top compression ring gap
B   Second compression ring gap
C   Oil ring gap

ENGINE FRONT

PISTON TOP VIEW

24071-2C-27.5B HAYNES

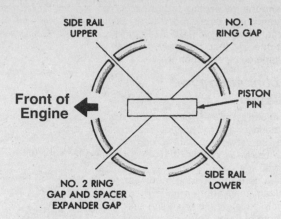

SIDE RAIL UPPER

NO. 1 RING GAP

Front of Engine

PISTON PIN

NO. 2 RING GAP AND SPACER EXPANDER GAP

SIDE RAIL LOWER

26.5b Ring end gap positions (with three-piece oil rings)

fits into the recess in the rod. Don't hammer the bearing insert into place and be very careful not to nick or gouge the bearing face. Don't lubricate the bearing at this time.

4   Clean the back side of the other bearing insert and install it in the rod cap. Again, make sure the tab on the bearing fits into the recess in the cap, and don't apply any lubricant. It's critically important that the mating surfaces of the bearing and connecting rod are perfectly clean and oil free when they're assembled.

5   Stagger the piston ring gaps around the piston **(see illustrations)**.

6   Slip a section of plastic or rubber hose over each connecting rod cap bolt.

7   Lubricate the piston and rings with clean engine oil and attach a piston ring compressor to the piston. Leave the skirt protruding about 1/4-inch (6 mm) to guide the piston into the cylinder. The rings must be compressed until they're flush with the piston.

8   Rotate the crankshaft until the number one connecting rod journal is at BDC (bottom dead center) and apply a coat of engine oil to the cylinder walls.

9   With the mark or notch on top of the piston facing the front of the engine, gently insert the piston/connecting rod assembly into the number one cylinder bore and rest

the bottom edge of the ring compressor on the engine block.

10   Tap the top edge of the ring compressor to make sure it's contacting the block around its entire circumference.

11   Gently tap on the top of the piston with the end of a wooden or plastic hammer handle **(see illustration)** while guiding the end of the connecting rod into place on the crankshaft journal. The piston rings may try to pop out of the ring compressor just before entering the cylinder bore, so keep some pressure down on the ring compressor. Work slowly, and if any resistance is felt as the piston enters the cylinder, stop immediately. Find out what's hanging up and fix it before proceeding. Do not, for any reason, force the piston into the cylinder - you might break a ring and/or the piston.

12   Once the piston/connecting rod assembly is installed, the connecting rod bearing oil clearance must be checked before the rod cap is permanently bolted in place.

13   Cut a piece of the appropriate size Plastigage slightly shorter than the width of the connecting rod bearing and lay it in place on the number one connecting rod journal, parallel with the journal axis **(see illustration)**.

14   Clean the connecting rod cap bearing face, remove the protective hoses from the

connecting rod bolts and install the rod cap. Make sure the mating mark on the cap is on the same side as the mark on the connecting rod.

15   Install the nuts and tighten them to the torque listed in this Chapter's Specifications. Work up to it in three steps. **Note:** *Use a thin-wall socket to avoid erroneous torque readings that can result if the socket is wedged between the rod cap and nut. If the socket tends to wedge itself between the nut and the cap, lift up on it slightly until it no longer contacts the cap. Do not rotate the crankshaft at any time during this operation.*

16   Remove the nuts and detach the rod cap, being very careful not to disturb the Plastigage.

17   Compare the width of the crushed Plastigage to the scale printed on the Plastigage envelope to obtain the oil clearance **(see illustration)**. Compare it to this Chapter's Specifications to make sure the clearance is correct.

18   If the clearance is not as specified, the bearing inserts may be the wrong size (which means different ones will be required). Before deciding different inserts are needed, make sure no dirt or oil was between the bearing

26.11 Drive the piston into the cylinder bore with the end of a wooden or plastic hammer handle

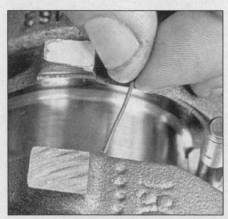

26.13 Lay the Plastigage strips on each rod bearing journal, parallel to the crankshaft centerline

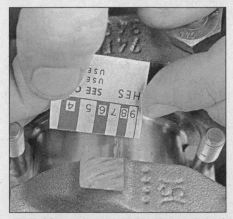

26.17 Measuring the width of the crushed Plastigage to determine the rod bearing oil clearance (be sure to use the correct scale - standard and metric ones are included)

inserts and the connecting rod or cap when the clearance was measured. Also, recheck the journal diameter. If the Plastigage was wider at one end than the other, the journal may be tapered (see Section 19).

Final connecting rod installation

19   Carefully scrape all traces of the Plastigage material off the rod journal and/or bearing face. Be very careful not to scratch the bearing - use your fingernail or the edge of a credit card.

20   Make sure the bearing faces are perfectly clean, then apply a uniform layer of clean moly-base grease or engine assembly lube to both of them. You'll have to push the piston into the cylinder to expose the face of the bearing insert in the connecting rod - be sure to slip the protective hoses over the rod bolts first.

21   Slide the connecting rod back into place on the journal, remove the protective hoses from the rod cap bolts, install the rod cap and tighten the nuts to the torque listed in this Chapter's Specifications. Again, work up to the torque in three steps.

22   Repeat the entire procedure for the remaining pistons/connecting rods.

23   The important points to remember are:

a) *Keep the back sides of the bearing inserts and the insides of the connecting rods and caps perfectly clean when assembling them.*

b) *Make sure you have the correct piston/rod assembly for each cylinder.*

c) *The arrow or mark on the piston must face the front of the engine.*

d) *Lubricate the cylinder walls with clean oil.*

e) *Lubricate the bearing faces when installing the rod caps after the oil clearance has been checked.*

24   After all the piston/connecting rod assemblies have been properly installed, rotate the crankshaft a number of times by hand to check for any obvious binding.

25   As a final step, the connecting rod endplay must be checked (see Section 13).

26   Compare the measured endplay to this Chapter's Specifications to make sure it's correct. If it was correct before disassembly and the original crankshaft and rods were reinstalled, it should still be right. If new rods or a new crankshaft were installed, the endplay may be inadequate. If so, the rods will have to be removed and taken to an automotive machine shop for re-sizing.

---

27   Initial start-up and break-in after overhaul

Warning: *Have a fire extinguisher handy when starting the engine for the first time.*

1   Once the engine has been installed in the vehicle, double-check the oil and coolant levels. Remove all of the spark plugs (see Chapter 1) from the engine.

2   Disable the fuel and ignition systems by disconnecting the primary electrical connectors at the ignition coil pack/modules (see Chapter 5) and the electrical connectors at the fuel injectors (see Chapter 4).

3   Install the spark plugs and then hook up the spark plug wires. Restore the fuel and ignition system functions.

4   Start the engine. It may take a few moments for the fuel system to build up pressure, but the engine should start without a great deal of effort. **Note:** *If the engine keeps backfiring, recheck the valve timing and spark plug wire routing.*

5   After the engine starts, it should be allowed to warm up to normal operating temperature. While the engine is warming up, make a thorough check for fuel, oil and coolant leaks.

6   Shut the engine off and recheck the engine oil and coolant levels.

7   Drive the vehicle to an area with no traffic, accelerate from 30 to 50 mph, then allow the vehicle to slow to 30 mph with the throttle closed. Repeat the procedure 10 or 12 times. This will load the piston rings and cause them to seat properly against the cylinder walls. Check again for oil and coolant leaks.

8   Drive the vehicle gently for the first 500 miles (no sustained high speeds) and keep a constant check on the oil level. It isn't unusual for an engine to use oil during the break-in period.

9   At approximately 500 to 600 miles, change the oil and filter.

10   For the next few hundred miles, drive the vehicle normally. Don't pamper it or abuse it.

11   After 2000 miles, change the oil and filter again and consider the engine broken in.

2B

Notes

Chapter 3
Cooling, heating and air conditioning systems

Contents

Specifications

General

Radiator cap pressure rating .... 11.8 to 15.6 psi (81.4 to 110 kPa)
Refrigerant type R-134a
Refrigerant capacity
  1996 through 2000 .... 1.50 to 1.61 pounds (675 to 725 g)
  2001 and later .... 1.43 to 1.54 pounds (655 to 705 g)
Compressor refrigerant oil type .... Polyalkylene glycol (PAG)
Compressor refrigerant oil capacity
  1996 through 2000 .... 170 to 190 cc
  2001 and later
    HS-15 compressor .... 140 to 160 cc
    10PA15C compressor .... 120 to 135 cc
Thermostat
  Opening temperature .... 177-degrees F (81-degrees C)
  Fully open at .... 205-degrees F (96.9-degrees C)
  Valve lift when fully open .... At least 0.33 inch (8.5 mm)
Coolant temperature sending unit resistance
  At 158 degrees F (60 degrees C) .... 90.5 to 117.5 ohms
  At 239 degrees F (115 degrees C) .... 21.3 to 36.3 ohms

Torque specifications

	Ft-lbs (unless otherwise indicated)	Nm
Coolant temperature sender	84 to 108 in-lbs	10 to 12
Thermostat housing cover bolts	108 to 168 in-lbs	15 to 20
Water pump bolts	15 to 20	20 to 27
Water pump pulley bolts	72 to 84 in-lbs	8 to 10

1   General information

Engine cooling system

All vehicles covered by this manual employ a pressurized engine cooling system with thermostatically controlled coolant circulation. An impeller type water pump mounted on the front (drivebelt end) of the engine block pumps coolant through the engine. The coolant flows around each cylinder as it moves through the cylinder head. Cast-in coolant passages direct coolant around the intake and exhaust ports, near the spark plug areas and in close proximity to the exhaust valve guides.

A wax pellet type thermostat is located in a housing near the transaxle end of the engine. During warm up, the closed thermostat prevents coolant from circulating through the radiator. As the engine nears normal operating temperature, the thermostat opens and allows hot coolant to travel through the radiator, where it's cooled before returning to the engine.

The cooling system is sealed by a pressure type radiator cap, which raises the boiling point of the coolant and increases the cooling efficiency of the radiator. If the system pressure exceeds the cap pressure relief value, the excess pressure in the system forces the spring-loaded valve inside the cap off its seat and allows the coolant to escape through the overflow tube into a coolant reservoir. When the system cools, the excess coolant is automatically drawn from the reservoir back into the radiator.

The coolant reservoir does double duty as both the point at which fresh coolant is added to the cooling system to maintain the proper fluid level and as a holding tank for overheated coolant.

This type of cooling system is known as a closed design because coolant that escapes past the pressure cap is saved and reused.

Heating system

The heating system consists of a blower fan and heater core located in the heater box, the hoses connecting the heater core to the engine cooling system and the heater/air conditioning control panel on the dashboard. Hot engine coolant is circulated through the heater core. When the heater mode is activated, a flap door opens to expose the heater box to the passenger compartment. A fan switch on the control head activates the blower motor, which forces air through the core, heating the air.

Air conditioning system

The air conditioning system consists of a condenser mounted in front of the radiator, an evaporator mounted adjacent to the heater core, a compressor mounted on the engine, a filter-drier which contains a high pressure relief valve and the plumbing connecting all of the above components.

A blower fan forces the warmer air of the passenger compartment through the evaporator core (sort of a radiator-in-reverse), transferring the heat from the air to the refrigerant. The liquid refrigerant boils off into low pressure vapor, taking the heat with it when it leaves the evaporator.

2   Antifreeze - general information

Warning: *Do not allow antifreeze to come in contact with your skin or painted surfaces of the vehicle. Rinse off spills immediately with plenty of water. Antifreeze, if consumed, can be fatal to children and pets, so wipe up garage floor and drip pan coolant spills immediately. Keep antifreeze containers covered and repair leaks in your cooling system as soon as they are noticed.*

The cooling system should be filled with a water/ethylene glycol based antifreeze solution, which will prevent freezing down to at least -20 degrees F, or lower if local climate requires it. It also provides protection against corrosion and increases the coolant boiling point.

The cooling system should be drained, flushed and refilled at the specified intervals (see Chapter 1). Old or contaminated antifreeze solutions are likely to cause damage and encourage the formation of corrosion and scale in the system. Use distilled water with the antifreeze.

Before adding antifreeze, check all hose connections, because antifreeze tends to search out and leak through very minute openings. Engines don't normally consume coolant, so if the level goes down, find the cause and correct it.

The exact mixture of antifreeze-to-water which you should use depends on the relative weather conditions. The mixture should contain at least 50 percent antifreeze, but should never contain more than 70 percent antifreeze. Consult the mixture ratio chart on the antifreeze container before adding coolant. Hydrometers are available at most auto parts stores to test the coolant. Use antifreeze which meets the vehicle manufacturer's specifications.

3   Thermostat - check and replacement

Warning: *Do not remove the radiator cap, drain the coolant or replace the thermostat until the engine has cooled completely.*

Check

1   Before assuming the thermostat is to blame for a cooling system problem, check the coolant level, drivebelt tension (Chapter 1) and temperature gauge operation.
2   If the engine seems to be taking a long time to warm up (based on heater output or temperature gauge operation), the thermostat is probably stuck open. Replace the thermostat with a new one.

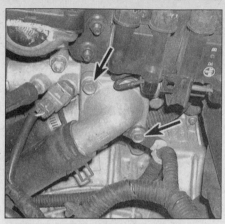

3.8 To remove the thermostat housing cover, remove these two bolts (arrows)

3   If the engine runs hot, use your hand to check the temperature of the upper radiator hose. If the hose isn't hot, but the engine is, the thermostat is probably stuck closed, preventing the coolant inside the engine from escaping to the radiator. Replace the thermostat. If the upper radiator hose is hot, it means that the coolant is flowing and the thermostat is open. Consult the Troubleshooting Section at the front of this manual for cooling system diagnosis. **Caution:** *Don't drive the vehicle without a thermostat. The computer may stay in open loop and emissions and fuel economy will suffer.*
4   Further testing of the thermostat can be accomplished by removing the thermostat and suspending it in a container of water. Heat the water while observing the thermostat (do not allow the thermostat to contact the sides of the container during heating). If the thermostat does not fully open as the water boils, it is defective.

Replacement

Caution: *Some models are equipped with an anti-theft radio. Before performing a procedure that requires disconnecting the battery, make sure you have the activation code.*
Refer to illustrations 3.8 and 3.13
5   Disconnect the battery cable from the negative terminal of the battery.
6   Drain the cooling system (see Chapter 1). If the coolant is relatively new or in good condition, save it and reuse it.
7   Follow the upper radiator hose to the engine to locate the thermostat housing.
8   Loosen the hose clamp **(see illustration)**, then detach the hose from the fitting. If it's stuck, grasp it near the end with a pair of large adjustable pliers and twist it to break the seal, then pull it off. If the hose is old or deteriorated, cut it off and install a new one.
9   Inspect the condition of the outer surface of the thermostat cover inlet that mates with the hose. If it's corroded or pitted, replace the thermostat housing cover.
10   Remove the thermostat housing cover bolts **(see illustration 3.8)** and then remove the cover. If the cover is stuck, tap it with a

3.13 Make sure that the thermostat is installed like this, with the spring facing in, toward the cylinder head

4.2 The drain cock valve (arrow) is located at the lower right rear corner of the radiator

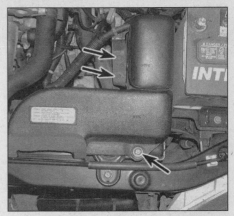

4.3 To detach the air duct, remove these bolts (arrows)

4.4a Radiator cooling fan electrical connector (arrow)

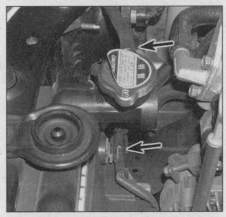

4.4b Condenser cooling fan electrical connector (lower arrow) (vehicles with air conditioning); don't forget to disconnect the reservoir hose (upper arrow) from the radiator filler neck

4.5a To disconnect the upper radiator hose from the radiator, loosen this hose clamp (arrow) and pull off the hose

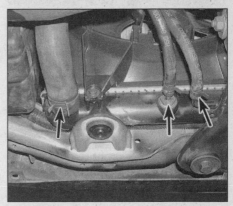

4.5b To disconnect the lower radiator hose from the radiator, loosen this hose clamp (left arrow) and pull off the hose; to disconnect the fluid cooler lines (vehicles with an automatic transaxle) from the radiator, loosen these hose clamps (right arrows) and pull off the hoses

soft-face hammer to jar it loose. Be prepared for some coolant to spill as the gasket seal is broken.

11   Note how the thermostat is installed (which end is facing out) and then remove it.

12   Stuff a rag into the thermostat housing, and then remove all traces of old gasket material and sealant from the housing and cover with a gasket scraper. Remove the rag from the thermostat housing and then clean the gasket mating surfaces with lacquer thinner or acetone.

13   Install the new thermostat in the housing. Make sure that the correct end faces out - the spring end is normally directed into the engine - and that the bleed hole is at the top (see illustration).

14   Apply a thin, uniform layer of RTV sealant to both sides of the new gasket and position it on the housing.

15   Install the cover and bolts. Tighten the bolts to the torque listed in this chapter's specifications.

16   Reattach the hose to the fitting and tighten the hose clamp securely.

17   Refill the cooling system (Chapter 1).

18   Start the engine and allow it to reach normal operating temperature, then check for leaks and proper thermostat operation (as described in Steps 2 through 4).

4   Radiator - removal and installation

Warning: *Wait until the engine is completely cool before beginning this procedure.*

Removal

Caution: *Some models are equipped with an anti-theft radio. Before performing a procedure that requires disconnecting the battery, make sure you have the activation code.*
Refer to illustrations 4.2, 4.3, 4.4a, 4.4b, 4.5a, 4.5b, 4.8 and 4.9

1   Disconnect the cable from the negative terminal of the battery.

2   Drain the cooling system (see Chapter 1). The drain cock valve (see illustration) is located at the lower right rear corner of the radiator. If the coolant is relatively new or in good condition, save it and reuse it.

3   Remove the air duct (see illustration).

4   Disconnect the electrical connector from the radiator cooling fan (see illustration). On vehicles with air conditioning, disconnect the condenser cooling fan connector (see illustration).

5   Loosen the hose clamps and then detach the upper and lower hoses (see illustrations) from the radiator. If they're stuck, grasp each hose near the end with adjustable pliers, twist it to break the seal, and then pull it off. Be careful not to distort the radiator fit-

4.8 To detach the radiator from the crossmember, remove these mounting bolts (arrows)

4.9 Carefully remove the radiator and cooling fan(s) as a single assembly

tings! If the hoses are old or deteriorated, cut them off and install new ones. Disconnect the reservoir hose from the radiator filler neck **(see illustration 4.4b)**.

6   If the vehicle is equipped with an automatic transaxle, place a drain pan under the fittings and disconnect the fluid cooler lines from the bottom of the radiator **(see illustration 4.5b)**.

7   Plug all open lines and fittings.

8   Remove the radiator mounting bolts and brackets **(see illustration)**.

9   Carefully lift out the radiator and cooling fan(s) as a single assembly **(see illustration)**. Don't spill coolant on the vehicle or scratch the paint.

10   Separate the cooling fan(s) from the radiator (see Section 5).

11   Inspect the radiator for leaks and damage. If it needs repair, have a radiator shop or dealer service department perform the work as special techniques are required.

12   Remove bugs and dirt from the radiator with compressed air and a soft brush. Don't bend the cooling fins as this is done.

Installation

13   Installation is the reverse of the removal procedure.

14   After installation, fill the cooling system with the proper mixture of antifreeze and water. Refer to Chapter 1 if necessary.

15   Start the engine and check for leaks. Allow the engine to reach normal operating temperature, indicated by the upper radiator hose becoming hot. Recheck the coolant level and add more if required.

16   If you're working on an automatic transaxle equipped vehicle, check the transaxle fluid level and add fluid as needed.

---

5   Cooling fans - check and replacement

Check

1   The circuit for the radiator cooling motor is controlled by the radiator fan relay, which in turn is controlled by the PCM. The PCM monitors engine temperature through the Engine Coolant Temperature (ECT) sensor. When the ECT sensor indicates that the engine is overheating, the PCM energizes the radiator fan relay, which turns on the circuit for the radiator fan motor.

2   The circuit for the condenser cooling fan motor is controlled by the condenser fan

relay, which is connected to the circuit for the A/C control relay. When the air conditioning system is turned on, the A/C control relay turns on the circuit that engages the compressor clutch, which activates the air conditioning system. When the A/C control relay is turned on, it also turns on the condenser fan relay, which turns on the circuit for the condenser fan motor.

3   First, check the fuses (see Chapter 12). If the fuses are okay, check the relays. All three relays - radiator fan relay, condenser fan relay and A/C control relay) are located inside the engine compartment fuse/relay box (see Chapter 12).

4   To test either fan motor, unplug the motor connector **(see illustration 4.4a)** and use fused jumper wires to connect the fan directly to the battery. If the fan does not operate, replace the motor.

5   If the fuse, relay and motor are okay, but the fan doesn't come on when the engine is hot, the problem is in the cooling fan motor circuit, or in the PCM itself. To troubleshoot the fan motor circuit, refer to the Wiring Diagrams at the end of Chapter 12.

6   If the fuse, relay, motor and fan motor circuit are good, have the PCM checked by a dealer service department.

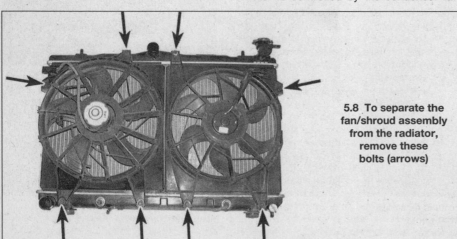

5.8 To separate the fan/shroud assembly from the radiator, remove these bolts (arrows)

5.9 Remove the clip (arrow) with a small screwdriver and then detach the fan blade assembly from the motor shaft

5.10 To detach the fan motor from the shroud, remove these screws (arrows)

Replacement

Refer to illustrations 5.8, 5.9 and 5.10

7   Remove the radiator and cooling fans as a single assembly (see Section 4).

8   Remove the bolts and separate the fan/shroud assembly from the radiator **(see illustration)**.

9   Remove the clip and detach the fan blade assembly from the motor shaft **(see illustration)**.

10   Remove the screws and detach the fan motor from the shroud **(see illustration)**.

11   Installation is the reverse of removal.

6   Coolant temperature sending unit - check and replacement

Refer to illustration 6.1

Warning: *The engine must be completely cool before removing the sending unit.*

1   The coolant temperature sending unit **(see illustration)** is threaded into the thermostat housing at the front left corner of the cylinder head. **Note:** *Don't confuse the coolant temperature sending unit with the Engine Coolant Temperature (ECT) sensor, which is also located on the thermostat housing. The coolant temperature sending unit is located in front of (ahead of) the ECT sensor. Also, the coolant temperature sending unit electrical connection is a single spade-type terminal; the ECT sensor has a two-terminal electrical connector.*

Check

2   If the coolant temperature gauge is inoperative, check the fuses first (Chapter 12). If the temperature gauge indicates a high operating temperature after the engine has warmed up, see the Troubleshooting Section in the front of the manual.

3   If the temperature gauge indicates HOT shortly after the engine is started cold, disconnect the wire at the coolant temperature sending unit. If the gauge reading drops, replace the sending unit. If the reading remains high, the wire to the gauge might be shorted to ground, or the gauge might be defective.

4   If the coolant temperature gauge fails to indicate anything after the engine has been fully warmed up (about 10 minutes), and if the fuse is okay, shut off the engine, disconnect the wire from the sending unit and, using a jumper wire, connect it to a clean ground on the engine. Turn on the ignition without starting the engine. If the gauge now indicates HOT, replace the sending unit.

5   If the gauge still doesn't indicate anything, either the circuit is open, or the gauge is defective (see Chapter 12).

6   Start the engine and warm it up. Stop the engine and turn the ignition switch to the OFF position.

7   Unplug the wire from the coolant temperature sending unit and then connect the leads of an ohmmeter between the sending unit terminal and a good ground on the engine.

8   Compare your measurement with the sending unit resistance listed in this Chapter's Specifications. If the ohmmeter indicates a different figure, then the sending unit is defective. Replace it. **Note:** *A sending unit which has been causing the temperature gauge to indicate a COLD condition regardless of how long the engine has been running, has an open circuit. A sender which has been causing the temperature gauge to indicate a HOT condition all the time has a short circuit.*

Replacement

9   With the engine completely cool, remove the cap from the radiator to release any pressure, then replace the cap. This reduces coolant loss during sending unit replacement.

10   Disconnect the wiring harness from the sending unit.

11   Prepare the new sending unit for installation by applying thread sealant or Teflon, tape to the threads.

12   Unscrew the sending unit from the engine and quickly install the new one to prevent coolant loss.

13   Tighten the sending unit securely and connect the wiring harness.

14   Refill the cooling system and run the engine. Check for leaks and proper temperature gauge operation at the instrument panel.

7   Coolant reservoir - removal and installation

Refer to illustration 7.2

1   Remove the cap from the coolant reservoir and remove the overflow hose.

2   Remove the coolant reservoir retaining bolts **(see illustration)** and lift out the coolant reservoir.

3   Installation is the reverse of removal.

3

6.1 The coolant temperature sending unit (arrow) is threaded into the thermostat housing just ahead of the coolant temperature sensor (an information sensor for the PCM - don't confuse the two)

7.2 To detach the coolant reservoir, remove these three bolts (arrows)

8.4 The water pump weep hole (arrow) is located on the underside of the pump

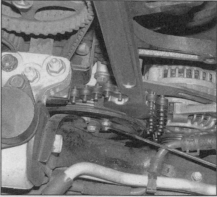

9.4 Using a chain wrench or a strap wrench, immobilize the water pump pulley, loosen and remove the pulley bolts and then remove the pulley

9.6a Note the position of the alternator bracket on the water pump and then remove the two bracket bolts (arrows) (these are also water pump bolts), remove the other upper pump bolt (arrow) . . .

9.6b . . . and then remove the three lower water pump mounting bolts (arrows)

8   Water pump - check

Refer to illustrations 8.4

1   A failure in the water pump can cause serious engine damage due to overheating.

2   There are three ways to check the operation of the water pump while it's installed on the engine. If the pump is defective, it should be replaced with a new or rebuilt unit.

3   With the engine running at normal operating temperature, squeeze the upper radiator hose. If the water pump is working correctly, a pressure surge should be felt as the hose is released. **Warning:** *Keep your hands away from the fan blades!*

4   The water pump is equipped with a weep or vent hole **(see illustration)**. If a failure occurs in the pump seal, coolant will leak from the hole. In most cases you'll need a flashlight to find the hole on the water pump from underneath to check for leaks.

5   If the water pump shaft bearings fail, they often emit a howling sound at the front of the engine while it's running. (Don't confuse the sound of pump bearing failure with the squealing sound of drivebelt slippage.) Try to rock the water pump pulley up and down. If you can move it up and down, the shaft and/or the bearings are excessively worn.

9   Water pump - removal and installation

Refer to illustrations 9.4, 9.6a, 9.6b, 9.7a, 9.7b and 9.12

Warning: *Wait until the engine is completely cool before beginning this procedure.*

Caution: *Some models are equipped with an anti-theft radio. Before performing a procedure that requires disconnecting the battery, make sure you have the activation code.*

1   Disconnect the cable from the negative terminal of the battery.

2   Drain the cooling system (see Chapter 1). If the coolant is relatively new or in good condition, save it and reuse it.

3   Remove the accessory drivebelt (see Chapter 1).

4   Loosen the water pump pulley bolts **(see illustration)**. Remove the water pump pulley bolts and then remove the pulley.

5   Remove the alternator (see Chapter 5).

6   Note the position of the alternator bracket on the water pump; it must be installed in the same position when installing the water pump. Remove the alternator bracket bolts (they're also water pump bolts) and then remove the other four bolts from the water pump **(see illustrations)**.

7   Loosen the hose clamp and then disconnect the water pump coolant inlet pipe connection hose. Detach the coolant inlet pipe from the block **(see illustration)** and then disconnect the coolant inlet pipe from the water pump mounting boss **(see illustration)**. Remove and discard the old O-ring. (This step is not necessary to remove the water pump, but it's a good idea to remove the inlet pipe, inspect its condition and replace the O-ring anytime you replace the pump.)

8   Clean the bolt threads and the threaded holes in the engine to remove corrosion and sealant.

9   Compare the new pump to the old one to make sure they're identical.

10   Remove all traces of old gasket material from the engine with a gasket scraper.

11   Clean the engine and water pump mating surfaces with lacquer thinner or acetone.

12   Affix the new gasket to the gasket mating surface of the pump with Gasgacinch, **(see illustration)**, or a similar gasket adhesive.

13   Carefully attach the pump and gasket to

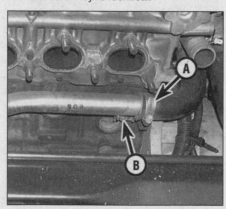

9.7a Loosen the hose clamp (A), pull off the coolant hose, remove the coolant inlet pipe bracket bolt (B), detach the coolant inlet pipe from the block . . .

9.7b . . . pull the coolant inlet pipe to the rear to detach it from the water pump mounting boss and then remove and discard the old O-ring (arrow)

the engine and thread the bolts into the holes finger tight.

14   Reposition the alternator bracket and then install the rest of the water pump mounting bolts. Tighten the water pump mounting bolts to the torque listed in this chapter's specifications in 1/4-turn increments. Overtightening them might distort the pump.

15   Install a new O-ring in the groove at the front end of the coolant inlet pipe and lubricate the O-ring with coolant. Insert the coolant inlet pipe into the water pump mounting boss and then secure it to the block with the retaining bolt. Tighten the bolt securely. Reconnect the connection hose to the coolant inlet pipe. Tighten the hose clamp securely.

16   Install the alternator (see Chapter 5).

17   Install the water pump pulley and tighten the bolts securely.

18   Install the accessory drivebelt (see Chapter 1).

19   Tighten the water pump pulley bolts to the torque listed in this Chapter's Specifications.

20   Refill the cooling system and check the drivebelt tension (Chapter 1).

21   Reconnect the negative battery cable.

22   Start the engine and check for leaks.

10   Heater blower motor - circuit check and component replacement

Check

1   If the blower motor does not operate at any speed, disconnect the electrical connector to the blower motor (see "Component replacement" below) and connect a test light between the two terminals of the harness side of the blower motor connector. Turn the ignition switch to ON and put the blower switch in the HIGH position. The test light should glow brightly, indicating that the blower motor power and ground circuits are okay. Plug in the electrical connector to the blower motor. If the blower motor does not operate when connected, replace the blower motor.

2   If the test light did not come on in Step 1, refer to the wiring diagrams at the end of Chapter 12 and determine which terminals in the blower motor harness connector are the

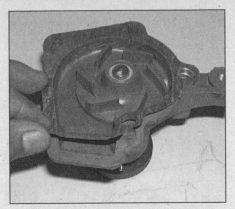

9.12 Place the gasket in position on the water pump (use a little gasket adhesive to ensure that the gasket doesn't fall off or get pinched or kinked when you install the pump)

power terminal (connected to the fuse box) and the ground terminal (grounded through the blower resistor and/or switch). Connect the test light to a good chassis ground, turn the ignition switch On, place the blower switch in the High position and probe the power terminal. If the test light still doesn't come on, check the fuse and the blower relay (both are located inside the engine compartment fuse box) and inspect the blower motor wiring (see the wiring diagrams at the end of Chapter 12). If the test light did come on in Step 1, power is available to the blower motor; use an ohmmeter or self-powered continuity tester to check for continuity to ground at the ground terminal. If the ground circuit is open, check the circuit for continuity from the blower motor, through the blower switch to the chassis ground point.

Blower motor resistor (1996 through 2000 models)
Refer to illustration 10.3

3   If the blower motor operates at one or more speeds, but not at all speeds, disconnect the electrical connector from the blower resistor and measure the continuity between the indicated resistor terminals **(see illustration)**.

a) Between terminals 1 and 3 - 0.4 ohms
b) Between terminals 2 and 3 - 1 ohm
c) Between terminals 3 and 4 - 2.565 to 2.835 ohms

If the resistance is incorrect between any of the indicated terminals, replace the blower motor resistor. If the resistor is okay, but the fan motor is not functioning correctly, remove the air conditioning and heater control assembly from the dash (see Section 17) and check for continuity between the appropriate blower switch terminals while placing the switch in each speed position (see wiring diagrams at the end of Chapter 12). Check for continuity in each individual wire from the blower resistor to the blower switch. Also check for continuity to chassis ground at the blower switch harness connector ground wire (usually a black wire). Trace the ground wire to the ground point on the chassis and repair the ground, if necessary.

Blower relay, high relay and power transistor (2001 models)
Refer to illustrations 10.4a and 10.4b

4   If the blower motor operates at one or more speeds, but not at all speeds, disconnect the electrical connectors from the blower relay, and from the high relay, and then measure the continuity between the indicated terminals **(see illustration)**:

Blower relay resistance

a) With the air conditioning system turned to ON, there should be continuity between terminals 1 and 2.
b) With battery voltage applied to terminals 1 and 2, there should be continuity between terminals 3 and 4.

High relay resistance

a) With the air conditioning system turned to ON, there should be continuity between terminals 1 and 4.
b) With battery voltage applied to terminals 1 and 4, there should be continuity between terminals 2 and 3.

If the resistance of either of the relays is incorrect, replace that relay.

Power transistor voltage

If both of the relays are okay, check the power transistor. Using a couple of T-pins, backprobe terminals 1 and 2 of the power transistor electrical connector **(see illustration)**, and then hook up a voltmeter to the backprobe pins. Start the engine, turn on the heater blower motor and check the voltage at each switch position.

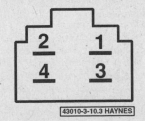

10.3 Blower motor resistor electrical connector terminal guide (1996 through 2000 models)

10.4a Blower relay and high relay electrical connector terminal guide (2001 models)

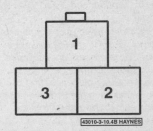

10.4b Power transistor electrical connector terminal guide (2001 models)

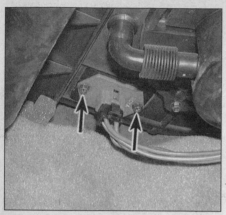

10.5 To detach the blower resistor from the underside of the lower blower case, simply unplug the electrical connector and then remove the two retaining screws (arrows) (1996 through 2000 model shown, later similar)

Fan speed	Voltage
First speed	3.8 volts
Second speed	5.3 volts
Third speed	6.7 volts
Fourth speed	8.1 volts
Fifth speed	9.5 volts
Sixth speed	10.6 volts
Seventh speed	13.5 volts

If all three components are okay, but the fan motor is not functioning correctly, remove the air conditioning and heater control assembly from the dash (see Section 17) and check for continuity between the appropriate blower switch terminals while putting the switch in each speed position (see wiring diagrams at the end of Chapter 12). Check for continuity in each individual wire from the blower switch to the blower relays and the power transistor. Also check for continuity to chassis ground at the blower switch harness connector ground wire (usually a black wire). Trace the ground wire to the ground point on the chassis and repair the ground, if necessary.

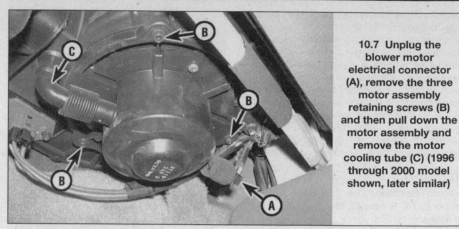

10.7 Unplug the blower motor electrical connector (A), remove the three motor assembly retaining screws (B) and then pull down the motor assembly and remove the motor cooling tube (C) (1996 through 2000 model shown, later similar)

Component replacement
1996 through 2000 models
Blower motor resistor
Refer to illustration 10.5
5   The blower resistor (see illustration) is located on the underside of the lower blower case. To replace it, simply unplug the electrical connector and then remove the two retaining screws. Installation is the reverse of removal.

Heater blower motor
Refer to illustrations 10.7, 10.10 and 10.11
6   Unplug the blower resistor electrical connector (see illustration 10.5).
7   Unplug the blower motor electrical connector (see illustration).
8   Remove the three motor assembly retaining screws (see illustration 10.7) and then remove the motor assembly.
9   After pulling down the motor assembly, detach and remove the motor cooling tube (see illustration 10.7), which directs air from the blower wheel to the motor.
10   Remove the two motor cover retaining screws (see illustration) and then remove the cover from the motor assembly.
11   Remove the fan retaining clip (see illustration) and detach the fan from the motor shaft.
12   Installation is the reverse of removal.

2001 models
Blower relay
13   The blower relay is located on the underside of the blower lower case. To replace it, simply unplug the electrical connector and then remove the relay bracket screw. Installation is the reverse of removal.

High relay
14   The high relay is located on the underside of the blower lower case. To replace it, simply unplug the electrical connector and then remove the relay bracket screw. Installation is the reverse of removal.

Power transistor
15   The power transistor is located on the underside of the lower blower case. To replace it, simply unplug the electrical connector and then remove the two retaining screws. Installation is the reverse of removal.

Heater blower motor
16   The blower motor replacement procedure for 2001 models is similar to the earlier procedure for 1996 through 2000 models. Refer to Steps 6 through 12 above.

11   Heater core - removal and installation

Warning 1: *These models are equipped with a Supplemental Restraint System (SRS), more commonly known as airbags. Disable the airbag system before working in the vicinity of airbag system components to avoid the possibility of accidental deployment of the airbag, which could result in personal injury (see Chapter 12).*
Warning 2: *The air conditioning system is under high pressure. Do not loosen any hose fittings or remove any components until after the system has been discharged. Air conditioning refrigerant must be correctly discharged into an EPA-approved recovery/recycling unit at a dealer service department or an automotive air conditioning repair facility. Always wear eye protection when disconnecting air conditioning system fittings.*
Warning 3: *Wait until the engine is completely cool before beginning this procedure.*

10.10 To separate the motor cover from the motor assembly, remove these two screws (arrows) (1996 through 2000 model shown, later similar)

10.11 To separate the fan from the motor shaft, remove this retaining clip (arrow) (1996 through 2000 model shown, later similar)

Caution: *Some models are equipped with an anti-theft radio. Before performing a procedure that requires disconnecting the battery, make sure you have the activation code.*

Note: *The removal and repair of the heater and related components is an involved procedure. Read the following Section thoroughly before beginning this procedure. Allow plenty of time to complete the operation. During disassembly, make notes on the routing of all wiring and cables, and the locations of all components, to ensure correct reassembly.*

Removal

Refer to illustrations 11.4, 11.7, 11.9, 11.11, 11.13, 11.14, 11.15a, 11.15b, 11.17, 11.18a, 11.18b and 11.19

1   If the vehicle is equipped with air conditioning, have the refrigerant discharged and recovered by a dealer service department or an automotive air conditioning shop.
2   Disconnect the cable from the negative terminal of the battery.
3   Set the heater control to 'HOT' and then drain the cooling system (see Chapter 1).
4   Working on the engine compartment side of the firewall, mark the heater hoses to ensure correct installation, loosen the hose clamps and then disconnect the heater hoses from the heater core tubes **(see illustration)**. Plug the hoses to prevent dirt from entering the cooling system. You'll also see a vacuum line connected to a vacuum pipe at the firewall, right below the larger of the two heater hoses. Disconnect this line and plug it to prevent dirt and moisture from entering the line.
5   If the vehicle is equipped with air conditioning, disconnect the refrigerant lines from the evaporator connection tubes (see Section 16). Plug these lines to prevent dirt and moisture from entering the air conditioning system.
6   Remove the air conditioning and heater

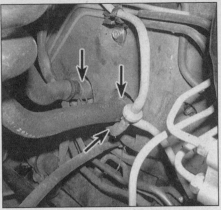

11.4 To detach the heater hoses (upper arrows) from the heater core tubes, loosen the hose clamps and then pull off the hoses; also disconnect the vacuum line (lower arrow)

control assembly (see Section 17) and the radio (see Chapter 12). Remove the instrument panel assembly (see Chapter 11).
7   Disconnect the vacuum line from the door motor in front of the blower assembly **(see illustration)**. Note the routing of this line between the door motor and the heater unit. When reassembling the under-dash heater and air conditioning components, it must be routed exactly the same way.
8   If the vehicle is equipped with air conditioning, remove the evaporator assembly (see Section 16).
9   If the vehicle is equipped with cruise control, Electronic Time and Alarm Control (ETAC) and/or keyless entry systems, unplug the electrical connectors from the cruise control module, the ETAC module and/or the keyless entry module **(see illustration)**.
10   Remove the bolts that attach the cruise

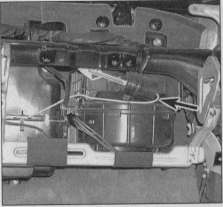

11.7 Note the routing of the vacuum line between the heater unit and the door motor and then disconnect it from the door motor (arrow); when reassembling the under-dash heater and air conditioning components, the vacuum line must be routed just like this

control and the ETAC/keyless entry module brackets to the left vertical member of the center fascia panel support bracket **(see illustration 11.9)**.
11   Remove the screws that attach the air conditioning and heater control assembly bracket to the left vertical member of the center fascia panel support bracket **(see illustration)**.
12   Remove the bolts that attach the right vertical member of the center fascia panel support bracket to the vehicle **(see illustration 11.9)** and then remove the right vertical member and the three horizontal support brackets as a single assembly.
13   Peel back the carpeting on the right side and then remove the bolts that attach the crossbar support bar to the vehicle **(see**

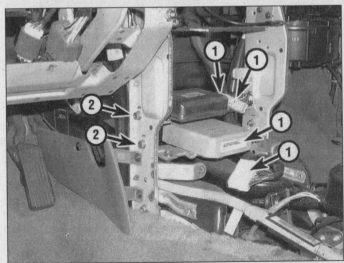

11.9 Unplug the electrical connector(s) from any electronic modules (1), then unbolt them (2) from each side of the brackets and carefully remove them

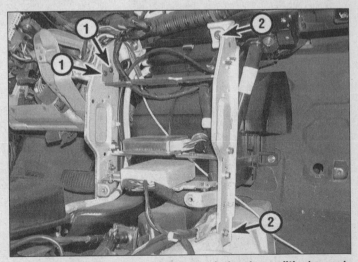

11.11 Remove the screws (1) that attach the air conditioning and heater control assembly bracket to the left vertical member of the center fascia panel support bracket, remove the bolts (2) that attach the right vertical member of the center fascia panel support bracket to the vehicle and then remove the right vertical member and the three horizontal support brackets as a single assembly

3

11.13 Peel back the carpeting on the right side, remove the bolts (arrows) that attach the crossbar support bar to the vehicle and then remove the support bar

11.14 Detach the rear floor vent duct (A) from the rear floor vent (B) and from the heater assembly (C) and then pull the duct to the rear and remove it; then peel back the carpeting on the left side and remove the right rear floor vent duct (it's not necessary to remove the surrounding foam - just pull out the ducts through the foam)

illustration) and then remove the support bar.

14   Peel back the carpeting on the left side. Detach the rear floor vent ducts **(see illustration)** from the rear floor vents and from the heater assembly and then pull each duct to the rear and remove it. (Just pull out the ducts through the surrounding foam - it's not necessary to remove the foam.)

15   Remove the mounting nut and bolt **(see illustration)** from the right side of the heater unit and remove the mounting nut from the upper left side **(see illustration)**.

16   Remove the heater assembly from the vehicle.

17   Disconnect the plastic vacuum hose from the metal vacuum line on the left side of the heater case **(see illustration)**.

18   Disengage the heater core cover retaining clips from the heater case and then remove the heater core cover **(see illustrations)**.

19   Pull the heater core out of the case **(see illustration)**.

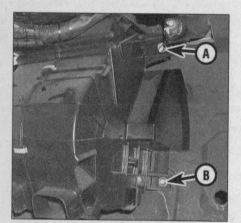

11.15a To detach the heater assembly from the vehicle, remove the mounting nut (A) and bolt (B) from the right side of the heater case . . .

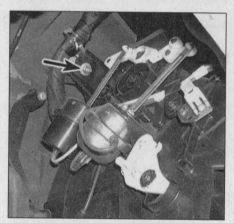

11.15b . . . remove the mounting nut (arrow) from the upper left side and then remove the heater assembly from the vehicle.

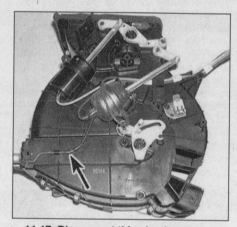

11.17 Disconnect this plastic vacuum hose (arrow) from the metal vacuum line on the left side of the heater case

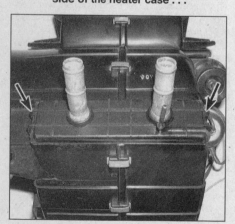

11.18a Disengage the heater core cover retaining clips (arrows) . . .

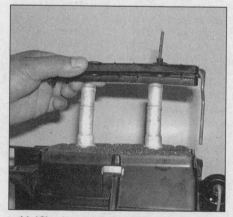

11.18b . . . and then remove the heater core cover

11.19 Pull the heater core out of the case

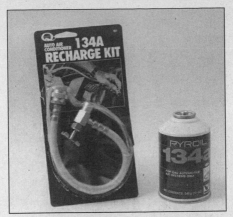

12.11 R-134a refrigerant and recharge kits are available from auto parts stores; follow the instructions that come with the kit

Installation

20   Installation is the reverse of removal. As you reassemble the heater unit:

a) *Make sure that the air control doors operate correctly. If any of the doors bind, correct the problem before installing the heater unit into the vehicle.*

b) *Make sure that all wiring, cables and vacuum lines are routed as noted during disassembly.*

c) *Make sure that the air ducting is securely reconnected.*

21   Fill the cooling system with the correct type and amount of coolant (see Chapter 1). On models equipped with air conditioning, have the system evacuated and recharged.

12   Air conditioning system - check and maintenance

Warning: *The air conditioning system is under high pressure. Do not loosen any hose fittings or remove any components until after the system has been discharged. Air conditioning refrigerant must be correctly discharged into an EPA-approved recovery/recycling unit at a dealer service department or an automotive air conditioning repair facility. Always wear eye protection when disconnecting air conditioning system fittings.*

Caution: *Two different types of air conditioning refrigerant are used on the models covered by this manual. 1993 and earlier models use R-12 refrigerant, while 1994 and later models use the non-ozone-depleting R-134a refrigerant. The R-134a refrigerant and its lubricating oil are not compatible with the R-12 system and under no circumstances should the two different types of refrigerant or lubricating oil be intermixed. The system charging fittings are different so that accidental connection of the unlike system charging hoses cannot be made.*

Note: *Because of Federal regulations proposed by the Environmental Protection Agency, R-12 refrigerant is no longer avail-*

able to the home mechanic. Models with R-12 systems should be serviced at a by a dealership or other correctly equipped repair facility.

1   The following maintenance checks should be performed on a regular basis to ensure that the air conditioner continues to operate at peak efficiency.

a) *Check the compressor drivebelt. If it's worn or deteriorated, replace it (see Chapter 1).*

b) *Check the drivebelt tension and, if necessary, adjust it (see Chapter 1).*

c) *Check the system hoses. Look for cracks, bubbles, hard spots and deterioration. Inspect the hoses and all fittings for oil bubbles and seepage. If there's any evidence of wear, damage or leaks, replace the hose(s).*

d) *Inspect the condenser fins for leaves, bugs and other debris. Use a "fin comb" or compressed air to clean the condenser.*

e) *Make sure the system has the correct refrigerant charge.*

2   It's a good idea to operate the system for about 10 minutes at least once a month, particularly during the winter. Long term non-use can cause hardening, and subsequent failure, of the seals.

3   Because of the complexity of the air conditioning system and the special equipment necessary to service it, in-depth troubleshooting and repairs are not included in this manual. However, simple checks and component replacement procedures are provided in this Chapter.

4   The most common cause of poor cooling is simply a low system refrigerant charge. If a noticeable drop in cool air output occurs, one of the following quick checks will help you determine if the refrigerant level is low.

5   Warm the engine up to normal operating temperature.

6   Place the air conditioning temperature selector at the coldest setting and put the blower at the highest setting. Open the doors (to make sure the air conditioning system doesn't cycle off as soon as it cools the passenger compartment).

7   After the system reaches operating temperature, feel the two pipes connected to the evaporator at the firewall. The pipe (thinner tubing) leading from the condenser outlet to the evaporator should be warm, and the evaporator outlet line (the thicker tubing that leads back to the compressor) should be cold. If the two pipes are the same temperature (or close to the same temperature), the system charge is low.

8   If the system is equipped with a sight glass (on top of the receiver-drier), check for the presence of air bubbles in the refrigerant. If the refrigerant passing through the sight glass looks foamy, the system charge is low.

9   Further inspection or testing of the system is beyond the scope of the home mechanic and should be left to a professional.

Adding refrigerant

Refer to illustration 12.11

Caution: *Make sure any refrigerant, refrigerant oil or replacement component your purchase is designated as compatible with environmentally-friendly R-134a systems.*

10   1993 and earlier models use R-12 refrigerant. Because of federal restrictions on the sale of R-12 refrigerant, it isn't practical for refrigerant to be added by the home mechanic. When the system needs recharging, take the vehicle to a dealer service department or professional air conditioning shop for evacuation, leak testing and recharging. On 1994 and later models using R-134a refrigerant, make sure any refrigerant, oil or replacement component is designated for R-134a systems.

11   Buy an R-134a automotive charging kit at an auto parts store **(see illustration)**. A charging kit includes a 12-ounce can of refrigerant, a tap valve and a short section of hose that can be attached between the tap valve and the system low side service valve. Because one can of refrigerant may not be sufficient to bring the system charge up to the proper level, it's a good idea to buy an additional can. **Warning:** *Never add more than two cans of refrigerant to the system.*

12   Hook up the charging kit by following the manufacturer's instructions. **Warning:** *DO NOT hook the charging kit hose to the system high side! The fittings on the charging kit are designed to fit **only** on the low side of the system.*

13   Back off the valve handle on the charging kit and screw the kit onto the refrigerant can, making sure first that the O-ring or rubber seal inside the threaded portion of the kit is in place. **Warning:** *Wear protective eyewear when dealing with pressurized refrigerant cans.*

14   Remove the dust cap from the low-side charging valve and then attach the quick-connect fitting on the kit hose.

15   Warm up the engine and turn on the air conditioning. Keep the charging kit hose away from the fan and other moving parts. **Note:** *The charging process requires the compressor to be running. If the clutch cycles off, you can put the air conditioning switch on High and leave the car doors open to keep the clutch on and compressor working.*

16   Turn the valve handle on the kit until the stem pierces the can, then back the handle out to release the refrigerant. You should be able to hear the rush of gas. Add refrigerant to the low side of the system, keeping the can upright at all times, but shaking it occasionally. Allow stabilization time between each addition. **Note:** *The charging process will go faster if you wrap the can with a hot-water-soaked shop rag to keep the can from freezing up.*

17   If you have an accurate thermometer, you can place it in the center air conditioning duct inside the vehicle and keep track of the output air temperature. A charged system that is working correctly should cool down to

3

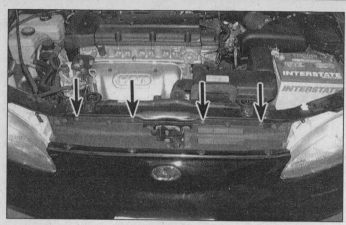

13.2 To detach the upper radiator grille, remove these four screws (arrows)

13.3 Unplug the electrical connector (arrow) from the dual-pressure switch

approximately 40-degrees F. If the ambient (outside) air temperature is very high, say 110 degrees F, the duct air temperature may be as high as 60 degrees F, but generally the air conditioning is 30-40 degrees F cooler than the ambient air.

18   When the can is empty, turn the valve handle to the closed position and release the connection from the low-side port. Replace the dust cap.

19   Remove the charging kit from the can and store the kit for future use with the piercing valve in the UP position, to prevent inadvertently piercing the can on the next use.

13   Air conditioning receiver-drier - removal and installation

Warning: *The air conditioning system is under high pressure. Do not loosen any hose fittings or remove any components until after the system has been discharged. Air conditioning refrigerant must be correctly discharged into an EPA-approved recovery/recycling unit at a dealer service department or an automotive air conditioning repair facility. Always wear eye protection when disconnecting air conditioning system fittings.*

Removal

Refer to illustrations 13.2, 13.3, 13.4a and 13.4b

1   Before you can remove the receiver-drier, which is a reservoir and a filter/dehumidifier for the refrigerant, you must have the system discharged and recovered by a dealer service department or an automotive air conditioning shop.

2   The receiver-drier is located at the right (passenger side) of the condenser. To access it, remove the upper radiator grille **(see illustration)**.

3   Unplug the electrical connector from the dual-pressure switch **(see illustration)**.

4   Disconnect the two refrigerant lines from the receiver-drier and then disconnect

13.4a To disconnect the two refrigerant lines from the receiver-drier, remove these nuts (upper arrows); to disconnect the line in the foreground from the condenser, remove the bolt (lower arrow); to remove the receiver-drier assembly, remove this bolt (center arrow) from the mounting bracket

the refrigerant lines from the condenser and from the fitting at the right end of the condenser **(see illustrations)**. Remove both lines and then immediately cap the open fittings to keep out dirt and moisture.

5   Remove the bolt from the receiver-drier mounting bracket **(see illustration 13.4a)** and then lift it out of the engine compartment.

Installation

6   Install new O-rings (if equipped) on the refrigerant line fittings and lubricate them with clean refrigerant oil.

7   Installation is the reverse of removal.

8   If a new receiver-drier is installed, add the correct amount and type of refrigerant oil to the system (see this Chapter's Specifications).

9   Have the system evacuated, recharged and leak tested.

13.4b To disconnect the other line from the condenser, remove this nut (arrow)

14   Air conditioning compressor - removal and installation

Warning: *The air conditioning system is under high pressure. Do not loosen any hose fittings or remove any components until after the system has been discharged. Air conditioning refrigerant must be correctly discharged into an EPA-approved recovery/recycling unit at a dealer service department or an automotive air conditioning repair facility. Always wear eye protection when disconnecting air conditioning system fittings.*

Removal

Caution: *Some models are equipped with an anti-theft radio. Before performing a procedure that requires disconnecting the battery, make sure you have the activation code.*

Refer to illustrations 14.4 and 14.5

1   Have the system discharged and recovered by a dealer service department or by an automotive air conditioning shop.

2   Disconnect the cable from the negative terminal of the battery.

3   Set the parking brake and block the rear tires. Raise the front of the vehicle and support it securely on jackstands.

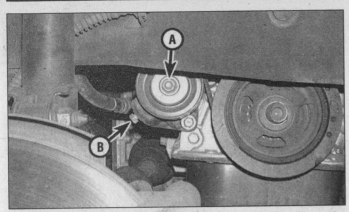

14.4 From underneath the vehicle, remove the tension from the drivebelt by loosening the locknut (A) and then backing off the tensioner bolt (B)

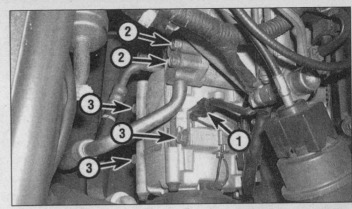

14.5 Disconnect the compressor clutch electrical connector (1), remove the bolts (2) that connect the suction and discharge lines and then remove the three compressor mounting bolts (3)

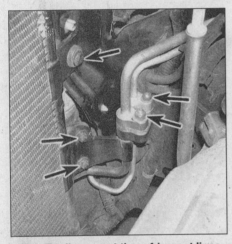

15.6 To disconnect the refrigerant lines from the junction at the condenser, remove these nuts (right arrows); to detach the right side of the condenser from the vehicle, remove the right mounting bolt (upper arrow) and the two liquid line junction bracket nuts (center and lower arrows)

4   From underneath the vehicle, loosen the locknut on the tensioner **(see illustration)** and then turn the tensioner counterclockwise to loosen the belt tension. Remove the compressor drivebelt (see Chapter 1, if necessary).

5   Disconnect the electrical connector from the compressor clutch **(see illustration)**.

6   Detach the refrigerant lines from the compressor **(see illustration 14.5)** and immediately cap the open fittings to prevent the entry of dirt and moisture.

7   Remove the compressor mounting bolts **(see illustration 14.5)** and then remove the compressor from the engine compartment. Note the location and thickness of any shims or spacers and reinstall them in the same location. **Note:** *Keep the compressor level during handling and storage. If the compressor has seized, or if you find metal particles in the refrigerant oil, the system must be flushed out by an air conditioning specialist and the receiver-drier must be replaced.*

Installation

8   If you are installing a new compressor, refer to the compressor manufacturer's instructions for adding refrigerant oil to the system.

9   Prior to installation, turn the center of the clutch six times to disperse any oil that has collected in the head.

10   Install the compressor in the reverse order of removal. Install new fitting O-rings.

11   Have the system evacuated, recharged and leak tested.

---

15   Air conditioning condenser - removal and installation

Warning: *The air conditioning system is under high pressure. Do not loosen any hose fittings or remove any components until after the system has been discharged. Air conditioning refrigerant must be correctly discharged into an EPA-approved recovery/recycling unit at a dealer service department or an automotive air conditioning repair facility. Always wear eye protection when disconnecting air conditioning system fittings.*

Removal

Refer to illustrations 15.6 and 15.7

1   Have the system discharged and recovered by a dealer service department or by an automotive air conditioning shop.

2   Remove the air intake duct assembly (see Chapter 4).

3   Remove the radiator upper mounting bolts and brackets (see Section 4).

4   Remove the upper grille **(see illustration 13.2)**.

5   Remove the receiver-drier, both liquid lines and the receiver-drier mounting bracket (see Section 13).

6   Disconnect the refrigerant lines from the junction block at the condenser **(see illustration)**. Besides the two liquid line nuts shown in the accompanying illustration, there's a third nut on the underside of the junction that must be removed **(see illustration 13.4b)**. Immediately cap the open fittings to prevent

the entry of dirt and moisture.

7   Remove the left condenser mounting bolt **(see illustration)**, remove the right mounting bolt and the two liquid line bracket nuts **(see illustration 15.6)** and then lift the condenser out of the vehicle. Store the condenser upright to prevent oil loss.

Installation

Refer to illustration 15.8

8   If you're going to reuse the old con-

15.7 To detach the left side of the condenser from the vehicle, remove this mounting bolt (arrow)

15.8 Straighten and clean bent condenser fins with a fin comb (available at most auto parts stores)

3

denser, straighten any bent condenser fins with a fin comb **(see illustration)** and then blow out the debris with compressed air. **Caution:** *Use a face shield and goggles when using compressed air to clean the condenser.*

9   Installation is the reverse of removal.
10   If a new condenser was installed, add the correct amount and type of refrigerant oil to the system (see this Chapter's Specifications).
11   Have the system evacuated, recharged, and leak tested.

16   Air conditioning evaporator - removal and installation

Warning: *The air conditioning system is under high pressure. Do not loosen any hose fittings or remove any components until the system has been discharged. Air conditioning refrigerant should be correctly discharged into an approved recovery/recycling unit by a dealer or an automotive air conditioning repair facility. Always wear eye protection when disconnecting air conditioning system fittings.*

Removal

Caution: *Some models are equipped with an anti-theft radio. Before performing a proce-* dure that requires disconnecting the battery, make sure you have the activation code.
Refer to illustrations 16.3, 16.5, 16.6, 16.7, 16.8, 16.9, 16.10a, 16.10b, 16.11 and 16.12

1   Have the system discharged and recovered by a dealer service department or by an automotive air conditioning shop.
2   Disconnect the negative battery cable.
3   Working from the engine compartment side of the firewall, disconnect the air conditioning lines from the evaporator inlet and outlet pipes **(see illustration)**. Cap the open fittings after disassembly to prevent the entry of air or dirt.
4   Inside the vehicle, remove the dash (see Chapter 11).
5   Remove the glove box support bracket **(see illustration)**.
6   Disconnect the thermostatic switch electrical connector **(see illustration)** and then disconnect the vacuum line between the door motor and the heater unit **(see illustration 11.7)**.
7   Remove the upper and lower evaporator case mounting bolts **(see illustration)**.
8   Remove the evaporator unit from the

16.3 To disconnect the air conditioning lines from the evaporator inlet and outlet pipes, remove these two nuts (arrows) (right nut not visible in this photo)

16.5 To remove the glove box support bracket, remove these bolts (arrows)

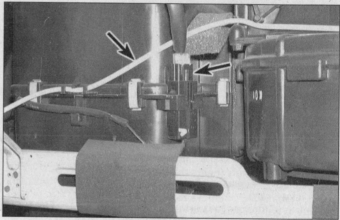

16.6 Unplug the electrical connector (right arrow) from the thermostatic switch, disconnect the vacuum line from the door motor (see illustration 11.7) and then detach the vacuum line (left arrow) from the evaporator case

16.7 To detach the evaporator case, remove these three mounting bolts (arrows)

16.8 Remove the evaporator unit from the vehicle

vehicle (see illustration).

9   Remove the sponge pad (see illustration) which insulates the evaporator inlet and outlet pipes.

10   Cut the foam that lines the openings on both sides of the evaporator case (see illustration). Unclip the upper and lower evaporator cases (see illustration) and then separate the upper case from the lower case.

11   Detach the thermostatic switch from the evaporator case and detach the thermistor mounting clip from the evaporator unit, and then remove the thermostatic switch and the thermistor as a single assembly (see illustration).

12   Remove the evaporator unit from the lower case and then remove the expansion valve assembly from the evaporator (see illustration).

13   If the evaporator core needs to be cleaned, wash it with soapy water and a soft brush or blow it off with (low-pressure) compressed air. Warning: *Be sure to wear eye protection when using compressed air.* Inspect the evaporator core and fittings for cracks or any other damage. Replace the evaporator if it's damaged in any way.

Installation

14   Evaporator installation is the reverse of removal. Replace any O-rings with ones that are specifically for the type of refrigerant in your system and lubricate them with refrigerant oil prior to installation. Warning: *Do not apply compressor oil to the fitting nuts.* Tighten the evaporator cooling unit inlet and outlet fittings securely.

15   Have the system evacuated, recharged and leak tested. If a new evaporator was installed, add the correct amount and type of refrigerant oil to the system (see this Chapter's Specifications).

16.9 Remove the sponge pad which insulates the evaporator inlet and outlet pipes

16.10a Foam insulates the two openings (to the heater case and the blower case, respectively) on the left and right sides of the evaporator case; neatly cut this foam where it crosses the split line between the case halves

16.10b There are seven clips (some of the clips not visible in this photo are in illustration 16.9) on the evaporator; pry them off with a screwdriver

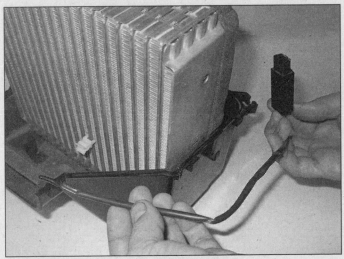

16.11 Detach the thermostatic switch from the evaporator case and detach the thermistor mounting clip from the evaporator unit, and then remove the thermostatic switch and the thermistor as a single assembly

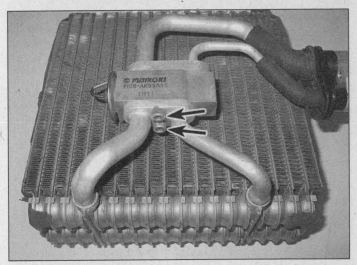

16.12 After removing the evaporator from the lower case, remove the expansion valve retaining bolts (arrows) and then separate the expansion valve assembly from the evaporator

3

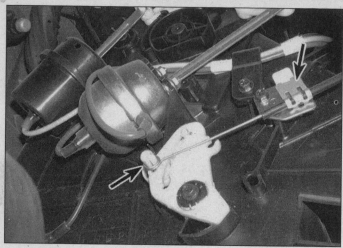

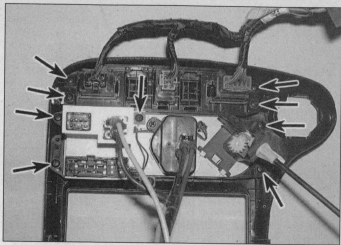

17.1 To disconnect the temperature control cable from the temperature door shaft arm, simply disengage it from this pin (lower left arrow) and then unclip (pull off) the cable retaining clip (upper right arrow) from the upper edge of the retaining clip bracket and disengage the cable from the clip and bracket

17.3 Remove the five screws (arrows) that attach the switch assembly for the hazard flasher, cruise control and rear window defogger to the center instrument panel bezel and then remove the four screws (arrows) that attach the air conditioning and heater control assembly to the bezel

17 Air conditioning and heater control assembly - removal, installation and cable adjustment

Removal and installation

Refer to illustrations 17.1 and 17.3

1   Disconnect the lower end of the temperature control cable from the heater **(see illustration)**.

2   Remove the center instrument panel bezel (see Chapter 11).

3   Remove the switch assembly for the hazard flasher, cruise control and rear window defogger switch **(see illustration)**.

4   Remove the air conditioning and-heater control assembly mounting screws **(see illustration 17.2)**.

5   Carefully remove the air conditioning and heater control assembly from the center instrument panel bezel.

6   Installation is the reverse of removal. When you're done, be sure to adjust the temperature control cable as follows.

Temperature control cable adjustment

7   Slide the temperature control lever to COLD.

8   Turn the temperature-door-shaft arm (the white plastic arm) all the way to the left (counterclockwise) and then reconnect the end of the temperature control cable to the pin on the arm **(see illustration 17.1)**.

9   Pull the cable sheath to the right (away from the temperature door-shaft arm) to take up any slack in the cable and then snap the cable clamp back into place.

Chapter 4
Fuel and exhaust systems

Contents

4

Specifications

Fuel system pressure
    1996 through 2000
        Pressure regulator vacuum line connected .... 37 psi (255 kPa)
        Pressure regulator vacuum line disconnected .... 44.37 psi (300 kPa)
    2001 and later .... 49.8 psi (350 kPa)
Fuel injector resistance (approximate) .... 16 ohms

Torque specifications

	Ft-lbs (unless otherwise indicated)	Nm
Fuel pressure line-to-fuel filter retaining bolt	18 to 25	25 to 35
Fuel pressure line-to-fuel tank retaining bolt	22 to 29	30 to 40
Fuel pressure regulator screws	36 to 52 in-lbs	4 to 6
Fuel rail bolts	84 to 132 in-lbs	10 to 15
Throttle body to air intake plenum nuts/bolts	132 to 180 in-lbs	15 to 20

1 General information

Refer to illustration 1.1

Warning: *Gasoline is extremely flammable, so take extra precautions when you work on any part of the fuel system. Don't smoke or allow open flames or bare light bulbs near the work area, and don't work in a garage where a gas-type appliance (such as a water heater or a clothes dryer) is present. Since gasoline is carcinogenic, wear latex gloves when there's a possibility of being exposed to fuel, and, if you spill any fuel on your skin, rinse it off immediately with soap and water. Mop up any spills immediately and do not store fuel-soaked rags where they could ignite. The fuel system is under constant pressure, so, if any fuel lines are to be disconnected, the fuel pressure in the system must be relieved first. When you perform any kind of work on the fuel system, wear safety glasses and have a Class B type fire extinguisher on hand.*

All models covered by this manual are equipped with a Multiport Fuel Injection (MFI) system **(see illustration)**. The MFI system uses timed impulses to sequentially inject the

1.1 Fuel injection components

1	Air cleaner assembly	4	Air intake plenum and intake manifold (one-piece)
2	Air intake duct	5	Fuel injectors
3	Throttle body		

fuel directly into the intake ports of each cylinder. The MFI system consists of an in-tank electric fuel pump, a fuel filter, a fuel pressure regulator, a fuel rail, four fuel injectors and the fuel lines connecting all these components. The injectors are controlled by the Powertrain Control Module (PCM). The PCM monitors various engine parameters and delivers the exact amount of fuel, in the correct sequence, into the intake ports. This Chapter covers the air and fuel delivery components of the system. Refer to Chapter 6 for information regarding the engine management system and emission control systems.

Access to the electric in-tank fuel pump is provided through an access hole under the rear seat cushion. The fuel level sending unit is an integral component of the fuel pump assembly and can be separated from the fuel

pump only after the pump has been removed from the fuel tank.

The exhaust system consists of an exhaust manifold, a pair of catalytic converters, an exhaust pipe and a muffler. Each of these components is replaceable. For further information regarding the catalytic converters, refer to Chapter 6.

2   Fuel pressure relief procedure

Caution: *Some models are equipped with an anti-theft radio. Before performing a procedure that requires disconnecting the battery, make sure you have the activation code.*

Refer to illustrations 2.1, 2.2 and 2.3

1   Remove the rear seat cushion **(see**

illustration)**.**
2   Remove the fuel pump access cover **(see illustration)**.
3   Disconnect the fuel pump electrical connector **(see illustration)**.
4   Start the engine and wait for it to stall. After it stalls, turn the ignition switch to the OFF position. Any residual fuel pressure in the fuel system is now relieved.
5   Before performing work on the fuel system, disconnect the cable from the negative terminal of the battery.
6   To restore fuel pressure, simply plug in the fuel pump electrical connector and then start the engine. There will be a slightly-longer-than-usual delay as the system builds up pressure, and then the engine will start. Fuel pressure is now restored.

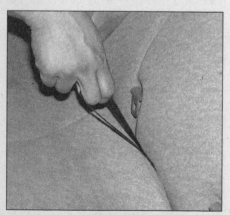

2.1 Pull up the seat cushion with this strap

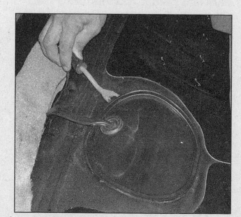

2.2 To remove the fuel pump access cover, break loose the sealant with a suitable prying tool

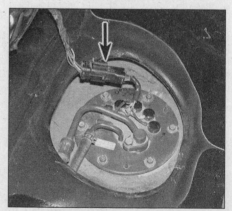

2.3 To deactivate the fuel pump, disconnect the fuel pump electrical connector (arrow)

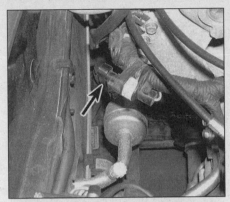

3.3a The fuel pump check connector (arrow) is located at the rear of the engine compartment, behind and below the air intake plenum

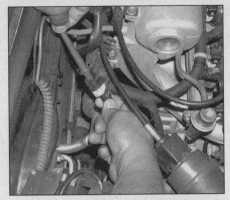

3.3b . . . to use the fuel pump check connector, remove the plug and connect a jumper cable from the battery or some other suitable 12-volt source

3.9 Remove the cable tie (lower arrow) that attaches the fuel pressure line to the fuel return line, put a shop rag around the fuel line retaining bolt on top of the fuel filter and then remove the bolt (upper arrow) and disconnect the fuel line from the filter

3 Fuel pump/fuel pressure - check

Warning: *See the* **Warning** *in Section 1.*

Preliminary check

Refer to illustrations 3.3a and 3.3b

1   If you suspect insufficient fuel delivery check the following items first:

a) *Check the battery and make sure it's fully charged (see Chapter 5).*
b) *Check the fuel pump fuse.*
c) *Check the fuel filter for restriction.*
d) *Inspect all fuel lines to ensure that the problem is not simply a leak in a line.*

2   Place the transmission in Park (automatic) or neutral (manual) and apply the parking brake. Have an assistant cycle the ignition key On and Off several times (or attempt to start the engine, if the engine does not start) while you listen for the sound of the fuel pump operating inside the fuel tank. Remove the rear seat cushion and the fuel pump access cover (see Section 2) and then listen to, or feel the top of, the fuel pump module. You should hear a "whirring" sound, indicating that the fuel pump is operating. If the fuel pump is operating, proceed to the pressure check.

3   If there is no sound from the pump, disconnect the fuel pump check connector **(see**

illustration). Using a jumper cable, hook up the battery to the check connector **(see illustration)** and power up the fuel pump. The pump should operate. If it doesn't, check the fuel pump circuit, referring to Chapter 12 and the wiring diagrams. Check the related fuses, the fuel pump relay and the related wiring to ensure power is reaching the fuel pump connector. Check the ground circuit for continuity.

4   If the power and ground circuits are good and the fuel pump does not operate, remove the fuel pump (see Section 5) and check for open circuits in the fuel pump module wiring and connectors. If the wiring and connectors are good, replace the fuel pump.

Pressure check

Refer to illustrations 3.9, 3.12a, 3.12b, 3.16, 3.17 and 3.18

5   Relieve the system fuel pressure (see Section 2).

6   Disconnect the negative battery cable.
Caution: *Some models are equipped with an anti-theft radio. Before performing a procedure that requires disconnecting the battery, make sure you have the activation code.*

7   Reconnect the fuel pump connector (that you disconnected to relieve system fuel pressure).

2000 and earlier models

8   Locate the fuel filter, which is located in

the left rear corner of the engine compartment, below the master cylinder.

9   Remove the cable tie **(see illustration)** that attaches the fuel pressure line to the fuel return line.

10   Unplug the brake fluid level sensor electrical connector from the master cylinder (see Chapter 9).

11   Put a shop rag around the fuel line retaining bolt on top of the fuel filter **(see illustration 3.9)**, and then remove the bolt and disconnect the fuel line from the filter.

12   Connect a fuel pressure gauge to the fuel filter in place of the fuel line **(see illustrations)**.

2001 and later models

13   Using the proper adapters (available at most auto parts stores) connect the fuel pressure gauge to the fuel rail.

All models

14   Reconnect the negative battery cable. Start the engine and make sure that there are no leaks at the fuel pressure gauge connection. If there are, turn off the engine immediately and tighten the fittings.

15   Measure the fuel pressure and compare this measurement to the fuel pressure listed in this Chapter's Specifications.

4

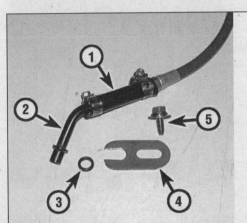

3.12a To connect your fuel pressure gauge to the fuel filter, fabricate your own adapter setup . . .

1   *Adapter hose and hose clamps*
2   *Short section of 5/16-inch (8 mm) diameter pipe with flange (to prevent O-rings from sliding up pipe) at one end (doesn't have to be bent, like this piece)*
3   *Two O-rings that fit snugly over end of pipe, up against pipe flange*
4   *Fabricate a hold-down flange from a piece of scrap*
5   *Use the stock fuel line-to-fuel filter flange hold-down bolt*

3.12b . . . and then use it to connect a fuel pressure gauge to the fuel filter

16   Disconnect the vacuum line from the fuel pressure regulator **(see illustration)**. Measure the fuel pressure again and compare your measurement to the fuel pressure listed in this Chapter's Specifications. **Note:** *This step only applies to 2000 and earlier models. On later models the fuel pressure regulator is incorporated into the fuel pump assembly.*

17   If the fuel pressure is incorrect in Step 15 or 16, use the following chart to diagnose the problem **(see illustration)**.

18   Stop the engine and note the indicated fuel pressure gauge reading. Fuel pressure should hold for about five minutes. If the gauge reading goes down more quickly, note the rate at which it drops and then use the following chart to diagnose the problem **(see illustration)**.

19   Relieve system fuel pressure (see Sec-

3.16 Disconnect the vacuum line from the fuel pressure regulator - the fuel pressure should immediately increase (2000 and earlier models only)

tion 2).

20   Disconnect the fuel pressure gauge.

21   Replace the O-ring at the end of the fuel high-pressure line, reconnect the fuel line to the fuel filter and tighten the retaining bolt to

the torque listed in this Chapter's Specifications.

22   Reconnect the fuel pump connector and the negative battery cable, start the engine and check for leaks.

Fuel pressure status	Likely cause	Solution
Fuel pressure too low	Clogged fuel filter	Replace the fuel filter (see Chapter 1).
Fuel pressure too low	Fuel leak on return side of system, caused by poor seating of fuel pressure regulator diaphragm (2000 and earlier models only)	Replace the fuel pressure regulator (see Section 14).
Fuel pressure too low	Low fuel pump discharge pressure	Check the in-tank fuel hose for an obstruction. If fuel hose is okay, replace the fuel pump (see Section 5).
Fuel pressure too high	Sticking fuel-pressure regulator	Replace the fuel pressure regulator (see Section 14).
Fuel pressure too high	Blocked or bent fuel return hose or pipe (2000 and earlier models only)	Blow out the obstruction in the hose or pipe with compressed air, or replace the hose or pipe (see Section 4).
No difference in fuel pressure with pressure regulator vacuum line connected or disconnected (2000 and earlier models only)	Blocked or damaged vacuum line or port on fuel pressure regulator	Blow out the obstruction in the vacuum line or port, or replace the vacuum line or pressure regulator.
No difference in fuel pressure with pressure regulator vacuum line connected or disconnected (2000 and earlier models only)	Stuck fuel pressure regulator diaphragm, or diaphragm not seating correctly	Replace the fuel pressure regulator (see Section 14).

3.17 Fuel pressure troubleshooting chart - engine running

Fuel pressure status	Likely cause	Solution
Fuel pressure drops slowly after engine is stopped	Leaking injector(s)	Replace the injector(s) (see Section 15).
Fuel pressure drops immediately after engine is stopped	Defective check valve in fuel pump	Replace the fuel pump (see Section 5).

3.18 Fuel pressure troubleshooting chart - bleed-down after engine has been turned off

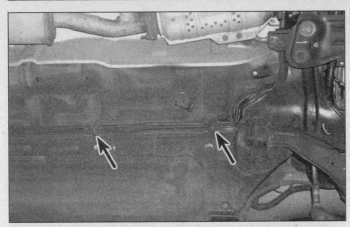

4.2 The metal fuel pressure and return lines connecting the fuel tank to the fuel injection system are routed underneath the vehicle and are secured to the pan by small, flexible retainers (arrows) that can be bent open to disengage the lines and then closed again when you're done

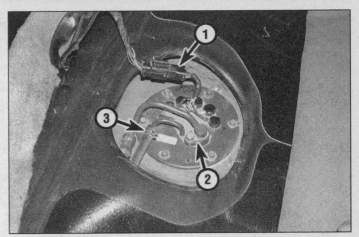

5.3 Unplug the fuel pump/fuel sending unit electrical connector (1), remove the fuel high pressure line flange bolt (2), loosen the fuel return hose clamp (3) and then disconnect both the line and the hose

4 Fuel lines and fittings - repair and replacement

Refer to illustration 4.2

Warning: *See the* **Warning** *in Section 1.*

1 Always relieve the fuel pressure before servicing fuel lines or fittings (see Section 2).

2 Special metal fuel supply and (on 2000 and earlier models) return lines extend from the fuel tank to the engine compartment. The fuel lines are secured to the underbody with retainers that can be straightened out to disengage the lines, and then bent back into their normal configuration to secure the lines **(see illustration)**. Rubber hose is used in a few places on the return side of the system. The metal fuel lines are virtually impervious to everything except the occasional rock that's flung up into the undercarriage with enough force to dent, or even puncture, a line. Rubber hoses are far more susceptible to deterioration, and should be inspected periodically - anytime that the vehicle is raised for service, for example. (Of course, anytime you smell gasoline, you should inspect the fuel lines and the fuel tank IMMEDIATELY.)

3 If you find contamination in the system or in the fuel filter during disassembly, disconnect the lines and blow them out. And inspect the "sock" (the fuel strainer) on the fuel pump pick-up for damage and deterioration.

4 Don't route fuel lines or hoses within four inches of any part of the exhaust system or within ten inches of the catalytic converter. Fuel line must never be allowed to chafe against the engine, body or frame. A minimum of 1/4-inch clearance must be maintained around a fuel line.

5 Because fuel lines used on fuel-injected vehicles are under high pressure, all fittings must be tightly connected and in good condition.

6 In the event of fuel line damage, we strongly urge you to replace the damaged lines with factory replacement parts. Other lines might not be designed to withstand the high operating pressure of this system.

7 When replacing a fuel line, remove all fasteners attaching the fuel line to the vehicle body and route the new line exactly as originally installed.

8 When replacing rubber hose, always use hose specifically designed for high-pressure fuel injection systems, and replace the hose clamp with a new one.

5 Fuel pump - removal and installation

Refer to illustrations 5.3, 5.5 and 5.6

Warning: *See the* **Warning** *in Section 1.*

Caution: *Some models are equipped with an* anti-theft radio. Before performing a procedure that requires disconnecting the battery, make sure you have the activation code.

1 Relieve the fuel system pressure (see Section 2).

2 Disconnect the negative battery cable.

3 Disconnect the electrical connector from the fuel pump/fuel sending unit **(see illustration)**.

4 Disconnect the high pressure hose and the fuel return hose from the fuel pump **(see illustration 5.3)**.

5 Remove the fuel pump mounting flange screws **(see illustration)**.

6 Lift the fuel pump and the fuel level sending unit as a single assembly from the tank **(see illustration)**.

7 If you're replacing either the fuel pump or the fuel level sending unit, separate the two units (see Section 6).

8 Installation is the reverse of removal.

5.5 To detach the fuel pump/fuel sending unit assembly from the fuel tank, remove these screws (arrows) from the fuel pump mounting flange

5.6 Remove the fuel pump/fuel sending unit assembly from the fuel tank

4

6   Fuel level sending unit - check and replacement

Warning: *See the* **Warning** *in Section 1.*

Check

Refer to illustrations 6.2a and 6.2b

1   Remove the fuel pump/fuel level sending unit assembly (see Section 5).

2   Connect the probes of an ohmmeter to the fuel level sending unit terminals of the fuel pump module electrical connector **(see illustrations)**.

3   Position the float in the down (empty) position and note the reading on the ohmmeter.

4   Move the float up to the full position while watching the ohmmeter.

5   If the fuel level sending unit resistance does not change smoothly as the float moves from EMPTY to FULL, replace the fuel level sending unit.

Replacement

Refer to illustrations 6.7a through 6.7e

6   Remove the fuel pump/fuel level send-

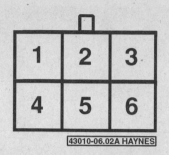

43010-06.02A HAYNES

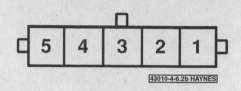

43010-4-6.2b HAYNES

6.2a Fuel pump/fuel level sending unit electrical connector terminal guide (1996 through 2000 models)

1   *Ground for fuel level sending unit*
2   *Thermistor voltage signal to low fuel level warning indicator light*
3   *Fuel pump voltage supply (from fuel pump relay)*
4   *Not used*
5   *Ground for fuel pump and for thermistor (for low fuel level warning indicator light)*
6   *Fuel level sending unit voltage signal to fuel gauge on instrument cluster*

6.2b Fuel pump/fuel level sending unit electrical connector terminal guide (2001 models)

1   *Ground for fuel level sending unit and for thermistor (for low fuel level warning indicator light)*
2   *Thermistor voltage signal to low fuel level warning indicator light*
3   *Fuel level sending unit voltage signal to fuel gauge on instrument cluster*
4   *Ground for fuel pump*
5   *Fuel pump voltage supply (from fuel pump relay)*

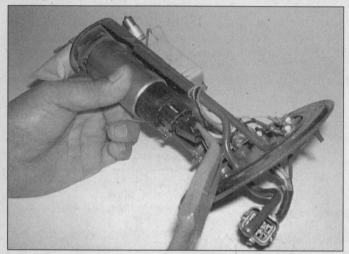

6.7a To separate the fuel pump and the fuel level sending unit, disconnect the electrical connector . . .

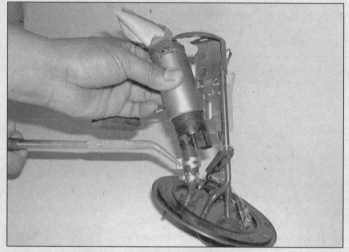

6.7b . . . loosen the hose clamps and remove the hose . . .

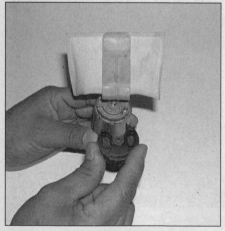

6.7c . . . remove the rubber isolator . . .

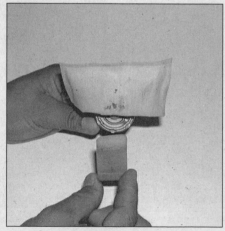

6.7d . . . remove the sock support . . .

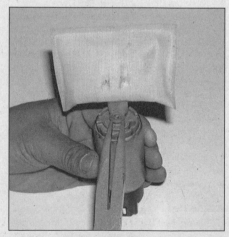

6.7e . . . and remove the sock retainer

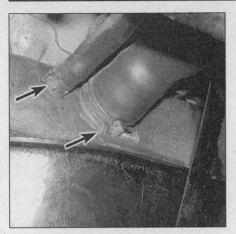

7.7 Loosen the hose clamps (arrows), then disconnect the fuel filler neck hose and the vapor hose from the fuel tank

7.9 Remove the fuel tank strap bolts (arrows)

8 Fuel tank cleaning and repair - general information

1   The fuel tank is not repairable. If it becomes damaged, it must be replaced.
2   Cleaning the fuel tank (due to fuel contamination) should be performed by a professional with the proper training to carry out this critical and potentially dangerous work. Even after cleaning and flushing, explosive fumes may remain inside the fuel tank.
3   If the fuel tank is removed from the vehicle, it should not be placed in an area where sparks or open flames could ignite the fumes coming out of the tank. Be especially careful inside a garage where a gas-type appliance is located.

ing unit (see Section 5), if you haven't already done so.
7   Separate the fuel level sending unit from the fuel pump **(see illustrations)**. Reassembly is the reverse of disassembly.
8   Installation is the reverse of removal.

7 Fuel tank - removal and installation

Refer to illustrations 7.7 and 7.9
Warning: *See the* **Warning** *in Section 1.*
Caution: *Some models are equipped with an anti-theft radio. Before performing a procedure that requires disconnecting the battery, make sure you have the activation code.*

1   Relieve the fuel system pressure (see Section 2). Remove the fuel tank filler cap to relieve fuel tank pressure.
2   Disconnect the cable from the negative terminal of the battery.
3   Unplug the electrical connector from the fuel pump/fuel sending unit **(see illustration 5.3)**.

4   Disconnect the fuel high pressure hose and the return hose from the fuel pump **(see illustration 5.3)**.
5   Use a siphoning kit (available at most auto parts stores) to siphon the fuel into an approved gasoline container.
6   Raise the vehicle and support it securely on jackstands.
7   Loosen the hose clamps **(see illustration)** and then disconnect the fuel filler neck hose and the vapor hoses from the fuel tank. Clearly label the two smaller hoses to ensure correct reassembly. Be sure to plug the hoses to prevent leakage and contamination of the fuel system.
8   Support the fuel tank with a floor jack. Place a wood block between the jack head and the fuel tank to protect the tank.
9   Remove the fuel tank strap bolts **(see illustration)**.
10   Swing the fuel tank retaining straps down until they are out of the way.
11   Lower the tank enough to disconnect any remaining hoses or connectors.
12   Remove the tank from the vehicle.
13   Installation is the reverse of removal.

9 Air cleaner assembly - removal and installation

Refer to illustration 9.2
1   Unclamp the air intake tube from the air cleaner cover, remove the air cleaner cover and remove the air filter element (see Chapter 1). **Note:** *Always inspect the condition of the filter element when you remove it. Replace the element if necessary.*
2   Remove the bolts **(see illustration)** that attach the air cleaner housing to the inner fender panel.
3   Remove the air cleaner housing from the engine compartment.
4   Installation is the reverse of removal.

10 Accelerator cable - removal and installation

Removal

Refer to illustrations 10.1, 10.2, 10.3, 10.4 and 10.5
1   Detach the accelerator cable from the three cable clips **(see illustration)**.

4

9.2 To detach the air cleaner housing from the inner fender panel, remove these bolts (arrows)

10.1 Detach the accelerator cable from these three clips (arrows)

10.2 Hold the accelerator cable locknut with a back-up wrench, loosen the cable adjusting nut, then disengage the cable from the cable bracket (disengage the cruise control cable from the cable bracket the same way)

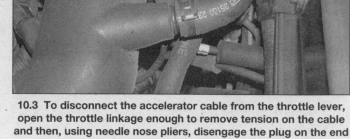

10.3 To disconnect the accelerator cable from the throttle lever, open the throttle linkage enough to remove tension on the cable and then, using needle nose pliers, disengage the plug on the end of the cable from its groove in the throttle cam (disengage the cruise control cable from the cam the same way)

2   Loosen the accelerator cable adjusting nut **(see illustration)**, then disengage the cable from the cable bracket.
3   Disengage the accelerator cable from the throttle lever **(see illustration)**.
4   Detach the accelerator cable from the firewall **(see illustration)**.
5   Working inside the vehicle, disengage the accelerator cable from the accelerator pedal **(see illustration)**.
6   From outside the vehicle, pull the accelerator cable through the firewall.

Installation

7   Installation is the reverse of removal. Make sure that there are no kinks or sharp bends in the cable.
8   After installing the cable, adjust free play, as follows:

a) *Verify that the throttle cable has no slack in it.*
b) *If the cable is slack, adjust it as follows:*
c) *Turn the adjusting nut counterclockwise until the throttle lever is free.*

d) *Remove any sharp bends from the accelerator cable.*
e) *Loosen the locknut and turn the throttle cable adjusting nut clockwise to the point at which the throttle lever just begins to move, then back off the adjusting nut one turn and tighten the locknut securely.*

---

11   Fuel injection system - general information

The fuel injection system consists of the air intake system, the fuel delivery system, the engine management system and the emission control systems. The engine management system uses a computer, known as the Powertrain Control Module (PCM), and an array of information sensors (coolant temperature sensor, throttle position sensor, mass airflow sensor, oxygen sensor, etc.) to determine the correct air/fuel ratio under all operating conditions. The emission control systems monitor and reduce emissions - hydrocarbons, carbon monoxide, oxides of nitrogen, etc. - produced by normal combustion.
The fuel injection system, the engine control system and the emission control systems are highly integrated. For information on the engine management system and the emission control systems, refer to Chapter 6.

Air intake system

The air intake system consists of the air cleaner housing, the air filter element, the air intake duct, the throttle body, the air intake plenum and the intake manifold runners (the plenum and the manifold runners are a one-piece design).

Engine management system and emission control systems

The engine management and emission control systems are described in detail in Chapter 6.

10.4 To detach the accelerator cable from the firewall, remove these two cable flange bolts (arrows)

10.5 To disconnect the accelerator cable from the accelerator pedal, disengage the cable plug (arrow) from its groove in top of the accelerator pedal

12.7 Use a stethoscope to determine whether the injectors are working correctly; they should make a steady clicking sound that rises and falls with engine speed changes

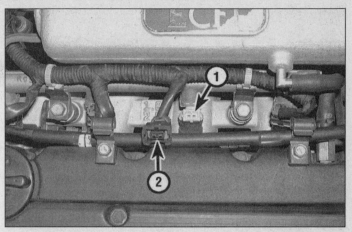

12.8 Fuel injector harness connector terminal guide

1   *Injector (male) side of connector (terminal 1 on left)*
2   *Harness (female) side of connector (terminal 1 on right)*

Fuel delivery system

The fuel delivery system consists of the fuel tank, the in-tank fuel pump, the fuel pressure regulator, the fuel rail, the fuel injectors and the hoses and lines connecting all of these components.

The fuel pump is an electric type located in the fuel tank. Fuel is drawn through a "sock" (inlet screen) into the pump. From the pump, fuel is pumped under pressure through the fuel filter and then into the fuel rail before being discharged into the intake ports by the fuel injectors. The fuel pressure regulator maintains a constant fuel pressure to the injectors. On 1996 through 2000 models, the pressure regulator is mounted on the fuel rail. On these models, excess fuel is released through the fuel pressure regulator and then through a return hose back to the fuel tank. On 2001 models, the pressure regulator is an integral part of the fuel pump assembly in the tank, so there is no return hose on these models.

The injectors are solenoid-actuated, pintle-type units consisting of a solenoid, plunger, needle valve and housing. When current is applied to the solenoid coil, the needle valve raises and pressurized fuel sprays out the nozzle. The quantity of fuel injected by each injector each time it opens is determined by the length of time the valve is open (the length of time during which current is supplied to the solenoid coils).

The fuel pump control relay is located on the relay panel at the left end of the dash, above the passenger compartment fuse panel. The fuel pump relay connects battery voltage to the fuel pump. The PCM controls the fuel pump relay. If the PCM senses there is NO signal from the engine speed sensor (as with the engine not running or cranking), the PCM will de-energize the relay.

12 Fuel injection system - check

Refer to illustrations 12.7, 12.8 and 12.9
Note: *The following procedure is based on*

the assumption that the fuel pressure is adequate (see Section 3).
1   Check all electrical connectors that are related to the system. Check the ground wire connections for tightness (see the wiring diagrams at the end of Chapter 12). Loose connectors and poor grounds can cause many problems that resemble more serious malfunctions.
2   Check to see that the battery is fully charged, as the control unit and sensors depend on an accurate supply voltage in order to properly meter the fuel.
3   Check the air filter element - a dirty or partially blocked filter will severely impede performance and economy (see Chapter 1).
4   Check the related fuses. If a blown fuse is found, replace it and see if it blows again. If it does, search for a wire shorted to ground in the harness.
5   Check the air intake duct to the intake manifold for leaks, which will result in an excessively lean mixture. Also check the condition of all vacuum hoses connected to the intake manifold and/or throttle body.
6   Remove the air intake duct from the throttle body and check for dirt, carbon or other residue build-up. If it's dirty, clean it with carburetor cleaner spray, a toothbrush and a shop towel.
7   With the engine running, place an automotive stethoscope against each injector, one at a time, and listen for a clicking sound, indicating operation **(see illustration)**. If you don't have a stethoscope, place the tip of a screwdriver against the injector and listen through the handle. If you hear the injectors operating, the electrical circuits are functioning, but the injectors may be dirty or fouled from carbon deposits - commercial cleaning products may help or they may require replacement. If one or more injectors are not operating, proceed with the injector check.
8   Turn the ignition switch to OFF. Disconnect one of the injector connectors **(see illustration)** and check for battery voltage at terminal no. 1 on the harness side of the injector connector with the ignition key turned to ON.

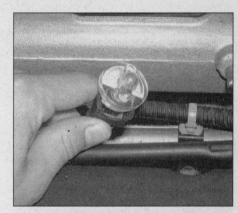

12.9 Install a "noid" light (available at most auto parts stores) into each injector electrical connector and verify that it blinks when the engine is cranking

If battery voltage is not present, check the fuse, fuel pump relay and related wiring (see Chapter 12).
9   Install an injector test light ("noid" light) into the disconnected injector electrical connector **(see illustration)**. Crank the engine over. Confirm that the light flashes. This tests the ECM control of the injectors. If the light does not flash, have the ECM checked at a dealer service department or other properly equipped repair facility. Test each injector connector, if necessary.
10   Disconnect the injector electrical connectors and measure the resistance of each injector **(see illustration 12.8)**. Compare the measurements with the resistance value listed in this Chapter's Specifications.
11   The remainder of the engine control system checks can be found in Chapter 6.

13 Throttle body - removal and installation

Warning: *Wait until the engine is completely cool before beginning this procedure.*

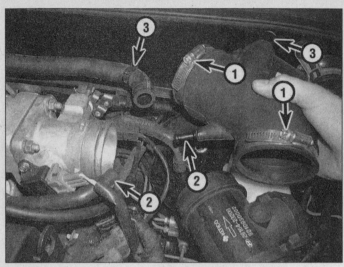

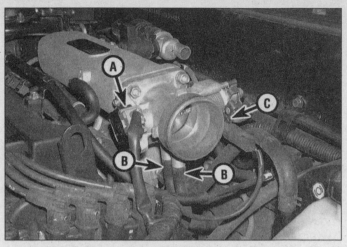

13.2 To remove the air intake duct, loosen the hose clamp screws (1), disconnect the breather hose (2) and the IAC hose (3),and then disconnect the duct from the throttle body and from the MAF sensor and then set it aside

13.3 Before removing the throttle body, be sure to disconnect the following:

A   *Throttle Position Sensor (TPS)*
B   *Coolant hoses*
C   *Idle switch (models with an automatic transaxle only)*

Caution: *Some models are equipped with an anti-theft radio. Before performing a procedure that requires disconnecting the battery, make sure you have the activation code.*

Removal

Refer to illustrations 13.2, 13.3 and 13.5

1   Disconnect the cable from the negative terminal of the battery.

2   Loosen the air intake duct hose clamps **(see illustration)** and disconnect the air intake duct from the throttle body.

3   Disconnect the electrical connectors from the Throttle Position Sensor (TPS) and, on models with an automatic transaxle, the idle switch **(see illustration)**. On 2001 models, unplug the electrical connector from the Idle Speed Control (ISC) actuator (see Chapter 6). If the throttle body is going to be washed in solvent, remove the TPS, the idle switch (automatics) and the ISC actuator (2001 models).

4   Disconnect the accelerator cable from the throttle lever (see Section 10). On models with cruise control, also disconnect the cruise control cable (the cruise control cable is attached to the throttle linkage and to the cable bracket exactly the same way as the accelerator cable - see Section 10).

5   Remove the four throttle body retaining nuts **(see illustration)** or bolts (2001 models).

6   Remove the throttle body from the air intake plenum far enough to disconnect the coolant hoses **(see illustration 13.3)** from the underside of the throttle body. Be sure to mark the hoses to ensure correct reassembly. Plug the hoses to prevent coolant loss.

7   Remove the gasket and discard it (you must use a new gasket when reinstalling the throttle body.

Installation

8   Install the TPS and, on 2001 models, the

ISC actuator (see Chapter 6), if you removed them. If the vehicle is an automatic, install the idle switch, if you removed it.

9   Reconnect the coolant hoses to their respective pipes on the underside of the throttle body. Make sure that the hoses are in good condition and that the hose clamps are tight.

10   Ensure that the gasket mating surfaces of the throttle body and the air intake plenum are clean and dry, place the new gasket in position, install the throttle body and then tighten the retaining nuts or bolts to the torque listed in this Chapter's Specifications.

11   If the vehicle is an automatic, reconnect the idle switch connector.

12   Reconnect the accelerator cable to the throttle cam. On models with cruise control, reconnect the cruise control cable.

13   Reconnect the electrical connectors to the TPS and (on 2001 models) the ISC actuator.

14   Reconnect the air intake duct and tighten the hose clamp screws securely.

15   Adjust the accelerator cable (see Sec-

tion 10).

16   Check the coolant level and refill as necessary.

17   Reconnect the battery negative cable.

14   Fuel pressure regulator - removal and installation

Refer to illustration 14.3

Warning: *See the* **Warning** *in Section 1.*

Caution: *Some models are equipped with an anti-theft radio. Before performing a procedure that requires disconnecting the battery, make sure you have the activation code.*

Note: *This procedure applies to 2000 and earlier models only. The fuel pressure regulator on 2001 and later models is integral with the fuel pump assembly (see Section 5 for replacement).*

1   Relieve the system fuel pressure (see Section 2). Disconnect the cable from the negative terminal of the battery.

2   Disconnect the vacuum hose from the

13.5 On 1996 through 2000 models (shown), remove the four throttle body retaining nuts (arrows) or, on 2001 models, the throttle body retaining bolts

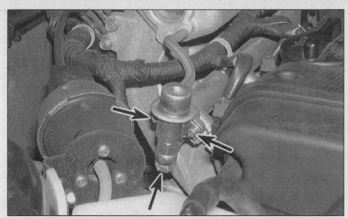

14.3 To disconnect the fuel return line from the fuel pressure regulator, remove the banjo bolt (lower arrow) from the bottom of the fuel pressure regulator; to detach the regulator from the fuel rail, remove the two screws (upper arrows)

15.4 To disconnect the fuel injector electrical connectors, release the lock wire on each connector by pulling it out to its "released" position (it will snap out and remain out until depressed) and then unplug the connector

15.5 Remove the two bolts (upper arrows) that attach the fuel pressure line flange to the fuel rail and disconnect the pressure line from the fuel rail; loosen the hose clamp (lower arrow) and disconnect the fuel return hose from the fuel return line

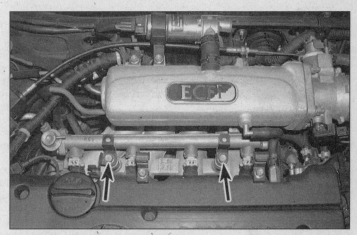

15.7a To detach the fuel rail from the intake manifold, remove these mounting bolts (arrows)

4

port on the regulator **(see illustration 3.16)**.

3   Remove the banjo bolt **(see illustration)** and disconnect the fuel return line from the bottom of the fuel pressure regulator. Discard the old sealing washers.

4   Remove the fuel pressure regulator retaining screws **(see illustration 14.3)** and remove the fuel pressure regulator from the fuel rail. Discard the old gasket.

5   Installation is the reverse of removal. Be sure to use a new o-ring and new sealing washers. Tighten the pressure regulator screws to the torque listed in this Chapter's Specifications.

6   Start the engine and check for leaks.

---

15   Fuel rail and injectors - removal and installation

Warning: *See the* **Warning** *in Section 1.*

Caution: *Some models are equipped with an anti-theft radio. Before performing a procedure that requires disconnecting the battery, make sure you have the activation code.*

Removal

Refer to illustrations 15.4, 15.5, 15.7a, 15.7b, 15.8a, 15.8b and 15.8c

1   Relieve the system fuel pressure (see Section 2).

2   Disconnect the negative battery cable.

3   Disconnect the vacuum hose from the fuel pressure regulator **(see illustration 3.16)**.

4   Disconnect the main injector harness electrical connector and the injector connectors **(see illustration)**. Detach the wiring harness retainers from the fuel rail and set the harness aside. **Note:** *Apply a numbered tag to each connector with the corresponding cylinder number.*

5   Remove the two bolts that attach the fuel pressure line flange to the fuel rail **(see illustration)** and disconnect the pressure line from the fuel rail.

6   Loosen the hose clamp and disconnect the fuel return hose from the fuel return line **(see illustration 15.5)**.

7   Clean any debris from around the injectors. Remove the fuel rail mounting bolts **(see illustration)**. Gently rock the fuel rail and

15.7b Be sure to remove and inspect the fuel rail insulators (arrows); if they're cracked or deteriorated, replace them before installing the fuel rail

injectors to loosen the injectors. Remove the fuel rail and fuel injectors as an assembly. Remove the fuel rail insulators **(see illustration)**. Inspect the insulators for cracks. If the

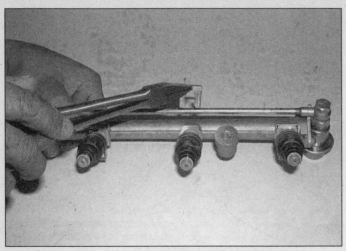

15.8a Using a small screwdriver or a pair of needle nose pliers, remove the retaining clip from each injector . . .

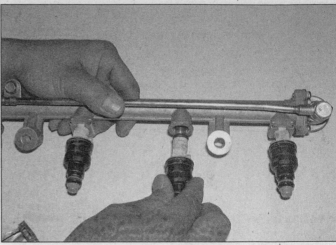

15.8b . . . then pull the injector out of the fuel rail assembly

insulators are cracked or otherwise damaged, replace them.

8   Remove the retaining clip and remove the injector(s) from the fuel rail assembly **(see illustrations)**. Remove and discard the O-rings and seals. **Note:** *Whether you're replacing an injector or a leaking O-ring, it's a good idea to remove all the injectors from the fuel rail and replace all the O-rings.*

Installation

9   Coat the new O-rings with clean engine oil and install them on the injectors, and then insert each injector into its corresponding bore in the fuel rail. Install the injector retaining clips.

10   Install the fuel insulators, then install the injector and fuel rail assembly on the intake manifold. Fully seat the injectors, then tighten the fuel rail mounting bolts to the torque listed in this Chapter's Specifications.

11   Connect the fuel return hose to the fuel return line. Make sure that the hose clamp is very tight. If it isn't, replace it.

12   Connect the fuel pressure line flange bolts and tighten them securely.

13   Connect the electrical connectors to each injector, referring to the numbered tags.

14   Connect the main injector harness connector.

15   Connect the vacuum line to the fuel pressure regulator.

16   Connect the negative battery cable.

17   Turn the ignition switch to ON, but don't start the engine. When the ignition key is turned to ON, it activates the fuel pump for about two seconds, which builds up fuel pressure in the fuel lines and the fuel rail. Repeat this step two or three times and then check the fuel pressure line, fuel return hose, the fuel rail and the fuel injectors for fuel leakage.

16   Exhaust system - general information

Refer to illustration 16.1
Warning: *Inspection and repair of exhaust*

system components should be done only after enough time has elapsed after driving the vehicle to allow the system components to cool completely. Also, when working under the vehicle, make sure it is securely supported on jackstands.

1   The exhaust system consists of the exhaust manifold, the upstream and downstream catalytic converters, the muffler, the tailpipe and all connecting pipes, brackets, hangers and clamps. The exhaust system is attached to the body with mounting brackets and rubber hangers **(see illustration)**. If any of these hangers deteriorate to the point at which they tear apart under the weight of the exhaust system, the exhaust system will sag, allowing the pipes and/or the muffler to touch other parts of the vehicle, usually the axle. If you hear excessive noise and vibration being transmitted through the vehicle body, especially under a load (accelerating up a steep hill, for example), then one or more of the rubber exhaust hangers may have broken.

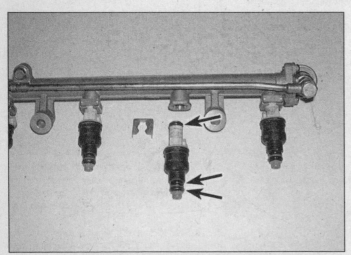

15.8c Remove the O-rings (arrows) from each injector and replace them with new ones

16.1 Make sure that each exhaust system rubber hanger (arrow) is in good shape; when one hanger rips apart from old age, the others will soon follow because the weight of the exhaust system imposes an extra load on the remaining hangers

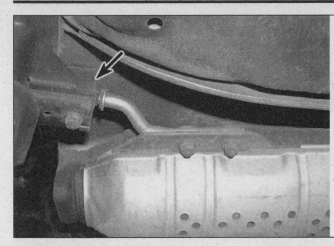

16.5 The catalytic converter hanger bracket is supported by this rubber insulator (arrow); because it's close to high heat all the time, this insulator is prone to premature failure, so inspect it regularly

Muffler and pipes

2   Conduct regular inspections of the exhaust system to keep it safe and quiet. Look for any damaged or bent parts, open seams, holes, loose connections, excessive corrosion or other defects which could allow exhaust fumes to enter the vehicle. Also check the catalytic converter when you inspect the exhaust system. Deteriorated exhaust system components should not be repaired; they should be replaced with new parts.

3   If the exhaust system components are extremely corroded or rusted together, welding equipment will probably be required to remove them. The convenient way to accom-plish this is to have a muffler repair shop remove the corroded sections with a cutting torch. If, however, you want to save money by doing it yourself (and you don't have a welding outfit with a cutting torch), simply cut the exhaust pipes with a hacksaw at the separation point. If you do decide to tackle the job at home, be sure to wear safety goggles to protect your eyes from metal chips and work gloves to protect your hands.

4   Here are some simple guidelines to follow when repairing the exhaust system:

a) *Work from the back to the front when removing exhaust system components.*

b) *Apply penetrating oil to the exhaust system component fasteners to make them easier to remove.*

c) *Use new gaskets, hangers and clamps when installing exhaust system components.*

d) *Apply anti-seize compound to the threads of all exhaust system fasteners during reassembly.*

e) *Be sure to allow sufficient clearance between newly installed parts and all points on the underbody to avoid over-heating the floor pan and possibly damaging the interior carpet and insulation. Pay particularly close attention to the catalytic converter and heat shield.*

Catalytic converter

Refer to illustration 16.5

Warning: *The converter gets very hot during operation. Make sure it has cooled down before you touch it.*

Note: *See Chapter 6 for additional information on the catalytic converter.*

5   Anytime the vehicle is raised for any sort of service, be sure to inspect the rubber insulator for the catalytic converter hanger **(see illustration)**. Because of its close proximity to high temperatures, this insulator is more prone than a typical exhaust hanger to dry out, crack and tear. Periodically inspect the heat shield for cracks, dents and loose or missing fasteners.

6   Inspect the converter for cracks or other damage.

7   If the catalytic converter requires replacement, refer to Chapter 6.

4

Notes

Chapter 5
Engine electrical systems

Contents

5

Specifications

Charging system

System type	12-volt, negative ground
Charging voltage	12.5 to 14.7 volts

Ignition system

System type	Distributorless electronic ignition
Firing order	1-3-4-2
Ignition coil resistance (approximate)	
Primary windings	0.45 to 0.55 ohms
Secondary windings	10.3 to 13.9 K-ohms
Spark plug wire resistance (approximate)	
Cylinder No. 1	15.3 K-ohms
Cylinder No. 2	12.4 K-ohms
Cylinder No. 3	10.7 K-ohms
Cylinder No. 4	8.8 K-ohms

Torque specifications

	Ft-lbs (unless otherwise indicated)	Nm
Alternator mounting bolts		
Lower bolt	15 to 18	20 to 25
Upper (adjustment) bolt	108 to 132 in-lbs	12 to 15
Starter motor mounting bolts	20 to 25	27 to 34

1   General information

The engine electrical systems include all ignition, charging and starting components. Because of their engine-related functions, these components are discussed separately from chassis electrical accessories (see Chapter 12) such as the lights, the instruments, etc.

Precautions

Always observe the following precautions when working on the electrical system:

a) *Be extremely careful when servicing engine electrical components. They can be easily damaged if you check, connect or handle them incorrectly.*

b) *Never leave the ignition switch switched on for long periods of time when the engine is not running.*

c) *Never disconnect the battery cables while the engine is running.*

d) *Maintain correct polarity when connecting battery cables from another vehicle during jump starting see the "Booster battery (jump) starting" section at the front of this manual.*

e) *Always disconnect the negative battery cable from the battery before working on the electrical system, but read the following battery disconnection procedure first.*

It's also a good idea to review the safety-related information regarding the engine electrical systems located in the *"Safety first!"* section at the front of this manual, before beginning any operation included in this Chapter.

Battery disconnection

Several systems on the vehicle require battery power to be available at all times, either to ensure their continued operation (such as radio, alarm system, power door locks, windows, etc.) or to maintain control unit memories (such as that in the engine management system's Powertrain Control Module

[PCM]) which would be lost if the battery were to be disconnected. Therefore, whenever the battery is to be disconnected, first note the following to ensure that there are no unforeseen consequences of this action:

a) *Some models are equipped with an anti-theft radio. Before performing a procedure that requires disconnecting the battery, make sure you have the proper activation code.*

b) *The engine management system's PCM will lose the information stored in its memory when the battery is disconnected (see Chapter 6).*

c) *On vehicles with power door locks, it is a wise precaution to remove the key from the ignition and to keep it with you, so that it does not get locked inside if the power door locks should engage accidentally when the battery is reconnected.*

Devices known as "memory-savers" can be used to avoid some of the above problems. Precise details vary according to the device used. Typically, it is plugged into the cigarette lighter and is connected by its own wires to a spare battery; the vehicle's own battery is then disconnected from the electrical system, leaving the "memory-saver" to pass sufficient current to maintain audio unit security codes and PCM memory values, and also to run permanently live circuits such as the clock and radio memory, all the while isolating the battery in the event of a short-circuit occurring while work is carried out.

Warning 1: *Some of these devices allow a considerable amount of current to pass, which can mean that many of the vehicle's systems are still operational when the main battery is disconnected. If a "memory-saver" is used, ensure that the circuit concerned is actually "dead" before carrying out any work on it!*

Warning 2: *If work is to be performed around any of the airbag system components, the battery must be disconnected and no "memory-saver" can be used. If a memory-saver device is used, power will be supplied to the*

airbag and personal injury may result if the airbag is accidentally deployed.

The battery is located at the left front corner of the engine compartment. To disconnect the battery for service procedures requiring power to be cut from the vehicle, loosen the negative cable clamp nut and detach the negative cable from the negative battery post (see Section 3). Isolate the cable end to prevent it from accidentally coming into contact with the battery post.

2   Battery - emergency jump starting

Refer to the *Booster battery (jump) starting* procedures at the front of this manual.

3   Battery - removal and installation

Warning: *Hydrogen gas is produced by the battery, so keep open flames and lighted cigarettes away from it at all times. Always wear eye protection when working around a battery. Rinse off spilled electrolyte immediately with large amounts of water.*

Caution 1: *Some models are equipped with an anti-theft radio. Before performing a procedure that requires disconnecting the battery, make sure you have the activation code.*

Caution 2: *Disconnecting the battery can cause driveability problems. See Section 1 for the use of an auxiliary voltage input device before disconnecting the battery.*

Check

Refer to illustrations 3.1a, 3.1b and 3.1c

1   A battery cannot be accurately tested until it is at or near a fully charged state. Disconnect the negative battery cable from the battery and perform the following tests:

a) *Battery state of charge test - Visually inspect the indicator eye (if equipped) on the top of the battery. If the indicator eye is dark in color, charge the battery as described in Chapter 1. If the battery is equipped with removable caps, check the battery electrolyte. The electrolyte level should be above the upper edge of the plates. If the level is low, add distilled water. DO NOT OVERFILL. The excess electrolyte may spill over during periods of heavy charging. Test the specific gravity of the electrolyte using a hydrometer (see illustration). Remove the caps and extract a sample of the electrolyte and observe the float inside the barrel of the hydrometer. Follow the instructions from the tool manufacturer and determine the specific gravity of the electrolyte for each cell. A fully charged battery will indicate approximately 1.270 (green zone) at 68-degrees F (20-degrees C). If the specific gravity of the electrolyte is low (red zone), charge the battery as described in Chapter 1.*

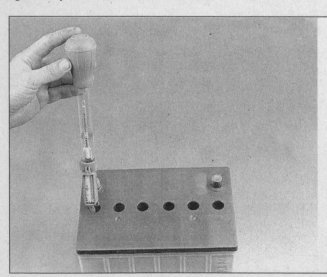

3.1a Use a battery hydrometer to draw electrolyte from the battery cell. Some hydrometers, like the one shown here, include a thermometer to make temperature corrections

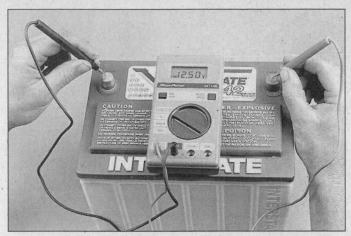

3.1b To test the open circuit, or standing, voltage of the battery, connect the black probe of the voltmeter to the negative terminal and the red probe to the positive terminal of the battery. A fully charged battery should indicate about 12.5 volts, depending on the ambient air temperature

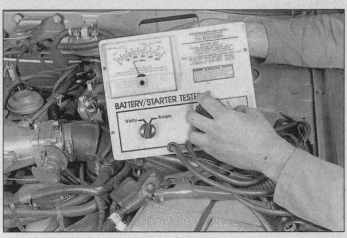

3.1c Some battery load testers, like the one shown here, are equipped with an ammeter, which allows you to dial in the battery load. Less expensive testers are only equipped with a load switch and a voltmeter

b) *Open circuit voltage test - Using a digital voltmeter, perform an open circuit voltage test* **(see illustration)**. *Connect the negative probe of the voltmeter to the negative battery post and the positive probe to the positive battery post. The battery voltage should be greater than 12.5 volts. If the battery is less than the specified voltage, charge the battery before proceeding to the next test. Do not proceed with the battery load test until the battery is fully charged.*

c) *Battery load test - An accurate check of the battery condition can only be performed with a load tester (available at most auto parts stores). This test evaluates the ability of the battery to operate the starter and other accessories during periods of heavy amperage draw (load). Install a special battery load testing tool onto the battery terminals* **(see illustration)**. *Load test the battery according to the tool manufacturer's instructions. This tool utilizes a carbon pile to increase the load demand (amperage draw) on the battery. Maintain the load on the battery for 15 seconds and observe that the battery voltage does not drop below 9.6 volts. If the battery condition is weak or defective, the tool will indicate this condition immediately.* **Note:** *Cold temperatures will cause the minimum voltage requirements to drop slightly. Follow the chart given in the tool manufacturer's instructions to compensate for cold climates. Minimum load voltage for freezing temperatures (32 degrees F/0-degrees C) should be approximately 9.1 volts.*

d) *Battery drain test - This test will indicate whether there's a constant drain on the vehicle's electrical system that can cause the battery to discharge. Make sure all accessories are turned Off. If the vehicle has an underhood light, verify it's working properly, then disconnect it.*

Connect one lead of a digital ammeter to the disconnected negative battery cable clamp and the other lead to the negative battery post. A drain of approximately 100 milliamps or less is considered normal (due to the engine control compudigital clocks, digital radios and other components which normally cause a key-off battery drain). An excessive drain (approximately 500 milliamps or more) will cause the battery to discharge. The problem circuit or component can be located by removing the fuses, one at a time, until the excessive drain stops and normal drain is indicated on the meter.

Replacement

Refer to illustrations 3.2 and 3.4

Caution: *Always disconnect the negative cable first and hook it up last or the battery may be shorted by the tool being used to loosen the cable clamps.*

2   Loosen the cable clamp nut **(see illustration)** and remove the negative battery cable from the negative battery post. Isolate the cable end to prevent it from accidentally coming into contact with the battery post.

3   Loosen the cable clamp nut and remove the positive battery cable from the positive battery post.

4   Remove the battery hold-down clamp **(see illustration)**.

5   Lift out the battery. Be careful - it's heavy. **Note:** *Battery straps and handlers are available at most auto parts stores for a reasonable price. They make it easier to remove and carry the battery.*

6   While the battery is out, inspect the battery tray for corrosion. If corrosion exists, clean the deposits with a mixture of baking soda and water to prevent further corrosion. Flush the area with plenty of clean water and dry thoroughly.

7   If you are replacing the battery, make sure you replace it with a battery with the identical dimensions, amperage rating, cold

3.2 Loosen the negative cable clamp nut (right arrow) and remove the negative battery cable from the negative battery post. Isolate the cable end to prevent it from accidentally coming into contact with the battery post. Loosen the positive cable clamp nut (left arrow) and remove the positive battery cable from the positive battery post

3.4 To remove the battery from the battery tray, remove the battery hold-down clamp bolt (arrow) and clamp, and then lift out the battery

5

4.4a To disconnect the positive battery cable from the starter solenoid terminal, remove this nut (arrow)

4.4b To disconnect the negative battery cable from the engine, remove this bolt (arrow)

cranking rating, etc.

8   When installing the battery, make sure the center notch in the battery foot is aligned with the hold-down clamp hole in the battery tray. Install the hold-down clamp and tighten the bolt securely, but don't over-tighten the bolt.

9   The remainder of installation is the reverse of removal. Connect the positive cable first, then the negative cable.

4   Battery cables - replacement

Refer to illustrations 4.4a and 4.4b

Caution 1: *Some models are equipped with an anti-theft radio. Before performing a procedure that requires disconnecting the battery, make sure you have the activation code.*

Caution 2: *Disconnecting the battery can cause driveability problems. See Section 1 for the use of an auxiliary voltage input device before disconnecting the battery.*

1   Periodically inspect the entire length of each battery cable for damage, cracked or burned insulation and corrosion. Poor battery cable connections can cause starting problems and decreased engine performance.

2   Check the cable-to-terminal connections at the ends of the cables for cracks, loose wire strands and corrosion. The presence of white, fluffy deposits under the insulation at the cable terminal connection is a sign that the cable is corroded and should be replaced. Check the terminals for distortion, missing mounting bolts and corrosion.

3   When removing the cables, always disconnect the negative cable from the negative battery post first and hook it up last or the battery may be shorted by the tool used to loosen the cable clamps. Even if only the positive cable is being replaced, be sure to disconnect the negative cable from the negative battery post first (see Chapter 1 for further information regarding battery cable maintenance).

4   Disconnect the old cables from the battery **(see illustration 3.2)**, then disconnect

the other end of each cable. The positive cable is connected to the starter motor solenoid and the negative cable is connected to one of the transaxle-to-engine bolts **(see illustrations)**. Note the routing of each cable to ensure correct installation.

5   If you are replacing either or both of the battery cables, take them with you when buying new cables. It is vitally important that you replace the cables with identical parts. Cables have characteristics that make them easy to identify: Positive cables are usually red and larger in cross-section; ground cables are usually black and smaller in cross-section.

6   Clean the threads of the starter solenoid or ground connection with a wire brush to remove rust and corrosion. Apply a light coat of battery terminal corrosion inhibitor or petroleum jelly to the threads to prevent future corrosion.

7   Attach the cable to the terminal and tighten the mounting nut/bolt securely.

8   Before connecting a new cable to the battery, make sure that it reaches the battery post without having to be stretched.

9   After installing the cables, connect the negative cable to the negative battery post.

5   Ignition system - general information and precautions

1   The ignition system is designed to ignite the fuel/air charge entering each cylinder at the exact moment for maximum efficiency. It does this by producing a high voltage spark between the electrodes of each spark plug.

2   All models are equipped with a Distributorless Ignition System (DIS). The DIS system is a complete electronically controlled ignition system that does not incorporate a distributor. The DIS system consists of a Camshaft Position (CMP) sensor, an externally mounted ignition coil assembly, the Powertrain Control Module (PCM), the spark plug wires and the spark plugs. The DIS system features a waste-spark method of spark distribution.

Each cylinder is paired with its companion cylinder in the firing order (1-4, 3-2). The cylinder under compression fires simultaneously with its opposing cylinder, which is on the exhaust stroke. Since the cylinder on the exhaust stroke requires very little of the available voltage to fire its plug, the majority of the voltage is used to fire the plug under compression. The system is equipped with one ignition coil pack, containing two separate coils. When either coil is triggered it supplies ignition voltage to two (companion) cylinders simultaneously.

3   This ignition system has no moving parts (no distributor); all engine timing and spark distribution is handled electronically. This system has fewer parts to replace and provides more accurate spark timing than conventional distributor type ignition systems. During engine operation, the PCM receives signals from the CMP sensor to determine the correct spark advance and firing sequence of the ignition coils.

4   When working on the ignition system, take the following precautions:

a) *Do not keep the ignition switch on for more than 10 seconds if the engine will not start.*

b) *Always connect a tachometer in accordance with the manufacturer's instructions. Some tachometers may be incompatible with this ignition system. Consult a dealer service department before buying a tachometer for use with this vehicle.*

c) *Never allow the ignition coil terminals to touch ground. A grounded coil could result in damage to the coil and/or the PCM.*

d) *Do not disconnect the battery when the engine is running.*

6   Ignition system - check

Refer to illustrations 6.2, 6.4, 6.5a, 6.5b and 6.8

1   If a malfunction occurs and the vehicle won't start, do not immediately assume that the ignition system is causing the problem. First, check the following items:

a) *Make sure the battery cable clamps, where they connect to the battery, are clean and tight.*

b) *Test the condition of the battery (see Section 3). If it does not pass all the tests, replace it with a new battery.*

c) *Check the external ignition coil wiring and connections.*

d) *Check the related fuses inside the fuse box (see Chapter 12). If they're burned, determine the cause and repair the circuit.*

2   If the engine turns over but won't start, make sure there is sufficient secondary ignition voltage to fire the spark plug. Disconnect a spark plug wire from one of the spark plugs and attach a calibrated ignition system tester (available at most auto parts stores) to the

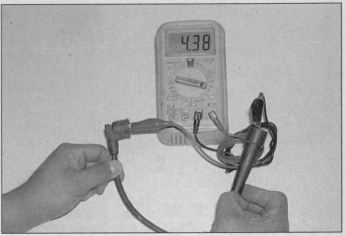

6.2 To use a calibrated ignition tester, disconnect a wire from a spark plug, connect the tester to the spark plug boot, clip the tester to a convenient ground and crank the engine over - if there's enough power to fire the plug, bright blue sparks will be visible between the electrode tip and the tester body (weak sparks or intermittent sparks are the same as no sparks)

6.4 Using an ohmmeter, check each spark plug wire for an open circuit or for high resistance

spark plug boot. Connect the clip on the tester to a bolt or metal bracket on the engine **(see illustration)**.

3   If spark occurs, sufficient voltage is reaching the plug to fire it (repeat the check at the remaining spark plug wires or ignition coils to verify that the spark plug wires, connectors and ignition coils are good). If the ignition system is operating properly the problem lies elsewhere; i.e. a mechanical or fuel system problem. However, the plugs themselves may be fouled, so remove and check them as described in Chapter 1.

4   If no spark occurs, disconnect the spark plug wires from the suspected ignition coil and check the high-tension terminals for damage. Using an ohmmeter, check each plug wire for an open circuit or for high resistance **(see illustration)** and compare your measurement with the values listed in this Chapter's Specifications.

5   Check for battery voltage to the ignition coil with the ignition key turned to ON (engine not running). Disconnect the coil electrical connector and check for power between the following terminals:

a)   *On 1996 through 1999 models, measure voltage between terminal 3 of the coil connector and ground* **(see illustration)**.
b)   *On 2000 models, measure voltage between terminal 1 of the coil connector and ground* **(see illustration 6.5a)**.
c)   *On 2001 models, measure voltage between terminal 2 and ground* **(see illustration)**.

6   Battery voltage should be available with the ignition key turned to ON. If there is no battery voltage present, check the fuses, the wiring and/or the circuit (including the ground side of the circuit) between the fuse box and the ignition coil. **Note:** *For testing and additional information on the ignition system circuits, refer to the wiring diagrams at the end of Chapter 12.*

7   If battery voltage is available to the ignition coil, check the resistance of the primary sides of each coil as follows:

a)   *To check the primary resistance of the coils on 1996 through 2000 models, measure the resistance between terminals 3 and 2 (primary side of the coil for the No. 1 and No. 4 cylinders) and between terminals 3 and 1 (primary side of the coil for the No. 2 and No. 3 cylinders)* **(see illustration 6.5a)**.

b)   *To check the primary resistance of the coils on 2000 models, measure the resistance between terminals 1 and 2 (primary side of the coil for the No. 1 and No. 4 cylinder) and between terminals 1 and 3 (primary side of the coil for cylinders No. 2 and No. 3)* **(see illustration 6.5a)**.
c)   *To check the primary resistance of the coils on 2001 models, measure the resistance between terminals 1 and 2 of each coil* **(see illustration 6.5b)**.

Compare your measurements with the coil primary resistance listed in this Chapter's Specifications. If the secondary resistance is incorrect for either coil, replace the ignition coil assembly.

8   If the primary resistance is okay, check the resistance of the secondary sides of each coil as follows. To check the secondary resistance, unplug the primary (low voltage) electrical connector(s) from the coil, remove the spark plug wires from the coil and then measure the resistance between the high tension terminals for the No. 1 and No. 4 cylinders,

6.5a Ignition coil terminal guide (1996 through 2000 models)

43010-5-6.5B HAYNES

6.5b Ignition coil terminal guide (2001 and later models) (there are two connectors, one for each coil, and they're identical, but be sure to check primary resistance at each connector)

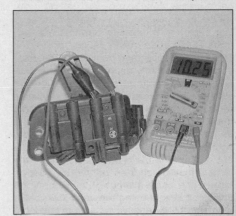

6.8 To check the secondary resistance, measure the resistance between the high tension terminals for the No. 1 and No. 4 cylinders, and for the No. 2 and No. 3 cylinders

5

7.4 To detach the coil assembly from the engine, remove these two bolts (arrows)

and for the No. 2 and No. 3 cylinders **(see illustration). Caution:** *Failure to unplug the coil primary electrical connector(s) before measuring secondary resistance can, if the coil secondary winding is shorted, damage the PCM or other sensitive components in the engine management system.* Compare your measurements with the coil secondary resistance listed in this Chapter's Specifications. If the secondary resistance is incorrect for either coil, replace the ignition coil assembly.

7 Ignition coil - replacement

Refer to illustration 7.4

Caution: *Some models are equipped with an anti-theft radio. Before performing a procedure that requires disconnecting the battery, make sure you have the activation code.*

1 Disconnect the negative battery cable.
2 Unplug the coil electrical connector.
3 Unplug the spark plug wires from the coils (see Chapter 1).
4 Remove the coil mounting bolts **(see illustration)**.
5 Remove the coil assembly.
6 Installation is the reverse of removal.

8 Charging system - general information and precautions

The charging system includes the alternator, an integral voltage regulator, the battery, a fusible link and the wiring between all the components. The charging system supplies electrical power for the ignition system, the lights, the radio, etc. The alternator is driven by a drivebelt at the front of the engine.

The purpose of the voltage regulator is to limit the alternator's voltage to a preset value. This prevents power surges, circuit overloads, etc., during peak voltage output.

The fusible links on these models are essentially higher-amperage fuses, located in the engine compartment fuse/relay box. The alternator fusible link on all models is rated at 100 amps.

The charging system doesn't normally require periodic maintenance. However, the drivebelt, battery and wires and connections should be inspected at specified intervals (see Chapter 1).

The dashboard warning light should come on when the ignition key is turned to Start, then go off immediately. If it remains on, there is a malfunction in the charging system (see Section 9).

Be very careful when making electrical connections to a vehicle equipped with an alternator and note the following:

a) *When reconnecting wires to the alternator from the battery, be sure to note the polarity.*
b) *Before using arc welding equipment to repair any part of the vehicle, disconnect the wires from the alternator and the battery terminals.*
c) *Never start the engine with a battery charger connected.*
d) *Always disconnect both battery leads before using a battery charger.*
e) *The alternator is driven by a drivebelt which could cause serious injury if your hands, hair or clothes become entangled in it with the engine running.*
f) *The alternator is connected directly to the battery, and could arc or cause a fire if overloaded or shorted out.*
g) *Wrap a plastic bag over the alternator and secure it with rubber bands before steam cleaning the engine.*

9 Charging system - check

1 If a malfunction occurs in the charging circuit, do not immediately assume that the alternator is causing the problem. First check the following items:

a) *The battery cables where they connect to the battery. Make sure the connections are clean and tight.*
b) *Check the battery as described in Section 3. If the battery is defective, replace the battery.*
c) *Check the external alternator wiring and connections.*
d) *Check the drivebelt condition and tension (see Chapter 1).*

e) *Check the alternator mounting bolts for tightness.*
f) *Run the engine and check the alternator for abnormal noise.*

2 The charging system warning light on the instrument cluster should illuminate when the ignition key is switched on and go off when the engine is running.
3 If the warning light does not illuminate when the ignition key is switched on, switch the ignition off and disconnect the wiring connector from the alternator (do not disconnect the large output wire). Connect the black wire terminal in the harness connector to a good engine ground point using a jumper wire and switch the ignition on. The warning light should illuminate - if it doesn't, there is an open circuit in the black wire between the alternator and the instrument cluster, or the instrument cluster is defective.
4 If the warning light illuminates, replace the alternator.
5 If the warning light is illuminated with the engine running, switch the engine off and disconnect the wiring connector from the alternator (do not disconnect the large output wire). Switch the ignition on and check the warning light. If the warning light is still on, the black wire from the alternator to the instrument cluster is grounded or the instrument cluster is defective. If the warning light went out, switch the ignition off, reconnect the connector and proceed with the charging system check.
6 Connect a voltmeter to the positive and negative battery terminals. Check the battery voltage with the engine off. It should be approximately 12.4 to 12.6 volts if the battery is fully charged.
7 Start the engine and check the battery voltage again. It should now be greater than the voltage recorded in Step 2, but not more than 14.5 volts. Turn On all the vehicle accessories (air conditioning, rear window defogger, blower motor, etc.) and increase the engine speed to 2000 rpm - the voltage should not drop below the voltage recorded in Step 2.
8 If the indicated voltage is greater than the specified charging voltage, replace the alternator (see Section 10).
9 If the indicated voltage reading is less than the specified charging voltage, the alternator is probably defective. Have the charging system checked at a dealer service department or other properly equipped repair facility. **Note:** *Many auto parts stores will bench test an alternator off the vehicle. Refer to your local auto parts store regarding their policy, many will perform this service free of charge.*

10 Alternator - removal and installation

Caution: *Some models are equipped with an anti-theft radio. Before performing a procedure that requires disconnecting the battery, make sure you have the activation code.*

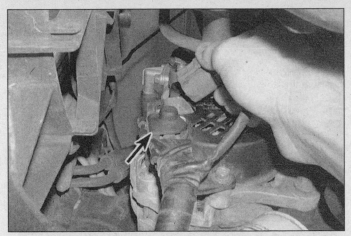

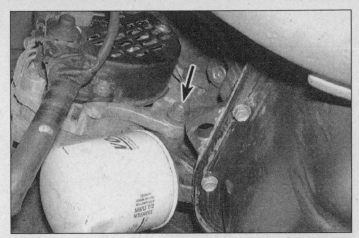

10.3 Unplug the big electrical connector from the alternator, remove the rubber plug (arrow) from the B+ terminal and then disconnect the wire from the B+ terminal

10.4a Loosen the alternator lower mounting nut (arrow) . . .

Removal

Refer to illustrations 10.3, 10.4a and 10.4b

1   Disconnect the cable from the negative terminal of the battery.

2   Raise the vehicle and support it securely on jack stands.

3   Disconnect the wire harness from the alternator electrical connections **(see illustration)**.

4   Loosen the alternator lower mounting bolt **(see illustration)**. Working from above, loosen the upper adjustment lockbolt **(see illustration)**, back off the adjustment bolt, swivel the alternator toward the engine and then release the drivebelt from the alternator pulley.

5   Unscrew and remove the alternator upper and lower mounting bolts and washers, then remove the alternator from its mounting bracket.

Installation

6   If you are replacing the alternator, take the old one with you when purchasing a new unit. Make sure the new/rebuilt unit looks identical to the old alternator. Look at the terminals - they should be the same in number, size and location as the terminals on the old alternator. Finally, look at the identification numbers - they will be stamped into the housing or printed on a tag attached to the housing. Make sure the numbers are the same on both alternators.

7   Many new/rebuilt alternators DO NOT have a pulley installed, so you may have to switch the pulley from the old unit to the new/rebuilt one. When buying an alternator, find out the shop's policy regarding pulleys - some shops will perform this service free of charge.

8   Installation is the reverse of removal. Tension the auxiliary drivebelt (see Chapter 1) and tighten the alternator mounting bolts to the torque listed in this Chapter's Specifications.

11 Starting system - general information and precautions

The starting system consists of the battery, the starter motor, the starter solenoid and the wires connecting them. The solenoid is mounted directly on the starter motor.

The solenoid/starter motor assembly is bolted to the transaxle bellhousing.

When the ignition key is turned to the Start position, the starter solenoid is actuated through the starter control circuit. The starter solenoid then connects the battery to the starter. The battery supplies the electrical energy to the starter motor, which does the actual work of cranking the engine.

The starter motor on a vehicle equipped with a manual transmission can only be operated when the clutch pedal is depressed; the starter on a vehicle equipped with an automatic transmission can only be operated when the transmission selector lever is in Park or Neutral.

Always observe the following precautions when working on the starting system:

a) *Excessive cranking of the starter motor can overheat it and cause serious damage. Never operate the starter motor for more than 15 seconds at a time without pausing to allow it to cool for at least two minutes.*

b) *The starter is connected directly to the battery and could arc or cause a fire if mishandled, overloaded or shorted out.*

c) *Always detach the cable from the negative terminal of the battery before working on the starting system.*

12 Starter motor and circuit - check

Refer to illustration 12.4

1   If a malfunction occurs in the starting circuit, do not immediately assume that the starter is causing the problem. First, check

10.4b . . . loosen the upper adjustment lockbolt (right arrow), back off the adjustment bolt (lower arrow) and then swivel the alternator toward the engine to release the drivebelt

the following items:

a) *Make sure the battery cable clamps, where they connect to the battery, are clean and tight.*

b) *Check the condition of the battery cables (see Section 4). Replace any defective battery cables with new parts.*

c) *Test the condition of the battery (see Section 3). If it does not pass all the tests, replace it with a new battery.*

d) *Check the starter motor wiring and connections.*

e) *Check the starter motor mounting bolts for tightness.*

f) *Check the related fuses in the fuse box (see Chapter 12). If they're blown, determine the cause and repair the circuit.*

g) *Check the ignition switch circuit for correct operation (see Chapter 12).*

h) *Check the starter relay (see Chapter 12).*

i) *Check the operation of the Park/Neutral position switch (see Chapter 7B) or the clutch start switch (see Chapter 8). These systems must operate correctly to provide battery voltage to the starter solenoid.*

5

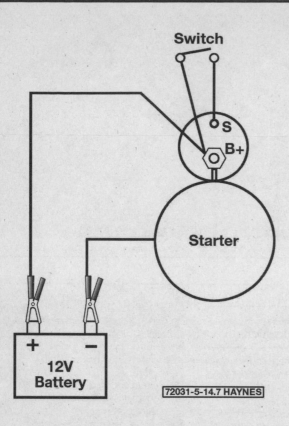

12.4 Starter motor bench testing details

13.5 To disconnect the electrical harness from the starter solenoid, unplug the connector (left arrow) for the starter switch and then unscrew the nut (right arrow) and disconnect the battery cable

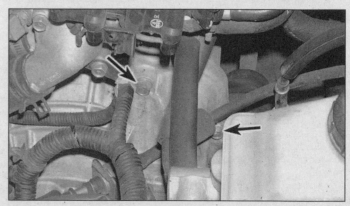

13.6 To detach the starter motor, remove these two mounting bolts (arrows) (2000 and earlier models shown)

2   If the starter does not activate when the ignition switch is turned to the start position, check for battery voltage to the starter solenoid. This will determine if the solenoid is receiving the correct voltage from the ignition switch. Install a 12-volt test light or a voltmeter to the starter solenoid terminal. While an assistant turns the ignition switch to the start position, observe the test light or voltmeter. The test light should shine brightly or battery voltage should be indicated on the voltmeter. If voltage is not available to the starter solenoid, refer to the wiring diagrams in Chapter 12 and check the fuses, switches and starter relay in series with the starting system. If voltage is available but there is no movement from the starter motor, remove the starter from the engine (see Section 13) and bench test the starter (see Step 4).

3   If the starter turns over slowly, check the starter cranking voltage and the current draw from the battery. This test must be performed with the starter assembly on the engine. Crank the engine over (for 10 seconds or less) and observe the battery voltage. It should not drop below 8.5 volts. Also, observe the current draw using an ammeter. Typically a starter amperage draw should not exceed 200 amps. If the starter motor amperage draw is excessive, have it tested by a dealer service department or other qualified repair shop. There are several conditions that

may affect the starter cranking potential. The battery must be in good condition and the battery cold-cranking rating must not be underrated for the particular application. Be sure to check the battery specifications carefully. The battery terminals and cables must be clean and not corroded. Also, in cases of extreme cold temperatures, make sure the battery and/or engine block is warmed before performing the tests.

4   If the starter is receiving voltage but does not activate, remove and check the starter motor assembly on the bench. Most likely the starter motor or solenoid is defective. In some rare cases, the engine may be seized so be sure to try and rotate the crankshaft pulley (see Chapter 2A or 2B) before proceeding. With the starter assembly mounted in a vise on the bench, install one jumper cable from the positive terminal of a test battery to the B+ terminal on the starter. Install another jumper cable from the negative terminal of the battery to the body of the starter **(see illustration)**. Install a starter switch and apply battery voltage to the solenoid S terminal (for 10 seconds or less) and observe the solenoid plunger, shift lever and overrunning clutch extend and rotate the pinion drive. If the pinion drive extends but does not rotate, the solenoid is operating but the starter motor is defective. If there is no movement but the solenoid clicks, the

solenoid and/or the starter motor is defective. If the solenoid plunger extends and rotates the pinion drive, the starter assembly is operating properly.

13 Starter motor - removal and installation

Refer to illustrations 13.5 and 13.6

1   Disconnect the cable from the negative terminal of the battery.

2   If you're working on a 2000 or earlier model, remove the air intake duct and the air cleaner assembly (see Chapter 4).

3   If you're working on a 2001 or later model, detach the shift cable(s) from the transaxle.

4   Disconnect the speedometer cable from the transaxle (see Chapter 7).

5   Unscrew the nut and disconnect the battery cable from the starter motor, then disconnect the wiring from the solenoid **(see illustration)**.

6   Remove the starter motor mounting bolts **(see illustration)**, supporting the starter motor as the bolts are removed, and remove the starter motor.

7   Installation is the reverse of removal. Tighten the starter mounting bolts to the torque listed in this Chapter's Specifications.

Chapter 6
Emissions and engine control systems

Contents

6

Specifications

Acceleration sensor output voltage	
2000 and earlier models	
At idle..	2.3 to 2.7 volts
While driving	0.5 to 4.5 volts
2001 and later models	
At idle..	2.3 to 2.7 volts
While driving	1.3 to 3.5 volts
Camshaft Position (CMP) sensor output voltage	
At idle (800 rpm)	0 to 5 volts
At 3000 rpm..	0 to 5 volts
Crankshaft Position (CKP) sensor resistance	486 to 594 ohms, at 68-degrees F (20-degrees C)
Engine coolant sensor (ECT) sensor resistance	
At -22 degrees F (-30 degrees C)......................................	22.22 to 31.78 k-ohms
At 14-degrees F (-10 degrees C)..	8.16 to 10.74 k-ohms
At 32-degrees F (0-degrees C)...	5.18 to 6.60 k-ohms
At 68-degrees F (20-degrees C)...	2.27 to 2.73 k-ohms
At 104-degrees F (40-degrees C).......................................	1.059 to 1.281 k-ohms
At 140-degrees F (60-degrees C).......................................	0.538 to 0.650 k-ohms
At 176-degrees F (80-degrees C).......................................	0.298 to 0.322 k-ohms
At 194-degrees F (90-degrees C).......................................	0.219 to 0.243 k-ohms
Fuel Tank Pressure (FTP) sensor output voltage (under acceleration)....	0.5 minimum, 4.5 volts maximum
Heated Oxygen Sensor (HO2S) heater resistance	30 ohms or more (at normal operating temperature)
Idle Speed Control (ISC) actuator resistance (at 68-degrees F [20-degrees C])	
Across terminals 1 and 2..	10.5 to 14 ohms
Across terminals 2 and 3..	10 to 12.5 ohms

Intake Air Temperature (IAT) sensor output voltage (1996 through 2000)
  At 32-degrees F (0-degrees C) .... 3.3 to 3.7 volts
  At 68-degrees F (20-degrees C) .... 2.4 to 2.8 volts
  At 104-degrees F (40-degrees C) .... 1.6 to 2.0 volts
  At 176-degrees F (80-degrees C) .... 0.5 to 0.9 volt
Intake Air Temperature (IAT) sensor resistance (2001 and later models)
  At 32-degrees F (0-degrees C) .... 4.5 to 7.5 ohms
  At 68-degrees F (20-degrees C) .... 2.0 to 3.0 ohms
  At 104-degrees F (40-degrees C) .... 0.7 to 1.6 ohms
  At 176-degrees F (80-degrees C) .... 0.2 to 0.4 ohms
Knock sensor resistance .... Approximately 5 M-ohms at 68-degrees F (20-degrees C)
Manifold Absolute Pressure (MAP) sensor output voltage (2001 and later models)
  Ignition switch ON (engine not running) .... 4 to 5 volts
  Engine running, at idle .... 0.4 to 2.0 volts
Mass Air Flow (MAF) sensor output voltage
  At idle .... 0.7 to 1.1 volt
  At 3,000 rpm .... 1.3 to 2.0 volts
Throttle position sensor resistance .... 700 to 3,000 ohms

Torque specifications

	Ft-lbs (unless otherwise indicated)	Nm
Crankshaft Position (CKP) sensor bolt	74 to 97 in-lbs	9 to 11
Engine Coolant Temperature (ECT) sensor		
1996 through 2000 models	132 to 168 in-lbs	15 to 20
2001 and later models	15 to 30	20 to 40
Heated oxygen sensor (HO2S)	37 to 44	50 to 60
Knock sensor bolt	144 to 228 in-lbs	16 to 28
Throttle Position Sensor (TPS) screws	14 to 21 in-lbs	1.5 to 2.5

1.1 Typical emission and engine control system components

1   Idle Speed Control (ISC) actuator
2   Positive Crankcase Ventilation (PCV) valve
3   Throttle Position Sensor (TPS)
4   Mass Air Flow (MAF) sensor
5   Intake Air Temperature (IAT) sensor
6   Engine Coolant Temperature (ECT) sensor
7   Camshaft Position (CMP) sensor (on back side of cylinder head)

1.7a The Vehicle Emission Control Information (VECI) label is located in the engine compartment and contains information on the emission devices on your vehicle

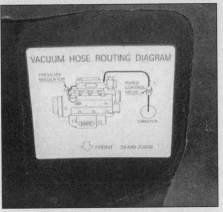

1.7b Vacuum hose routing diagram of the emissions system vacuum hoses

1 General information

Refer to illustrations 1.1, 1.7a and 1.7b

To prevent pollution of the atmosphere from incompletely burned and evaporating gases, and to maintain good driveability and fuel economy, a number of emission control systems and devices are incorporated **(see illustration)**. They include the:

Electronic engine control system: Powertrain Control Module (PCM), information sensors and output actuators
Catalytic converter
Evaporative emission control system
Positive Crankcase Ventilation (PCV) system

All of these systems are linked, directly or indirectly, to the emission control system.

The Sections in this Chapter include general descriptions, checking procedures within the scope of the home mechanic (when possible) and component replacement procedures for each of the systems listed above.

Before assuming that an emissions control system is malfunctioning, check the fuel and ignition systems carefully. The diagnosis of some emission control devices requires specialized tools, equipment and training. If checking and servicing become too difficult or if a procedure is beyond your ability, consult a dealer service department or other properly equipped repair facility. Remember, the most frequent cause of emissions problems is simply a loose or broken vacuum hose or wire, so always check the hose and wiring connections first.

This doesn't mean, however, that emission control systems are particularly difficult to maintain and repair. You can quickly and easily perform many checks and service procedures at home with common test equipment and hand tools. **Note:** *Because of a Federally mandated warranty which covers the emission control system components, check with your dealer about warranty coverage before working on any emissions-related systems. Once the warranty has expired, you may wish to perform some of the component checks and/or replacement procedures in this Chapter to save money.*

Pay close attention to any special precautions outlined in this Chapter. It should be noted that the illustrations of the various systems may not exactly match the system installed on the vehicle you're working on because of changes made by the manufacturer during production or from year-to-year.

A Vehicle Emissions Control Information (VECI) label and a vacuum hose routing diagram are located in the engine compartment **(see illustrations)**. The VECI label contains important emissions specifications and adjustment information. When servicing the engine or emissions systems, the VECI label in your particular vehicle should always be checked for up-to-date information.

2 On-Board Diagnostic (OBD) system and trouble codes

Diagnostic tool information

Refer to illustrations 2.1 and 2.2

1 Use a digital multimeter **(see illustration)** to check fuel injection and emission components. When working with electronic circuits, many of which are very low voltage (5 volts or less), an accurate reading is essential. Most analog multimeters can't measure volts, ohms or amps to two or three decimal places (and the few that can are difficult to read), yet even an inexpensive digital multimeter can easily make accurate measurements to two or three decimal places. That's because digital multimeters are equipped with internal circuitry of very high resistance (usually 10 million ohms). A voltmeter is hooked up in parallel with the circuit being tested, so it is critical that none of the voltage being measured be allowed to travel through the parallel path set up by the meter itself. This problem doesn't occur when measuring larger amounts of voltage (9- to 12-volt circuits), but if you are measuring a low-voltage circuit - oxygen sensor signal voltage, for example - a fraction of a volt is significant when diagnosing a problem.

2 Hand-held scanners **(see illustration)** are powerful and versatile tools for analyzing engine management systems used on later model vehicles. A scan tool must be compatible with (be able to communicate with) the

6

2.1 Digital multimeters can be used for testing all types of circuits; because of their high impedance, they are much more accurate than analog meters for measuring low-voltage computer circuits

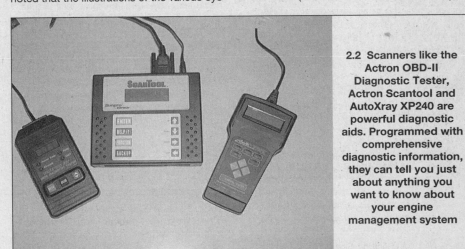

2.2 Scanners like the Actron OBD-II Diagnostic Tester, Actron Scantool and AutoXray XP240 are powerful diagnostic aids. Programmed with comprehensive diagnostic information, they can tell you just about anything you want to know about your engine management system

PCM of the vehicle you are servicing. Some scan tools - the generic, usually less expensive units that most readers will buy - are designed to be compatible with a specific year, make and model. More expensive professional units can accept interchangeable cartridges which allow one scan tool to interface with a manufacturer (Ford, GM, Chrysler, etc.). Some scan tools accept cartridges that enable the tool to be compatible with all vehicles manufactured in a country or geographic region (Germany, Japan or the USA, for example; or Asia, Europe, etc.).

3   A somewhat more sophisticated scan tool is needed to access a vehicle equipped with the Federally-mandated On-Board Diagnostics-II (OBD-II) system (which applies to all of the vehicles covered by this manual). Several tool manufacturers have already introduced relatively inexpensive generic OBD-II scan tools for the home mechanic. Ask the parts salesman at a local auto parts store for additional information concerning availability and cost.

On-Board Diagnostic system general description

4   All models described in this manual are equipped with the On-Board Diagnostic (OBD-II) system. The OBD-II system consists of an on-board computer, known as the Powertrain Control Module (PCM), information sensors and output actuators. The PCM is calibrated to optimize the emissions, fuel economy and driveability of the specific vehicle in which it's installed.

5   The information sensors monitor various functions of the engine and send data to the PCM. Comparing this incoming data to its "map" (the program stored in the computer's memory), the PCM constantly alters the operating conditions of the engine (spark timing, fuel injection pulse width, etc.) through an array of relays, solenoids and other output actuators.

6   Because of a Federally mandated warranty which covers the emissions system components, and because any owner-induced damage to the PCM, the sensors and/or the control devices could void the warranty, it isn't a good idea to attempt diagnosis or replacement of the PCM at home while the vehicle is under warranty. Take the vehicle to a dealer service department if the PCM or a system component malfunctions.

Information sensors

7   **Acceleration sensor** – The acceleration sensor prevents the PCM from incorrectly identifying a misfire when the vehicle is being driven over a rough road.

8   **Camshaft Position (CMP) sensor** - The camshaft position sensor provides information on camshaft position. The PCM uses this information, along with the engine speed sensor information, to control the ignition timing and fuel injection synchronization.

9   **Crankshaft Position (CKP) Sensor** - The CKP sensor senses crankshaft position

(TDC) during each engine revolution. The PCM uses this information to control the ignition system.

10   **Engine Coolant Temperature (ECT) sensor** - The ECT sensor senses engine coolant temperature. The PCM uses this information to control fuel injection duration and ignition timing.

11   **Heated Oxygen Sensor (HO2S)** - The oxygen sensors generate a voltage signal that varies with the difference between the oxygen content of the exhaust and the oxygen in the surrounding air. All vehicles covered by this manual are equipped with two oxygen sensors, an upstream HO2S and a downstream HO2S. The PCM uses the signal from the upstream HO2S to determine whether the fuel system is running rich or lean; it uses the signal from the downstream HO2S to determine whether the catalytic converter is doing its job. Both HO2S units are heated, in order to reach their normal operating temperature as quickly as possible.

12   **Idle switch** - Used only on models with an automatic transaxle, the idle switch signals the PCM when the throttle is in the fully closed position. The PCM uses this information to control the engine idle speed.

13   **Intake Air Temperature (IAT) sensor** - The IAT sensor senses the temperature of the air entering the intake manifold. The PCM uses this information to control fuel injection duration.

14   **Knock sensor** - The knock sensor is a piezoelectric element that detects engine detonation or "pinging." The PCM supplies a voltage signal to the knock sensor. When the block vibrates, it applies pressure to the piezoelectric element, which varies its voltage output back to the PCM in accordance with the change in pressure. The PCM uses this variable voltage signal from the knock sensor to identify detonation, and responds by retarding the spark advance to avoid engine damage.

15   **Manifold Absolute Pressure(MAP)/Intake Air Temperature (IAT) sensor** - Used on 2001 and later models, the MAP/IAT sensor combines the functions of MAP and IAT sensors into one component. A MAP sensor measures intake manifold pressure and vacuum on the absolute scale (zero psi, instead of 14.7 psi). (There is no MAF sensor on these models.)

16   **Mass Air Flow (MAF) sensor** - The MAF sensor measures the mass of the air entering the engine. It does this by monitoring the heat transfer from a hot film probe installed across the stream of air flowing through the sensor. As the air flow through the sensor increases or decreases, it alters the amount of heat transferred from the hot film probe surface to the air flow. As the heat transfer changes, so does the resistance of the hot film probe. A 5-volt control signal from the PCM is supplied to the hot-film probe. The reference signal (the output) from the hot film probe back to the PCM varies in accordance with the resistance of the hot film probe. Think of the hot film probe as a vari-

able resistor whose resistance is proportional to the air flow. The PCM uses this information to control fuel delivery.

17   **Throttle Position Sensor (TPS)** - The throttle position sensor senses throttle movement and position. This signal enables the PCM to determine when the throttle is closed, in a cruise position, or wide open. The PCM uses this information to control fuel delivery and ignition timing. The throttle position sensor is a component of the throttle control module.

18   **Vehicle Speed Sensor (VSS)** - The vehicle speed sensor provides information to the PCM to indicate vehicle speed. On 1996 through 2000 models, the Vehicle Speed Sensor (VSS), which is an integral part of the speedometer, is a magnetic pick-up coil that converts the transaxle gear revolutions into a pulsing AC voltage output to the PCM. The VSS emits four pulses per revolution of the cable. On 2001 and later models, the VSS is a Hall effect switch located at the speedometer driven gear on the transaxle. On these models, the VSS converts the rotations of the driven gear into an on-off voltage signal to the PCM.

Output actuators

19   **Check Engine light** - The PCM will illuminate the Check Engine light if a malfunction in the electronic engine control system occurs.

20   **EVAP Canister Close Valve (CCV)** - The EVAP CCV seals off the canister when instructed to do so by the PCM.

21   **EVAP canister purge valve solenoid** - The evaporative emission canister purge valve solenoid is operated by the PCM to purge the fuel vapor canister and route fuel vapor to the intake manifold for combustion.

22   **Fuel injectors** - The PCM opens the fuel injectors individually in firing order sequence. The PCM also controls the time the injector is held open (pulse width). The pulse width of the injector (measured in milliseconds) determines the amount of fuel delivered. For more information on the fuel delivery system and the fuel injectors, including injector replacement, refer to Chapter 4.

23   **Fuel pump control relay** - The fuel pump control relay controls the fuel pump circuit. When the ignition switch is turned to the ON position, the relay is activated momentarily by the PCM, in order to energize the fuel pump so that it can pressurize the system fuel line. The fuel pump control relay is always activated by the PCM when the ignition switch is in the START or RUN position. For more information on fuel pump check and replacement, refer to Chapter 4.

24   **Fuel Tank Pressure (FTP) sensor** - The FTP sensor monitors the pressure inside the fuel tank.

25   **Ignition coils** - The PCM controls spark delivery and ignition timing depending on engine operation conditions. Refer to Chapter 5 for more information on the ignition system.

26 **MFI control relay** - The MFI control relay controls the fuel injector circuit. The MFI control relay is always activated by the PCM when the ignition switch is in the START or RUN position.

27 **Heated Oxygen Sensor (HO2S) heaters** - All HO2S units are equipped with a heating element. Heating the HO2S allows it to reach operating temperature quickly. The PCM controls these heaters.

Obtaining diagnostic trouble codes

Refer to illustration 2.30

Note: *The diagnostic trouble codes on all models can only be extracted from the Powertrain Control Module (PCM) using a specialized scan tool. Have the vehicle diagnosed by a dealer service department or other qualified automotive repair facility if the proper scan tool is not available.*

28 The PCM monitors the circuits of most of the information sensors and actuators described above. When a malfunction is detected in one of these circuits, a trouble code is "set" (stored) in the PCM.

29 The PCM also illuminates the CHECK ENGINE light (also known as the Malfunction Indicator Lamp, or MIL) when it stores a trouble code. The MIL is located on the instrument cluster. The MIL will remain illuminated

2.30 The diagnostic connector (arrow) is located under the dash

until the problem is repaired and the code is cleared or the PCM does not detect any malfunction for several consecutive drive cycles.

30 The diagnostic trouble codes for the On-Board Diagnostic (OBD) system can only be extracted from the PCM using a scan tool, which interfaces with the OBD system by plugging into the diagnostic connector **(see illustration).**

Clearing diagnostic trouble codes

31 After the system has been repaired, the codes must be cleared from the PCM memory using a scan tool. Do not attempt to clear the codes by disconnecting battery power. If battery power is disconnected from the PCM, the PCM will lose the current engine operating parameters and driveability will suffer until the PCM is programmed with a scan tool.

32 Always clear the codes from the PCM before starting the engine after a new electronic emission control component is installed onto the engine. The PCM stores the operating parameters of each sensor. The PCM may set a trouble code if a new sensor is allowed to operate before the parameters from the old sensor have been erased.

Diagnostic trouble code identification

33 The accompanying list of diagnostic trouble codes is a compilation of all the codes that may be encountered using a generic scan tool. Additional trouble codes may be available with the use of the manufacturer specific scan tool. Not all codes pertain to all models and not all codes will illuminate the Check Engine light when set. All models require a scan tool to access the diagnostic trouble codes.

Trouble codes

Code	Code Identification
P0030 (2001 and later models)	Oxygen sensor heater circuit malfunction (bank 1, sensor 1), plausibility check
P0036 (2001 and later models)	Oxygen sensor heater circuit malfunction (bank 1, sensor 2), plausibility check
P0102	Mass air flow sensor circuit, low input
P0103	Mass air flow sensor circuit, high input
P0105 (2001 and later models)	Manifold absolute pressure circuit malfunction
P0106 (2001 and later models)	Manifold absolute pressure circuit range/performance problem
P0110 (2001 and later models)	Intake air temperature circuit malfunction
P0112	Intake air temperature circuit, low input
P0113	Intake air temperature circuit, high input
P0115 (2001 and later models)	Engine coolant temperature circuit malfunction
P0116	Engine coolant temperature circuit, range or performance problem
P0117	Engine coolant temperature circuit, low input
P0118	Engine coolant temperature circuit, high input
P0120 (2001 and later models)	Throttle position sensor circuit malfunction
P0121	Throttle position sensor circuit, range or performance problem
P0122	Throttle position sensor circuit, low input
P0123	Throttle position sensor circuit, high input
P0125	Insufficient coolant temperature for closed loop fuel control
P0128 (2001 and later models)	Engine coolant thermostat malfunction

6

Trouble codes (continued)

Code	Code Identification
P0130	Oxygen sensor circuit malfunction (pre-converter sensor)
P0131	Oxygen sensor circuit, low voltage (pre-converter sensor)
P0132	Oxygen sensor circuit, high voltage (pre-converter sensor)
P0133	Oxygen sensor circuit, slow response (pre-converter sensor)
P0134	Oxygen sensor circuit, no activity detected (pre-converter sensor)
P0135	Oxygen sensor heater circuit malfunction (pre-converter sensor)
P0136	Oxygen sensor circuit malfunction (post-converter sensor)
P0137	Oxygen sensor circuit, low voltage (post-converter sensor)
P0138	Oxygen sensor circuit, high voltage (post-converter sensor)
P0139 (2001 and later models)	Oxygen sensor circuit, slow response (post-converter sensor)
P0140 (2001 and later models)	Oxygen sensor circuit, no activity detected (post-converter sensor)
P0141	Oxygen sensor heater circuit malfunction (post-converter sensor)
P0170 (2001 and later models)	Fuel trim malfunction
P0201	Injector circuit malfunction, cylinder No. 1
P0202	Injector circuit malfunction, cylinder No. 2
P0203	Injector circuit malfunction, cylinder No. 3
P0204	Injector circuit malfunction, cylinder No. 4
P0230 (2001 and later models)	Fuel pump circuit malfunction
P0300	Random/multiple cylinder misfire detected
P0301	Cylinder no. 1 misfire detected
P0302	Cylinder no. 2 misfire detected
P0303	Cylinder no. 3 misfire detected
P0304	Cylinder no. 4 misfire detected
P0325 (2001 and later models)	Knock sensor circuit malfunction
P0326	Knock sensor circuit, range problem
P0335	Crankshaft position sensor circuit malfunction
P0336	Crankshaft position sensor circuit, range problem
P0340 (2001 and later models)	Camshaft position sensor circuit malfunction
P0342	Camshaft position sensor circuit, low input
P0343	Camshaft position sensor circuit, high input
P0351 (2001 and later models)	Ignition coil A primary/secondary circuit malfunction
P0352 (2001 and later models)	Ignition coil B primary/secondary circuit malfunction
P0353 (2001 and later models)	Ignition coil C primary/secondary circuit malfunction
P0354 (2001 and later models)	Ignition coil D primary/secondary circuit malfunction
P0422	Catalyst system efficiency below threshold
P0440 (2001 and later models)	Evaporative emission control system malfunction
P0441	Evaporative emission control system, purge valve stuck open
P0442	Evaporative emission control system, small leak detected
P0443	Evaporative emission control system, PCSV circuit malfunction
P0444	Evaporative emission control system, purge control valve circuit open
P0445	Evaporative emission control system, purge control valve circuit shorted

Trouble codes (continued)

Code	Code Identification
P0446	Evaporative emission control system, canister close valve stuck closed
P0446 (2001 and later models)	Evaporative emission control system, vent control problem
P0447	Evaporative emission control system, ventilation control valve circuit shorted to ground
P0448	Evaporative emission control system, ventilation control valve circuit shorted to battery voltage
P0450 (2001 and later models)	Evaporative emission control system, pressure sensor malfunction
P0451	Evaporative emission control system, pressure sensor range/performance problem
P0452	Evaporative emission control system, pressure sensor signal low
P0453	Evaporative emission control system, pressure sensor signal high
P0454 (2001 and later models)	Evaporative emission control system, pressure sensor intermittent malfunction
P0455	Evaporative emission control system, incorrect purge flow
P0456	Evaporative emission control system, small leak detected
P0501	Vehicle speed sensor circuit, range or performance problem
P0506	Idle control system, rpm lower than expected
P0507 (2001 and later models)	Idle control system, rpm higher than expected
P0560 (2001 and later models)	System voltage malfunction
P0600 (2001 and later models)	Serial communication link malfunction
P0605 (2001 and later models)	PCM - self-test failure

3   Powertrain Control Module (PCM) - removal and installation

Refer to illustrations 3.4 and 3.5

1   Check to see if there are any trouble codes stored in the PCM (see Section 2). Any codes stored in the PCM will be erased when the PCM is disconnected.

2   Disconnect the negative battery cable.

3   Remove the knee bolster (see Chapter 11).

4   Locate the PCM **(see illustration)**.

5   Swing down the PCM mounting bracket (it pivots from the right), pull down the PCM **(see illustration)** and then disconnect the electrical connector from the PCM.

6   Remove the PCM.

7   Installation is the reverse of removal.

4   Mass Air Flow (MAF) sensor - check and replacement

Note: *This procedure applies to 2000 and earlier models only.*

Check

Refer to illustrations 4.1 and 4.2

1   The MAF sensor **(see illustration)** is located in the intake duct between the air

6

3.4 The PCM is mounted near the fuse box; to remove the PCM, pull down on the mounting bracket (arrow), which pivots from the right end . . .

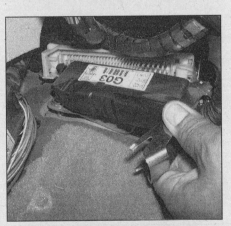

3.5 . . . pull down the PCM, then disconnect the electrical connector and remove the PCM

4.1 The MAF sensor is located in the intake duct between the air cleaner housing and the throttle body; to remove it, simply loosen the hose clamp screws (arrows)

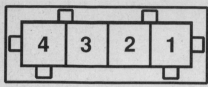

MASS AIR FLOW CONNECTOR

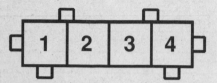

HARNESS SIDE CONNECTOR

43010-6-4.2 HAYNES

4.2 MAF sensor electrical connector terminal guide

4.3 To unplug the electrical connector from the MAF sensor, depress the wire retainer with your thumb and pull

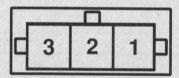

KNOCK SENSOR SIDE CONNECTOR

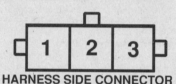

HARNESS SIDE CONNECTOR

43010-6-5.2 HAYNES

5.2 Knock sensor electrical connector terminal guide (1996 through 2000 model connector shown; 2001 model connector has only two terminals)

5.1 The knock sensor (arrow) is located on the front of the block; to detach the sensor from the block, remove the sensor retaining bolt

6.1 On 1996 through 2000 models, the Intake Air Temperature (IAT) sensor (arrow) is located on the air cleaner housing (on 2001 models, it's located on the air intake plenum, and is integrated with the MAP sensor)

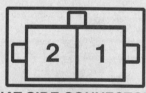

IAT SIDE CONNECTOR

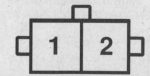

HARNESS SIDE CONNECTOR

43010-6-6.2 HAYNES

6.2 Intake Air Temperature (IAT) sensor electrical connector terminal guide (1996 through 2000 models)

cleaner housing and the throttle body.

2   Without disconnecting the MAF sensor electrical connector, backprobe terminal 1 of the MAF sensor side of the connector **(see illustration)** with a suitable probe and connect a voltmeter. Check the output voltage at idle and then check it at 3,000 rpm. Compare your measurement with the voltage values listed in this Chapter's Specifications. If the MAF sensor output voltage varies greatly from the specified values, replace it.

Replacement

Refer to illustration 4.3

3   Unplug the MAF sensor electrical connector **(see illustration)**.

4   Loosen the hose clamps **(see illustration 4.1)** and remove the MAF from the intake duct.

5   Installation is the reverse of removal.

5   Knock sensor - check and replacement

Check

Refer to illustration 5.1 and 5.2

1   The knock sensor **(see illustration)** is mounted on the front of the engine cylinder block.

2   Disconnect the electrical connector and using an ohmmeter, measure the knock sensor resistance. On 1996 through 2000 models, measure the resistance between terminals 2 and 3 on the sensor side of the connector **(see illustration)**. On 2001 models, the knock sensor connector has only two terminals - measure the resistance between them. Compare your measurement to the knock sensor resistance listed in this Chapter's Specifications. If the indicated resistance is lower than the specified resistance, replace the knock sensor.

Replacement

Refer to illustration

3   Unplug the knock sensor electrical con-

nector.

4   Remove the knock sensor retaining bolt **(see illustration 5.1)**.

5   Remove the knock sensor from the engine cylinder block.

6   Installation is the reverse of removal.

6   Intake Air Temperature (IAT) sensor - check and replacement

Check

Refer to illustrations 6.1 and 6.2

1   On 1996 through 2000 models, the IAT sensor **(see illustration)** is located on the air cleaner housing. On 2001 models, it's mounted on the air intake plenum, and is integral with the MAP sensor. The check and replacement procedure for the 2001 type MAP/IAT sensor is in Section 14.

2   Backprobe terminal 1 of the IAT sensor electrical connector **(see illustration)** with a suitable probe, such as a paper clip or a piece of wire, and then hook up the positive lead of a voltmeter to the backprobe and clip the negative lead to a suitable ground. Remove the IAT sensor from the air cleaner

6.3a To unplug the electrical connector from the IAT sensor, first pry up the wire retainer . . .

6.3b . . . and then pull off the connector

6.4 To remove the IAT sensor from the air cleaner housing, simply pry it out of its rubber grommet; while the IAT sensor is removed, inspect the grommet for cracks

housing (see below) but don't unplug the sensor electrical connector. Using a hair dryer to heat up the sensor and a digital pyrometer or a suitable thermometer (such as a cooking thermometer) to measure the temperature of the hot air passing over the sensor, turn the ignition switch to ON and measure the output voltage of the sensor as it

7.2 To release the electrical connector from the TPS, push in on the wire retainer

heats up. Compare your measurements to the IAT sensor output voltage listed in this Chapter's Specifications. If the IAT sensor doesn't operate as described, replace it.

Replacement

Refer to illustrations 6.3a, 6.3b and 6.4

3   Unplug the IAT sensor electrical connector **(see illustrations)**.
4   To remove the IAT sensor from the air cleaner housing, simply pry it out of the rubber grommet **(see illustration)**.
5   Before installing the IAT sensor, inspect the rubber grommet and make sure that it's in good condition. A torn or cracked grommet can allow an air leak, which will affect driveability and performance.
6   Installation is the reverse of removal.

7   Throttle Position Sensor (TPS) - check and replacement

Check

Refer to illustrations 7.2, 7.3a and 7.3b

1   The Throttle Position Sensor (TPS) is located on the throttle body.
2   Disconnect the electrical connector

from the TPS **(see illustration)**.
3   Connect an ohmmeter between terminal 2 and terminal 3 on the TPS side of the connector **(see illustrations)** and measure the resistance between these terminals with the throttle plate closed. Compare your measurement to this Chapter's Specifications. If the resistance is within the specified range, proceed to the next test. If it isn't, replace the TPS.
4   Connect the ohmmeter between terminals 1 and 3 and then note the resistance as you slowly open the throttle plate. Verify that the resistance value changes smoothly and proportionately. If the TPS resistance does not change smoothly, replace the TPS.

Replacement

Refer to illustrations 7.7, 7.8a and 7.8b

5   Disconnect the cable from the negative terminal of the battery.
6   Disconnect the TPS electrical connector.
7   Loosen and remove the retaining screws **(see illustration)** from the throttle position sensor. Disengage the TPS from the throttle

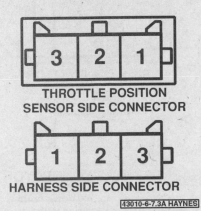

7.3a Throttle Position Sensor (TPS) electrical connector terminal guide (1996 through 2000 models)

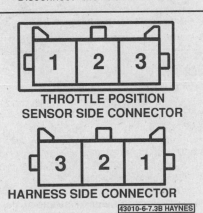

7.3b Throttle Position Sensor (TPS) electrical connector terminal guide (2001 and later models)

7.7 To detach the TPS from the throttle body, remove these two retaining screws (arrows)

6

valve spindle and remove it from the vehicle.
8   When installing the TPS, make sure that the flat surface inside the TPS is correctly mated to the flat surface on the throttle valve spindle **(see illustrations)** and then tighten the retaining screws to the torque listed in this Chapter's Specifications.
9   The remainder of installation is the reverse of removal.

8   Engine Coolant Temperature (ECT) sensor - check and replacement

Refer to illustrations 8.1and 8.3

1   The Engine Coolant Temperature (ECT) sensor **(see illustration)** is installed in a coolant passage which is located at the front left corner of the cylinder head.
2   Drain the cooling system (see Chapter 1).
3   Unplug the electrical connector from the ECT sensor **(see illustration)**.
4   Unscrew and remove the ECT sensor.
5   Suspend the ECT sensor in a container of water and heat the water on a stove while monitoring the water temperature with a cooking thermometer. Do not allow the sensor to touch the sides or bottom of the container. Connect an ohmmeter to the sensor terminals and measure the resistance of the sensor as the water is heated. Compare your measurements with the values listed in this Chapter's Specifications. Replace the sensor if the measured resistance varies greatly from the specified resistance values.
6   Before installing the ECT sensor, make sure that you put on the brass sealing washer, and then tighten the ECT sensor to the torque listed in this Chapter's Specifications.
7   After installing the ECT sensor, fill the cooling system (see Chapter 1), then start the engine and check for leaks.

9   Heated Oxygen Sensor (HO2S) - check and replacement

General information

Refer to illustrations 9.1a and 9.1b

1   All vehicles covered in this manual are equipped with an "upstream" and a "downstream" Heated Oxygen Sensor (HO2S). The upstream HO2S **(see illustration)** is located ahead of the catalytic converter (on 2001 and later models, the upstream HO2S is located in the exhaust manifold); the downstream HO2S **(see illustration)** is located behind the converter.
2   The upstream HO2S monitors the oxygen content of the exhaust gas stream. The HO2S reacts with the oxygen content in the exhaust stream to produce a voltage output from 100 millivolts (high oxygen, lean mixture) to 800 millivolts (low oxygen, rich mixture). The PCM monitors this voltage output to determine the optimal air/fuel mixture. The PCM alters the air/fuel mixture ratio by con-

7.8a When installing the TPS, make sure that the flat surface (arrow) inside the recess in the backside of the TPS . . .

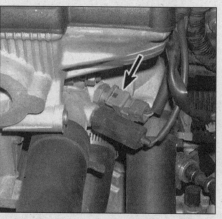

8.1 The Engine Coolant Temperature (ECT) sensor (arrow) is located at the front left corner of the cylinder head

trolling the pulse width (open time) of the fuel injectors. A mixture of 14.7 parts air to 1 part fuel is the ideal ratio for minimizing exhaust emissions, thus allowing the catalytic converter to operate at maximum efficiency. It is this ratio of 14.7 to 1 which the PCM and the HO2S attempt to maintain at all times.

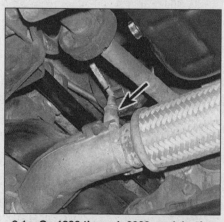

9.1a On 1996 through 2000 models, the upstream Heated Oxygen Sensor (HO2S) (arrow) is located ahead of the catalytic converter (on 2001 and later models, the upstream HO2S is located in the exhaust manifold)

7.8b . . . is correctly aligned with the flat surface (arrow) on the throttle valve spindle

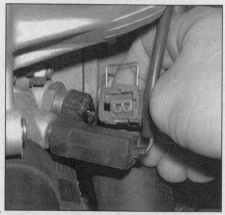

8.3 To unplug the electrical connector from the ECT sensor, pry up the wire retainer, then pull the connector off

3   The HO2S must be hot to operate correctly (approximately 600-degrees F). During the initial warm-up period, the PCM operates in open loop mode - that is, it controls fuel delivery in accordance with a programmed default value instead of feedback information from the oxygen sensor.

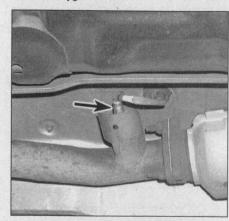

9.1b On all models, the downstream HO2S (arrow) is located behind the converter

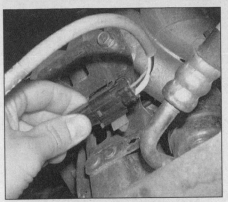

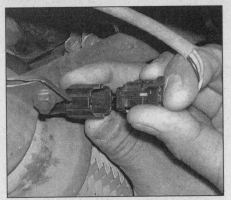

9.6a To unplug the upstream HO2S connector (arrow), detach it from its bracket . . .

9.6b . . . and then pull it down and unplug it

9.6c The downstream HO2S connector (arrow) is located under the center console

4   The correct operation of the oxygen sensor is contingent on four conditions:

a) *Electrical* - *The low voltages and low currents generated by the sensor depend upon good, clean connections. When a you suspect that the HO2S is malfunctioning, always check the connections first.*

b) *Outside air supply* - *In order to function correctly, the HO2S must have air circulation to the internal part of the sensor. Whenever the sensor is removed or replaced, make sure that the air passages are not restricted.*

c) *Correct operating temperature* - *The PCM will not react to the HO2S signal until the HO2S reaches approximately 600-degrees F. This factor must be taken into consideration when evaluating the performance of the HO2S.*

d) *Unleaded fuel* - *The HO2S will operate correctly only with unleaded fuel. Make sure that the fuel you're using is unleaded.*

5   The downstream HO2S works the same way as the upstream HO2S, but the PCM uses the signal from the downstream HO2S to monitor the efficiency of the catalytic converter, and to predict imminent failure *before* it occurs.

Check

Refer to illustrations 9.6a, 9.6b, 9.6c, 9.7a, 9.7b,

Caution: *The HO2S is very sensitive to excessive circuit loads and circuit damage of any kind. For safest testing, disconnect the HO2S connector, install jumper wires between the two connectors and connect your voltmeter to the jumper wires. If jumper wires aren't available, carefully backprobe the wires in the connector shell with suitable probes (such as T-pins). Do not puncture the HO2S wires or try to backprobe the HO2S itself. Use only a digital voltmeter to test an HO2S.*

Note: *Performing the following test might set a diagnostic trouble code and illuminate the Check Engine light. If it does, be sure to clear the code after performing the test and making any necessary repairs (see Section 2).*

6   The upstream HO2S connector **(see illustrations)** is located underneath the engine compartment, so you'll need to raise the front of the vehicle and place it securely on jackstands before proceeding. The downstream HO2S connector **(see illustration)** is located under the center console, inside the vehicle; to access this connector, remove the center console (see Chapter 11).

7   Using T-pins or short sections of stiff wire, backprobe terminals 1 and 2 of the HO2S electrical connector **(see illustrations)** and then hook up the leads of a voltmeter to the probes. Turn the ignition ON but do not start the engine. The meter should read approximately 400 to 450 millivolts (0.40 to 0.45 volt). If it doesn't, trace and repair the circuit from the HO2S to the PCM. **Note:** *Refer to the wiring diagrams at the end of this manual for additional information on the HO2S circuits.*

8   Start the engine and let it warm up to normal operating temperature; again check the oxygen sensor signal voltage.

a) *Voltage from an upstream HO2S should range from 100 to 800 millivolts (0.1 to 0.8 volt) and switch actively between high and low readings.*

b) *Voltage from a downstream HO2S should also read between 100 to 800 millivolts (0.1 to 0.8 volt) but it should not switch actively. The downstream HO2S voltage may stay toward the center of its range (about 400 millivolts) or remain at the upper or lower limits of the range for relatively longer periods of time.*

9   Check the battery voltage supply and ground circuits to the oxygen sensor heater. Disconnect the electrical connector and con-

6

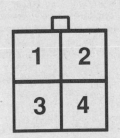

OXYGEN SENSOR SIDE CONNECTOR

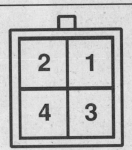

HARNESS SIDE CONNECTOR

43010-6-9.7A HAYNES

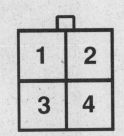

HARNESS SIDE CONNECTOR

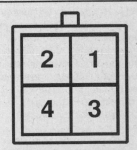

OXYGEN SENSOR SIDE CONNECTOR

43010-6-9.7B HAYNES

9.7a HO2S electrical connector terminal guide (1996 through 2000 models)

9.7b HO2S electrical connector terminal guide (2001 models)

9.14 Remove and install the HO2S with a special oxygen sensor socket that has a slot on one side for the harness

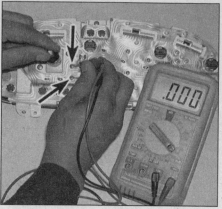

10.3 To test the Vehicle Speed Sensor (VSS), hook up an ohmmeter to the test terminals (arrows), and then rotate the speedometer drive while observing the display on the meter, which should switch from continuity to no continuity four times per revolution

10.7a Vehicle Speed Sensor (VSS) connector terminal guide (2001 and later models with a manual transaxle)

1   *Ground*
2   *Output (to instrument cluster, cruise control module and data link connector)*
3   *Voltage supply*

nect a voltmeter between terminal 4 and ground **(see illustration 9.7a or 9.7b)**. Turn the ignition to ON. The meter should indicate approximately 12 volts. If battery voltage is not present, check the power and ground circuits to the sensor (don't forget to check the fuses first).

10   Before the HO2S cools down, check the oxygen sensor heater for an open circuit: unplug the HO2S electrical connector and hook up an ohmmeter between terminals 3 and 4 on the HO2S side of the connector **(see illustration 9.7a or 9.7b)**. Measure the resistance of the HO2S heater and then compare your measurement to the HO2S heater resistance listed in this Chapter's Specifications. If the heater resistance is excessive, replace the oxygen sensor.

11   If the HO2S checks out okay, but there's a driveability problem or a diagnostic trouble code related to the HO2S circuit, check the wiring harness and connectors between the HO2S and the PCM for an open or short circuit. If no problems are found, have the vehicle checked by a dealer service department.

Replacement

Refer to illustration 9.14

12   The exhaust pipe contracts when cool, and the HO2S may be hard to loosen when the engine is cold. To make HO2S removal easier, start and run the engine for a minute or two and then shut it off. Be careful not to burn yourself during the following procedure. Also observe these guidelines when replacing an HO2S.

a) *The HO2S has a permanently attached pigtail and electrical connector which cannot be removed from the HO2S. Damage or removal of the pigtail or electrical connector will permanent disable the HO2S.*

b) *Keep grease, dirt and other contaminants away from the electrical connector and the louvered end of the HO2S.*

c) *Do not use cleaning solvents of any kind on the HO2S.*

d) *Do not drop or roughly handle the HO2S.*

13   Raise the front of the vehicle and place it securely on jackstands.

14   Using a suitable wrench or specialized oxygen sensor socket, unscrew the HO2S from the exhaust manifold **(see illustration)**.

15   Use anti-seize compound on the threads of the HO2S to facilitate future removal. The threads of a new HO2S should already be coated with anti-seize compound. If they aren't, be sure to apply anti-seize compound before installing the HO2S.

16   Install the HO2S and tighten it to the torque listed in this Chapter's Specifications.

17   Reconnect the electrical connector to the HO2S, then lower the vehicle.

---

10   Vehicle Speed Sensor (VSS) - check and replacement

1996 through 2000 models

Check

Refer to illustration 10.3

1   The Vehicle Speed Sensor (VSS), which is an integral part of the speedometer, is a magnetic pick-up coil that converts the transaxle gear revolutions into a pulsing signal voltage output for the PCM. (The VSS emits four pulses per revolution of the cable.)

2   Remove the instrument cluster (see Chapter 12).

3   Hook up an ohmmeter to the indicated terminals on the backside of the instrument cluster **(see illustration)** and rotate the speedometer drive. Note whether the continuity fluctuates on and off, four times per revolution of the cable, as you do so. If it doesn't, replace the VSS.

Replacement

4   If the VSS is defective, replace the instrument cluster (see Chapter 12).

2001 and later models

Check

Refer to illustrations 10.7a and 10.7b

5   The Vehicle Speed Sensor (VSS), which is mounted on the transaxle, is a Hall effect switch that generates pulse signals in response to the rotating driven gear. The sensor is triggered by a toothed rotor on the transaxle output shaft. As the output shaft rotates, the sensor produces a fluctuating voltage, the frequency of which is proportional to vehicle speed. Unlike the magnetic pick-up coil device used on earlier VSS units, the Hall effect switch emits a square-wave (on-off) signal. The PCM uses the VSS input signal for several different engine and transmission control functions. The VSS signal also drives the speedometer on the instrument panel. A defective VSS can cause various driveability and transaxle problems.

6   Raise the front of the vehicle and support it securely on jackstands. Unplug the connector and inspect the condition of the terminals inside the connector. Look for corrosion and dirt. Clean the connector as necessary. Also, inspect the wires leading to the VSS. Make sure they're tight and there are no breaks in the wires. Repair as required.

7   Plug in the electrical connector. Using suitable probes, backprobe the ground and output terminals of the VSS connector **(see illustrations)** (see Chapter 12 for additional information on how to backprobe a connector). Connect a voltmeter to the probes and turn the ignition key On. Hold the right front tire steady and rotate the left front tire by hand while watching the voltmeter. The sensor should produce a fluctuating voltage of zero to approximately 5.0 volts. If it doesn't, replace the VSS.

Replacement

8   Raise the vehicle and support it securely on jackstands.

9   Disconnect the electrical connector from the VSS.

10   Remove the VSS mounting bolt and

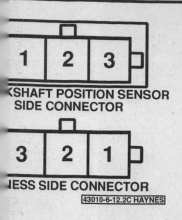

KSHAFT POSITION SENSOR
SIDE CONNECTOR

NESS SIDE CONNECTOR

43010-6-12.2C HAYNES

rankshaft Position (CKP) sensor
ical connector terminal guide
(2001 and later models)

---

ement

ug the CKP sensor electrical con-
emove the CKP sensor mounting
illustration 12.1) and remove the
or from the block.
lation is the reverse of removal. Be
hten the CKP sensor mounting bolt
que listed in this Chapter's Specifi-

**eleration sensor - check and
acement**

ustrations 13.1 and 13.2
acceleration sensor **(see illustra-**
cated at the left rear corner of the
mpartment. The acceleration sen-
nts the PCM from misinterpreting a
d as a misfire signal.
probe terminal no.1 of the accelera-
r electrical connector **(see illustra-**
Chapter 12 for additional information
backprobe a connector) and hook
neter between terminal no. 1 and
se leads long enough to allow you to
voltmeter on the dash or somewhere
vehicle where you can see it safely,
taking your eyes off the road.
the engine and allow it to warm up
ling normally. Note the voltage out-
he acceleration sensor and com-
measurement to the idling voltage
is Chapter's Specifications.
the vehicle on a drive and measure
e output of the acceleration sensor
compare your measurement to the
tage listed in this Chapter's Speci-

e voltage is outside the specified
idle or while driving, replace the
n sensor.

ement

ug the acceleration sensor electri-
tor.
ve the acceleration sensor retain-

**13.1 The acceleration sensor is located at
the left rear corner of the engine
compartment; to detach the acceleration
sensor from its mounting bracket, remove
these two bolts (arrows)**

ing bolts **(see illustration 13.1)**.
8   Remove the acceleration sensor.
9   Installation is the reverse of removal.

---

14   Manifold Absolute Pressure (MAP)/Intake Air Temperature (IAT) sensor (2001 and later models) - check and replacement

Check

**Manifold Absolute Pressure (MAP)
sensor**

Refer to illustrations 14.1 and 14.2
1   The Manifold Absolute Pressure (MAP)
sensor **(see illustration)** is located on the air
intake plenum. The MAP sensor is a pres-
sure-sensitive variable resistor that measures
changes in intake manifold pressure caused
by changes in engine load and speed. The
MAP sensor converts these changes into a
variable voltage output. The MAP sensor also
measures barometric pressure during starting and, under some conditions, allows the
PCM to automatically compensate for
changes in altitude. The PCM provides 5-
volts to power the MAP sensor, which provides a path to ground through its variable
resistor. The amount of voltage dropped
across the resistor is interpreted by the PCM
as the change in intake manifold pressure.
The PCM uses this information to help control fuel delivery and ignition timing.
2   Backprobe terminals 1 and 4 of the MAP
sensor electrical connector **(see illustration)**
(see Chapter 12 for additional information on
how to backprobe a connector). Hook up a
voltmeter to the backprobed wires. Turn the
ignition switch to ON and note the indicated
MAP sensor output voltage. Compare your
measurement to the MAP sensor output voltage listed in this Chapter's Specifications.
3   Start the engine and allow it to warm up
to its normal idle. Once again, note the indicated voltage and compare your measurement to the voltage listed in this Chapter's

---

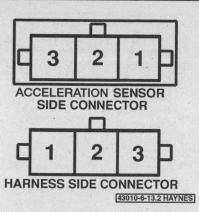

ACCELERATION SENSOR
SIDE CONNECTOR

HARNESS SIDE CONNECTOR

43010-6-13.2 HAYNES

**13.2 Acceleration sensor electrical
connector terminal guide**

**14.1 The Manifold Absolute Pressure
(MAP)/Intake Air Temperature (IAT) sensor
is located on the air intake plenum; to
detach the MAP/IAT sensor from the
plenum, unplug the electrical
connector and remove the two
bolts (2001 and later models)**

Specifications.
4   If the voltage is outside the specified
range with the ignition switch on, or at idle,
replace the MAP/IAT sensor.

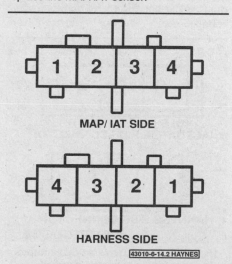

MAP/ IAT SIDE

HARNESS SIDE

43010-6-14.2 HAYNES

**14.2 MAP/IAT sensor electrical connector
terminal guide (2001 and later models)**

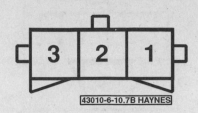

10.7b Vehicle Speed Sensor (VSS) connector terminal guide (2001 and later models with an automatic transaxle)

1   *Voltage supply*
2   *Ground*
3   *Output (to instrument cluster, cruise control module and data link connector)*

withdraw the VSS from the transaxle case.
11   Replace the VSS O-ring.
12   Installation is the reverse of removal.

11   Camshaft Position (CMP) sensor - check and replacement

Check

Refer to illustrations 11.1, 11.2a and 11.2b

1   The Camshaft Position (CMP) sensor **(see illustration)** is located at the right rear corner of the cylinder head. The CMP sensor signals the PCM when the No. 1 cylinder is at Top Dead Center (TDC) on its compression stroke. The PCM uses this information to fire the injectors in the correct sequence and at the right time.
2   Using a suitable probe, backprobe terminal 2 of the CMP sensor electrical connector **(see illustrations)** (see Chapter 12 for additional information on how to backprobe a connector). Connect a voltmeter and measure the sensor output voltage at idle (800 rpm) and at 3000 rpm. The sensor output voltage should fluctuate between zero

12.1 The Crankshaft Position (CKP) sensor is located on the front of the cylinder block; to remove the CKP sensor, remove the retaining bolt (arrow)

11.1 The Camshaft Position (CMP) sensor (lower arrow) is located at the right rear corner of the cylinder head; the electrical connector (upper arrow) is located right above the injector for cylinder No. 1

and 5 volts at both idle and at 3000 rpm. If the CMP sensor does not operate as described, replace it.

Replacement

3   Unplug the CMP sensor electrical connector, remove the sensor mounting bolt and remove the CMP sensor from the cylinder head.
4   Installation is the reverse of removal.

12   Crankshaft Position (CKP) sensor - check and replacement

Check

Refer to illustrations 12.1, 12.2a, 12.2b and 12.2c

1   The Crankshaft Position (CKP) sensor **(see illustration)** is located on the front side of the engine block, near the flywheel/driveplate. The CKP sensor monitors the position of the crankshaft, from which the PCM is able to compute engine RPM.

12.2a Crankshaft Position (CKP) sensor electrical connector (arrow)

**CAMSHAF
SID**

HARNESS

**11.2a Camsh
electrical c
(1996 th**

**CAMSHAF
SID**

HARNESS

**11.2b Camsh
electrical c
(2001**

2   Disconnec
connector **(see i**
resistance betw
sensor **(see illu**
measurement w
Chapter's Spec
resistance is ou
resistance, repla

**CRANKSHAF
SIDE**

HARNESS

**12.2b Cranksh
electrical c
(1996 thr**

CRAN

HAR

**12.2c
elec**

Repla

3   Unp
nector, r
bolt **(see**
CKP sen
4   Insta
sure to ti
to the to
cations.

13   Acc
rep

Check

Refer to

1   The
tion) is l
engine c
sor preve
rough roa
2   Bac
tion sens
tion) **(see**
on how t
up a vol
ground. U
place the
inside the
i.e. witho
3   Sta
until it's
put from
pare you
listed in
4   Tak
the volta
again an
driving v
fications
5   If th
range a
accelera

Repla

6   Unp
cal conn
7   Re

15.1a On 1996 through 2000 models, the Idle Speed Control (ISC) actuator (arrow) is located right behind the air intake plenum

15.2a To unplug the ISC electrical connector, depress the wire retainer and pull off the connector (1996 through 2000 model shown, 2001 models similar)

Intake Air Temperature (IAT) sensor

5   The Intake Air Temperature (IAT) sensor **(see illustration 14.1)** is also located on the air intake plenum, and shares the same housing with the MAP sensor. The IAT sensor is a

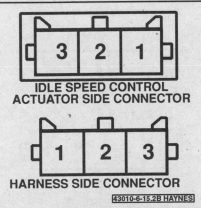

15.2b Idle Speed Control (ISC) actuator electrical connector terminal guide (all models)

15.1b On 2001 and later models, the Idle Speed Control (ISC) actuator is mounted on the front of the air intake plenum; to remove the ISC actuator, unplug the electrical connector, remove the two mounting screws (arrows) and disconnect the ISC actuator from the hose underneath

negative temperature coefficient (NTC) thyristor (a thermo-resistor that decreases its resistance as the air temperature goes up). The PCM provides a 5-volt signal to the IAT sensor. As the engine warms up, so does the intake air, and the IAT sensor resistance decreases accordingly, allowing an increasing portion of the 5-volt signal from the PCM to return to ground through the PCM. The PCM uses this variable output voltage from the IAT sensor to calculate the appropriate amount of fuel to deliver through the injectors.

6   Remove the MAP/IAT sensor from the air intake plenum and hook up an ohmmeter to terminals 3 and 4 **(see illustration 14.2)**. Heat up the IAT sensor with a hair dryer. As the IAT sensor heats up, note the resistance across terminals 3 and 4 and compare your measurements to the resistance values listed in this Chapter's Specifications.

7   If the IAT sensor resistance doesn't decrease as specified, replace the MAP/IAT sensor.

Replacement

8   Unplug the MAP/IAT sensor electrical connector.

9   Remove the MAP/IAT sensor retaining bolts **(see illustration 14.1)** and detach the MAP/IAT sensor from the plenum.

10   Installation is the reverse of removal.

15   Idle Speed Control (ISC) actuator - check and replacement

Check

Refer to illustrations 15.1a, 15.1b, 15.2a and 15.2b

1   On 1996 through 2000 models, the Idle Speed Control (ISC) actuator **(see illustration)** is located behind air intake plenum. On 2001 and later models, the Idle Speed Control (ISC) actuator **(see illustration)** is located on the front of the air intake plenum. The ISC actuator, which is under PCM control, controls the amount of air entering the intake plenum at idle.

2   Disconnect the ISC actuator electrical connector **(see illustration)** and measure the resistance across terminals 1 and 3, then terminals 2 and 3 **(see illustration)**. Compare your measurements with the values listed in this Chapter's Specifications. If the indicated resistance is incorrect for either pair of terminals, replace the ISC actuator.

Replacement

1996 through 2000 models

Refer to illustrations 15.4 and 15.5

3   Unplug the ISC actuator electrical connector **(see illustration 15.2a)**.

4   Loosen the hose clamps **(see illustration)** and disconnect the air hoses from the actuator.

5   To disengage the ISC actuator from its mounting bracket, pull straight up **(see illustration)**. (It's not necessary to remove the bracket itself.)

6   Installation is the reverse of removal.

15.4 Before removing the ISC actuator, loosen the hose clamps and disconnect both hoses (1996 through 2000 models)

15.5 To detach the ISC actuator from the air intake plenum, simply pull it straight up - it's not necessary to remove the bracket (1996 through 2000 models)

6

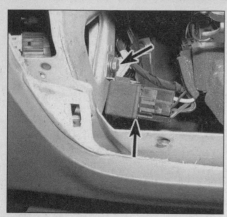

16.1 The Multiport Fuel Injection (MFI) control relay is located under the steering column (trim panel and reinforcement removed); to remove the MFI control relay, unplug the electrical connector and remove this retaining bolt (arrow)

2001 and later models

7   Unplug the electrical connector.
8   Remove the ISC actuator mounting screws **(see illustration 15.1b)**.
9   Disconnect the ISC actuator from the hose.
10   Installation is the reverse of removal.

16   Multiport Fuel Injection (MFI) control relay - check and replacement

Refer to illustrations 16.1, 16.4a and 16.4b

1   The MFI control relay is located under the steering column on 2000 and earlier models **(see illustration)** or in the underhood fuse/relay box on 2001 and later models. When the ignition key switch is turned to ON, current flows from the ignition switch through the MFI control relay to ground, activating the MFI control relay, which supplies power to the PCM, the fuel injectors and most of the MFI system information sensors and output actuators.
2   On 2000 and earlier models, remove the left knee bolster (see Chapter 11) and the metal reinforcement behind it.
3   Remove the relay.
4   Using an ohmmeter, check continuity between terminals 1 and 5 on the MFI control relay **(see illustrations)**. There should be no continuity.
5   Using jumper wires, connect the battery positive terminal to terminal 4 and the negative terminal to terminal 2 on the MFI relay and check continuity between terminals 1 and 5 again. There should be continuity when the relay is energized.
6   Disconnect the jumper wires and check continuity between terminals 3 and 5 on the relay. There should be no continuity.
7   Reconnect the jumper wires as in Step 5 and check continuity between terminals 3 and 5. There should be continuity

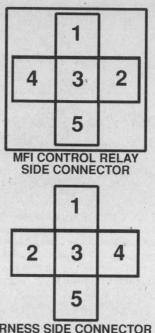

MFI CONTROL RELAY SIDE CONNECTOR

HARNESS SIDE CONNECTOR
43010-6-16.4A HAYNES

16.4a   Multiport Fuel Injection (MFI) control relay electrical connector terminal guide (1996 through 2000 models)

8   If the MFI control relay doesn't operate as described, replace it.
9   Installation is the reverse of removal.

17   Positive Crankcase Ventilation (PCV) system

Refer to illustration 17.2

1   The Positive Crankcase Ventilation (PCV) system reduces hydrocarbon emissions by scavenging crankcase vapors. It does this by circulating fresh air from the air cleaner through the crankcase, where it mixes with blow-by gases and is then rerouted through a PCV valve to the intake manifold.
2   The only components of the PCV system are the PCV valve **(see illustration)** and a pair of hoses. One hose connects the air intake duct to the valve cover; this hose carries fresh air from the intake to the crankcase. The other hose connects the PCV valve, which is installed in the valve cover, to the air intake plenum; this hose carries crankcase vapors from the engine to the intake plenum.
3   When the throttle valve is closed during deceleration and idle, intake vacuum is high. When intake vacuum is high (also referred to as a "low load" condition), the PCV valve restricts the flow of crankcase vapors in order to prevent an excessively rich mixture during deceleration and to maintain idle quality. When the throttle valve is open during acceleration and steady cruising speeds, intake vacuum is low ("high load" condition). Under these conditions, the PCV valve opens more

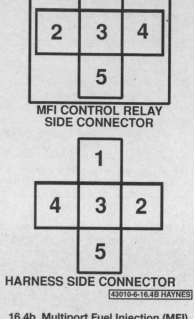

MFI CONTROL RELAY SIDE CONNECTOR

HARNESS SIDE CONNECTOR
43010-6-16.4B HAYNES

16.4b   Multiport Fuel Injection (MFI) control relay electrical connector terminal guide (2001 and later models)

to facilitate flow. If abnormal operating conditions (such as piston ring problems) arise, the system is designed to allow excessive amounts of blow-by gases to flow back through the crankcase vent hose into the air intake duct, where it mixes with intake air.
4   Checking and replacement of the PCV valve and filter is covered in Chapter 1.

18   Evaporative Emission Control (EVAP) system - check and component replacement

Warning: *Gasoline is extremely flammable, so take extra precautions when you work on any part of the fuel system. Don't smoke or allow open flames or bare light bulbs near the work area, and don't work in a garage where*

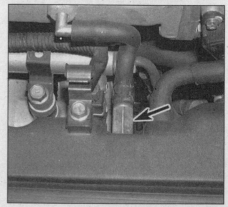

17.2   The PCV valve (arrow) is located in the valve cover

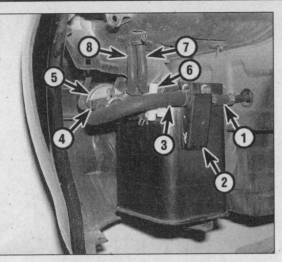

18.7a On 1996 through 2000 models, the EVAP canister is located in front of the left wheel well; to access the canister, remove the left inner fender panel

1   Air filter inlet hose
2   Air filter
3   Air filter-to-CCV hose
4   CCV electrical connector
5   Close Canister Valve (CCV)
6   Two-way valve
7   Fuel tank-to-EVAP canister hose
8   EVAP canister-to-canister purge solenoid valve hose

18.7b On 2001 and later models, the EVAP canister is located at the left rear corner of the underside of the vehicle; to remove the EVAP canister, remove these two bolts (arrows), remove the plastic protective cover and then lower the canister

a gas-type appliance (such as a water heater or a clothes dryer) is present. Since gasoline is carcinogenic, wear latex gloves when there's a possibility of being exposed to fuel, and, if you spill any fuel on your skin, rinse it off immediately with soap and water. Mop up any spills immediately and do not store fuel-soaked rags where they could ignite. The fuel system is under constant pressure, so, if any fuel lines are to be disconnected, the fuel pressure in the system must be relieved first. When you perform any kind of work on the fuel system, wear safety glasses and have a Class B type fire extinguisher on hand.

General description

1   The Evaporative Emission Control (EVAP) system absorbs fuel vapors from the fuel tank and, during engine operation, releases them into the engine intake system, where they mix with the incoming air/fuel mixture. The main components of the EVAP system are the fuel tank, the Fuel Tank Pressure (FTP) sensor, the EVAP canister (filled with activated charcoal to absorb fuel vapors), the canister purge solenoid valve, the Canister Close Valve (CCV), and the vapor and purge lines that connect these components to each other and to the fuel tank and the engine.

2   After passing through a one-way valve, fuel tank vapors are carried through a vapor hose to the EVAP canister. The activated charcoal in the canister absorbs and stores the vapors. There they remain until the next time the engine is running and warmed up, at which time the PCM energizes the canister purge solenoid valve, which opens the canister purge valve. Fuel vapors from the canister are then drawn through a hose by intake manifold vacuum into the intake manifold and then to the combustion chamber where they are burned up during normal engine operation.

3   The PCM doesn't simply turn the canister purge solenoid valve on and off; it regulates the rate of vapor flow from the canister to the intake manifold by controlling the "duty cycle" of the solenoid. (The duty cycle is a measurement of the amount of time during which the solenoid is energized, or turned on,

expressed as a percentage of the complete on-off cycle of the solenoid. In other words, the duty cycle is the ratio of the pulse width to the complete cycle width.) During cold running conditions, the PCM does not energize the solenoid. After the engine has warmed up to the correct operating temperature, the PCM purges the vapors to the intake manifold in accordance with the operating condition of the engine. The PCM will energize the purge control valve solenoid about 5 to 10 times per second. The flow rate is determined by the "pulse width," or length of time, that the solenoid is energized.

4   The EVAP system is equipped with a Fuel Tank Pressure (FTP) sensor that can detect a leak in the EVAP system. The FTP detects the difference in pressure between the ambient pressure (about 14.7 psi at sea level) and the pressure inside the fuel tank (which increases in relation to ambient pressure, as the fuel heats up). If the FTP sensor detects excessive pressure, it signals the PCM, which opens the Canister Close Valve (CCV).

Check and replacement

Note 1: The evaporative emissions control system, like all emission control systems, is protected by a Federally-mandated warranty. The EVAP system probably won't fail during the service life of the vehicle; however, if it does, the hoses or charcoal canister are usually to blame.

Note 2: A factory scan tool is required to thoroughly check the EVAP system. If the following simple checks fail to solve the problem, have the system diagnosed by a dealer service department or other qualified repair shop.

5   First, check the hoses. A damaged, disconnected, kinked or missing hose is the most likely cause of a malfunctioning EVAP system. Refer to the Vacuum Hose Routing Diagram (see Section 1) to determine whether the hoses are correctly routed and attached. Repair any damaged hoses or replace any missing hoses as necessary.

6   Check the related wiring (see the Wiring Diagrams at the end of Chapter 12).

EVAP canister

Refer to illustrations 18.7a, 18.7b and 18.8

7   The EVAP canister **(see illustrations)** is located in front of the left wheel well (1996 through 2000 models) or underneath the left rear part of the floorpan (2001 and later models). Inspect all hoses leading to and from the canister for loose connections, damage and kinks.

8   Remove the canister **(1996 through 2000 models, see accompanying illustration; 2001 models, see illustration 18.7b)** and then inspect it for distortion, cracks and any sign of leaking fuel vapor.

9   If there is any sign of damage to the canister, replace it.

18.8 To remove the EVAP canister on 1996 through 2000 models, disconnect the hoses shown in illustration 18.7a, then remove these two bolts (arrows) and pull down the canister to disengage it from the upper end of the mounting bracket (when you unbolt the canister, the outer of the two lower brackets - the one that slots into the underside of the canister - will fall off, so don't lose it)

6

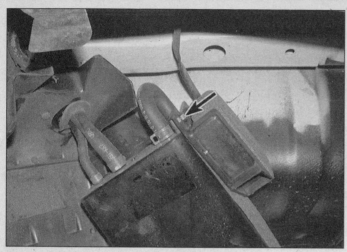

18.10 To remove the air filter from the canister on 2001 and later models, remove the bolt that secures the CCV to the filter (see illustration 18.11b) and then remove this bolt (arrow)

18.11a On 1996 through 2000 models, the Canister Close Valve (CCV) (arrow) is located on the upper edge of the EVAP canister, in the hose between the air filter and the two-way valve

Air filter

Refer to illustration 18.10

10   When the EVAP canister is vented to the intake manifold by the canister purge solenoid valve, fresh air is drawn into the canister to help flush fuel vapors from the charcoal in which they're stored inside the canister. The air filter (**1996 through 2000 models, see illustration 18.7a; 2001 models, see accompanying illustration**), which is located on the side of the EVAP canister, prevents dirt and debris from contaminating the EVAP canister. To detach the filter from the canister on 1996 through 2000 models, loosen the two hose clamps, disconnect the hoses from the filter, remove the two nuts that secure the air filter housing to the canister and then remove the filter. To detach the filter from the canister on 2001 models, remove the bolt that secures the CCV to the filter (**see illustration 18.11b**), remove the bolt that secures the filter to the canister (**see illustration 18.10**) and then remove the filter. Inspect the filter for cracks, distortion and other damage. Make sure the filter isn't clogged. If the filter is damaged, replace it.

Canister Close Valve (CCV)

Refer to illustrations 18.11a, 18.11b and 18.12

11   The Canister Close Valve (CCV) (**see illustrations**) is located at the upper edge of the EVAP canister, in the hose between the air filter and the two-way valve.

12   Start the engine and allow it to warm up. At idle, disconnect the CCV electrical connector and, using a pair of jumper wires, connect the two halves of terminal 2 with one of the jumper wires (**see illustration**). Use the other jumper wire to connect terminal 1 on the CCV side of the connector to the negative battery terminal and then verify that the CCV is closed. Disconnect the jumper wire between terminal 1 and the negative battery terminal and then verify that the CCV is open. How can you tell whether the CCV is open, or closed? Place a very thin piece of paper flat against the end of the hose and note whether the hose sucks the paper toward it, or not. If the hose sucks the paper toward it, the CCV is open; if the hose doesn't suck the paper, the CCV is closed.

13   If the CCV doesn't operate as described, replace it.

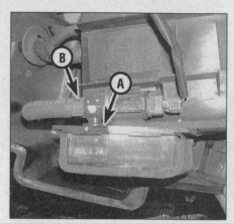

18.11b On 2001 and later models, the Canister Close Valve (CCV) is located on top of the EVAP canister; to remove it, unplug the electrical connector (A), loosen the hose clamp (B), disconnect the hose, remove this bolt (arrow) and detach the CCV from the air filter

```
 2   1
43010-18.12 HAYNES
```

18.12 Canister Close Valve (CCV) electrical connector terminal guide

18.14 The two-way valve (arrow) is located in the hose between the CCV and the EVAP canister (1996 through 2000 model shown; on 2001 and later models, the two-way valve is located underneath the vehicle, ahead of the EVAP canister, between the fuel tank pressure sensor and canister)

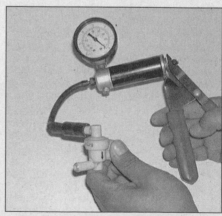

18.15 To test the two-way valve, hook up a hand-held vacuum pump and verify that air can travel through the valve in the direction of the arrow, but not in the opposite direction

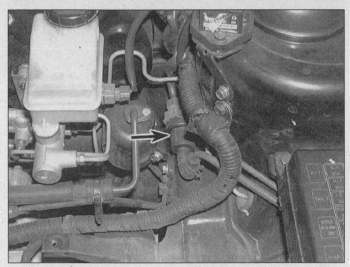

18.17 The canister purge solenoid valve (arrow) is located in the left rear corner of the engine compartment, next to the left strut tower on 2000 and earlier models

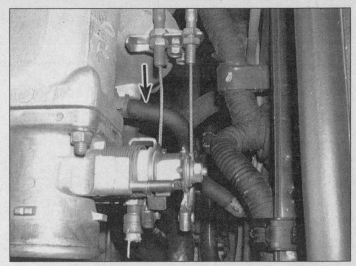

18.18a The purge port for the canister purge solenoid valve is located on the backside of the air intake plenum; to verify that the port isn't clogged up, disconnect the purge hose (arrow) from the purge port . . .

Two-way valve

Refer to illustrations 18.14 and 18.15

14 The two-way valve **(see illustration)** is located in the same hose as the air filter and the CCV, between the CCV and the EVAP canister.

15 Loosen the two hose clamps and pull the hoses off the two-way valve. To test the two-way valve, verify that air can pass through the valve in the direction of the directional arrow on the valve **(see illustration)**, and cannot pass through the valve in the opposite direction of the directional arrow. (Ideally, this test should be performed with a hand-operated pump, but if you have no pump, carefully wipe off the two-way valve and blow through it.)

16 If the two-way valve doesn't operate as described, replace it.

Canister purge solenoid valve

Refer to illustrations 18.17, 18.18a, 18.18b and 18.19

17 The canister purge solenoid valve **(see illustration)**, which controls the flow of vapors through the purge hose between the canister and the intake manifold, is located in the left rear corner of the engine compartment, next to the left strut tower (1996 through 2000 models) or behind the air intake plenum (2001 and later models).

18 Before testing the canister purge solenoid valve, make sure that the purge port at the intake manifold is not clogged. Disconnect the purge hose **(see illustration)**, connect a vacuum gauge in its place **(see illustration)**, start the engine and verify that there is a steady vacuum indicated by the gauge. If there isn't, the purge port might be clogged.

Try blowing out the port with compressed air and then retest it. If the port is still clogged, remove the intake manifold (see Chapter 4) and clean it thoroughly.

19 Detach the red-striped vacuum hose (the hose connected to the rear end of the valve) from the canister purge solenoid valve, and then connect a hand-operated vacuum pump to the solenoid valve in its place **(see illustration)**.

20 Unplug the electrical connector from the canister purge solenoid valve. Using a pair of jumper wires, apply battery voltage and ground to the terminals on the valve. Apply vacuum to the valve and verify that the valve releases the vacuum.

21 Disconnect the jumper cables, apply vacuum to the solenoid valve again and verify that the valve retains vacuum.

22 If the canister purge solenoid valve

6

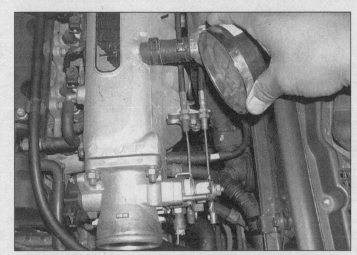

18.18b . . . connect a vacuum gauge in its place, start the engine and verify that there is a steady vacuum indicated by the gauge; if there isn't, the port is clogged and must be cleaned

18.19 The canister purge solenoid valve should hold vacuum when not energized, and shouldn't hold vacuum when energized

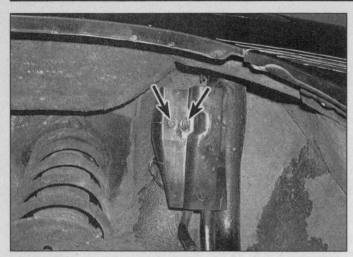

18.25a The Fuel Tank Pressure (FTP) sensor, which is located in the left rear wheel well, is protected by this cover; to remove the cover, remove these two screws (arrows)

18.25b To detach the FTP sensor from its mounting bracket, remove these two bolts (arrows) (the bolt heads, not visible in this photo, face up, and must be removed from the upper side of the sensor)

doesn't operate as described, replace it.

23   Measure the resistance between the terminals of the solenoid valve electrical connector on the solenoid side and compare your measurement to the resistance listed in this Chapter's Specifications.

24   If the resistance is incorrect, replace the canister purge solenoid valve.

Fuel Tank Pressure (FTP) sensor

Refer to illustrations 18.25a, 18.25b and 18.27
Note: *Verify that the fuel tank contains at least 15 percent of its normal capacity before proceeding. Otherwise, the results will be inaccurate.*

25   The Fuel Tank Pressure (FTP) sensor **(see illustrations)** is located near the fuel tank.

26   Start the engine and allow it to reach its normal idle (800 rpm).

27   Using T-pins or some other suitable wires, back-probe terminals 1 and 2 of the FTP sensor connector **(see illustration)** and then hook up a voltmeter to the probe wires (see Chapter 12 for additional information on how to backprobe a connector).

28   After the engine has been idling for at least 20 minutes, accelerate the engine and note the voltage. Compare your measurement to the voltage listed in this Chapter's Specifications.

29   If the FTP sensor doesn't operate as described, replace it.

19   On-Board Refueling Vapor Recovery (ORVR) system (1998 and later models) - general information

On 1998 and later models, the EVAP system (see Section 18) includes an On-Board Refueling Vapor Recovery (ORVR) system, which prevents fuel vapors from escaping into the atmosphere during refueling and

instead directs them to the EVAP canister. If the ORVR system malfunctions, have it diagnosed and repaired by a dealer service department.

20   Catalytic converter - check and component replacement

Refer to illustration 20.1
Note: *Because of a Federally mandated warranty which covers emissions-related components such as the catalytic converter, check with a dealer service department before replacing the converter at your own expense.*

1   The catalytic converter **(see illustration)** is an emission control device added to the exhaust system to reduce pollutants from the exhaust gas stream. A three-way catalyst design is used. The catalytic coating on the reduction part of the catalyst consists of platinum and rhodium, which lowers the levels of oxides of nitrogen (NOx). The catalytic coating on the oxidation part of the catalyst consists of platinum and palladium, which

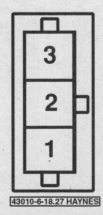

18.27 Fuel Tank Pressure (FTP) sensor electrical connector terminal guide

reduces hydrocarbons (HC) and carbon monoxide (CO).

2   On 1996 and 1997 models, there is one catalytic converter, which is located underneath the vehicle, right behind the upstream heated oxygen sensor (HO2S). There are two converters on 1998 and later models. The first converter is either bolted to the exhaust manifold (1998 through 2000 models), or is an integral part of the exhaust manifold (2001 and later models). The second converter is in the same location as the single converter used on 1996 and 1997 models, i.e. underneath the vehicle, right behind the upstream HO2S. Both converters function in exactly the same manner, but the upstream converter heats up much more quickly than the downstream converter, so the interval of time during which the vehicle "runs dirty" during cold-start warm-ups is considerably less than that of earlier vehicles with only one catalyst.

Check

3   Whenever the vehicle is raised for servicing of underbody components, inspect the catalytic converter for leaks, corrosion, dents and other damage. Inspect the welds/flange bolts that attach the front and rear ends of the converter to the exhaust system. If damage is discovered, the converter should be replaced.

4   A catalytic converter might become clogged. The easiest way to determine whether a converter is restricted is to use a vacuum gauge to diagnose the effect of a blocked exhaust on intake vacuum.

a) *Connect a vacuum gauge to an intake manifold vacuum source.*

b) *Warm the engine to operating temperature, place the transmission in Park and apply the parking brake.*

c) *Note and record the vacuum reading at idle.*

d) *Open the throttle until the engine speed is about 2000 rpm.*

20.1 A typical catalytic converter (arrow); on 1996 and 1997 models, this is the only converter used; on 1998 and later models, this is the second, or "downstream," converter (the upstream converter on these models is right below the exhaust manifold)

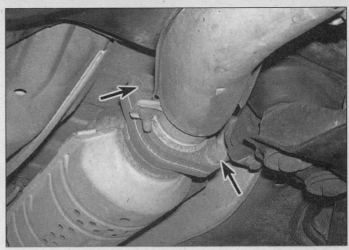

20.7a To detach the converter (1996 and 1997 models) or the downstream converter (1998 and later models) from the exhaust system, remove these nuts and bolts (arrows) from the forward flange . . .

e) *Release the throttle quickly and record the vacuum reading.*
f) *Perform the test three more times, recording the reading after each test.*
g) *If the reading after the fourth test is more than one in-Hg lower than the reading recorded at idle, the catalytic converter, muffler or exhaust pipes may be plugged or restricted.*

5   No further testing of the catalytic converter is recommended. The test equipment for a catalytic converter is specialized and expensive. If you suspect that a converter is malfunctioning, take it to a dealer service department and have it checked out.

Replacement

Note: *Refer to the exhaust system servicing section in Chapter 4A for additional information.*
6   Raise the vehicle and support it securely on jackstands.

1996 and 1997 models, and downstream converter on 1998 and later models

Refer to illustrations 20.7a and 20.7b
6   Disconnect the electrical connector(s) from the oxygen sensor(s) (see Section 9).

7   Because they're subjected to intense heat, as well as dirt, debris, mud and water, the nuts and bolts that attach the mounting flanges of the catalyst to the exhaust pipe flanges are among the most-difficult-to-remove fasteners on the vehicle. Apply a liberal amount of penetrant to the exhaust pipe-to-catalytic converter nuts and bolts **(see illustrations)**. Wait a while for the penetrant to do its work and then remove the exhaust pipe-to-catalyst nuts and bolts, separate the exhaust pipes from the converter and remove the converter. Installation is the reverse of removal. Be sure to clean any carbon deposits from the exhaust pipe flanges and use new gaskets when installing the new converter. Tighten the bolts securely.

1998 and later models (upstream converter)

8   Remove the nuts and bolts that attach the upper exhaust pipe to the lower flange of the converter. Be sure to apply penetrant to the fasteners to loosen them up (see comments in Step 7 regarding catalyst fasteners). Separate the upper end of the exhaust pipe from the catalyst and push it aside.
9   On 1998 through 2000 models, unbolt the catalyst from the exhaust manifold (again,

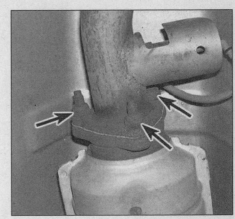

20.7b . . . and then remove these nuts and bolts (arrows) from the rear flange

use liberal doses of penetrant to help loosen the fasteners). On 2001 and later models, the upstream converter is an integral part of the exhaust manifold. Remove the exhaust manifold (see Chapter 2A).
10   Clean the carbon deposits from the mounting flanges and install new gaskets.
11   Installation is the reverse of removal.

6

Notes

Chapter 7 Part A
Manual transaxle

Contents

Specifications

Torque specifications

	Ft-lbs (unless otherwise indicated)	Nm
Shift cable to body bolts	108 to 132 in-lbs	12 to 15
Shift lever base plate mounting nuts		
2000 and earlier models	108 to 132 in-lbs	12 to 15
2001 models	7 to 10 in-lbs	9 to 14
Center member	44 to 59	60 to 80
Transaxle-to-engine bolts	32 to 39	43 to 55
Transaxle mount bracket-to-transaxle	43 to 58	60 to 80
Transaxle mount bracket-to-body	65 to 80	90 to 110

7A

1   General information

The models covered by this manual are equipped with either a five-speed manual transaxle or an automatic transaxle. Information on the manual transaxle is included in this Part of Chapter 7. Information on the automatic transaxle can be found in Chapter 7, Part B. You'll also find certain procedures common to both transaxles - such as oil seal replacement - in Chapter 7B.

The manual transaxle is a synchronized, 5-speed design. The transaxle model number is stamped onto a plate on the transaxle. Refer to *Vehicle identification numbers* at the front of this manual for the location of the plate.

Depending on the expense involved in having a transaxle overhauled, it might be a better idea to consider replacing it with either a new or rebuilt unit. Your local dealer or transaxle shop should be able to supply information concerning cost, availability and exchange policy. Regardless of how you decide to remedy a transaxle problem, you can still save a lot of money by removing and installing the unit yourself.

2   Shift lever assembly and cables - removal and installation

Warning: *The models covered by this manual are equipped with Supplemental Restraint systems (SRS), more commonly known as airbags. Always disable the airbag system before working in the vicinity of any airbag system component to avoid the possibility of accidental deployment of the airbag, which could cause personal injury (see Chapter 12).*

Shift lever

Refer to illustration 2.2
1   Remove the center console (see Chapter 11).
2   Remove shift and select cable retainers and disconnect both cables from the shift lever **(see illustration)**.
3   Remove the retaining bolts/nuts and detach the shift lever assembly.
4   Installation is the reverse or removal.

Cables

5   Detach the shift and select cable from the shift lever assembly (see Step 2).
6   Remove the retaining clips and cotter pins and detach the cable ends of the transaxle.
7   Remove the cable retainer bolts from the firewall and detach the cable assembly from the vehicle.
8   Installation is the reverse of removal.

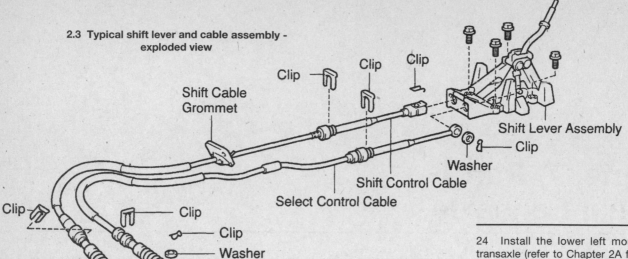

2.3 Typical shift lever and cable assembly - exploded view

---

3   Manual transaxle - removal and installation

Caution: *Some models are equipped with an anti-theft radio. Before performing a procedure that requires disconnecting the battery, make sure you have the activation code.*

Removal

1   Disconnect the negative cable and then the positive cable from the battery.
2   Remove the air intake duct and the air cleaner housing (see Chapter 4).
3   Disconnect the back-up light switch.
4   Disconnect the clutch fluid line, unbolt the clutch release cylinder and support it out of the way with a piece of wire (see Chapter 8). **Caution:** *Be careful not to bend or kink the clutch fluid pressure line and do NOT depress the clutch pedal while the clutch release cylinder is removed.*
5   Disconnect the speedometer cable. On 2001 models, remove the battery and battery tray.
6   Disconnect and remove the shift cables from the transaxle (see Section 2).
7   Remove the upper transaxle mounting bolts and the starter motor bolts.
8   Secure the engine using an engine support fixture **(see illustration 6.8 in Chapter 7B)**. If an engine support fixture is not available, connect an engine hoist and a lifting chain assembly.
9   Raise the vehicle and support it securely on jackstands.
10   Remove the front wheels.
11   Remove the splash shield and drain the transaxle lubricant (see Chapter 1).
12   Disconnect the control arms from the steering knuckles (see Chapter 10).
13   Remove the driveaxles (see Chapter 8).
14   Remove the center member and the

transaxle stay from the engine (2000 and earlier models.
15   Remove front mounting transaxle bracket from the vehicle.
16   Remove the clutch access cover.
17   Support the transaxle with a transaxle jack. Secure the transaxle to the jack with a safety chain. Raise the jack just enough to take the weight off the mounts. **Note:** *Special transmission adapters are available that fit onto regular floor jacks. These can be obtained at tool stores or equipment rental yards.*
18   Remove the lower transaxle mounting bolts.
19   Make a final check that all wires and hoses have been disconnected from the transaxle, then carefully pull the transaxle and jack away from the engine. Once the input shaft is clear, lower the transaxle and remove it from under the vehicle.
20   With the transaxle removed, the clutch components are now accessible and can be inspected. In most cases, new clutch components should be routinely installed when the transaxle is removed (see Chapter 8).

Installation

21   If removed, install the clutch components (see Chapter 8.)
22   With the transaxle secured to the jack by a chain, raise it into position behind the engine, then carefully slide it forward, engaging the dowel pins on the transaxle with the corresponding holes in the block and the input shaft with the clutch plate hub splines. Do not use excessive force to install the transaxle - if the input shaft does not slide into place, readjust the angle of the transaxle so it is level and/or turn the input shaft so the splines engage properly with the clutch plate hub.
23   Install the lower engine-to-transaxle mounting bolts and the rear engine mount bracket bolts. Refer to Chapter 2A for the installation procedure and the torque specifications.

24   Install the lower left mount onto the transaxle (refer to Chapter 2A for the torque specifications).
25   Connect the shift cables to the transaxle.
26   Install the driveaxles (see Chapter 8).
27   Install the transaxle center member and tighten the bolts to the torque listed in this Chapter's Specifications.
28   Connect the control arm to the steering knuckles (see Chapter 10).
29   Install the splash shield and front wheels and lower the vehicle.
30   Install the remaining transaxle mounting bolts and tighten them to the torque listed in this Chapter's Specifications.
31   Install the front engine mount bolts (see Chapter 2A) for the installation procedure and the torque specifications.
32   The remainder of installation is the reverse of removal.
33   Refill the transaxle with the specified type and amount of lubricant (see Chapter 1).
34   Check the clutch operation and bleed the hydraulic system, if necessary (see Chapter 8).
35   Road test the vehicle for proper operation and check for leaks.
36   Have the front wheel alignment checked.

---

4   Manual transaxle overhaul - general information

Overhauling a manual transaxle is difficult for the do-it-yourselfer. Not only must you disassemble and reassemble many small parts, but you must also measure numerous clearances and, if necessary, change them with select-fit shims, thrust washers and spacer collars.

If transaxle problems arise, you can save a lot of money by removing and installing the transaxle yourself. Then buy a rebuilt transaxle (check with local auto parts stores and transmission shops). The cost for an overhaul almost always exceeds the cost of a rebuilt unit. If rebuilt units aren't available, have the transaxle rebuilt by a shop that specializes in rebuilding these units.

Chapter 7 Part B
Automatic transaxle

Contents

Specifications

General

Fluid type and capacity .... See Chapter 1

Torque specifications

	Ft-lbs (unless otherwise indicated)	Nm
Center member bolts (2000 and earlier models)	44 to 59	60 to 80
Front subframe (2001 models)		
Transaxle mount bushing nut	65 to 80	90 to 110
Transaxle bracket to-side member bolts	30 to 36	40 to 50
Subframe-to-chassis mounting bolts	45 to 50	61 to 67
Transaxle-to-engine bolts		
8 mm	22 to 25	30 to 35
10 mm	43 to 58	60 to 80
12 mm	31 to 40	43 to 55
Torque converter cover	60 to 70 in-lbs	8 to 10
Torque converter-to-driveplate bolts	33 to 38	46 to 53
Shift lever bracket-to-floor	84 to 110 in-lbs	9 to 14

1.2a An underside view of the automatic transaxle and related components (2000 and earlier model shown)

1   Center member
2   Transaxle fluid pan

1   General information

Refer to illustration 1.2a and 1.2b

All models covered by this manual are equipped with either a manual transaxle or an automatic transaxle. Information on the automatic is included in this Part of Chapter 7. Information on the manual transaxle can be found in Chapter 7, Part A. You'll also find certain procedures common to both transaxles - such as oil seal replacement - in this chapter.

The automatic transaxle is an electronically controlled, 4-speed unit **(see illustrations)**. The transaxle model number is stamped onto a plate on the transaxle. Refer to *Vehicle identification numbers* at the front of this manual for the location of the plate. Be sure to consult with a dealer parts specialist or other qualified automotive parts representative when ordering replacement transaxle parts.

The transaxle is equipped with transaxle solenoids that are controlled by the computer. These transaxle actuators (solenoids) are mounted in the valve body.

1.2b Underside view of the automatic transaxle and related components (2001 and later model shown)

1   Subframe
2   Subframe bolts
3   Transaxle drain plug

Due to the complexity of the clutches and the hydraulic control system, and because of the special tools and expertise required to perform an automatic transaxle overhaul, it should not be undertaken by the home mechanic. Therefore, the procedures in this Chapter are limited to general diagnosis, routine maintenance, adjustment and transaxle removal and installation.

If the transaxle requires major repair work, it should be left to a dealer service department or an automotive or transmission repair shop. You can, however, remove and install the transaxle yourself and save the expense, even if the repair work is done by a transmission shop (but be sure a proper diagnosis has been made before removing the transaxle).

2 Diagnosis - general

Note: *Automatic transaxle malfunctions may be caused by five general conditions: poor engine performance, improper adjustments, hydraulic malfunctions, mechanical malfunctions or malfunctions in the computer or its signal network. Diagnosis of these problems should always begin with a check of the easily repaired items: fluid level and condition (see Chapter 1), shift control cable adjustment and transaxle range sensor adjustment. Next, perform a road test to determine if the problem has been corrected or if more diagnosis is necessary. If the problem persists after the preliminary tests and corrections are completed, additional diagnosis should be done by a dealer service department or transmission repair shop. Refer to the Troubleshooting section at the front of this manual for information on symptoms of transaxle problems.*

Preliminary checks

1 Drive the vehicle to warm the transaxle to normal operating temperature.
2 Check the fluid level as described in Chapter 1:

   a) *If the fluid level is unusually low, add enough fluid to bring the level within the designated area of the dipstick, then check for external leaks (see below).*
   b) *If the fluid level is abnormally high, drain off the excess, then check the drained fluid for contamination by coolant. The presence of engine coolant in the automatic transmission fluid indicates that a failure has occurred in the internal radiator walls that separate the coolant from the transmission fluid (see Chapter 3).*
   c) *If the fluid is foaming, drain it and refill the transaxle, then check for coolant in the fluid, or a high fluid level.*

3 Check the engine idle speed. **Note:** *If the engine is malfunctioning, do not proceed with the preliminary checks until it has been repaired and runs normally.*
4 Check the throttle control cable for freedom of movement (see Chapter 4).
5 Inspect the shift control linkage (see

Section 4). Make sure that it's properly adjusted and that the linkage operates smoothly.

Fluid leak diagnosis

6 Most fluid leaks are easy to locate visually. Repair usually consists of replacing a seal or gasket. If a leak is difficult to find, the following procedure may help.
7 Identify the fluid. Make sure it's transmission fluid and not engine oil or brake fluid (automatic transmission fluid is a deep red color).
8 Try to pinpoint the source of the leak. Drive the vehicle several miles, then park it over a large sheet of cardboard. After a minute or two, you should be able to locate the leak by determining the source of the fluid dripping onto the cardboard.
9 Make a careful visual inspection of the suspected component and the area immediately around it. Pay particular attention to gasket mating surfaces. A mirror is often helpful for finding leaks in areas that are hard to see.
10 If the leak still cannot be found, clean the suspected area thoroughly with a degreaser or solvent, then dry the area.
11 Drive the vehicle for several miles at normal operating temperature and varying speeds. After driving the vehicle, visually inspect the suspected component again.
12 Once the leak has been located, the cause must be determined before it can be properly repaired. If a gasket is replaced but the sealing flange is bent, the new gasket will not stop the leak. The bent flange must be straightened.
13 Before attempting to repair a leak, check to make sure that the following conditions are corrected or they may cause another leak. **Note:** *Some of the following conditions cannot be fixed without highly specialized tools and expertise. Such problems must be referred to a transmission shop or a dealer service department.*

Gasket leaks

14 Check the fluid pan (2000 and earlier models) or front cover periodically. Make sure the bolts are tight, no bolts are missing, the gasket is in good condition and the cover is not damaged.
15 If the leak is from the pan or front cover area, the bolts may be too tight, the sealing surface of the transaxle housing may be damaged, the gasket may be damaged or the transaxle casting may be cracked or porous. If sealant instead of gasket material has been used to form a seal between the pan/cover and the transaxle housing, it may be the wrong sealant.

Seal leaks

16 If a transaxle seal is leaking, the fluid level or pressure may be too high, the vent may be plugged, the seal bore may be damaged, the seal itself may be damaged or improperly installed, the surface of the shaft protruding through the seal may be damaged

or a loose bearing may be causing excessive shaft movement.
17 Make sure the dipstick tube seal is in good condition and the tube is properly seated. Periodically check the area around the speedometer gear or sensor for leakage. If transmission fluid is evident, check the O-ring for damage.

Case leaks

18 If the case itself appears to be leaking, the casting is porous and will have to be repaired or replaced.
19 Make sure the oil cooler hose fittings are tight and in good condition.

Fluid comes out vent pipe or fill tube

20 If this condition occurs, the transaxle is overfilled, there is coolant in the fluid, the case is porous, the dipstick is incorrect, the vent is plugged or the drain-back holes are plugged.

3 Shift lever - removal and installation

Refer to illustrations 3.3, 3.4 and 3.5
Warning: *The models covered by this manual are equipped with Supplemental Restraint systems (SRS), more commonly known as airbags. Always disable the airbag system before working in the vicinity of the impact sensors, steering column or instrument panel to avoid the possibility of accidental deployment of the airbag, which could cause personal injury (see Chapter 12). The yellow wiring harnesses and connectors routed through the console and instrument panel are for this system. Do not use electrical test equipment on any of the airbag system wiring or tamper with them in any way.*
1 Remove the center console (see Chapter 11).
2 On 2000 and earlier models, remove the two screws, detach the shift knob and disconnect the overdrive switch connector.
3 Disconnect the cables from the shift lock and shift cables from the shift lever assembly **(see illustration)**.

7B

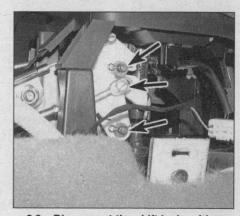

3.3a Disconnect the shift lock cables (arrows) from the lever assembly

3.4 Disconnect the shift cable (A), then remove the through-bolt from the shift lever (B)

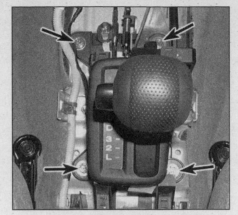

3.5 Remove the shift lever bracket mounting bolts (arrows)

4.3 Before adjusting the shift cable, loosen the swivel nut (A) that connects the cable to the lever on the transaxle and note if the holes in the end of the shift range switch arm and the housing line up (B)

4   Remove the shift cable from the shift lever assembly, then remove the through-bolt from the shift lever **(see illustration)**.

5   Remove the shift lever bracket mounting bolts **(see illustration)**. Remove the shift lever assembly from the vehicle.

6   Installation is the reverse of removal. Be sure to tighten the nuts securely.

4   Shift cable - adjustment and replacement

Warning: *The models covered by this manual are equipped with Supplemental Restraint systems (SRS), more commonly known as airbags. Always disable the airbag system before working in the vicinity of the impact sensors, steering column or instrument panel to avoid the possibility of accidental deployment of the airbag, which could cause personal injury (see Chapter 12). The yellow wiring harnesses and connectors routed through the console and instrument panel are for this system. Do not use electrical test equipment on any of the airbag system wiring or tamper with them in any way.*

Adjustment

Refer to illustration 4.3

1   When the shift lever inside the vehicle is moved from the Neutral position to the other positions, it should move smoothly and accurately to each position and the shift indicator should indicate the correct gear position. If the indicator isn't aligned with the correct position, adjust the shift cable as follows:

2   Move the lever inside the vehicle to the Neutral position.

3   Open the hood and loosen the swivel nut on the manual shift lever on the transaxle noting if the holes in the switch arm and housing line up **(see illustration)**.

4   Place the shift range lever on the transaxle in Neutral.

5   Loosen the switch housing bolts and turn the range switch until the holes in the switch and the lever line up, then tighten the swivel nut and switch bolts securely.

6   Check the operation of the transaxle in each shift lever position (try to start the engine in each gear - the starter should operate in the Park and Neutral positions only).

Replacement

Refer to illustrations 4.7 and 4.8

7   Disconnect the cable from the shift lever **(see illustration 3.4)** and remove the large C-clip retaining the it to shift bracket **(see illustration)**.

8   Working on the transaxle, remove the nut and C-clip retaining the cable to the transaxle shift lever and housing bracket **(see illustration)**.

9   Remove the two shift cable grommet bolts securing the shift cable grommet to the bulkhead.

10   Remove the shift cable from the vehicle.

Installation

11   Insert the shift cable through the opening in the bulkhead.

12   Working in the console area of the passenger compartment, pull the cable into place and install the C-clip into the bracket on the shift lever assembly. Install the cable end onto the selector lever.

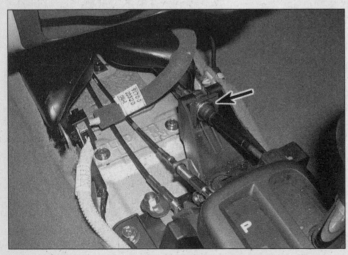

4.7 To remove the shift cable, remove the large C-clip retainer (arrow) from the shift bracket

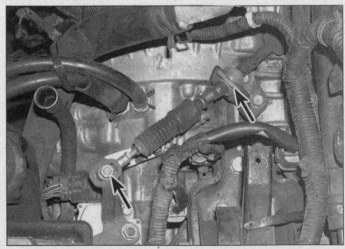

4.8 Remove nut from the shift lever and the C-clip from the bracket (arrows) and detach the shift cable

13   Working in the transaxle area, install the shift cable onto the lever of the transaxle range sensor. Install the C-clip to lock the shift cable into the bracket.

14   Working on the bulkhead, position the shift cable grommet and install the two bolts and tighten them securely.

15   Working in the console area of the passenger compartment, install the shift position indicator assembly and tighten the screws securely.

16   Adjust the shift cable as described in Steps 1 through 6.

17   Install the floor console (see Chapter 11).

18   Move the shift lever to each gear to verify the correct shifting position.

5   Driveaxle oil seals - replacement

Refer to illustration 5.6

1   Oil leaks frequently occur due to wear of the driveaxle oil seals. Replacement of these seals is relatively easy, since the repair can usually be performed without removing the transaxle from the vehicle.

2   The driveaxle oil seals are located at the sides of the transaxle, where the driveaxles are attached. If leakage at the seal is suspected, raise the vehicle and support it securely on jackstands. If the seal is leaking, lubricant will be found on the sides of the transaxle, below the seals.

3   Refer to Chapter 8 and remove the driveaxles.

4   Using a screwdriver or prybar, carefully pry the oil seal out of the transaxle bore.

5   If the oil seal cannot be removed with a screwdriver or prybar, a special oil seal removal tool (available at auto parts stores) will be required.

6   Using a large section of pipe or a large deep socket (slightly smaller than the outside diameter of the seal) as a drift, install the new oil seal **(see illustration)**. Drive it into the bore squarely and make sure it's completely seated. Coat the seal lip with transaxle lubricant.

5.6 Tap the new seal into place with a large socket or piece of pipe and a hammer - the outside diameter of the pipe or socket should be slightly smaller than the seal

7   Install the driveaxle(s). Be careful not to damage the lip of the new seal.

6   Automatic transaxle - removal and installation

Removal

Refer to illustrations 6.7, 6.8, 6.11, 6.15a and 6.15b

Caution: *Some models are equipped with an anti-theft radio. Before performing a procedure that requires disconnecting the battery, make sure you have the activation code.*

1   Disconnect the negative cable and then the positive cable from the battery. For easier access to upper transaxle components, remove the battery and the battery tray (see Chapter 5).

2   Remove the air intake duct and the air cleaner housing (see Chapter 4).

3   Disconnect the shift cable from the transaxle (see Section 4).

4   Disconnect the transaxle ground cable and the transaxle range sensor.

6.7 Remove the upper transaxle-to-engine bolt (arrow) (2000 and earlier models)

5   Disconnect the transaxle harness connector from the side of the transaxle.

6   Drain the transaxle fluid (see Chapter 1), then disconnect the transaxle fluid cooler lines from the transaxle.

7   On 2000 and earlier models, remove the upper transaxle-to-engine mounting bolt **(see illustration)**.

8   Raise the vehicle and support it securely on jackstands. Secure the engine using an engine support brace that is installed above the engine compartment **(see illustration)**. If an engine support brace is not available, install an engine lift and a lifting chain assembly. This will keep the engine stable during the entire transaxle removal procedure.

9   Remove the transaxle mount bracket.

10   Remove the front wheels.

2000 and earlier models

11   Remove the bolts from the center member and the transaxle roll stopper **(see illustration)**.

12   Disconnect the lower control arms from the steering knuckles and remove the driveaxles.

13   Remove the transaxle stay, followed by the bell housing access cover.

7B

6.8 Install an engine support brace across the engine compartment

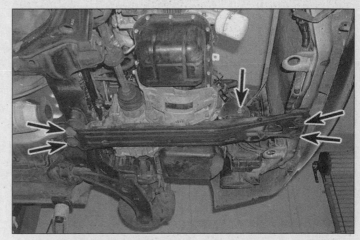

6.11 On 2000 and earlier models, remove the bolts from the transaxle roll stopper and the center member (arrows)

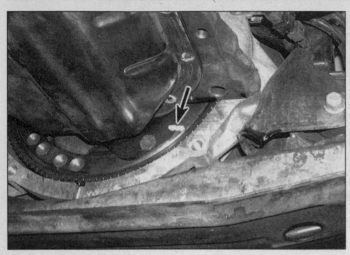

6.15a Mark the torque converter-to-drive plate relationship (arrow) . . .

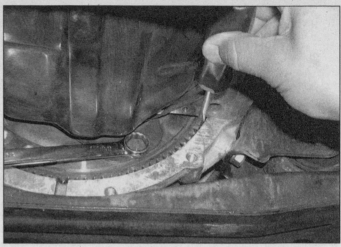

6.15b . . . and rotate the crankshaft to remove each mounting bolt

2001 and later models

14   Remove the steering gear assembly and the stabilizer bar, then disconnect the lower ball joints (see Chapter 10) and remove the driveshafts (see Chapter 8). Remove the starter motor. Paint or scribe subframe-to-chassis reference marks to ensure correct reassembly. Remove the mounting bolts and lower the subframe.

All models

15   Unbolt and remove the cover, then remove the torque converter bolts. A screwdriver wedged in the ring gear teeth will keep the torque converter from rotating while the bolts are loosened. Rotate the engine for access to all of the bolts (see illustrations).
16   Support the transaxle with an approved transaxle jack and safety chains. Floor jacks are often not stable enough to support and lower the transaxle from the vehicle.
17   Make a final check that all wires and hoses have been disconnected from the transaxle.

18   Remove the mounting and retaining bolts and lower the transaxle from the vehicle or subframe with a jack.

Installation

19   If removed, install the torque converter into the transaxle.
20   With the transaxle secured to the jack by a chain, raise it into position behind the engine, then carefully slide it forward, engaging the dowel pins on the transaxle with the corresponding holes in the block and the bolt holes in the driveplate with the flywheel. Do not use excessive force to install the transaxle - if the torque converter does not slide into place, readjust the angle of the transaxle so it is level.
21   Install the engine-to-transaxle mounting bolts.
22   Install the shift cable onto the transaxle (see Section 4).
23   On 2000 and earlier models, install the roll stopper and center member. Tighten the center member bolts to the torque listed in

this Chapter's Specifications. Install the driveaxle and connect the lower ball joints. Tighten suspension and driveaxle components to the torques listed in the Chapter 10 Specifications.
24   On 2001 and later models, install the starter motor. Install the stabilizer bar and the steering gear assembly, then install the driveshafts and connect the lower ball joints. Install the subframe, aligning the mark(s) made during removal and tighten the bolts to the torque listed in this Chapter's Specifications (see illustration 1.2b).
25   Install the remaining engine-to-transaxle mounting bolts.
26   Install the splash shield and front wheels and lower the vehicle.
27   The remainder of installation is the reverse of removal.
28   Refill the transaxle with the specified type and amount of lubricant (see Chapter 1).
29   Road test the vehicle for proper operation and check for leaks.
30   Have the front end aligned.

Chapter 8
Clutch and driveaxles

Contents

Specifications

General

Clutch pedal freeplay	1/4 to 1/2 inch (6 to 12 mm)
Clutch pedal standard height	
2000 and earlier models	7-1/2 inches (190.1 mm)
2001 and later models	6-9/16 inches (166.9 mm)

Driveaxles

Driveaxle length	
Manual transaxle	
1996 through 1998 models	
Left axle	15-45/64 inches (399 mm)
Right axle	26-15/16 inches (684 mm)
1999 and 2000 models	
Left axle	15-41/64 inches (397.5 mm)
Right axle	26-53/64 inches (681.5 mm)
2001 models	
Left	20-13/64 inches (513.2 mm)
Right	31-11/32 inches (796.2 mm)
Automatic transaxle	
1996 through 1998 models	
Left	15-43/64 inches (398.1 mm)
Right	26-21/32 inches (679.1 mm)
1999 and 2000 models	
Left axle	15-11/16 inches (398.2 mm)
Right axle	26-25/32 inches (677.2 mm)
2001 models	
Left	20-13/64 inches (513.2 mm)
Right	31-11/32 inches (798.2 mm)

Torque specifications

	Ft-lbs (unless otherwise indicated)	Nm
Clutch master cylinder mounting fasteners	72 to 108 in-lbs	8 to 12
Clutch release cylinder mounting bolts	11 to 16	15 to 22
Clutch pressure plate bolts	11 to 16	15 to 22
Driveaxle/hub nut	148 to 192	200 to 260

8

1   General information

The information in this Chapter deals with the components from the rear of the engine to the front wheels, except for the transaxle, which is dealt with in the previous Chapter. For the purposes of this Chapter, these components are grouped into two categories - clutch and driveaxles. Separate Sections within this Chapter offer general descriptions and checking procedures for components in each of the two groups.

Since nearly all the procedures covered in this Chapter involve working under the vehicle, make sure it's securely supported on sturdy jackstands or on a hoist where the vehicle can be easily raised and lowered.

2   Clutch - description and check

1   All vehicles with a manual transaxle use a single dry-plate, diaphragm-spring type clutch. The clutch disc has a splined hub, which allows it to slide along the splines of the transmission input shaft. Spring pressure exerted by the diaphragm in the pressure plate holds the clutch and pressure plate in contact.

2   The clutch release system is operated by hydraulic pressure. The hydraulic release system consists of the clutch pedal, a master cylinder and fluid reservoir, the hydraulic line, a release (or slave) cylinder which actuates the clutch release lever and the clutch release (or throwout) bearing.

3   When pressure is applied to the clutch pedal to release the clutch, hydraulic pressure is exerted against the outer end of the clutch release lever. As the lever pivots the shaft fingers push against the release bearing. The bearing pushes against the fingers of the diaphragm spring of the pressure plate assembly, which in turn releases the clutch plate.

4   Terminology can be a problem when discussing the clutch components because common names are in some cases different from those used by the manufacturer. For example, the driven plate is also called the clutch plate or disc, the clutch release bearing is sometimes called a throwout bearing, the release cylinder is sometimes called the operating or slave cylinder.

5   Other than to replace components with obvious damage, some preliminary checks should be performed to diagnose clutch problems. These checks assume that the transaxle is in good working condition.

a)   *The first check should be of the fluid level in the clutch master cylinder (see Chapter 1). If the fluid level is low, add fluid as necessary and inspect the hydraulic system for leaks. If the master cylinder reservoir has run dry, bleed the system as described in Section 5 and retest the clutch operation.*

b)   *To check "clutch spin-down time," run the engine at normal idle speed with the transmission in Neutral (clutch pedal up - engaged). Disengage the clutch (pedal down), wait several seconds and shift the transmission into Reverse. No grinding noise should be heard. A grinding noise would most likely indicate a problem in the pressure plate or the clutch disc.*

c)   *To check for complete clutch release, run the engine (with the parking brake applied to prevent movement) and hold the clutch pedal approximately 1/2-inch from the floor. Shift the transmission between 1st gear and Reverse several times. If the shift is rough, component failure is indicated. Check the release cylinder pushrod travel. With the clutch pedal depressed completely, the release cylinder pushrod should extend substantially. If it doesn't, check the fluid level in the clutch master cylinder.*

d)   *Visually inspect the pivot bushing at the top of the clutch pedal to make sure there is no binding or excessive play.*

e)   *Crawl under the vehicle and make sure the clutch release lever is solidly mounted on the ball stud (2001 and later models).*

3   Clutch master cylinder - removal and installation

Caution: *Some models are equipped with an anti-theft radio. Before performing a procedure that requires disconnecting the battery, make sure you have the activation code.*

Removal

1   Disconnect the cable from the negative battery terminal.

2   Working under the dashboard, remove the cotter pin from the clutch master cylinder pushrod clevis. Pull out the clevis pin to disconnect the pushrod from the pedal.

3   Remove as much fluid as possible from the clutch fluid reservoir with a suction gun or large syringe. Be careful not to drip any fluid on the vehicle's paint. On 2000 and earlier models, detach the fluid feed line from the master cylinder.

4   Using a flare-nut wrench, disconnect the hydraulic line fitting at the cylinder. Have rags handy, as some fluid will be lost as the line is removed. Cap or plug the ends of the line to prevent fluid leakage and the entry of contaminants.

5   Remove the mounting fasteners and detach the cylinder from the firewall. **Caution:** *Don't allow brake fluid to come into contact with the paint, as it will damage the finish.*

Installation

6   Place the master cylinder in position on the firewall and install the mounting fasteners finger tight.

7   Connect the hydraulic line fitting to the clutch master cylinder and tighten it finger tight (since the cylinder is still a bit loose, it'll be easier to start the threads into the cylinder).

8   Tighten the mounting fasteners to the torque listed in this Chapter's Specifications, then tighten the hydraulic line fitting securely.

9   On 2000 and earlier models, attach the fluid feed hose from the reservoir to the clutch master cylinder and tighten the hose clamp.

10   Connect the pushrod to the clutch pedal, using a new cotter pin to secure the clevis pin.

11   Fill the reservoir with brake fluid conforming to DOT 3 specifications and bleed the clutch system as outlined in Section 5.

12   Connect the negative battery cable.

4   Clutch release cylinder - removal and installation

Caution: *Some models are equipped with an anti-theft radio. Before performing a procedure that requires disconnecting the battery, make sure you have the activation code.*

Removal

1   Disconnect the negative cable from the battery.

2000 and earlier models

2   Open the hood, remove the clip and the retaining pin then detach the release cylinder push rod from the clutch release lever.

3   Disconnect the hydraulic line at the release cylinder using a flare-nut wrench. Have a small can and rags handy, as some fluid will be spilled as the line is removed. Plug the line to prevent excessive fluid loss and contamination.

4   Unscrew the bolts and remove the clutch release cylinder.

2001 and later models

5   Raise the vehicle and support it securely on jackstands.

6   Disconnect the hydraulic line at the release cylinder using a flare-nut wrench. Have a small can and rags handy, as some fluid will be spilled as the line is removed. Plug the line to prevent excessive fluid loss and contamination.

7   Remove the two release cylinder mounting bolts.

8   Remove the release cylinder.

Installation

9   On 2001 and later models, lubricate the pocket in the release fork with multi-purpose grease.

10   On all models, install the release cylinder on the clutch housing and install the bolts, but leave them a little loose until after the hydraulic line fitting threads have been started. On 2000 and earlier models, connect the pushrod to the release lever and install

5.5 When bleeding the clutch hydraulic system, a hose is connected to the bleeder valve at the release cylinder and then submerged in brake fluid. When the pedal is depressed and the valve is opened, air will be seen as bubbles in the hose and container (typical setup shown)

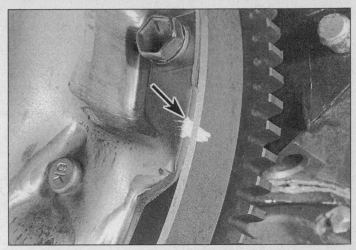

6.5 Mark the relationship of the pressure plate to the flywheel (if you're planning to re-use the old pressure plate)

the retaining pin, washer and clip. On 2001 and later models, make sure the pushrod is seated in the release fork pocket.

11   Connect the hydraulic line fitting to the release cylinder, using your fingers only at this time (since the cylinder is still a bit loose, it'll be easier to start the threads into the cylinder).

12   Tighten the mounting bolts to the torque listed in this Chapter's Specifications.

13   Tighten the hydraulic fitting securely, using a flare-nut wrench.

14   Check the fluid level in the brake fluid reservoir, adding brake fluid conforming to DOT 3 specifications until the level is correct.

15   Bleed the system as described in Section 5, then recheck the brake fluid level.

16   Connect the negative battery cable.

5   Clutch hydraulic system - bleeding

Refer to illustration 5.5

1   Bleed the hydraulic system whenever any part of the system has been removed or the fluid level has fallen so low that air has been drawn into the master cylinder. The bleeding procedure is very similar to bleeding a brake system.

2   Fill the clutch master cylinder reservoir with new brake fluid conforming to DOT 3 specifications. **Caution:** *Do not re-use any of the fluid coming from the system during the bleeding operation or use fluid which has been inside an open container for an extended period of time.*

3   If you're working on a 2001 or later model, raise the vehicle and support it securely on jackstands to gain access to the release cylinder, which is located on the front of the transaxle.

4   Remove the dust cap that fits over the

bleeder valve and push a length of plastic hose over the valve. Place the other end of the hose into a clear container with about two inches of brake fluid. The hose end must be in the fluid at the bottom of the container.

5   Have an assistant depress the clutch pedal and hold it. Open the bleeder valve on the release cylinder, allowing fluid to flow through the hose **(see illustration)**. Close the bleeder valve when the flow of fluid (and bubbles) ceases. Once closed, have your assistant release the pedal.

6   Repeat this process until all air is evacuated from the system, indicated by a solid stream of fluid being ejected from the bleeder valve each time with no air bubbles in the hose or container. Keep a close watch on the fluid level inside the clutch master cylinder reservoir - if the level drops too far, air will get into the system and you'll have to start all over again.

7   Install the dust cap and, on 2001 and later models, lower the vehicle. Check the clutch fluid level again, and add some, if necessary, to bring it to the appropriate level. Check carefully for proper operation before placing the vehicle into normal service.

6   Clutch components - removal, inspection and installation

Warning: *Dust produced by clutch wear and deposited on clutch components may contain asbestos, which is hazardous to your health. DO NOT blow it out with compressed air and DO NOT inhale it. DO NOT use gasoline or petroleum-based solvents to remove the dust. Brake system cleaner should be used to flush the dust into a drain pan. After the clutch components are wiped clean with a rag, dispose of the contaminated rags and cleaner in a covered, marked container.*

Removal

Refer to illustrations 6.5 and 6.6

1   Access to the clutch components is normally accomplished by removing the transaxle, leaving the engine in the vehicle. If the engine is being removed for major overhaul, check the clutch for wear and replace worn components as necessary. However, the relatively low cost of the clutch components compared to the time and trouble spent gaining access to them warrants their replacement anytime the engine or transaxle is removed, unless they are new or in near-perfect condition. The following procedures are based on the assumption the engine will stay in place.

2   Remove the transaxle from the vehicle (see Chapter 7, Part A). Support the engine while the transaxle is out. Preferably, an engine support fixture or a hoist should be used to support it from above. However, if a jack is used underneath the engine, make sure a piece of wood is positioned between the jack and oil pan to spread the load. **Caution:** *The pick-up for the oil pump is very close to the bottom of the oil pan. If the pan is bent or distorted in any way, engine oil starvation could occur.*

3   The clutch fork and release bearing can remain attached to the transaxle housing for the time being.

4   To support the clutch disc during removal, install a clutch alignment tool through the clutch disc hub.

5   Carefully inspect the flywheel and pressure plate for indexing marks. The marks are usually an X, an O or a white letter. If they cannot be found, scribe or paint marks yourself so the pressure plate and the flywheel will be in the same alignment during installation **(see illustration)**.

6   Turning each bolt a little at a time, loosen the pressure plate-to-flywheel bolts

8

6.6 Remove the pressure plate bolts (arrows) gradually and evenly in a criss-cross pattern

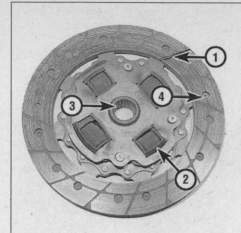

6.9 The clutch disc

1   **Lining** - this will wear down in use
2   **Springs or dampers** - check for cracking and deformation
3   **Splined hub** - the splines must not be worn and should slide smoothly on the transaxle input shaft splines
4   **Rivets** - these secure the lining and will damage the flywheel or pressure plate if allowed to contact the surfaces

(see illustration). Work in a criss-cross pattern until all spring pressure is relieved. Then hold the pressure plate securely and completely remove the bolts, followed by the pressure plate and clutch disc.

Inspection

Refer to illustrations 6.9, 6.11a and 6.11b

7   Ordinarily, when a problem occurs in the clutch, it can be attributed to wear of the clutch driven plate assembly (clutch disc). However, all components should be inspected at this time.

8   Inspect the flywheel for cracks, heat checking, grooves and other obvious defects. If the imperfections are slight, a machine shop can machine the surface flat and smooth, which is highly recommended regardless of the surface appearance. Refer to Chapter 2 for the flywheel removal and installation procedure.

9   Inspect the lining on the clutch disc. There should be at least 3/64-inch (1.1 mm) of lining above the rivet heads. Check for loose rivets, distortion, cracks, broken springs and other obvious damage **(see illustration)**. If there is any doubt about its condition, replace the clutch disc with a new one.

10   Replace the release bearing along with the clutch disc (see Section 7).

11   Check the machined surfaces and the diaphragm spring fingers of the pressure plate **(see illustrations)**. If the surface is grooved or otherwise damaged, replace the

NORMAL FINGER WEAR   EXCESSIVE WEAR   **EXCESSIVE FINGER WEAR**   **BROKEN OR BENT FINGERS**

6.11a Replace the pressure plate if excessive wear (or damage) is noted

6.11b Inspect the pressure plate surface for excessive score marks, cracks and signs of overheating

6.13 Center the clutch disc in the pressure plate with a clutch alignment tool

pressure plate. Also check for obvious damage, distortion, cracking, etc. Light glazing can be removed with emery cloth or sandpaper. If a new pressure plate is required, new and re-manufactured units are available.

Installation

Refer to illustration 6.13

12   Before installation, clean the flywheel and pressure plate machined surfaces with brake cleaner, lacquer thinner or acetone. It's important that no oil or grease is on these surfaces or the lining of the clutch disc. Handle the parts only with clean hands.

13   Position the clutch disc and pressure plate against the flywheel with the clutch held in place with an alignment tool **(see illustration)**. Make sure the disc is installed properly (most replacement clutch discs will be marked "flywheel side" or something similar - if not marked, install the clutch disc with the damper springs toward the transaxle).

14   Tighten the pressure plate-to-flywheel bolts only finger tight, working around the pressure plate.

15   Center the clutch disc by ensuring the alignment tool extends through the splined hub and into the pilot bearing in the crankshaft. Wiggle the tool up, down or side-to-side as needed to center the disc. Tighten the pressure plate-to-flywheel bolts a little at a time, working in a criss-cross pattern to prevent distorting the cover. After all of the bolts are snug, tighten them to the torque listed in this Chapter's Specifications. Remove the alignment tool.

16   Using high-temperature grease, lubricate the inner groove of the release bearing (see Section 7). Also place grease on the release lever contact areas and the transaxle input shaft bearing retainer.

17   Install the clutch release bearing (see Section 7).

18   Install the transaxle and all components removed previously.

7   Clutch release bearing and fork - removal, inspection and installation

Warning: *Dust produced by clutch wear and deposited on clutch components may contain asbestos, which is hazardous to your health. DO NOT blow it out with compressed air and DO NOT inhale it. DO NOT use gasoline or petroleum-based solvents to remove the dust. Brake system cleaner should be used to flush the dust into a drain pan. After the clutch components are wiped clean with a rag, dispose of the contaminated rags and cleaner in a covered, marked container.*

Removal

Refer to illustration 7.3

1   Unbolt the clutch release cylinder (see Section 4), but don't disconnect the fluid line between the master cylinder and the release cylinder. Suspend the release cylinder out of the way with a piece of wire. **Caution:** *Don't depress the clutch pedal with the release cylinder unbolted.* On 2000 and earlier models, remove the release lever from the release shaft to allow transaxle removal.

2   Remove the transaxle (see Chapter 7, Part A).

3   On 2000 and earlier models, use snap ring pliers to remove the snap ring retaining the release bearing to the pressure plate. On 2001 and later models, pull the clutch release fork off the ball stud and slide the release bearing off the input shaft along with release fork **(see illustration)**.

Inspection

Refer to illustration 7.4

4   Hold the bearing by the outer race and rotate the inner race while applying pressure **(see illustration)**. If the bearing doesn't turn smoothly or if it's noisy, replace it with a new

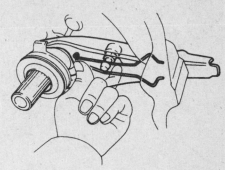

7.3 Reach behind the release lever and disengage the lever from the ball stud by pulling on the retention spring, then remove the lever and bearing (2001 and later models)

one. Wipe the bearing with a clean rag and inspect it for damage, wear and cracks. It's common practice to replace the bearing with a new one whenever a clutch job is performed, to decrease the possibility of a bearing failure in the future. Don't immerse the bearing in solvent - it's sealed for life and to do so would ruin it.

5   Check the release lever for cracks and bends.

Installation

Refer to illustrations 7.6, 7.7a and 7.7b

6   Fill the inner groove of the release bearing with high temperature grease. Also apply a light coat of the same grease to the transaxle input shaft splines, ball stud (2001 and later models) and the front bearing retainer **(see illustration)**.

7   Lubricate the release lever contact points and release cylinder pushrod socket with high temperature grease **(see illustrations)**.

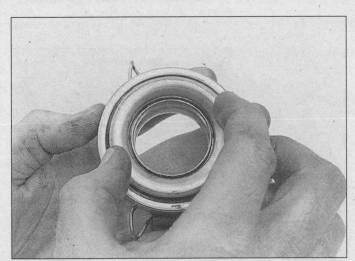

7.4 To check the bearing, hold it by the outer race and rotate the inner race while applying pressure; if the bearing doesn't turn smoothly or if it is noisy, replace the bearing

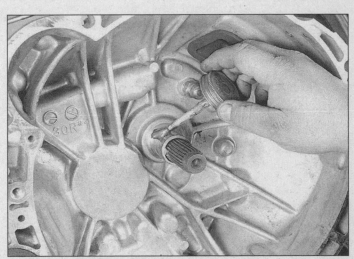

7.6 Apply a light coat of high-temperature grease to the bearing surface of the retainer (before installing the transaxle, apply the same grease to the input shaft splines and, on 2001 and later models, the release lever ball stud)

8

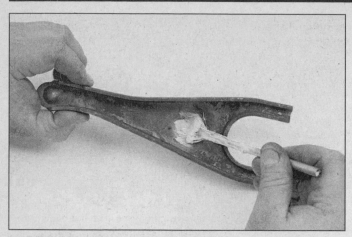

7.7a Using high temperature grease, lubricate the ball stud socket in the back of the release lever . . .

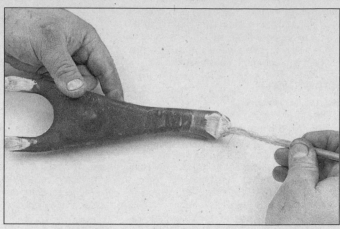

7.7b . . . the lever ends and the depression for the release cylinder pushrod (2001 and later models)

8   On 2001 and later models, attach the release bearing to the release fork.

9   On 2000 and earlier models lightly lubricate the pressure plate diaphragm fingers, install the release bearing and secure it with the snap-ring. On 2001 and later models, slide the release bearing onto the transaxle input shaft front bearing retainer while passing the end of the release fork through the opening in the clutch housing. Push the clutch release fork onto the ball stud until it's firmly seated. Apply a light coat of high temperature grease to the face of the release bearing.

10   The remainder of installation is the reverse of the removal procedure.

8   Clutch pedal - adjustment

Pedal height

Refer to illustration 8.1

1   The height of the clutch pedal is the distance the pedal sits off the floor **(see illustration)**. If the pedal height is not within the specified range, it must be adjusted. Measure the pedal height from the center of the clutch pedal pad to the floor (with the carpet in place).

2   To adjust the clutch pedal, loosen the locknut on the adjusting bolt and back the bolt out to increase the pedal height or turn the bolt in to decrease pedal height. Check the pedal height (see Step 1), then tighten the locknut.

Pedal freeplay

Refer to illustration 8.3

3   The freeplay is the pedal slack, or the distance the pedal can be depressed before it begins to have any effect on the clutch system **(see illustration)**. If the pedal freeplay is not within the specified range, it must be adjusted.

4   To adjust the pedal freeplay, loosen the locknut on the clutch pushrod **(see illustration 8.1)**. Turn the pushrod to adjust the pedal freeplay to the specified range and retighten the locknut.

9   Starter/clutch interlock switch - check and replacement

Check

1   Located at the upper end of the clutch pedal, the starter/clutch interlock switch closes when the clutch pedal is depressed with the ignition switch key in the Start position, allowing the starter motor to activate.

2   If the engine won't crank when the clutch pedal is depressed check the switch and, if necessary, replace it.

3   If the engine won't start when the clutch pedal is depressed, either there's no voltage from the ignition switch to the switch, or there's no continuity between the two terminals on the switch.

4   Check the voltage to the switch using a voltmeter or test light. Refer to the wiring diagrams at the end of Chapter 12. Voltage should be available with the ignition key ON (engine not running). If there isn't, look for an open or short circuit condition somewhere between the ignition switch and the clutch switch.

5   Check the switch for continuity. With the clutch pedal depressed and the key in Start, continuity should exist between terminals 1 and 2. With the clutch pedal released, continuity should not exist.

Replacement

6   Disconnect the electrical connector.

7   Loosen the locknut and separate the switch from its mounting bracket.

8   Installation is the reverse of removal.

10   Driveaxles - general information and inspection

1   Power is transmitted from the transaxle to the wheels through a pair of driveaxles. The inner end of the driveaxle is splined into the differential side gear. The outer ends of the driveaxles are splined to the axle hubs and secured by a large locknut.

2   The inner ends of the driveaxles are

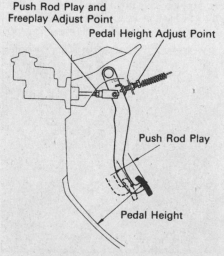

8.1 Clutch pedal height is the distance between the pedal pad and the floor

8.3 Clutch pedal freeplay is the distance from the natural resting point of the pedal to the point at which resistance is felt

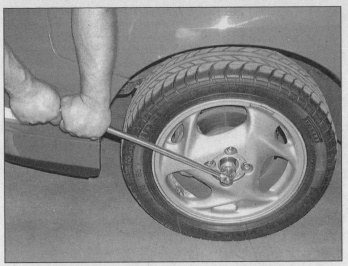

11.2 Loosen the driveaxle/hub nut with a long breaker bar - depending on the design of the wheel, it may be necessary to install the spare wheel and tire to access the hub nut

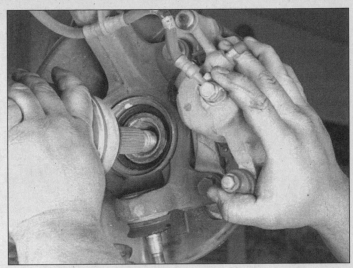

11.6a Swing the hub/knuckle out (away from the vehicle) and pull the driveaxle from the hub

equipped with sliding constant velocity joints, which are capable of both angular and axial motion. On automatic transaxle models a "tri-pot" inner joint is used. On manual transaxle models a "ball-and-cage" type inner joint is used. The inner joints can be disassembled and cleaned in the event of a boot failure (see Section 12), but if any parts are damaged, the joints must be replaced as a unit.

3   The outer CV joints are the "ball-and-cage" type, which have ball bearings running between an inner and outer race; these joints allow angular but not axial movement. The outer joints should be cleaned, inspected and repacked when replacing the boot, but they cannot be disassembled. If an outer joint is damaged, it must be replaced along with the axleshaft (the outer joint and axleshaft are sold as a single component).

4   The boots should be inspected periodically for damage and leaking lubricant. Torn CV joint boots must be replaced immediately or the joints can be damaged. Boot replacement involves removal of the driveaxle (see Section 11). **Note:** *Some auto parts stores carry "split" type replacement boots, which can be installed without removing the driveaxle from the vehicle. This is a convenient alternative, but it should only be considered a temporary fix. At any rate, the driveaxle still must be removed and the CV joint disassembled and cleaned to ensure the joint is free from contaminants such as moisture and dirt which will accelerate CV joint wear.* The most common symptom of worn or damaged CV joints, besides lubricant leaks, is a clicking noise in turns, a clunk when accelerating after coasting, and vibration at highway speeds. To check for wear in the CV joints and driveaxle shafts, grasp each axle (one at a time) and rotate it in both directions while holding the CV joint housings, feeling for play indicating worn splines or sloppy CV joints. Also check the driveaxle shafts for cracks, dents and distortion.

11 Driveaxles - removal and installation

Removal

Refer to illustrations 11.2, 11.6a and 11.6b

1   Remove the wheel cover or hub cap. Remove the cotter pin.

2   Break the hub nut loose with a socket and large breaker bar **(see illustration)**. **Note:** *If the socket will not fit through the opening in the center of the wheel, remove the wheel and install the spare tire/wheel.*

3   Loosen the wheel lug nuts, raise the vehicle and support it securely on jackstands. Remove the wheel. Drain the transaxle lubricant (see Chapter 1).

4   Detach the stabilizer bar link(s) from the control arm(s) (see Chapter 10).

5   Separate the lower control arm from the steering knuckle (see Chapter 10). Now remove the driveaxle/hub nut.

6   Swing the knuckle/hub assembly out (away from the vehicle) until the end of the

driveaxle is free of the hub **(see illustration)**. **Note:** *If the driveaxle splines stick in the hub, tap on the end of the driveaxle with a plastic hammer. Carefully pry the inner CV joint from the transaxle using a large screwdriver or prybar positioned between the CV joint housing and the transaxle housing* **(see illustration)**. *Support the outer end of the driveaxle with a piece of wire to avoid unnecessary strain on the inner CV joint.*

7   Support the CV joints and carefully remove the driveaxle from the vehicle.

Installation

Refer to illustrations 11.8a and 11.8b

8   Pry the old spring clip from the inner end of the driveaxle and install a new one **(see illustrations)**. Lubricate the differential seal with multi-purpose grease and raise the driveaxle into position while supporting the CV joints. **Note:** *Position the spring clip with the opening facing up; this will ease insertion of the driveaxle and prevent damage to the clip.*

11.6b Use a large screwdriver or a prybar to pop the inner CV joint out of the transaxle

11.8a Pry the old spring clip from the inner end of the driveaxle with a small screwdriver or awl

8

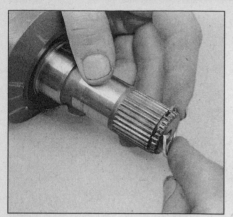

11.8b To install the new spring clip, start one end in the groove and work the clip over the shaft end, into the groove

12.3a Cut off the boot clamps and discard them - don't try to reuse old clamps

12.3b Slide the boot down the driveaxle, out of the way

9   Push the splined end of the inner CV joint into the differential side gear and make sure the spring clip locks in its groove.

10   Apply a light coat of multi-purpose grease to the outer CV joint splines, pull out on the steering knuckle assembly and install the stub axle into the hub.

11   Insert the balljoint stud into the steering knuckle and tighten the pinch bolt to the torque listed in the Chapter 10 Specifications.

12   Install the driveaxle/hub nut. Tighten the hub nut securely, but don't try to tighten it to the actual torque specification until you've lowered the vehicle to the ground.

13   Grasp the inner CV joint housing (not the driveaxle) and pull out to make sure the driveaxle has seated securely in the transaxle.

14   Connect the stabilizer bar link(s) (see Chapter 10).

15   Install the wheel and lug nuts, then lower the vehicle. Tighten the lug nuts to torque listed in the Chapter 1 Specifications.

16   Tighten the driveaxle/hub nut to the torque listed in this Chapter's Specifications and install a new cotter pin. Install the hub

cap or wheel cover.

17   Refill the transaxle with the recommended type and amount of lubricant (see Chapter 1).

12   Driveaxle boot - replacement

Note 1: *If the CV joints are worn or the boots are in need of replacement (check on the availability of parts), before beginning the job. Complete rebuilt driveaxles are available on an exchange basis, which eliminates much time and work.*

Note 2: *Some auto parts stores carry "split" type replacement boots, which can be installed without removing the driveaxle from the vehicle. This is a convenient alternative; however, the driveaxle should be removed and the CV joint disassembled and cleaned to ensure the joint is free from contaminants such as moisture and dirt which will accelerate CV joint wear.*

Note 3: *Models equipped with ABS are equipped with ABS sensor rings on the outer CV joints. Be sure to inspect the sensor rings*

for chipped or missing teeth. Replace the sensor ring if necessary.

1   Remove the driveaxle from the vehicle (see Section 11).

2   Mount the driveaxle in a vise. The jaws of the vise should be lined with wood or rags to prevent damage to the driveaxle.

Inner CV joint and boot

Tri-pot type (automatic transaxle models)

Disassembly

Refer to illustrations 12.3a, 12.3b, 12.4, 12.5, 12.6 and 12.7

3   Remove the boot clamps **(see illustration)**.

4   Pull the boot back from the inner CV joint, remove the retainer ring and slide the joint housing off. Be sure to mark the relationship of the tri-pot to the outer race **(see illustration)**.

5   Mark the tri-pot and axleshaft to ensure that they are reassembled properly **(see illustration)**.

6   Remove the snap-ring from the end of

12.4 Mark the relationship of the tri-pot assembly to the outer race

12.5 Use a center punch to place marks (arrows) on the tri-pot and the driveaxle to ensure that they are properly reassembled

12.6 Remove the snap-ring from the groove in the end of the axleshaft

12.7 Drive the tri-pot joint from the axleshaft with a brass punch and hammer – make sure you don't damage the bearing surfaces or the splines on the shaft

the axleshaft with a pair of snap-ring pliers **(see illustration)**.

7   Use a hammer and a brass punch to drive the tri-pot joint from the driveaxle **(see illustration)**.

Inspection

8   Clean the old grease from the outer race and the tri-pot bearing assembly. Carefully disassemble each section of the tri-pot assembly, one at a time so as not to mix up the parts, and clean the needle bearings with solvent.

9   Inspect the rollers, tri-pot, bearings and outer race for scoring, pitting or other signs of abnormal wear, which will warrant the replacement of the inner CV joint.

Reassembly

Refer to illustrations 12.10, 12.11, 12.13, 12.14, 12.15a, 12.15b, 12.15c, 12.15d and 12.15e

10   Slide the clamps and boot onto the axleshaft. It's a good idea to wrap the axleshaft splines with tape to prevent damaging the boot **(see illustration)**.

11   Place the tri-pot on the shaft (making sure the marks are aligned) and install the

12.10 Wrap the splined area of the axleshaft with tape to prevent damage to the boot(s) when installing it

snap-ring. Apply grease to the tri-pot assembly, the inside of the joint housing and the inside of the boot **(see illustration)**. Install the housing over the tri-pot.

12   Slide the boot into place, making sure both ends seat in their grooves.

13   Adjust the length of the joint to the

12.11 Pack the outer race with grease and slide it over the tri-pot assembly – make sure the match marks on the CV joint housing and tri-pot line up

length listed in this Chapter's Specifications **(see illustration)**.

14   Equalize the pressure within the boot **(see illustration)**.

15   Tighten and the boot clamps **(see illustrations)**. Proceed to Step 36.

12.13 Adjust the driveaxle length to the dimension listed in this Chapter's Specifications

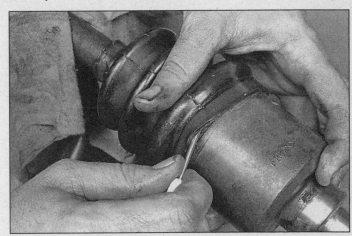

12.14 Equalize the pressure inside the boot by inserting a small, dull screwdriver between the boot and the housing

8

12.15a To install new fold-over type clamps, bend the tang down . . .

12.15b . . . and flatten the tabs to hold it in place

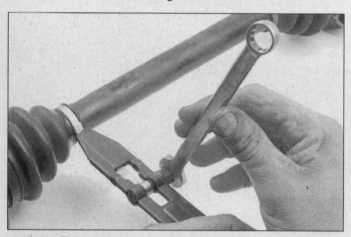

13.15c To install band-type clamps you'll need a special tool; install the band with its end pointing in the direction of axle rotation and tighten it securely, then pivot the tool up 90-degrees and tap the center of the clip with a center punch . . .

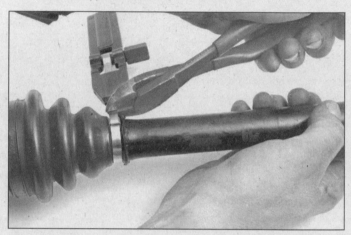

12.15d . . . then bend the end of the clamp back over the clip and cut off the excess

Ball-and-cage type (manual transaxle models)

Disassembly

Refer to illustrations 12.18, 12.19, 12.20 and 12.22

16   Remove both boot clamps **(see illustra-** tion 12.3a) and discard them.

17   Slide the boot away from the outer race (CV joint housing).

18   Pry the wire ring bearing retainer from the CV joint housing **(see illustration)**.

19   Pull the CV joint housing off the inner bearing assembly **(see illustration)**.

20   Remove the snap-ring from the groove in the axleshaft with a pair of snap-ring pliers **(see illustration)**.

21   Slide the inner race off the axleshaft.

22   Make index marks on the inner race and cage to insure correct alignment for reassembly **(see illustration)**.

12.15e If you're installing crimp-type boot clamps, you'll need a pair of special crimping pliers (available at most auto parts stores)

12.18 Pry the wire retainer ring from the CV joint housing with a small screwdriver

12.19 With the retainer removed, the CV joint housing can be
pulled off the ball-and-cage bearing assembly

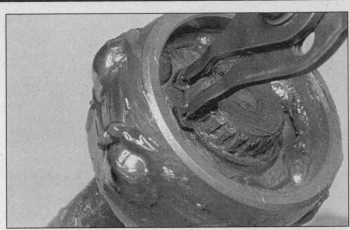

12.20 Remove the snap-ring from the end of the axleshaft

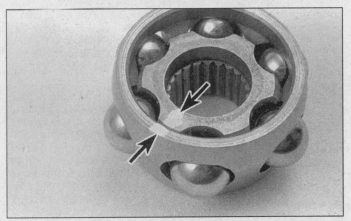

12.22 Make index marks on the inner race and cage so they will
both be facing the same direction when reassembled

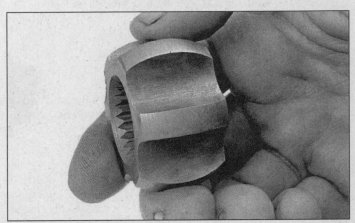

12.24a Inspect the inner race lands and grooves for pitting, score
marks, cracks and other signs of wear and damage

23   Using a screwdriver, pry the ball bearings from the cage. Be careful not to scratch
the inner race, the ball bearings or the cage.
Remove the cage.

Inspection
Refer to illustrations 12.24a and 12.24b
24   Clean the components with solvent to
remove all traces of grease. Inspect the cage

and races for pitting, score marks, cracks
and other signs of wear and damage **(see
illustrations)**. Shiny, polished spots are normal and will not adversely affect CV joint performance.

Reassembly
Refer to illustration 12.26 and 12.28
25   Wrap the axleshaft splines with tape to

avoid damaging the boot. Slide the small
boot clamp and boot onto the axleshaft, then
remove the tape. Slide the large boot clamp
over the boot.
26   Assemble the cage, inner race and ball
bearings. Move the cage up over the inner
race. Press the ball bearings into the cage
windows with your thumbs **(see illustration)**.

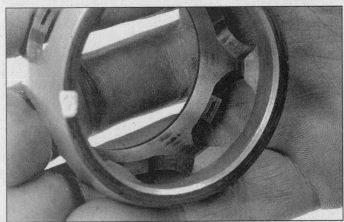

12.24b Inspect the cage for cracks, pitting and score marks
(shiny, polished spots are normal and will not adversely
affect CV joint performance)

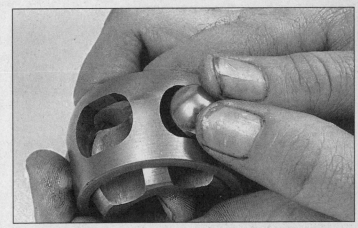

13.26 Press the balls into the cage through the windows

8

12.28 Note that the larger diameter side, or "bulge", is facing OUT

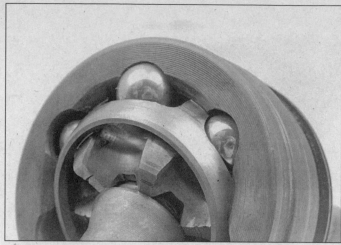

12.40 After the old grease has been rinsed away and the solvent has been blown out with compressed air, rotate the outer joint assembly through its full range of motion and inspect the bearing surfaces for wear and damage - if any of the ball bearings, the race or the cage look damaged, replace the driveaxle and outer joint assembly

27   Fill the ball-and-cage assembly with CV joint grease (normally included with the new boot kit).

28   Install the cage, race and ball bearing assembly onto the axleshaft with the smaller diameter side of the cage facing in and the larger side facing out **(see illustration)**.

29   Install the snap-ring in the groove. Make sure it's completely seated by pushing on the inner race.

30   Pack the CV joint inner housing with grease, by hand, until grease is worked completely into the housing.

31   Install the wire ring bearing retainer.

32   Wipe any excess grease from the axle boot groove on the CV joint housing. Seat the small diameter of the boot in the recessed area on the axleshaft. Push the other end of the boot onto the CV joint housing.

33   Adjust the length of the joint to the length listed in this Chapter's Specifications **(see illustration 12.13)**.

34   Equalize the pressure in the boot by inserting a dull screwdriver between the boot and the outer race **(see illustration 12.14)**. Don't damage the boot with the tool.

35   Tighten the boot clamps **(see illustrations 12.15a through 12.15e)**. Proceed to the next Step.

All inner CV joints

36   Install a new circlip on the inner CV joint stub axle **(see illustrations 11.8a and 11.8b)**.

37   Install the driveaxle (see Section 11).

Outer CV joint

Refer to illustration 12.40

38   Remove the boot clamps **(see illustration 12.3a)** and slide the boot back far enough to inspect the joint.

39   Thoroughly wash the outer CV joint in clean solvent and blow dry it with compressed air, if available. The outer joint can't be disassembled, so it's difficult to wash away all the old grease and to rid the bearing of solvent once it's clean. But it's imperative that the job be done thoroughly, so take your time and do it right.

40   Bend the outer CV joint housing at an angle to the driveaxle to expose the bearings, inner race and cage. Inspect the bearing surfaces for signs of wear. If the joint is worn, replace it, along with the axleshaft **(see illustration)**.

41   If the boot is damaged but the joint is OK, remove the inner CV joint and boot (see Steps 3 through 9 for tri-pot joints and

Steps 16 through 24 for ball-and-cage joints). If the shaft is equipped with a dynamic damper, mark or measure its position on the shaft, then remove the clamp and slide it off.

42   Slide the new outer boot onto the driveaxle. It's a good idea to wrap vinyl tape around the shaft splines to prevent damage to the boot **(see illustration 12.10)**. When the boot is in position, add the specified amount of grease (included in the boot replacement kit) to the outer joint and the boot (pack the joint with as much grease as it will hold and put the rest into the boot). Slide the boot on the rest of the way, equalize the pressure inside the boot and install the new clamps **(see illustrations 12.14 and 12.15a through 12.15e)**. Slide the dynamic damper (if equipped) and a new clamp onto the shaft, aligning it with the mark made in Step 40. Tighten the clamp.

43   Slide on the small clamp and inner boot and install the inner CV joint (see Steps 10 through 15 for tri-pot joints and 25 through 35 for ball-and-cage joints). Be sure to adjust the length of the inner joint before tightening the clamps.

44   Install the driveaxle (see Section 11).

Chapter 9   Brakes

Contents

Specifications

General

Brake pedal
  Height (with carpet in place)
    2000 and earlier models .... 7-31/64 inches (190 mm)
    2001 and later models .... 6-11/16 inches (70 mm)
  Freeplay .... 1/8 to 5/16 inch (3 to 8 mm)
Parking brake lever travel .... 7 to 9 clicks
Power brake booster pushrod-to-master cylinder piston clearance .... 0.0 inch (0.0 mm)

Disc brakes

Brake pad minimum thickness .... See Chapter 1
Disc minimum thickness .... Refer to minimum thickness cast into disc
Thickness variation (parallelism) .... No more than 0.0004 inch (0.01 mm)
Runout limit
  1996 models .... 0.006 inch (0.15 mm)
  1997 through 2000 models .... 0.0024 inch (0.06 mm)
  2001 and later models .... 0.003 inch (0.08)

Drum brakes

Brake lining minimum thickness .... See Chapter 1
Drum diameter (maximum) .... Refer to maximum diameter cast into drum

9

Torque specifications

	Ft-lbs (unless otherwise indicated)	Nm
General		
Brake hose-to-caliper (front or rear)	18 to 22	25 to 30
Master cylinder mounting nuts	72 to 108 in-lbs	8 to 12
Brake booster mounting nuts		
2000 and earlier models..	72 to 108 in-lbs	8 to 12
2001 and later models..	108 to 144 in-lbs	13 to 16
Wheel sensor mounting bolts		
Front	72 to 84 in-lbs	8 to 10
Rear		
1998 and earlier models	12 to 19	17 to 26
1999 and later models	132 in-lbs	16
Front disc brake		
Caliper mounting bolts	16 to 24	22 to 32
Caliper pin bolt	26 to 33	35 to 45
Caliper mounting bracket bolts		
1999 and earlier models..	44 to 63	69 to 85
2000 and later models..	51 to 55	69 to 75
Disc-to-hub nuts (2000 and earlier models)	37 to 44	50 to 60
Rear disc brake		
Caliper mounting bolts	16 to 24	22 to 32

1   General information

General

All vehicles covered by this manual are equipped with hydraulically operated, power-assisted brake systems. All front brake systems are disc type. Some models use drum type brakes at the rear, others are equipped with rear disc brakes.

All brakes are self-adjusting. The front and rear disc brakes automatically compensate for pad wear, while the rear drum brakes incorporate an adjustment mechanism which is activated as the brakes are applied, either through the pedal or the parking brake lever.

The hydraulic system is a split design, meaning there are two separate circuits that control the brakes. If one circuit fails, the other circuit will remain functional and a warning indicator will light up on the dashboard when a substantial amount of brake fluid is lost, showing that a failure has occurred.

Master cylinder

The master cylinder is bolted to the power brake booster, which is mounted on the driver's side of the firewall. To locate the master cylinder, look for the large fluid reservoir on top. The fluid reservoir is plastic, secured to the master cylinder by grommets and a screw.

The master cylinder is designed for the "split system" mentioned earlier and has separate piston assemblies for each circuit.

Proportioning valve

The proportioning valve assembly is located below the master cylinder. It regulates the hydraulic pressure to the rear brakes during heavy braking to eliminate rear wheel lock-up. Under normal braking conditions, it allows full pressure to the rear brake system until a predetermined pedal pressure is reached. Above that point, the pressure to the rear brakes is limited.

The proportioning valve is not serviceable. If a problem develops with the valve, it must be replaced as an assembly. Later ABS-equipped models use Electronic Brakeforce Distribution (EBD) instead of a proportioning valve. EBD is part of the ABS system and can perform the proportioning function much more precisely because it is computer operated.

Power brake booster

The power brake booster, which uses engine manifold vacuum and atmospheric pressure to provide assistance to the hydraulically operated brakes, is mounted on the firewall in the engine compartment.

Parking brake

A parking brake lever inside the vehicle operates a rod attached to a pair of rear cables, each of which is connected to its respective rear brake. When the parking brake lever is pulled up on drum brake models, each rear cable pulls on a lever attached to the brake shoe assembly, causing the shoes to expand against the drum. When the lever is pulled on models with rear disc brakes, the rear cables pull on levers that are attached to screw-type actuators in the caliper housings, which apply force to the caliper pistons, clamping the brake pads against the brake disc.

Precautions

There are some general cautions and warnings involving the brake system on these vehicles:

a) Use only brake fluid conforming to DOT 3 specifications.
b) The brake pads and linings may contain asbestos fibers, which are hazardous to your health if inhaled. Whenever you work on brake system components, clean all parts with brake system cleaner. Do not allow the fine dust to become airborne, and wear a filter/mask over your nose and mouth when cleaning or servicing brakes, regardless of the material the pads are made of.
c) Safety should be paramount whenever any servicing of the brake components is performed. Do not use parts or fasteners which are not in perfect condition, and be sure that all clearances and torque specifications are adhered to. If you are at all unsure about a certain procedure, seek professional advice. Upon completion of any brake system work, test the brakes carefully in a controlled area before putting the vehicle into normal service.
d) If a problem is suspected in the brake system, don't drive the vehicle until it's fixed.

2   Anti-lock Brake System (ABS) - general information and trouble codes

General information

Refer to illustration 2.3

1   In a conventional braking system, if you press the brake pedal too hard, the wheels can "lock up" (stop turning) and the vehicle can go into a skid. If the wheels lock up, you can lose control of the vehicle. The Anti-lock Brake System (ABS) prevents the wheels

from locking up by modulating (pulsing on and off) the pressure of the brake fluid at each brake.

2   The Anti-lock Brake System has two basic subsystems: One is an electrical system and the other is hydraulic. The electrical half has four "gear pulsers," four wheel sensors, a computer and an electrical circuit connecting all the components. The hydraulic part of the system consists of a hydraulic actuation assembly, the disc brake calipers and the hydraulic fluid lines between the hydraulic actuation assembly and the calipers.

3   In principle, the system is pretty simple: Each wheel has a wheel sensor monitoring a gear pulser (a ring with evenly spaced raised ridges cast into its circumference). The wheel sensor "counts" the ridges of the gear pulser as they pass by, converts this information into an electrical output and transmits it back to the computer **(see illustration)**. The computer constantly "samples" the voltage inputs from all four wheel sensors and compares them to each other. As long as the gear pulsers at all four wheels are rotating at the same speed, the Anti-lock Brake System is inactive. But when a wheel locks up, the voltage signal from that wheel sensor deviates from the signals coming from the other wheels. So the computer "knows" the wheel is locking up. It sends an electrical signal to the hydraulic actuator assembly, which releases the brake fluid pressure to the brake caliper at that wheel. As soon as the wheel unlocks and resumes turning at the same rate of speed as the other wheels, its wheel sensor voltage output once again matches the output of the other wheels and the computer deactivates the signal to the hydraulic actuator assembly.

4   In reality, the Anti-lock Brake System is far more complex than it sounds, so we don't recommend that you attempt to diagnose or service it. If the Anti-lock Brake System on your vehicle develops problems, take it to a dealer service department or other qualified shop.

ABS trouble codes

Refer to illustration 2.6

5   Normally, the ABS indicator light should come on when the engine is started, then go off immediately. Under certain conditions, however, the indicator light may remain on. If this occurs, the ABS computer has stored a diagnostic trouble code because it has detected a problem in the ABS system. There are two different methods used for accessing ABS trouble codes. 1998 and earlier models can be accessed through the Data Link Connector (DLC) in the engine compartment. 1999 and later models require a special scan tool connected to the 16-pin data link connector in the passenger compartment. If the special scan tool is not available, have the diagnostic codes extracted from the Powertrain Control Module (PCM) by a dealer service department or other qualified repair facility.

6   On 1998 and earlier models, to access the ABS self diagnosis system, connect a jumper wire between terminal 15 of the data link connector and a good ground. Turn the ignition to the ON position but do not start the engine.

7   The diagnostic code is the number of times the ABS light in the instrument cluster flashes. If no codes are stored, the ABS light will come on briefly and then go out. If any malfunction has been detected, the light will blink the first digit of the code at a long inter-

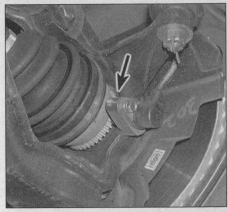

2.3   Location of the front ABS wheel speed sensor (arrow)

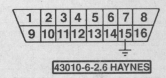

2.6   The data link connector is located under the driver's side of the dash

val. For example, a code 19 (defective wheel speed sensor), will first blink one long flash and then pause and blink nine short flashes.

8   The following code chart lists the ABS codes for the most common Anti-lock Brake System problems. Most ABS repairs must be performed by a dealer service department or other qualified automotive repair facility.

ABS Trouble Codes (1998 and earlier models only)

Code	Probable cause
19	Damaged or defective wheel sensor
21	Left front wheel solenoid
22	Left front wheel solenoid (open circuit or short to body ground)
23	Right front solenoid (short to body power)
24	Right front solenoid (open circuit or short to body ground)
25	Left rear solenoid (short to body power)
26	Left rear solenoid (open circuit or short to body ground)
27	Right rear solenoid (short to body power)
28	Right rear solenoid (open circuit or short to body ground)
31	Left front speed sensor air gap
32	Right front speed sensor air gap
33	Left rear speed sensor air gap
34	Right rear speed sensor air gap

9

ABS Trouble Codes (continued)

Code	Probable cause
35	ABS motor pump (locked-up or faulty)
36	ABS motor relay circuit malfunction (open circuit or short to body ground)
37	ABS pump motor relay (short to relay power)
38	ABS pump motor (short at the motor)
39	ABS pump motor (short to ground at the pump)
41	Fail-safe relay (short at the relay contacts)
42	Fail-safe relay (open at the relay contacts)
43	Fail-safe relay coil (current from the relay is too high or too low)
44	Service Reminder Indicator (SRI) (short at the SRI so it is permanently on)
45	Service Reminder Indicator (SRI) diode (open at the diode)
54	Service Reminder Indicator (SRI) (short to body power)
55	Service Reminder Indicator (SRI) diode (open at the indicator)
56	Low battery voltage
57	High battery voltage
62	Left front wheel sensor (open circuit or short to body power)
63	Right front wheel sensor (open circuit or short to body power)
64	Left rear wheel sensor (open circuit or short to body power)
65	Right rear wheel sensor (open circuit or short to body power)
66	Left front wheel sensor (short to body ground)
67	Right front wheel sensor (short to body ground)
68	Left rear wheel sensor (short to body ground)
69	Right rear wheel sensor (short to body ground)
71	Left front wheel sensor (missing sensor wheel teeth)
72	Right front wheel sensor (missing sensor wheel teeth)
73	Left rear wheel sensor (missing sensor wheel teeth)
74	Right rear wheel sensor (missing sensor wheel teeth)
77	ABSCM ERROR (ABS Control Module malfunction)

9   The ABS diagnostic codes on 1999 and later models are accessed using a special scan tool. Refer to Chapter 6 for additional information on scan tools and accessing diagnostic trouble codes. Most ABS system repairs must be performed by a dealer service department or other qualified automotive repair facility.

10   The diagnostic codes must be cleared from the computer memory after the repairs have been performed. The diagnostic codes can only be erased using the special scan tool. If the scan tool is not available, have the code clearing procedure performed by a dealership service department or other qualified repair facility.

3   Disc brake pads - replacement

Warning: *Disc brake pads must be replaced on both front wheels at the same time - never replace the pads on only one wheel. Also, the dust created by the brake system is harmful to your health. Never blow it out with compressed air and don't inhale any of it. An approved filtering mask should be worn when working on the brakes. Do not, under any circumstances, use petroleum-based solvents to clean brake parts. Use brake system cleaner only!*

Note: *This procedure applies to front and rear disc brakes.*

1   Remove the cap from the brake fluid reservoir.

2   Loosen the wheel lug nuts, raise the vehicle and support it securely on jackstands.

3   Remove the wheels. Work on one brake assembly at a time, using the assembled brake for reference if necessary.

4   Inspect the brake disc carefully as out-

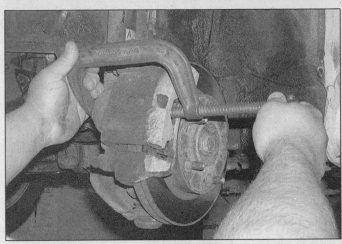

3.5 Using a large C-clamp, push the piston back into the caliper - note that one end of the clamp is on the back side of the caliper and the other end (screw end) is pressing on the outer brake pad

3.6a Before removing anything, spray the disc, caliper and brake pads with brake system cleaner to remove the dust produced by brake pad wear - DO NOT blow the dust off with compressed air!

3.6b Remove the caliper mounting bolt (lower arrow; upper arrow points to banjo fitting for the brake hose, which should not be disconnected unless you are removing the caliper or hose for replacement)

3.6c Swing the caliper up . . .

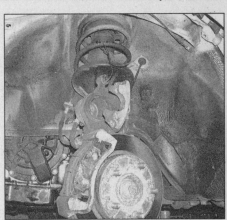

3.6d . . . and secure the caliper in this position with a piece of wire

lined in Section 5. If machining is necessary, follow the information in that Section to remove the disc, at which time the calipers and pads can be removed as well.

Front pads

Refer to illustrations 3.5 and 3.6a through 3.6p

5   Push the piston back into the bore to provide room for the new brake pads. A C-clamp can be used to accomplish this **(see illustration)**. As the piston is depressed to the bottom of the caliper bore, the fluid in the master cylinder will rise. Make sure it doesn't

overflow. If necessary, drain off some of the fluid.

6   Follow the accompanying photos, beginning with **illustration 3.6a**, for the actual pad replacement procedure. Be sure to stay in order and read the caption under each illustration. When you have completed the Steps described in the accompanying photos, proceed to Step 15.

3.6e Remove the lower and upper anti-rattle springs

3.6f Remove the outer brake pad and shim

3.6g Remove the inner brake pad and shim(s)

9

3.6h Remove and inspect the upper and lower pad retainer clips

3.6i The pad retainer clips should fit snugly in the caliper mounting bracket; if they don't, replace them. Apply a thin film of high-temperature grease to the retainer

3.6j Apply anti-squeal compound to the back of the pads

3.6k Install the new inner pad and shim(s); make sure the "ears" on the upper and lower ends of the pad are fully engaged with their respective grooves and the pad retainer clips

3.6l Install the new outer pad and shim (if the new pad has no shim, take the old shim off the old pad and install it on the new outer pad)

3.6m Install the upper and lower anti-rattle springs

3.6n Clean off the caliper pin and coat it with high-temperature grease

3.6o Lubricate the lower caliper pin with high-temperature grease, then swing the caliper down over the disc and new pads (if the piston hits the inner pad, depress the piston further into the caliper bore with your C-clamp)

3.6p Install the mounting bolt and tighten it to the torque listed in this Chapter's Specifications

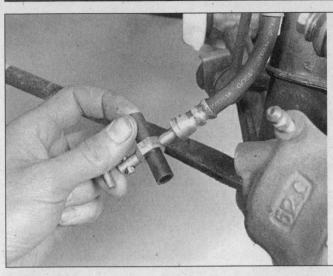

4.2 Using a short piece of rubber hose of the appropriate diameter, plug the brake line banjo fitting

Rear pads

7   Wash the brake assembly with brake system cleaner.

8   On early models it may be necessary to remove the center console and detach the parking brake cable from the lever to provide sufficient slack to allow the cable end to be detached from the caliper.

9   Detach the clip and disconnect parking brake cable from its bracket, then remove the two bolts, lift the caliper assembly off.

10   Remove the brake pads and use a special tool to rotate the caliper piston in until there is enough clearance for the new pads.

11   Apply a thin coat of disc brake anti-squeal compound, in accordance with the manufacturer's recommendations, on the backing plates of the new pads.

12   Install the new pads.

13   Lower the caliper into position over the disc, then install the mounting bolts, tightening them to the torque listed in this Chapter's Specifications.

14   Reconnect the parking brake cable.

5.3 The brake pads on this vehicle were obviously neglected, as they wore down to the rivets; the rivets then cut deep grooves into the disc, and now the disc must be replaced

Front or rear pads

15   Install the wheel and lug nuts, lower the vehicle and tighten the lug nuts to the torque listed in the Chapter 1 Specifications.

16   Apply and release the brake pedal several times to bring the pads into contact with the brake discs. Check the brake fluid level and add fluid, if necessary (see Chapter 1).

17   Check the operation of the brakes in an isolated area before driving the vehicle in traffic.

---

4   Brake caliper - removal and installation

Warning: *Dust created by the brake system is harmful to your health. Never blow it out with compressed air and don't inhale any of it. An approved filtering mask should be worn when working on the brakes. Do not, under any circumstances, use petroleum-based solvents to clean brake parts. Use brake system cleaner only!*

Note: *Always replace the calipers in pairs - never replace just one of them.*

Front

Removal

Refer to illustration 4.2

1   Loosen - but don't remove - the lug nuts on the front wheels. Raise the front of the vehicle and place it securely on jackstands. Remove the front wheels.

2   Disconnect the brake line from the caliper **(see illustration 3.6b)** and plug it to keep contaminants out of the brake system and to prevent losing any more brake fluid than necessary **(see illustration)**.

3   Remove the caliper mounting bolts.

4   Swing the caliper up and slide it off.

Installation

5   Install the caliper by reversing the removal procedure. Remember to replace the sealing washers on either side of the brake line fitting with new ones. Tighten the caliper mounting bolts and the banjo bolt to the torque listed in this Chapter's Specifications.

6   Bleed the brake system (see Section 10).

7   Install the wheels and lug nuts and lower the vehicle. Tighten the wheel lug nuts to the torque listed in the Chapter 1 Specifications.

Rear

Removal

8   Loosen - but don't remove - the lug nuts on the rear wheels. Raise the rear of the vehicle and place it securely on jackstands. Remove the rear wheels.

9   Release the parking brake and remove the clip from the parking brake cable on the back side of the caliper assembly.

10   Separate the parking brake cable from the lever on the caliper.

11   Unscrew the banjo bolt and detach the brake line from the caliper. Plug the fitting to prevent fluid loss and contamination **(see illustration 4.2)**.

12   Remove the caliper mounting bolts.

13   Pivot the caliper back and slide it off.

Installation

14   Install the caliper by reversing the removal procedure. Remember to replace the sealing washers on either side of the brake line fitting with new ones, and tighten the banjo bolt and caliper mounting bolt to the torque values listed in this Chapter's Specifications.

15   Bleed the brake system (see Section 10).

16   Install the wheels and lug nuts. Lower the vehicle and tighten the lug nuts to the torque listed in the Chapter 1 Specifications.

---

5   Brake disc - inspection, removal and installation

Note: *This procedure applies to both the front and (on vehicles so equipped) rear brake discs.*

Inspection

Refer to illustrations 5.3, 5.4a, 5.4b, 5.5a and 5.5b

1   Loosen the wheel lug nuts, raise the vehicle and support it securely on jackstands. Remove the wheel. If you're checking the rear disc, release the parking brake.

2   Remove the brake caliper (see Section 4), but don't disconnect the brake hose. After removing the caliper, suspend it out of the way with a piece of wire.

3   Visually inspect the disc surface for scoring or damage **(see illustration)**. Light scratches and shallow grooves are normal after use and may not always be detrimental to brake operation, but deep scoring requires refinishing by an automotive machine shop. Be sure to check both sides of the disc.

4   If you've noted pulsation during braking, suspect disc runout. To check disc runout, place a dial indicator at a point about 1/2-

9

5.4a Make sure the disc retaining screws or lug nuts are tight, then rotate the disc and check the runout with a dial indicator - if the reading exceeds the maximum allowable runout limit, the disc will have to be machined or replaced

5.4b Using a swirling motion, remove the glaze from the disc with emery cloth or sandpaper

5.5a The minimum allowable thickness is stamped into the disc (typical)

5.5b A micrometer is used to measure disc thickness

inch from the outer edge of the disc **(see illustration)**. Set the indicator to zero and turn the disc. The indicator reading should not exceed the specified allowable runout limit. If it does, have the disc refinished by an automotive machine shop. **Note:** *Professionals recommend that the discs be resurfaced regardless of the dial indicator reading, as this will impart a smooth finish and ensure a perfectly flat surface, eliminating any brake pedal pulsation or other undesirable symptoms related to questionable discs. At the very least, if you elect not to have the discs resurfaced, remove the glazing from the surface with emery cloth or sandpaper using a swirling motion* **(see illustration)**.

5   It is absolutely critical that the disc not be machined to a thickness less than the minimum allowable thickness. The minimum (or discard) thickness is stamped on the disc **(see illustration)**. The disc thickness can be checked with a micrometer **(see illustration)**. Check the thickness at several points.

Removal

6   Remove the brake caliper (if not already done), but don't disconnect the brake hose (see Section 4). Also remove the caliper mounting bracket.

7   If you're working on a 2000 or earlier model, remove the steering knuckle (see Chapter 10) and take it to a properly equipped shop and have the hub flange pressed out of the knuckle. The disc can then be unbolted from the hub.

8   If you're working on a 2001 or later model, simply slide the disc off the hub flange.

9   On rear disc brakes remove the retaining screw and remove the disc from the hub.

Installation

10   Installation is the reverse of the removal procedure. Tighten the mounting bracket and caliper bolts to the torque values listed in this Chapter's Specifications.

11   Install the wheel, then lower the vehicle to the ground. Tighten the lug nuts to the torque listed in the Chapter 1 Specifications. Depress the brake pedal a few times to bring the brake pads into contact with the disc. Bleeding of the system will not be necessary unless the fluid hose was disconnected from the caliper. Check the operation of the brakes carefully before placing the vehicle into normal service.

6   Drum brake shoes - replacement

Refer to illustrations 6.4a through 6.4z and 6.6

Warning: *Drum brake shoes must be replaced on both wheels at the same time - never replace the shoes on only one wheel. Also, the dust created by the brake system is harmful to your health. Never blow it out with compressed air and don't inhale any of it. An approved filtering mask should be worn when working on the brakes. Do not, under any circumstances, use petroleum-based solvents to clean brake parts. Use brake system cleaner only!*

Caution: *Whenever the brake shoes are*

replaced, the return and hold-down springs should also be replaced. Due to the continuous heating/cooling cycle that the springs are subjected to, they lose their tension over a period of time and may allow the shoes to drag on the drum and wear at a much faster rate than normal.

1   Loosen the wheel lug nuts, raise the rear of the vehicle and support it securely on jackstands.

2   Block the front wheels to keep the vehicle from rolling. Remove the rear wheels.

6.4a Details of the rear drum brake assembly

1   *Wheel cylinder*
2   *Shoe return spring*
3   *Adjuster screw assembly*
4   *Parking brake lever*
5   *Trailing brake shoe*
6   *Parking brake cable*
7   *Shoe return spring*
8   *Leading brake shoe*
9   *Adjuster spring*
10   *Hold-down spring*
11   *Adjuster lever pawl*

6.4b Before removing anything, clean the brake assembly with brake cleaner and allow it to dry - position a drain pan under the brake assembly to catch the residue - DO NOT USE COMPRESSED AIR TO BLOW BRAKE DUST OFF THE PARTS!

6.4c Unhook the adjuster spring . . .

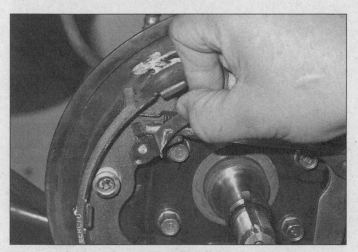

6.4d . . . then remove the adjuster lever pawl

6.4e Unhook the upper return spring from the brake shoes

Release the parking brake.
3   Remove the rear wheel bearing cap, spindle nut and washer, then slide the hub/drum assembly straight off the spindle (see Chapter 10).

4   Follow **illustrations 6.4a through 6.4z** for the inspection and replacement of the brake shoes. Be sure to stay in order and read the caption under each illustration. All four rear brake shoes must be replaced at the

same time, but to avoid mixing up parts, work on only one brake assembly at a time.
5   Before reinstalling the drum, make sure the brake shoes are retracted to allow easy installation of the drum.

6.4f Unhook the lower return spring from the brake shoes

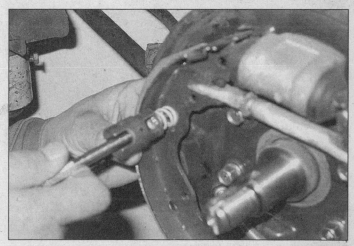

6.4g Push down on the hold-down spring, then turn it 90-degrees to align its slot with the blade on the pin, then remove the spring

9

6.4h Lift off the leading brake shoe

6.4i Remove the adjuster screw assembly

6.4j Remove the hold-down spring from the trailing brake shoe . . .

6.4k . . . then remove the shoe and detach the parking brake cable from the parking brake lever

6.4l Lubricate the brake shoe contact areas on the backing plate with high-temperature grease

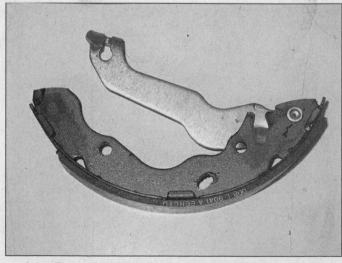

6.4m The parking brake lever and the trailing shoe are one assembly - don't try to separate them

6.4n Install the hold-down pins into the backing plate

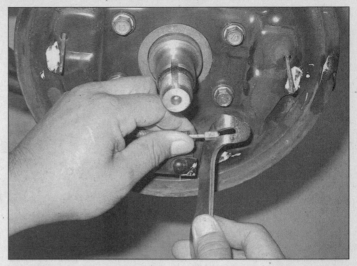

6.4o Connect the parking brake cable to the parking brake lever

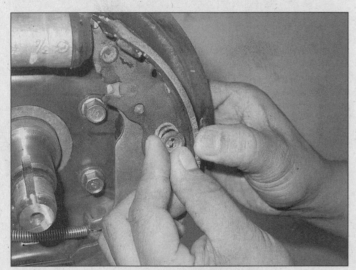

6.4p Place the trailing shoe and hold-down spring assembly
in position

6.4q Install the trailing shoe hold-down spring with the tool

6.4r Connect the lower return spring to the brake shoes

6.4s Install the leading shoe onto the backing plate, making sure
it engages correctly with the wheel cylinder . . .

9

6.4t ... and install the hold-down spring

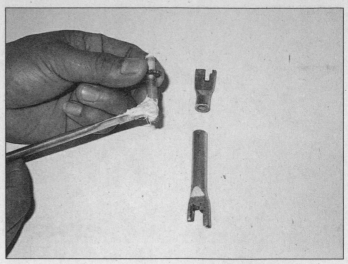

6.4u Prior to installing the adjuster screw assembly, lubricate the threads with high-temperature grease

6.4v Install the adjuster screw assembly

6.4w Connect the upper return spring to the brake shoes

6.4x Place the adjuster lever pawl in position

6.4y With the lever pawl in place ...

6.4z . . . install the adjuster spring

6.6 The maximum allowable diameter is cast into the drum (typical)

6   Prior to reinstalling, the drum should be checked for cracks, score marks, deep scratches and hard spots, which will appear as small, discolored areas. If the hard spots cannot be removed with fine emery cloth or if any of the other conditions listed above exist, the drum must be taken to an automotive machine shop to have it machined. **Note:** *Professionals recommend resurfacing the drums whenever a brake job is done. Resurfacing will eliminate the possibility of out-of-round drums. If the drums are worn so much that they can't be resurfaced without exceeding the maximum allowable diameter (stamped into the drum)* **(see illustration)**, then new ones will be required. At the very least, if you elect not to have the drums resurfaced, remove the glazing from the surface with sandpaper or emery cloth using a swirling motion.

7   Install the brake drum and bearing unit, the washer and a *new* spindle nut (see Chapter 10). Tighten the nut to the torque listed in the Chapter 10 Specifications.

8   Mount the wheel, install the lug nuts, then lower the vehicle. Tighten the lug nuts to the torque listed in the Chapter 1 Specifications.

9   Depress the brake pedal several times. Then, drive the vehicle backwards and forwards and apply the brakes forcefully a number of times. This action will bring the brake shoes into the proper adjustment.

10   Check brake operation carefully before driving the vehicle in traffic. **Warning:** *Do not operate the vehicle if you are in doubt about the effectiveness of the brake system.*

7   Wheel cylinder - removal and installation

Refer to illustration 7.4
Note: *Always replace wheel cylinders in pairs.*

Removal

1   Raise the rear of the vehicle and support

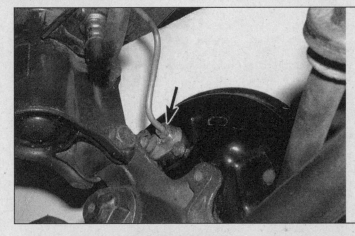

7.4 Unscrew the brake line fitting (arrow), then remove the two wheel cylinder bolts

it securely on jackstands. Block the front wheels to keep the vehicle from rolling.

2   Remove the brake shoe assembly (see Section 6).

3   Remove all dirt and foreign material from around the wheel cylinder.

4   Unscrew the brake line fitting **(see illustration)**. **Note:** *If available, use a flare-nut wrench to avoid rounding off the corners of the fitting. Don't pull the brake line away from the wheel cylinder.*

5   Remove the wheel cylinder mounting bolts.

6   Detach the wheel cylinder from the brake backing plate. Immediately plug the brake line to prevent fluid loss and contamination. **Note:** *If the brake shoe linings are contaminated with brake fluid, install new brake shoes and clean the drums with brake system cleaner.*

Installation

7   Apply RTV sealant to the mating surface of the wheel cylinder and the brake backing plate, place the cylinder in position and connect the brake line. Don't tighten the fitting completely yet.

8   Install the mounting bolts, tightening them to the torque listed in this Chapter's

Specifications. Tighten the brake line fitting securely. Install the brake shoe assembly (see Section 6).

9   Bleed the brakes (see Section 11).

10   Check brake operation before driving the vehicle in traffic. **Warning:** *Do not operate the vehicle if you are in doubt about the effectiveness of the brake system.*

8   Master cylinder - removal and installation

Removal

Refer to illustration 8.5

1   The master cylinder is located in the engine compartment, mounted to the power brake booster.

2   Remove the intake duct between the air filter housing and the throttle body.

3   Remove as much fluid as you can from the reservoir with a syringe, such as an old poultry baster. **Warning:** *If a baster is used, never again use it for the preparation of food.*

4   Place rags under the fluid fittings and prepare caps or plastic bags to cover the ends of the lines once they are disconnected. **Caution:** *Brake fluid will damage paint. Cover*

8.5 Use a flare-nut wrench to unscrew the threaded fittings at the master cylinder (A), then remove the mounting nuts (B)

8.8 The best way to bleed air from the master cylinder before installing it on the vehicle is with a pair of bleed tubes that direct brake fluid back into the reservoir during bleeding

all body parts and be careful not to spill fluid during this procedure.

5   Loosen the fittings at the ends of the brake lines where they enter the master cylinder **(see illustration)**. To prevent rounding off the corners on these nuts, the use of a flare-nut wrench, which wraps around the nut, is preferred. Pull the brake lines slightly away from the master cylinder and plug the ends to prevent contamination.

6   Disconnect the electrical connector at the brake fluid level switch on the master cylinder reservoir, then remove the nuts attaching the master cylinder to the power booster **(see illustration 8.5)**. Pull the master cylinder off the studs and out of the engine compartment. Again, be careful not to spill the fluid as this is done.

Installation

Refer to illustration 8.8

7   Bench bleed the master cylinder before installing it. Mount the master cylinder in a vise, with the jaws of the vise clamping on the mounting flange.

8   Attach a pair of master cylinder bleeder tubes to the outlet ports of the master cylinder **(see illustration)**.

9   Fill the reservoir with brake fluid of the recommended type (see Chapter 1).

10   Slowly push the pistons into the master cylinder (a large Phillips screwdriver can be used for this) - air will be expelled from the pressure chambers and into the reservoir. Because the tubes are submerged in fluid, air can't be drawn back into the master cylinder when you release the pistons.

11   Repeat the procedure until no more air bubbles are present.

12   Remove the bleed tubes, one at a time, and install plugs in the open ports to prevent fluid leakage and air from entering. Install the reservoir cap.

13   Install the master cylinder over the studs on the power brake booster and tighten the attaching nuts only finger tight at this time. **Note:** *Be sure to install a new O-ring into the*

sleeve of the master cylinder.

14   Thread the brake line fittings into the master cylinder. Since the master cylinder is still a bit loose, it can be moved slightly in order for the fittings to thread in easily. Do not strip the threads as the fittings are tightened.

15   Fully tighten the mounting nuts, then the brake line fittings. Tighten the nuts to the torque listed in this Chapter's Specifications.

16   Fill the master cylinder reservoir with fluid, then bleed the master cylinder. To bleed the cylinder on the vehicle, have an assistant depress the brake pedal and hold the pedal to the floor. Loosen the fitting to allow air and fluid to escape. Repeat this procedure on both fittings until the fluid is clear of air bubbles. **Caution:** *Have plenty of rags on hand to catch the fluid - brake fluid will ruin painted surfaces. After the bleeding procedure is completed, rinse the area under the master cylinder with clean water.*

17   Bleed the entire brake system as described in Section 10.

18   Test the operation of the brake system carefully before placing the vehicle into nor-

mal service. **Warning:** *Do not operate the vehicle if you are in doubt about the effectiveness of the brake system.*

9   Brake hoses and lines - inspection and replacement

Refer to illustrations 9.4a, 9.4b and 9.5

1   About every six months the flexible hoses which connect the steel brake lines with the rear brakes and front calipers should be inspected for cracks, chafing of the outer cover, leaks, blisters, and other damage.

2   Replacement steel and flexible brake lines are commonly available from dealer parts departments and auto parts stores. Do not, under any circumstances, use anything other than genuine steel brake lines or approved flexible brake hoses as replacement items.

3   When installing the brake line, leave at least 3/4-inch clearance between the line and any moving or vibrating parts.

4   To disconnect a hose and line, use a flare-nut wrench **(see illustration)**. Then

9.4a Use a flare-nut wrench to loosen the brake line-to-hose fitting . . .

9.4b . . . then remove the clip, unscrew the fitting and and slide the hose out of the bracket

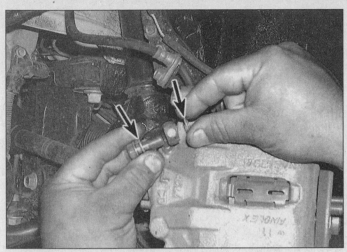

9.5 Always install new sealing washers on either side of the banjo fitting

10.8 When bleeding the brakes, a hose is connected to the bleed screw at the caliper or wheel cylinder and then submerged in brake fluid - air will be seen as bubbles in the tube and container (all air must be expelled before moving to the next wheel)

remove the clip and slide the hose out of the bracket **(see illustration)**.

5   To disconnect a hose from a caliper, unscrew the banjo bolt and discard the sealing washers. Always install new sealing washers when reconnecting the hose fitting **(see illustration)**.

6   Steel brake lines are usually retained along their span with clips. Always remove these clips completely before removing a rigid brake line. Always reinstall these clips, or new ones if the old ones are damaged, when replacing a brake line, as they provide support and keep the lines from vibrating, which can eventually break them.

7   When replacing brake lines, be sure to use the correct parts. NEVER use copper tubing! Purchase genuine steel brake lines from a dealer or auto parts store.

8   When installing a steel line, make sure it's securely supported in the brackets and has plenty of clearance between moving or hot components.

9   After installation, check the fluid level in the master cylinder and add fluid as necessary. Bleed the brake system as described in Section 10 and test the brakes carefully before driving the vehicle in traffic. **Warning:** *Do not operate the vehicle if you are in doubt about the effectiveness of the brake system.*

10 Brake hydraulic system - bleeding

Refer to illustration 10.8

Warning 1: *Wear eye protection when bleeding the brake system. If the fluid comes in contact with your eyes, immediately rinse them with water and seek medical attention.*
Warning 2: *The manufacturer states that on 1999 and later models with ABS, a special scan tool must be used to ensure that all air is bled from the ABS control unit. If you are working on a 1999 or later model equipped*

with ABS and, after following this procedure you don't have a firm brake pedal (or the ABS light on the instrument panel stays on), have the vehicle towed to a dealer service department or other properly equipped repair shop to have the system bled. DO NOT operate the vehicle if you have any doubts as to the effectiveness of the brake system or if the ABS light stays on.

1   Bleeding the hydraulic system is necessary to remove any air that manages to find its way into the system when it's been opened during removal and installation of a hose, line, caliper or master cylinder. It will probably be necessary to bleed the system at all four brakes if air has entered the system due to low fluid level, or if the brake lines have been disconnected at the master cylinder.

2   If a brake line was disconnected only at a wheel, then only that caliper or wheel cylinder must be bled.

3   If a brake line is disconnected at a fitting located between the master cylinder and any of the brakes, that part of the system served by the disconnected line must be bled.

4   Remove any residual vacuum from the power brake booster by applying the brake several times with the engine off.

5   Remove the master cylinder reservoir cover and fill the reservoir with brake fluid. Reinstall the cover. **Note:** *Check the fluid level often during the bleeding operation and add fluid as necessary to prevent the fluid level from falling low enough to allow air bubbles into the master cylinder.*

6   Have an assistant on hand, as well as a supply of new brake fluid, a clear container partially filled with clean brake fluid, a length of clear tubing to fit over the bleed screw and a wrench to open and close the bleed screw.

7   Beginning at the right rear wheel, loosen the bleed screw slightly, then tighten it to a point where it is snug but can still be loosened quickly and easily.

8   Place one end of the tubing over the

bleed screw and submerge the other end in brake fluid in the container **(see illustration)**.

9   Have the assistant push the brake pedal to the floor and hold the pedal firmly depressed.

10   While the pedal is held depressed, open the bleed screw just enough to allow a flow of fluid to leave the screw. Watch for air bubbles to exit the submerged end of the tube. When the fluid flow slows after a couple of seconds, close the screw and have your assistant release the pedal slowly.

11   Repeat Steps 9 and 10 until no more air is seen leaving the tube, then tighten the bleed screw and proceed to the left front wheel, then the left rear wheel and then to the right front wheel, in that order, and perform the same procedure. Be sure to check the fluid in the master cylinder reservoir frequently.

12   Never use old brake fluid. It contains moisture which can boil, rendering the brakes inoperative.

13   Refill the master cylinder with fluid at the end of the operation.

14   Check the operation of the brakes. The pedal should feel solid when depressed, with no sponginess. If necessary, repeat the entire process. **Warning:** *Do not operate the vehicle if you are in doubt about the effectiveness of the brake system.*

11 Power brake booster - check, removal and installation

Operating check

1   Depress the pedal and start the engine. If the pedal goes down slightly, operation is normal.

2   Depress the brake pedal several times with the engine running and make sure there is no change in the pedal reserve distance (the distance between the pedal and the floor).

9

11.10 The power brake booster is secured to the firewall with four nuts (arrows)

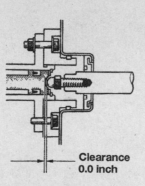

Clearance 0.0 inch

11.13a There should be no clearance between the booster pushrod and the master cylinder pushrod, but no interference either; if there is interference between the two, the brakes may drag; if there is clearance, there will be excessive brake pedal travel

11.13b Measure the distance that the pushrod protrudes from the brake booster at the master cylinder mounting surface (including the gasket)

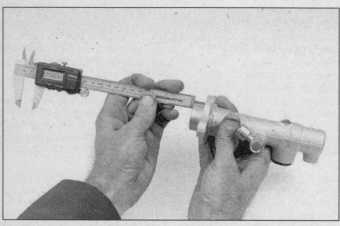

11.13c Measure the distance from the mounting flange to the end of the master cylinder

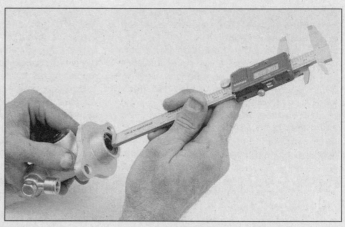

11.13d Measure the distance from the piston pocket to the end of the master cylinder

Airtightness check

3   Start the engine and turn it off after one or two minutes. Depress the brake pedal several times slowly. If the pedal goes down farther the first time but gradually rises after the second or third depression, the booster is airtight.

4   Depress the brake pedal while the engine is running, then stop the engine with the pedal depressed. If there is no change in the pedal reserve travel after holding the pedal for 30 seconds, the booster is airtight.

Removal

Refer to illustration 11.10

5   Power brake booster units should not be disassembled. They require special tools not normally found in most automotive repair stations or shops. They are fairly complex and because of their critical relationship to brake performance it is best to replace a defective booster unit with a new or rebuilt one.

6   To remove the booster, first remove the brake master cylinder as described in Section 8.

7   Disconnect the vacuum hose from the booster. Be careful not to damage the hose when removing it from the booster fitting.

8   Locate the pushrod clevis pin connecting the booster to the brake pedal.

9   Remove the retaining clip with pliers and pull out the clevis pin.

10   Remove the four mounting nuts holding the brake booster to the firewall **(see illustration).** You may need a light to see them, because they're up under the dash area.

11   Slide the booster straight out from the firewall until the studs clear the holes, then maneuver the booster out from the engine compartment.

Installation

Refer to illustrations 11.13a, 11.13b, 11.13c, 11.13d and 11.13e.

12   Installation procedures are basically the reverse of those for removal. Use new gaskets on either side of the spacer at the firewall. Tighten the booster mounting nuts to the torque listed in this Chapter's Specifications.

13   If a new power brake booster unit is being installed, check the pushrod clearance

(see illustration) as follows:

a) *Measure the distance that the pushrod protrudes from the master cylinder mounting surface on the front of the power brake booster, including the gasket, if equipped. Write down this measurement* **(see illustration).** *This is "dimension A."*

b) *Measure the distance from the mounting flange to the end of the master cylinder* **(see illustration).** *Write down this measurement. This is "dimension B."*

c) *Measure the distance from the end of the master cylinder to the bottom of the pocket in the piston* **(see illustration).** *Write down this measurement. This is "dimension C."*

d) *Subtract measurement B from measurement C, then subtract measurement A from the difference between B and C. This the pushrod clearance.*

e) *Compare your calculated pushrod clearance to the pushrod clearance listed in this Chapter's Specifications. If necessary, adjust the pushrod length to achieve the correct clearance* **(see illustration).**

11.13e To adjust the length of the booster pushrod, hold the serrated portion of the rod with a pair of pliers and turn the adjusting screw in or out, as necessary, to achieve the desired setting

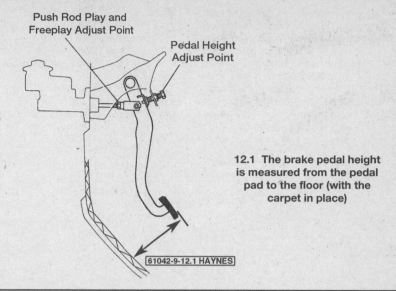

Push Rod Play and Freeplay Adjust Point

Pedal Height Adjust Point

12.1 The brake pedal height is measured from the pedal pad to the floor (with the carpet in place)

61042-9-12.1 HAYNES

15   After the final installation of the master cylinder, the brake pedal height and freeplay must be adjusted and the system must be bled. See the appropriate Sections of this Chapter for the procedures.

12 Brake pedal height and freeplay - adjustment

Pedal height

Refer to illustration 12.1
1   The height of the brake pedal is the distance the pedal sits off the floor **(see illustration)**. If the pedal height is not within the specified range, it must be adjusted. Measure the pedal height from the top of the brake pedal pad to the floor with the carpet in place.
2   To adjust the brake pedal height, loosen the locknut on the pedal height adjusting bolt and back the bolt out to increase the pedal height or turn the bolt in to decrease pedal height. After the pedal height is adjusted, the freeplay must be adjusted (see Step 4). Tighten the locknuts securely.

Pedal freeplay

Refer to illustration 12.3
3   The freeplay is the pedal slack, or the distance the pedal can be depressed before it begins to have any effect on the brake system **(see illustration)**. If the pedal freeplay is not within the specified range, it must be adjusted.
4   To adjust the pedal freeplay, loosen the locknut on the brake pushrod **(see illustration 12.1)**, then turn the pushrod to adjust the pedal freeplay to the specified range. Retighten the locknut.

13 Parking brake - adjustment

1   Remove the center console (see Chapter 11).
2   Block the front wheels, raise the rear of the vehicle and support it securely on jackstands. Apply the parking brake lever until you hear one click.
3   Turn the adjusting nut on the equalizer clockwise while rotating the rear wheels.

Stop turning the nut when the brakes just start to drag on the rear wheels.
4   Release the parking brake lever and check to see that the brakes don't drag when the rear wheels are turned. When properly adjusted, the travel on the parking brake lever should be as listed in this Chapter's Specifications. If it is not, loosen the locknut and the adjusting on the end of the cable at the parking brake lever. Turn the adjusting nut until the specified number of clicks are achieved and tighten the locknut.
5   Lower the vehicle and reinstall the console or cover.

14 Parking brake cable(s) - replacement

Refer to illustration 14.2
1   Block the front wheels and loosen the rear wheel lug nuts. Raise the rear of the vehicle and support it securely on jackstands.
2   On models with rear drum brakes,

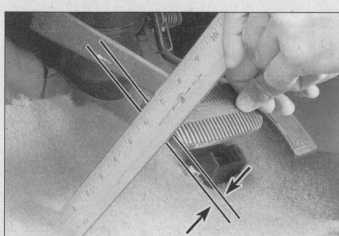

12.3 Brake pedal freeplay is the amount of brake pedal travel before the master cylinder is actuated

14.2 To detach the parking brake cable from a drum brake backing plate, compress the retainer tangs with a pair of pliers and pass the cable through the backing plate

9

remove the brake shoes (see Section 6) and disconnect the cable end from the lever on the trailing brake shoe **(see illustration 6.4k)**. Depress the tangs on the cable casing retainer and pass the cable through the backing plate using needle-nose pliers **(see illustration)** or a box-end wrench of the proper size to fit snugly over the retainer. This compresses all the tangs simultaneously. **Note:** *You can also use a small screw-type hose clamp. Tighten the clamp around the tangs, start the cable through the hole and remove the hose clamp.*

3   On models with rear disc brakes, refer to Section 3 to disconnect the cable from the caliper.

4   Unhook the forward end of the cable from the equalizer, then compress the retainer tangs and pass the cable through the bracket.

5   Unbolt the cable casing clamps from the underbody, noting how the cable is routed, then remove the cable from the vehicle.

6   If both cables are to be removed, repeat the above steps to remove the remaining cable.

7   Installation is the reverse of the removal procedure. After the cable(s) are installed, be sure to adjust them according to the procedure described in Section 13.

Chapter 10
Suspension and steering systems

Contents

Specifications

Torque specifications

	Ft-lbs (unless otherwise indicated)	Nm
Front suspension		
Control arm-to-crossmember fasteners		
2000 and earlier models		
Front pivot bolt	72 to 87	97 to 117
Rear bushing clamp bolt	58 to 72	78 to 97
Rear bushing clamp nuts	25 to 33	34 to 45
Rear pivot stud nut	92 to 114	125 to 154
2001 models		
Front bushing bolts	96 to 111	130 to 149
Rear bushing bolt	96 to 111	130 to 149
Control arm-to-steering knuckle balljoint nut	43 to 52	58 to 70
Stabilizer bar		
Link nuts	25 to 33	33 to 44
Clamp bolts	25 to 33	33 to 44
Strut/coil spring assembly		
Strut-to-steering knuckle bolts/nuts	81 to 95	109 to 128
Strut-to-body upper mounting nuts	29 to 36	39 to 48
Damper shaft nut	43 to 51	58 to 69

10

Torque specifications

	Ft-lbs (unless otherwise indicated)	Nm
Rear suspension		
Brake backing plate-to-rear knuckle bolts	37 to 44	50 to 59
Crossmember mounting bolts		
2000 and earlier models	44 to 59	59 to 79
2001 models	74 to 88	100 to 119
Hub nut		
1996 and 1997 models	130 to 159	175 to 214
1998 through 2000 models	147 to 169	200 to 230
2001 models	148 to 192	200 to 260
Rear suspension arms		
Lateral arms-to-crossmember bolt(s)/nut(s)		
2000 and earlier models	58 to 72	78 to 97
2001 models	96	130
Lateral arms-to-rear knuckle bolt(s)/nut(s)		
2000 and earlier models	58 to 72	78 to 97
2001 models	96	130
Trailing arm bolts		
Bracket-to-frame bolt	29 to 36	39 to 48
Arm-to-bracket bolt/nut	74 to 88	100 to 119
Arm-to-knuckle bolt	74 to 88	100 to 119
Stabilizer bar		
Stabilizer bushing clamp bolts	25 to 33	33 to 44
Stabilizer link nuts	25 to 33	33 to 44
Strut/coil spring assembly		
Strut-to-rear knuckle bolts/nuts	80 to 94	108 to 127
Strut-to-body upper mounting nuts		
2000 and earlier models	14 to 22	18 to 29
2001 models	29 to 37	39 to 50
Damper shaft nut	29 to 40	39 to 54
Steering		
Airbag module-to-steering wheel fasteners	48 in-lbs	5.4
Intermediate shaft U-joint pinch bolt	132 to 180 in-lbs	15 to 20
Power steering pump fluid lines		
Supply line fittings	108 to 144 in-lbs	12 to 16
High pressure line banjo bolt	40 to 48	54 to 65
Power steering pump pulley nut	41 to 51	55 to 69
Power steering pump bracket bolts	26 to 38	35 to 51
Steering column mounting bolts and nuts	120 to 144 in-lbs	13 to 17
Steering gear mounting bracket bolts	44 to 59	59 to 79
Steering wheel nut	30	41
Tie-rod end-to-steering knuckle nut	18 to 25	24 to 33
Tie-rod end jam nut (adjusting nut)	37 to 41	50 to 55

1   General information

Refer to illustrations 1.1, 1.2a and 1.2b

The front suspension system **(see illustration)** is a MacPherson strut design. The upper end of each strut is attached to the vehicle body. The lower end of the strut is connected to the upper end of the steering knuckle. The steering knuckle is attached to a balljoint mounted on the outer end of the control arm. A stabilizer bar is used on all models. The bar is attached to the frame with a pair of clamps and to the control arms with link rods.

The rear suspension system **(see illustration)** also uses MacPherson struts, a pair of lateral suspension arms (front and rear) and a trailing arm on each side. The upper ends of the struts are attached to the vehicle body and their lower ends are attached to the upper ends of the rear knuckles. The lower ends of the knuckles are attached to the outer ends of the lateral arms using through-bolts. A stabilizer bar is attached to the vehicle by a pair of brackets and to the struts by link rods **(see illustration)**.

The rack-and-pinion steering gear is located behind the engine/transaxle assembly, on the subframe. The steering gear actuates the tie-rods, which are attached to the steering knuckles. The inner ends of the tie-rods are protected by rubber boots that should be inspected periodically for secure attachment, tears and leaking lubricant.

The power assist system consists of a belt-driven pump and associated lines and hoses. The fluid level in the power steering pump reservoir should be checked periodically (see Chapter 1).

The steering wheel operates the steering shaft, which actuates the steering gear through universal joints. Looseness in the steering can be caused by wear in the steering shaft universal joints, the steering gear, the tie-rod ends and loose retaining bolts.

Frequently, when working on the suspension or steering system components, you may come across fasteners that seem impossible to loosen. These fasteners on the underside of the vehicle are continually subjected to water, road grime, mud, etc., and can become rusted or "frozen," making them extremely difficult to remove. In order to unscrew these stubborn fasteners without damaging them (or other components), be sure to use lots of penetrating oil and allow it to soak in for a while. Using a wire brush to clean exposed threads will also ease removal of the nut or bolt and prevent damage to the threads. Sometimes a sharp blow with a hammer and punch will break the bond between nut and bolt threads, but care must be taken to prevent the punch from slipping off the fastener and ruining the threads. Heating the stuck fastener and surrounding area

1.1 Front suspension and steering components (2000 and earlier models shown, later models similar)

1	*Steering gear*	3	*Balljoint*	5	*Strut/coil spring assembly*
2	*Control arm*	4	*Steering knuckle*	6	*Splash shield*

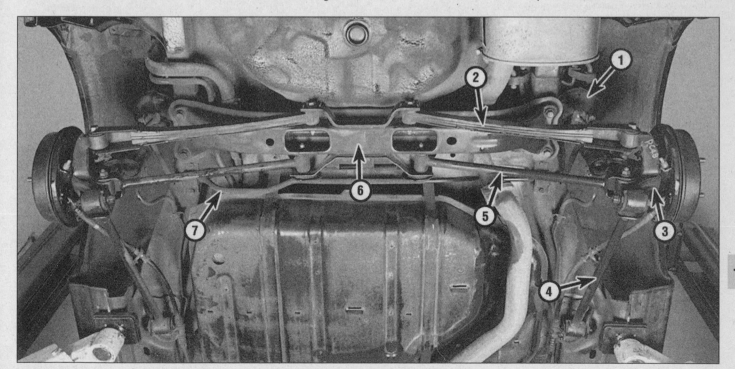

1.2a Rear suspension components (bottom view)

1	*Strut/coil spring assembly*	4	*Trailing arm*	6	*Crossmember*
2	*Rear lateral arm*	5	*Front lateral arm*	7	*Stabilizer bar*
3	*Knuckle*				

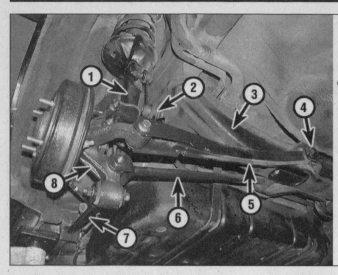

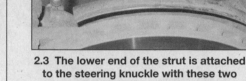

1.2b Rear suspension components (rear view)

1 Strut/coil spring assembly
2 Stabilizer bar link
3 Crossmember
4 Adjusting cam (earlier models)
5 Rear lateral arm
6 Front lateral arm
7 Trailing arm
8 Knuckle

2.3 The lower end of the strut is attached to the steering knuckle with these two nuts and bolts

with a torch sometimes helps too, but isn't recommended because of the obvious dangers associated with fire. Long breaker bars and extension, or "cheater," pipes will increase leverage, but never use an extension pipe on a ratchet - the ratcheting mechanism could be damaged. Sometimes tightening the nut or bolt first will help to break it loose. Fasteners that require drastic measures to remove should always be replaced with new ones.

Since most of the procedures dealt with in this Chapter involve jacking up the vehicle and working underneath it, a good pair of jackstands will be needed. A hydraulic floor jack is the preferred type of jack to lift the vehicle, and it can also be used to support certain components during various operations. **Warning:** *Never, under any circumstances, rely on a jack to support the vehicle while working on it. Whenever any of the suspension or steering fasteners are loosened or removed they must be inspected and, if necessary, replaced with new ones of the same part number or of original equipment quality and design. Torque specifications must be followed for proper reassembly and component retention. Never attempt to heat or straighten any suspension or steering components. Instead, replace any bent or damaged part with a new one.*

2   Strut/coil spring assembly (front) - removal, inspection and installation

Refer to illustrations 2.3 and 2.5

Removal

1   Loosen the front wheel lug nuts, raise the front of the vehicle and support it securely on jackstands. Remove the wheels.
2   Detach the brake hose bracket from the strut. If the vehicle is equipped with ABS, detach the speed sensor wiring harness from the strut by removing the clamp bracket bolt.
3   Remove the strut-to-knuckle nuts and if

necessary, knock the bolts out with a hammer and punch **(see illustration)**.
4   Separate the strut from the steering knuckle. Be careful not to overextend the inner CV joint and don't let the knuckle fall outward, as this could damage the brake hose.
5   An assistant would be helpful at this point to hold the strut as the nuts are loosened. Remove the strut upper mounting nuts **(see illustration)**. Remove the assembly out from the fenderwell.

Inspection

6   Check the strut body for leaking fluid, dents, cracks and other obvious damage which would warrant repair or replacement.
7   Check the coil spring for chips or cracks in the spring coating (this will cause premature spring failure due to corrosion). Inspect the spring seat for cuts, hardness and general deterioration.
8   If any undesirable conditions exist, proceed to the strut disassembly procedure (see Section 3).

Installation

9   Guide the strut assembly up into the fenderwell and insert the upper mounting studs through the holes in the strut tower. Once the studs protrude from the strut tower, install the nuts so the strut won't fall back through. This is most easily accomplished with the help of an assistant, as the strut is quite heavy and awkward.
10   Slide the steering knuckle into the strut flange and insert the bolts. Install the nuts and tighten them to the torque listed in this Chapter's Specifications.
11   Connect the brake hose bracket to the strut. If equipped with ABS, attach the wheel speed sensor bracket to the strut and tighten the bolt securely.
12   Install the wheel and lug nuts, then lower the vehicle and tighten the lug nuts to the torque listed in the Chapter 1 Specifications.
13   Tighten the upper mounting nuts to the torque listed in this Chapter's Specifications.

2.5 Strut upper mounting nuts

3   Strut/coil spring - replacement

1   If the struts or coil springs exhibit the telltale signs of wear (leaking fluid, loss of damping capability, chipped, sagging or cracked coil springs) explore all options before beginning any work. The strut/damper assemblies are not serviceable and must be replaced if a problem develops. However, strut assemblies complete with springs may be available on an exchange basis, which eliminates much time and work. Whichever route you choose to take, check on the cost and availability of parts before disassembling your vehicle. **Warning:** *Disassembling a strut is potentially dangerous and utmost attention must be directed to the job, or serious injury may result. Use only a high-quality spring compressor and carefully follow the manufacturer's instructions furnished with the tool. After removing the coil spring from the strut, set it aside in a safe, isolated area.*

Disassembly

Refer to illustrations 3.3, 3.4, 3.5 and 3.6
2   Remove the strut and spring assembly following the procedure described in Section 2 (front) or Section 9 (rear). Mount the strut assembly in a vise. Line the vise jaws with wood or rags to prevent damage to the

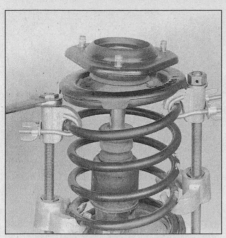

3.3 Install the spring compressor according to the tool manufacturer's instructions and compress the spring until all pressure is relieved from the upper spring seat

3.4 Remove the damper shaft nut

3.5 Lift the suspension support off the damper shaft

unit, and don't tighten the vise excessively.

3　Following the tool manufacturer's instructions, install the spring compressor (which can be obtained at most auto parts stores or equipment yards on a daily rental basis) on the spring and compress it sufficiently to relieve all pressure from the upper spring seat **(see illustration)**. This can be verified by wiggling the spring.

4　Pry out the dust cover with a screwdriver and remove the damper shaft nut **(see illustration)**.

5　Remove the upper suspension support **(see illustration)**. Inspect the bearing in the suspension support for smooth operation. If it does not turn smoothly, replace the suspension support. Check the rubber portion of the suspension support for cracking and general deterioration. If there is any separation of the rubber, replace it.

6　Lift the compressed spring from the damper shaft **(see illustration)**. Check the rubber spring seat for cracking and hardness, replacing it if necessary. **Warning:** *Carry the spring carefully and never place any part of your body near the end of the spring! Set the compressed spring aside in an isolated area.*

7　Separate the spring seat and rubber seal from the compressed spring if they are stuck to it.

8　Slide the dust boot off the damper shaft.

9　Check the lower insulator for wear, cracking and hardness and replace it if necessary.

Reassembly

Refer to illustrations 3.11 and 3.12

10　If the lower insulator is being replaced, set it into position with the dropped portion seated in the lowest part of the seat. Extend the damper rod to its full length and install the dust boot.

11　Carefully place the coil spring onto the lower insulator, with the end of the spring resting in the lowest part of the insulator **(see**

illustration).

12　Install the upper insulator and the spring seat **(see illustration)**. Make sure the D-shaped cutout in the spring seat mates properly with the damper shaft.

13　Install the dust seal and suspension support to the damper shaft.

14　Install the nut and, using a special tool or suitable wrench to keep the shaft from turning, tighten it to the torque listed in this Chapter's Specifications.

15　Install the strut/coil spring assembly (see Section 2 [front] or 9 [rear]).

4　Steering knuckle - removal and installation

Warning: *Dust created by the brake system is harmful to your health. Never blow it out with compressed air and don't inhale any of it. Do not, under any circumstances, use petroleum-based solvents to clean brake parts. Use brake system cleaner only.*

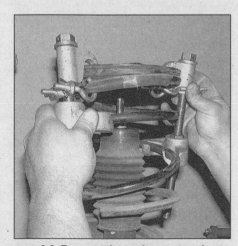

3.6 Remove the spring seat and compressed spring from the damper shaft

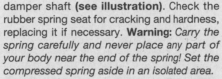

3.11 When installing the spring, make sure the end fits into the recessed portion of the lower seat (arrow)

3.12 Make sure the upper end of the coil spring fits into the recess in the spring seat

10

4.2 Use a breaker bar and socket to loosen the driveaxle/hub nut - install the spare tire onto the hub if the nut is not accessible through the wheel

6.2 To disconnect the stabilizer link from the stabilizer bar, remove the upper nut; to disconnect the link from the control arm, remove the nut that attaches the link to the control arm

Removal

Refer to illustration 4.2

1   Remove the cotter pin from the end of the driveaxle.

2   Use a breaker bar and socket and loosen the driveaxle/hub nut **(see illustration)**. **Note:** *If you can't get a socket on the driveaxle/hub nut through the opening in the center of the wheel, install the spare tire and lower the vehicle to the ground.*

3   Loosen the wheel lug nuts slightly, raise the front of the vehicle and support it securely on jackstands. Remove the wheel and the driveaxle/hub nut.

4   Disconnect the brake hose from the strut, then remove the brake caliper, caliper mounting bracket and, on 2001 and later models, the brake disc (see Chapter 9). **Note:** *Don't disconnect the brake hose from the caliper. Also, be sure to support the caliper with a piece of wire - don't let it hang by the brake hose.*

5   If the vehicle is equipped with ABS, unbolt the wheel speed sensor.

6   Remove the strut-to-steering knuckle nuts, but don't remove the bolts yet (see Section 2).

7   Separate the tie-rod end from the steering knuckle arm (see Section 16).

8   Separate the balljoint from the steering knuckle (see Section 7).

9   Push the driveaxle from the hub (see Chapter 8). Support the end of the driveaxle with a length of wire.

10   Remove the strut-to-knuckle bolts, then separate the knuckle from the strut.

Installation

11   Guide the knuckle and hub assembly into position, inserting the driveaxle into the hub.

12   Push the knuckle into the strut flange and install the bolts and nuts, but don't tighten them yet.

13   Attach the control arm balljoint to the

steering knuckle (see Section 7).

14   Attach the tie-rod end to the steering knuckle arm (see Section 16). Tighten the strut-to-knuckle nuts to the torque listed in this Chapter's Specifications.

15   Place the brake disc on the hub (2001 and later models only) and install the caliper mounting bracket and caliper (see Chapter 9). Tighten the mounting bracket bolts and the caliper bolts to the torque listed in Chapter 9 Specifications.

16   Install the driveaxle/hub nut and tighten it securely, but not completely yet.

17   Install the wheel and lug nuts, lower the vehicle and tighten the lug nuts to the torque listed in the Chapter 1 Specifications. Tighten the driveaxle/hub nut to the torque listed in the Chapter 8 Specifications. Install a new cotter pin.

5   Hub and wheel bearing assembly (front) - removal and installation

Due to the special tools and expertise required to press the hub and bearing from the steering knuckle, this job should be left to a professional mechanic. However, the steering knuckle and hub may be removed and the assembly taken to a dealer service department or other qualified repair shop. See Section 4 for the steering knuckle removal procedure.

6   Stabilizer bar (front) - removal and installation

Refer to illustrations 6.2 and 6.3

1   Loosen the wheel lug nuts, raise the front of the vehicle and support it securely on jackstands. Remove the wheels.

2   Disconnect both stabilizer bar links from the stabilizer bar **(see illustration)**.

3   Remove the stabilizer bar clamps **(see illustration)**.

4   On 2000 and earlier models, remove the steering gear assembly for access (see Section 18).

5   Remove the stabilizer bar, guiding it out from the right (passenger's) side of the vehicle.

6   Inspect the clamp bushings and the link balljoints. If the bushings are cracked or torn, replace them. If the link balljoints are loose, replace the links.

7   Installation is the reverse of removal. Be sure to tighten all fasteners to the torque values listed in this Chapter's Specifications.

7   Control arm - removal, inspection and installation

Removal

Refer to illustrations 7.4, 7.5 and 7.6

1   Loosen the wheel lug nuts, raise the vehicle and support it securely on jackstands. Remove the wheel.

2   Detach the stabilizer bar link from the control arm (see Section 6).

6.3 To disconnect the stabilizer bar from the subframe, remove the bushing clamp nuts and bolts (arrows) from both sides

7.4 Use a pickle fork tool to disconnect the balljoint stud from the steering knuckle

3   Loosen, but do not remove the balljoint nut.

4   Use a pickle fork tool to pop the balljoint stud from the steering knuckle **(see illustration)**. Separate the arm from the steering knuckle.

5   Remove the front pivot bolt **(see illustration)**.

6   Remove the rear bushing clamp bolts **(see illustration)**. Remove the control arm.

Inspection

7   Inspect the front and rear bushings for cracks and general deterioration. If the front bushing (or rear bushing on 2001 and later models) is in need of replacement, take the control arm to an automotive machine shop to have the old one pressed out and the new one pressed in. If the rear bushing on 2000 and earlier models is in need of replacement, remove the pivot stud nut from the rear of the control arm and slide the bushing and bracket assembly off the control arm pivot. Install the new bushing, lockwasher and nut, tightening the nut to the torque listed in this Chapter's Specifications.

8   Inspect the control arm for straightness. If it's bent, replace it. Do not attempt to straighten a bent control arm.

7.5 Remove the front pivot bolt (arrow)

Installation

9   Installation is the reverse of removal. Tighten all of the fasteners to the torque values listed in this Chapter's Specifications.

10   Install the wheel and lug nuts, lower the vehicle and tighten the lug nuts to the torque listed in the Chapter 1 Specifications.

8   Balljoints - replacement

If the balljoint is in need of replacement, take the control arm to an automotive machine shop to have the old one pressed out and the new one pressed in. See Section 7 for the control arm removal procedure.

9   Strut/coil spring assembly (rear) - removal, inspection and installation

Removal

Refer to illustrations 9.3 and 9.6

1   Loosen the rear wheel lug nuts, raise the rear of the vehicle and support it securely on jackstands. Remove the wheels.

2   Remove the brake hose clip from the

bracket and disconnect the stabilizer bar link on the strut. If the vehicle is equipped with ABS, remove the speed sensor harness bracket bolt.

3   Remove the strut-to-knuckle nuts **(see illustration)** and knock the bolts out with a hammer and punch.

4   Separate the strut from the knuckle. Don't allow the knuckle to fall outward, as this may damage the brake hose.

5   Remove the luggage compartment trim panel for access to the upper mounting nuts.

6   Have an assistant support the strut and spring assembly while you remove the three upper mounting nuts **(see illustration)**. Remove the assembly from the fenderwell.

Inspection

7   Inspect the strut and spring as outlined in Section 2. If any undesirable conditions exist, replace the strut or spring (see Section 3).

Installation

8   Guide the strut assembly up into the fenderwell and insert the upper mounting studs through the holes in the strut tower. Once the studs protrude from the strut tower, install the nuts so the strut won't fall back through. This is most easily accomplished with the help of an assistant, as the strut is quite heavy and awkward.

9   Slide the rear knuckle into the strut flange and insert the two bolts. Install the nuts and tighten them to the torque listed in this Chapter's Specifications.

10   Connect the brake hose to the strut bracket and install the clip, then connect the stabilizer bar link. If the vehicle is equipped with ABS, connect the speed sensor wiring harness bracket and tighten the bolt securely.

11   Install the wheel and lug nuts, then lower the vehicle and tighten the lug nuts to the torque listed in the Chapter 1 Specifications.

12   Tighten the upper mounting nuts to the torque listed in this Chapter's Specifications. Install the trim panel.

10

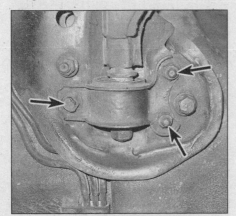

7.6 Remove the rear pivot bushing bolt and nuts (arrows) (2000 and earlier models shown)

9.3 To disconnect the strut from the rear knuckle, remove the two nuts and bolts (arrows)

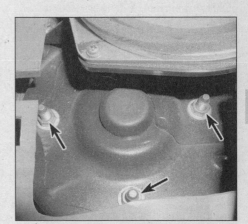

9.6 Remove the strut upper mounting nuts (arrows)

10.6 Once the brake assembly has been detached from the knuckle, the knuckle can be removed by removing the bolts and nuts that attach it to the rear knuckle and suspension arms (arrows)

12.2 If you're just removing the stabilizer bar, remove the nut that attaches it to the link (lower arrow); if you're removing the strut, remove the nut from the upper end of the link (upper arrow)

12.3 To disconnect the rear stabilizer bar bushing clamps, remove the bolts (arrows) from each clamp

10   Rear knuckle - removal and installation

Refer to illustration 10.6

1   Loosen the rear wheel lug nuts, raise the rear of the vehicle and support it securely on jackstands. Remove the wheels.

2   Remove the rear hub and bearing assembly (see Section 11).

3   On models with rear drum brakes, remove the clips securing the brake line to the strut (see Chapter 9). Detach the parking brake cable from the parking brake lever and the brake backing plate (see Chapter 9). **Note:** *The brake shoes can remain attached to the backing plate.*

4   Remove the bolts and detach the disc brake caliper assembly or drum brake backing plate from the knuckle (see Chapter 9). Lift the caliper or backing plate and brake shoe assembly off the knuckle and hang it from the strut spring with a length of wire. **Caution:** *Do not disconnect the brake line from the wheel cylinder, but be careful not to twist or otherwise damage the brake hose.*

5   On models with ABS, remove the rear wheel sensor.

6   Loosen the strut-to-knuckle nuts, then disconnect the suspension arms from the knuckle **(see illustration).**

7   Remove the strut-to-knuckle nuts and drive the bolts out with a hammer and punch, then detach the knuckle from the strut.

8   Installation is the reverse of removal. Be sure to tighten the suspension and brake backing plate fasteners to the torque values listed in this Chapter's Specifications. If equipped with rear disc brakes, tighten the caliper mounting bracket bolts and caliper mounting bolt to the torque values listed in the Chapter 9 Specifications. The brake hydraulic system will not require bleeding unless the brake line was detached from the caliper or wheel cylinder.

9   Install the wheel and lug nuts. Lower the vehicle and tighten the lug nuts to the torque listed in the Chapter 1 Specifications.

11   Hub and wheel bearing assembly (rear) - removal and installation

Note: *The hub and bearing assembly is a sealed unit and is not serviceable. If found to be defective it must be replaced with a new one.*

1   Loosen the rear wheel lug nuts, raise the rear of the vehicle and support it securely on jackstands. Remove the wheel.

2   On disc brake-equipped models, remove the caliper and brake disk (see Chapter 9).

3   Remove the center cap and unstake the hub nut.

4   Using a breaker bar and socket, loosen the hub nut.

5   Unscrew the hub nut.

6   Remove the brake drum/hub and bearing assembly from the knuckle (see Chapter 9).

7   Installation is the reverse of removal. Be sure to tighten the hub nut to the torque listed in this Chapter's Specifications, then stake the nut into the groove in the spindle. If equipped with disc brakes, tighten the caliper mounting bracket bolts and the caliper mounting bolt to the torque values listed in the Chapter 9 Specifications.

8   Install the wheel and lug nuts. Lower the vehicle and tighten the lug nuts to the torque listed in the Chapter 1 Specifications.

12   Stabilizer bar (rear) - removal and installation

Refer to illustrations 12.2 and 12.3

1   Loosen the rear wheel lug nuts, raise the rear of the vehicle and support it securely on jackstands. Remove the wheels.

2   Remove the stabilizer bar-to-link nuts **(see illustration).** Separate the links from the bar.

3   Remove the bushing clamp bolts and nuts from the rear crossmember **(see illus-**

tration). Remove the stabilizer bar.

4   Inspect the clamp bushings and the link balljoints. If the bushings are cracked or torn, replace them. If the link balljoints are loose, replace the links.

5   Installation is the reverse of removal. Be sure to tighten all fasteners to the torque values listed in this Chapter's Specifications.

6   Install the wheel and lug nuts. Lower the vehicle and tighten the lug nuts to the torque listed in the Chapter 1 Specifications.

13   Rear suspension arms - removal and installation

1   Loosen the rear wheel lug nuts, raise the rear of the vehicle and support it securely on jackstands. Remove the wheels.

2   On ABS-equipped models, remove the wheel speed sensors.

Trailing arms

Refer to illustrations 13.4 and 13.5

3   Remove the bolts and disconnect the parking brake cable from the trailing arm.

4   Remove the bolt that attaches the rear end of the arm to the knuckle **(see illustration).**

13.4 Remove the bolt that attaches the rear end of the trailing arm to the knuckle

13.5 To disconnect the forward end of the trailing arm from the body, remove the nut and pivot bolt (arrows)

5   Remove the pivot bolt and nut from the forward end of the trailing arm **(see illustration)**. Remove the trailing arm.
6   Installation is the reverse of removal.

Place a floor jack under the rear knuckle and raise the suspension to simulate normal ride height, then tighten the fasteners to the torque listed in this Chapter's Specifications.
7   Lower the vehicle and tighten the lug nuts to the torque listed in the Chapter 1 Specifications.

Lateral arms

Refer to illustration 13.8a, 13.8b, 13.9a and 13.9b
8   Mark the relationship of the toe-in adjusting cams on the inner ends of the rear lateral arms to the crossmember to preserve rear wheel alignment **(see illustrations)**.
9   Remove the through-bolts that attach the outer ends of the lateral arms to the rear knuckle **(see illustrations)**.
10   Remove the inner pivot nuts and bolts. Remove the rear lateral arm. **Note:** *On 2001 and later models it will be necessary to unbolt the crossmember from the floorpan to allow the pivot bolts to be removed.*
11   Installation is the reverse of removal.

Before tightening the lateral arm fasteners on 2000 and earlier models, align the match-marks you made in Step 8. On all models, place a floor jack under the rear knuckle and raise the suspension to simulate normal ride height, then tighten the fasteners to the torque values listed in this Chapter's Specifications.
12   Lower the vehicle and tighten the lug nuts to the torque listed in the Chapter 1 Specifications.
13   When you're done, drive the vehicle to an alignment shop and have the rear-wheel toe checked and, if necessary, adjusted.

14   Steering wheel - removal and installation

Warning: *The models covered by this manual are equipped with Supplemental Restraint Systems (SRS), more commonly known as airbags. Always disable the airbag system before working in the vicinity of any airbag*

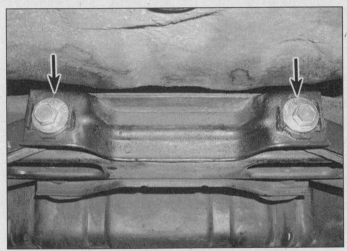

13.8a On 2000 and earlier models, mark the relationship of the toe adjusting cams to the crossmember (arrows)

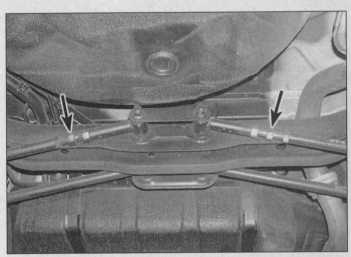

13.8b On 2001 and later models, mark the relationship of the adjusting nuts (arrows) on the inner ends of the rear lateral rods (this is only necessary if the arms are going to be disassembled)

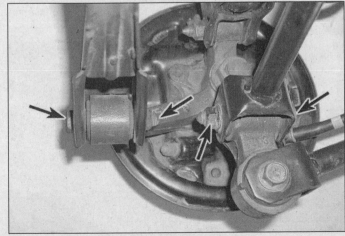

13.9a On 2000 and earlier models the front and rear lateral arms are connected to the knuckle by through-bolts and nuts (arrows)

13.9b On 2001 and later models both the front and rear lateral arms are connected to the knuckle by a single through-bolt and nut (arrows)

10

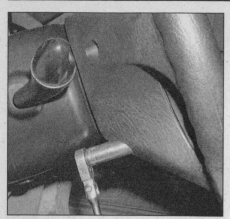

14.3 Remove the airbag mounting nuts

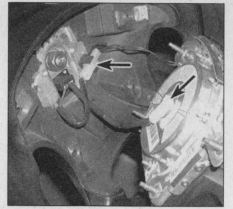

14.4 Carefully lift the airbag module and disconnect the airbag electrical connectors (arrows)

14.6 After the steering wheel retaining nut has been removed, mark the relationship of the steering wheel to the steering shaft (arrow)

system components to avoid the possibility of accidental deployment of the airbag, which could cause personal injury (see Chapter 12). **Caution:** *Some models are equipped with an anti-theft radio. Before performing a procedure that requires disconnecting the battery, make sure you have the activation code.*

Removal

Refer to illustrations 14.3, 14.4, 14.6 and 14.7
1   Park the vehicle with the front wheels pointing straight ahead.
2   Disconnect the cable from the negative battery terminal, then the positive battery terminal and wait at least two minutes before proceeding.
3   Remove the airbag module nuts from the backside of the steering wheel **(see illustration)**.
4   Unplug the airbag module connector while holding the airbag module assembly off to the side **(see illustration)**.
5   Lift the airbag module off the steering wheel. **Warning:** *Handle the airbag module with care, carry the module with the trim cover side facing away from your body and store it in an isolated area with the trim side facing up.*
6   Remove the steering wheel retaining nut, then mark the relationship of the steering

wheel to the steering shaft **(see illustration)**.
7   Use a steering wheel puller to separate the steering wheel from the steering shaft **(see illustration)**. When removing the wheel, make sure the electrical leads for the airbag module and the cruise control system don't snag on the wheel. **Warning:** *Do not turn the steering shaft while the steering wheel is removed.*

Installation

8   Make absolutely sure that the clockspring is centered with the arrow on the clockspring pointing up. This shouldn't be a problem as long as you have not turned the steering shaft while the wheel was removed.
9   If the airbag clockspring was accidentally rotated while the wheel was removed, re-center it by rotating the hub of the clockspring counterclockwise until it stops, then rotate it clockwise until it stops, counting the number of turns. Divide this number by two and rotate the hub counterclockwise by that amount. Now line up the pointers on the clockspring body and hub.
10   Pull the electrical leads for the airbag module through the steering wheel and install the wheel, making sure the matchmarks line up.

11   Install the steering wheel retaining nut and tighten it to the torque listed in this Chapter's Specifications.
12   Connect the airbag electrical connectors. Install the airbag module and tighten the mounting nuts/bolts to the torque listed in this Chapter's Specification.
13   Verify that the airbag circuit is operational by turning the ignition key to the On position. The "AIR BAG" warning light should illuminate for about seven seconds, then turn off.

15   Steering column - removal and installation

Warning 1: *The models covered by this manual are equipped with Supplemental Restraint Systems (SRS), more commonly known as airbags. Always disable the airbag system before working in the vicinity of any airbag system components to avoid the possibility of accidental deployment of the airbag, which could cause personal injury (see Chapter 12).*
Warning 2: *Make sure the steering shaft is not turned while the steering wheel is removed or you could damage the airbag sys-*

14.7 Use a steering wheel puller to separate the steering wheel from the steering shaft

15.2 Remove the clockspring mounting screws (arrows)

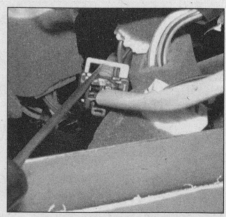

15.3 Disconnect the clockspring connector

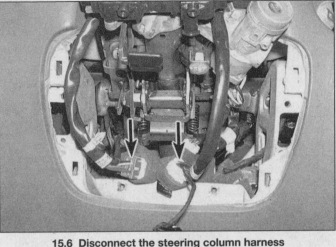

15.6 Disconnect the steering column harness connectors (arrows)

15.7 Remove the pinch bolt (A) and the steering column mounting bolts (B indicates lower mounting bolts)

tem clockspring. To prevent the shaft from turning, position the wheels straight ahead, turn the ignition key to the lock position and remove the key before beginning work. Due to the possible damage to the airbag system, we recommend only experienced mechanics attempt this procedure.

Caution: *Some models are equipped with an anti-theft radio. Before performing a procedure that requires disconnecting the battery, make sure you have the activation code.*

Removal

Refer to illustrations 15.2, 15.3, 15.6 and 15.7

1   Disconnect the cable from the negative battery terminal, then the positive battery terminal and wait at least two minutes. Remove the steering wheel (see Section 14).
2   Remove the clockspring mounting screws **(see illustration)**.
3   Disconnect the clockspring connector and separate the clockspring from the steering column **(see illustration)**.
4   Remove the combination switch (see Chapter 12).
5   Remove the lower instrument panel (see Chapter 11).

6   Disconnect the electrical connectors from the steering column wiring harness **(see illustration)**.
7   Remove the pinch bolt from the lower end of the steering column, then remove the steering column bracket bolts **(see illustration)**.
8   Remove the steering column.

Installation

9   Installation is the reverse of removal. Be sure to tighten all fasteners to the torque listed in this Chapter's Specifications. When installing the clockspring, be sure to center it following the procedure in Section 14.

---

16   Tie-rod ends - removal and installation

Removal

Refer to illustrations 16.2 and 16.3

1   Loosen the wheel lug nuts, raise the front of the vehicle and support it securely on jackstands. Block the rear wheels and set the parking brake. Remove the front wheel.

2   Loosen the jam nut enough to mark the position of the tie-rod end in relation to the threads **(see illustration)**.
3   Remove the cotter pin **(see illustration)** and loosen, but don't remove, the nut on the tie-rod end stud.
4   Disconnect the tie-rod end from the steering knuckle arm with a puller. Remove the nut and separate the tie-rod.
5   Unscrew the tie-rod end from the steering rod.

Installation

6   Thread the tie-rod end on to the marked position and insert the tie-rod stud into the steering knuckle arm. Install the castle nut on the stud and tighten it to the torque listed in this Chapter's Specifications. Install a new cotter pin. If necessary, tighten the nut a little more to allow cotter pin insertion (don't loosen the nut to do this).
7   Tighten the jam nut securely.
8   Install the wheel and lug nuts. Lower the vehicle and tighten the lug nuts to the torque listed in the Chapter 1 Specifications.
9   Have the alignment checked and, if necessary, adjusted.

16.2 Loosen the jam nut, then mark the position of the tie-rod end in relation to the threads

16.3 Remove the cotter pin

10

17.3 The outer end of each steering gear boot is secured by a spring-type clamp that can be slid off simply by pinching the ends together

17   Steering gear boots - replacement

Refer to illustration 17.3

1   Loosen the wheel lug nuts, raise the vehicle and support it securely on jackstands. Remove the wheel.

2   Remove the tie-rod end and jam nut (see Section 16).

3   Remove the outer clamp from the steering gear boot **(see illustration)** with a pair of pliers. Cut off the inner boot clamp with a pair of diagonal cutters. Slide the boot off.

4   Before installing the new boot, wrap the threads on the end of the steering rod with tape so the small end of the new boot isn't damaged.

5   Slide the new boot into position on the steering gear until it seats in the groove in the steering rod and install new clamps.

6   Remove the tape and install the tie-rod end (see Section 16).

7   Install the wheel and lug nuts. Lower the vehicle and tighten the lug nuts to the torque listed in the Chapter 1 Specifications.

18   Steering gear - removal and installation

Warning 1: *The models covered by this manual are equipped with Supplemental Restraint Systems (SRS), more commonly known as airbags. Always disable the airbag system before working in the vicinity of any airbag system components to avoid the possibility of accidental deployment of the airbag, which could cause personal injury (see Chapter 12).*

Warning 2: *Make sure the steering shaft is not turned while the steering wheel is removed or you could damage the airbag system clockspring. To prevent the shaft from turning, position the wheels straight ahead, turn the ignition key to the lock position and remove the key before beginning work, or thread the seat belt through the steering wheel and clip it into place.*

Removal

Refer to illustrations 18.2 and 18.7

1   In the engine compartment, remove the air intake hose from between the throttle body and air filter housing.

2   Place a drain pan under the steering gear. Disconnect the fluid pressure and return fittings on the steering gear, then cap the ends to prevent excessive fluid loss and contamination **(see illustration)**.

3   Working inside the vehicle, mark the relationship of the lower universal joint to the steering gear input shaft. Remove the lower shaft pinch bolt.

4   With the wheels pointing straight ahead, loosen the front wheel lug nuts, raise the front of the vehicle and support it securely on jackstands. Apply the parking brake and remove the wheels. Remove the engine splash shields.

5   Disconnect the tie-rod ends from the steering knuckles (see Section 16).

6   Remove the right side stabilizer bar bracket.

7   Remove the steering gear clamp mounting bolts **(see illustration)** and the hydraulic line clamp. Separate the intermediate shaft from the steering gear input shaft and remove the steering gear assembly through the right side fenderwell.

Installation

Note: *Make sure the steering gear is centered from side-to-side before installing it.*

8   Guide the steering gear into position and connect the U-joint, aligning the marks.

9   Install the mounting brackets and bolts and tighten them to the torque listed in this Chapter's Specifications.

10   Connect the stabilizer bar (see Section 6).

11   Connect the tie-rod ends to the steering knuckle arms (see Section 16).

12   Install the U-joint pinch bolt and tighten it to the torque listed in this Chapter's Specifications.

13   Connect the power steering pressure and return lines to the steering gear and fill the power steering pump reservoir with the recommended fluid (see Chapter 1).

14   The remainder of installation is the reverse of removal.

15   Be sure to tighten all suspension and steering fasteners to the torque listed in this Chapter's Specifications.

16   Install the wheels and lug nuts, then lower the vehicle and tighten the lug nuts to the torque listed in the Chapter 1 Specifications. Bleed the steering system (see Section 20).

19   Power steering pump - removal and installation

Caution: *Some models are equipped with an anti-theft radio. Before performing a procedure that requires disconnecting the battery, make sure you have the activation code.*

Removal

Refer to illustration 19.3

1   Disconnect the cable from the negative battery terminal.

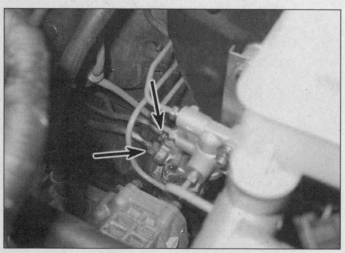

18.2 Disconnect the fluid line fittings (arrows) on the steering gear and cap them

18.7 To remove the steering gear assembly, remove the retaining clamp bolts (arrows)

2   Using a large syringe or suction gun, suck as much fluid out of the power steering fluid reservoir as possible. Place a drain pan under the vehicle to catch any fluid that spills out when the hoses are disconnected.

3   Remove the fluid reservoir supply hose, hose and the pressure hose banjo bolt from power steering pump **(see illustration).**

4   Loosen the lock bolt and the adjusting bolt and remove the power steering belt (see Chapter 1).

5   Remove the pump mounting bolts then remove the pump from the vehicle.

Installation

6   Installation is the reverse of removal. Adjust the drivebelt tension following the procedure described in Chapter 1.

7   Top up the fluid level in the reservoir (see Chapter 1) and bleed the system (see Section 20).

20 Power steering system - bleeding

1   Following any operation in which the power steering fluid lines have been disconnected, the power steering system must be bled to remove all air and obtain proper steering performance.

2   With the front wheels in the straight ahead position, check the power steering fluid level and, if low, add fluid until it reaches the Cold mark on the dipstick.

3   Start the engine and allow it to run at fast idle. Recheck the fluid level and add more if necessary to reach the Cold mark on the dipstick.

4   Bleed the system by turning the wheels from side to side, without hitting the stops. This will work the air out of the system. Keep the reservoir full of fluid as this is done.

5   When the air is worked out of the system, return the wheels to the straight ahead position and leave the vehicle running for several more minutes before shutting it off.

6   Road test the vehicle to be sure the steering system is functioning normally and noise free.

7   Recheck the fluid level to be sure it is up to the Hot mark on the dipstick while the engine is at normal operating temperature. Add fluid if necessary (see Chapter 1).

21 Wheels and tires - general information

Refer to illustration 21.1

1   All vehicles covered by this manual are equipped with metric-sized steel belted radial tires **(see illustration).** Use of other size or type of tires may affect the ride and handling of the vehicle. Don't mix different types of tires, such as radials and bias belted, on the same vehicle as handling may be seriously affected. It's recommended that tires be replaced in pairs on the same axle, but if only one tire is being replaced, be sure it's the same size, structure and tread design as the other.

2   Because tire pressure has a substantial effect on handling and wear, the pressure on all tires should be checked at least once a

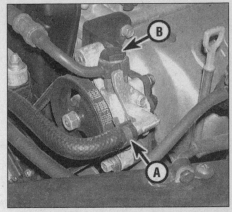

19.3 Remove the power steering fluid supply line (A) and the high pressure line banjo bolt (B) from the power steering pump

month or before any extended trips (see Chapter 1).

3   Wheels must be replaced if they are bent, dented, leak air, have elongated bolt holes, are heavily rusted, out of vertical symmetry or if the lug nuts won't stay tight. Wheel repairs that use welding or peening are not recommended.

4   Tire and wheel balance is important in the overall handling, braking and performance of the vehicle. Unbalanced wheels can adversely affect handling and ride characteristics as well as tire life. Whenever a tire is installed on a wheel, the tire and wheel should be balanced by a shop with the proper equipment.

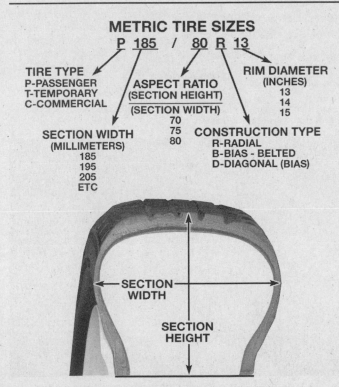

METRIC TIRE SIZES
P 185 / 80 R 13

TIRE TYPE
P-PASSENGER
T-TEMPORARY
C-COMMERCIAL

ASPECT RATIO
(SECTION HEIGHT)
(SECTION WIDTH)
70
75
80

RIM DIAMETER
(INCHES)
13
14
15

CONSTRUCTION TYPE
R-RADIAL
B-BIAS - BELTED
D-DIAGONAL (BIAS)

SECTION WIDTH
(MILLIMETERS)
185
195
205
ETC

SECTION
WIDTH

SECTION
HEIGHT

21.1 Metric tire size code

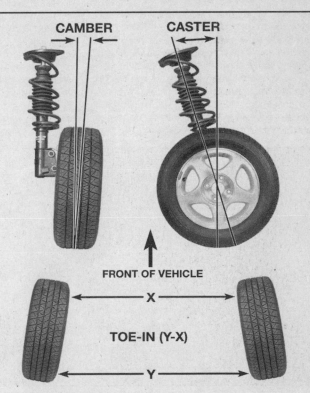

CAMBER   CASTER

FRONT OF VEHICLE

X

TOE-IN (Y-X)

Y

22.1 Camber, caster and toe-in angles

10

22   Wheel alignment - general information

Refer to illustration 22.1

A wheel alignment refers to the adjustments made to the wheels so they are in proper angular relationship to the suspension and the ground. Wheels that are out of proper alignment not only affect vehicle control, but also increase tire wear. The front end angles normally measured are camber, caster and toe-in **(see illustration)**. Camber and caster can't be adjusted, but should be measured to check for bent or worn parts; toe-in is adjustable by altering the position of the tie-rod ends on the tie-rods. The rear toe-in can also be adjusted, but the camber and caster cannot (however, camber and caster are usually measured to check for bent or worn suspension parts).

Getting the proper wheel alignment is a very exacting process, one in which complicated and expensive machines are necessary to perform the job properly. Because of this, you should have a technician with the proper equipment perform these tasks. We will, however, use this space to give you a basic idea of what is involved with a wheel alignment so you can better understand the process and deal intelligently with the shop that does the work.

Toe-in is the turning in of the wheels. The purpose of a toe specification is to ensure parallel rolling of the wheels. In a vehicle with zero toe-in, the distance between the front edges of the wheels will be the same as the distance between the rear edges of the wheels. The actual amount of toe-in is normally only a fraction of an inch. On the front end, toe-in is controlled by the tie-rod end position on the tie-rod. On the rear end, it's controlled by adjuster cams on the inner ends of the rear (number two) suspension arms (2000 and earlier models) or by threaded rods on the rear suspension arm. Incorrect toe-in will cause the tires to wear improperly by making them scrub against the road surface.

Camber is the tilting of the wheels from vertical when viewed from one end of the vehicle. When the wheels tilt out at the top, the camber is said to be positive (+). When the wheels tilt in at the top the camber is negative (-). The amount of tilt is measured in degrees from vertical and this measurement is called the camber angle. This angle affects the amount of tire tread which contacts the road and compensates for changes in the suspension geometry when the vehicle is cornering or traveling over an undulating surface.

Caster is the tilting of the front steering axis from the vertical. A tilt toward the rear is positive caster and a tilt toward the front is negative caster.

Chapter 11   Body

Contents

1   General information

These models feature a "unibody" layout, using a floor pan with front and rear frame side rails which support the body components, front and rear suspension systems and other mechanical components.

Certain components are particularly vulnerable to accident damage and can be unbolted and repaired or replaced. Among these parts are the body moldings, bumpers, the hood and trunk lid, doors and all glass.

Only general body maintenance practices and body panel repair procedures within the scope of the do-it-yourselfer are included in this Chapter.

2   Body - maintenance

1   The condition of your vehicle's body is very important, because the resale value depends a great deal on it. It's much more difficult to repair a neglected or damaged body than it is to repair mechanical components. The hidden areas of the body, such as the wheel wells, the frame and the engine compartment, are equally important, although they don't require as frequent attention as the rest of the body.

2   Once a year, or every 12,000 miles, it's a good idea to have the underside of the body steam cleaned. All traces of dirt and oil will be removed and the area can then be inspected carefully for rust, damaged brake lines, frayed electrical wires, damaged cables and other problems.

3   At the same time, clean the engine and the engine compartment with a steam cleaner or water-soluble degreaser.

4   The wheel wells should be given close attention, since undercoating can peel away and stones and dirt thrown up by the tires can cause the paint to chip and flake, allowing rust to set in. If rust is found, clean down to the bare metal and apply an anti-rust paint.

5   The body should be washed about once a week. Wet the vehicle thoroughly to soften the dirt, then wash it down with a soft sponge and plenty of clean soapy water. If the surplus dirt is not washed off very carefully, it can wear down the paint.

6   Spots of tar or asphalt thrown up from the road should be removed with a cloth soaked in kerosene. Scented lamp oil is available in most hardware stores and the smell is easier to work with than straight kerosene.

7   Once every six months, wax the body and chrome trim. If a chrome cleaner is used to remove rust from any of the vehicle's plated parts, remember that the cleaner also removes part of the chrome, so use it sparingly. On any plated parts where chrome cleaner is used, use a good paste wax over the plating for extra protection.

3   Vinyl trim - maintenance

Don't clean vinyl trim with detergents, caustic soap or petroleum-based cleaners. Plain soap and water works just fine, with a soft brush to clean dirt that may be ingrained. Wash the vinyl as frequently as the rest of the vehicle.

After cleaning, application of a high quality rubber and vinyl protectant will help prevent oxidation and cracks. The protectant can also be applied to weatherstripping, vacuum lines and rubber hoses, which often fail as a result of chemical degradation, and to the tires.

4   Upholstery and carpets - maintenance

1   Every three months remove the floormats and clean the interior of the vehicle (more frequently if necessary). Use a stiff whiskbroom to brush the carpeting and loosen dirt and dust, then vacuum the upholstery and carpets thoroughly, especially along seams and crevices.

2   Dirt and stains can be removed from carpeting with basic household or automotive carpet shampoos available in spray cans. Follow the directions and vacuum again, then use a stiff brush to bring back the "nap" of

11

the carpet.

3   Most interiors have cloth or vinyl uphol-stery, either of which can be cleaned and maintained with a number of material-specific cleaners or shampoos available in auto sup-ply stores. Follow the directions on the prod-uct for usage, and always spot-test any upholstery cleaner on an inconspicuous area (bottom edge of a backseat cushion) to ensure that it doesn't cause a color shift in the material.

4   After cleaning, vinyl upholstery should be treated with a protectant. **Note:** *Make sure the protectant container indicates the prod-uct can be used on seats - some products may make a seat too slippery.* **Caution:** *Do not use protectant on vinyl-covered steering wheels.*

5   Leather upholstery requires special care. It should be cleaned regularly with sad-dlesoap or leather cleaner. Never use alco-hol, gasoline, nail polish remover or thinner to clean leather upholstery.

6   After cleaning, regularly treat leather upholstery with a leather conditioner, rubbed in with a soft cotton cloth. Never use car wax on leather upholstery.

7   In areas where the interior of the vehicle is subject to bright sunlight, cover leather seating areas of the seats with a sheet if the vehicle is to be left out for any length of time.

5   Body repair - minor damage

Repair of flexible plastic body panels (front and rear bumper covers)

The following repair procedures are for minor scratches and gouges. Repair of more serious damage should be left to a dealer service department or qualified auto body shop. Below is a list of the equipment and materials necessary to perform the following repair procedures on plastic body panels. 3M and other manufacturers produce the materi-als listed, many of which are available from auto parts stores.

Wax, grease and silicone removing sol-vent
Cloth-backed body tape
Sanding discs
Drill motor with three-inch disc holder
Hand sanding block
Rubber squeegees
Sandpaper
Non-porous mixing palette
Wood paddle or putty knife
Curved-tooth body file
Flexible parts repair kit (includes adhe-sive material and fiberglass-type material)

1   Remove the damaged panel, if neces-sary or desirable. In most cases, repairs can be carried out with the panel installed.
2   Clean the area(s) to be repaired with a wax, grease and silicone removing solvent applied with a water-dampened cloth.

3   If the damage is structural, that is, if it extends through the panel, clean the back-side of the panel area to be repaired as well. Wipe dry.
4   Sand the rear surface about 1-1/2 inches (38 mm) beyond the break.
5   Cut two pieces of fiberglass cloth large enough to overlap the break by about 1-1/2 inches (38 mm). Cut only to the required length.
6   Mix the adhesive material according to the instructions and apply a layer of the mix-ture approximately 1/8-inch (3 mm) thick on the backside of the panel. Overlap the break by at least 1-1/2 inches (38 mm).
7   Apply one piece of fiberglass cloth to the adhesive and cover the cloth with addi-tional adhesive. Apply a second piece of fiberglass cloth to the adhesive and immedi-ately cover the cloth with additional adhesive in sufficient quantity to fill the weave.
8   Allow the repair to cure for 20 to 30 min-utes at 60-degrees to 80-degrees F (15 to 26-degrees C).
9   If necessary, trim the excess repair material at the edge.
10   Remove all of the paint film over and around the area(s) to be repaired. The repair material should not overlap the painted sur-face.
11   With a drill motor and a sanding disc (or a rotary file), cut a "V" along the break line approximately 1/2-inch (13 mm) wide. Remove all dust and loose particles from the repair area.
12   Mix and apply the repair material. Apply a light coat first over the damaged area; then continue applying material until it reaches a level slightly higher than the surrounding finish.
13   Cure the mixture for 20 to 30 minutes at 60-degrees to 80-degrees F (15 to 26-degrees C).
14   Roughly establish the contour of the area being repaired with a body file. If low areas or pits remain, mix and apply additional adhesive.
15   Block sand the damaged area with sandpaper to establish the actual contour of the surrounding surface.
16   If desired, the repaired area can be tem-porarily protected with several light coats of primer. Because of the special paints and techniques required for flexible body panels, it is recommended that the vehicle be taken to a paint shop for completion of the body repair.

Steel body panels

See photo sequence

Repair of minor scratches

17   If the scratch is superficial and does not penetrate to the metal of the body, repair is very simple. Lightly rub the scratched area with a fine rubbing compound to remove loose paint and built up wax. Rinse the area with clean water.
18   Apply touch-up paint to the scratch, using a small brush. Continue to apply thin layers of paint until the surface of the paint in

the scratch is level with the surrounding paint. Allow the new paint at least two weeks to harden, then blend it into the surrounding paint by rubbing with a very fine rubbing compound. Finally, apply a coat of wax to the scratch area.
19   If the scratch has penetrated the paint and exposed the metal of the body, causing the metal to rust, a different repair technique is required. Remove all loose rust from the bottom of the scratch with a pocket knife, then apply rust inhibiting paint to prevent the formation of rust in the future. Using a rubber or nylon applicator, coat the scratched area with glaze-type filler. If required, the filler can be mixed with thinner to provide a very thin paste, which is ideal for filling narrow scratches. Before the glaze filler in the scratch hardens, wrap a piece of smooth cot-ton cloth around the tip of a finger. Dip the cloth in thinner and then quickly wipe it along the surface of the scratch. This will ensure that the surface of the filler is slightly hollow. The scratch can now be painted over as described earlier in this Section.

Repair of dents

20   When repairing dents, the first job is to pull the dent out until the affected area is as close as possible to its original shape. There is no point in trying to restore the original shape completely as the metal in the dam-aged area will have stretched on impact and cannot be restored to its original contours. It is better to bring the level of the dent up to a point, which is about 1/8-inch (3 mm) below the level of the surrounding metal. In cases where the dent is very shallow, it is not worth trying to pull it out at all.
21   If the back side of the dent is accessible, it can be hammered out gently from behind using a soft-face hammer. While doing this, hold a block of wood firmly against the oppo-site side of the metal to absorb the hammer blows and prevent the metal from being stretched.
22   If the dent is in a section of the body which has double layers, or some other factor makes it inaccessible from behind, a different technique is required. Drill several small holes through the metal inside the damaged area, particularly in the deeper sections. Screw long, self tapping screws into the holes just enough for them to get a good grip in the metal. Now the dent can be pulled out by pulling on the protruding heads of the screws with locking pliers.
23   The next stage of repair is the removal of paint from the damaged area and from an inch or so of the surrounding metal. This is easily done with a wire brush or sanding disk in a drill motor, although it can be done just as effectively by hand with sandpaper. To complete the preparation for filling, score the surface of the bare metal with a screwdriver or the tang of a file or drill small holes in the affected area. This will provide a good grip for the filler material. To complete the repair, see the Section on filling and painting.

Repair of rust holes or gashes

24   Remove all paint from the affected area and from an inch or so of the surrounding metal using a sanding disk or wire brush mounted in a drill motor. If these are not available, a few sheets of sandpaper will do the job just as effectively.

25   With the paint removed, you will be able to determine the severity of the corrosion and decide whether to replace the whole panel, if possible, or repair the affected area. New body panels are not as expensive as most people think and it is often quicker to install a new panel than to repair large areas of rust.

26   Remove all trim pieces from the affected area except those which will act as a guide to the original shape of the damaged body, such as headlight shells, etc. Using metal snips or a hacksaw blade, remove all loose metal and any other metal that is badly affected by rust. Hammer the edges of the hole in to create a slight depression for the filler material.

27   Wire brush the affected area to remove the powdery rust from the surface of the metal. If the back of the rusted area is accessible, treat it with rust inhibiting paint.

28   Before filling is done, block the hole in some way. This can be done with sheet metal riveted or screwed into place, or by stuffing the hole with wire mesh.

29   Once the hole is blocked off, the affected area can be filled and painted. See the following subsection on filling and painting.

Filling and painting

30   Many types of body fillers are available, but generally speaking, body repair kits which contain filler paste and a tube of resin hardener are best for this type of repair work. A wide, flexible plastic or nylon applicator will be necessary for imparting a smooth and contoured finish to the surface of the filler material. Mix up a small amount of filler on a clean piece of wood or cardboard (use the hardener sparingly). Follow the manufacturer's instructions on the package, otherwise the filler will set incorrectly.

31   Using the applicator, apply the filler paste to the prepared area. Draw the applicator across the surface of the filler to achieve the desired contour and to level the filler surface. As soon as a contour that approximates the original one is achieved, stop working the paste. If you continue, the paste will begin to stick to the applicator. Continue to add thin layers of paste at 20-minute intervals until the level of the filler is just above the surrounding metal.

32   Once the filler has hardened, the excess can be removed with a body file. From then on, progressively finer grades of sandpaper should be used, starting with a 180-grit paper and finishing with 600-grit wet-or-dry paper. Always wrap the sandpaper around a flat rubber or wooden block, otherwise the surface of the filler will not be completely flat. During the sanding of the filler surface, the wet-or-dry paper should be periodically rinsed in water. This will ensure that a very smooth finish is produced in the final stage.

33   At this point, the repair area should be surrounded by a ring of bare metal, which in turn should be encircled by the finely feathered edge of good paint. Rinse the repair area with clean water until all of the dust produced by the sanding operation is gone.

34   Spray the entire area with a light coat of primer. This will reveal any imperfections in the surface of the filler. Repair the imperfections with fresh filler paste or glaze filler and once more smooth the surface with sandpaper. Repeat this spray-and-repair procedure until you are satisfied that the surface of the filler and the feathered edge of the paint are perfect. Rinse the area with clean water and allow it to dry completely.

35   The repair area is now ready for painting. Spray painting must be carried out in a warm, dry, windless and dust free atmosphere. These conditions can be created if you have access to a large indoor work area, but if you are forced to work in the open, you will have to pick the day very carefully. If you are working indoors, dousing the floor in the work area with water will help settle the dust that would otherwise be in the air. If the repair area is confined to one body panel, mask off the surrounding panels. This will help minimize the effects of a slight mismatch in paint color. Trim pieces such as chrome strips, door handles, etc., will also need to be masked off or removed. Use masking tape and several thickness of newspaper for the masking operations.

36   Before spraying, shake the paint can thoroughly, then spray a test area until the spray painting technique is mastered. Cover the repair area with a thick coat of primer. The thickness should be built up using several thin layers of primer rather than one thick one. Using 600-grit wet-or-dry sandpaper, rub down the surface of the primer until it is very smooth. While doing this, the work area should be thoroughly rinsed with water and the wet-or-dry sandpaper periodically rinsed as well. Allow the primer to dry before spraying additional coats.

37   Spray on the top coat, again building up the thickness by using several thin layers of paint. Begin spraying in the center of the repair area and then, using a circular motion, work out until the whole repair area and about two inches of the surrounding original paint is covered. Remove all masking material 10 to 15 minutes after spraying on the final coat of paint. Allow the new paint at least two weeks to harden, then use a very fine rubbing compound to blend the edges of the new paint into the existing paint. Finally, apply a coat of wax.

6   Body repair - major damage

1   Major damage must be repaired by an auto body shop specifically equipped to perform unibody repairs. These shops have the specialized equipment required to do the job properly.

2   If the damage is extensive, the body must be checked for proper alignment or the vehicle's handling characteristics may be adversely affected and other components may wear at an accelerated rate.

3   Due to the fact that some of the major body components (hood, fenders, doors, etc.) are separate and replaceable units, any seriously damaged components should be replaced rather than repaired. Sometimes the components can be found in a wrecking yard that specializes in used vehicle components, often at considerable savings over the cost of new parts.

7   Hinges and locks - maintenance

Once every 3000 miles, or every three months, the hinges and latch assemblies on the doors, hood and trunk (or liftgate) should be given a few drops of light oil or lock lubricant. The door latch strikers should also be lubricated with a thin coat of grease to reduce wear and ensure free movement. Lubricate the door and trunk (or liftgate) locks with spray-on graphite lubricant.

8   Windshield and fixed glass - replacement

Replacement of the windshield and fixed glass requires the use of special fast-setting adhesive/caulk materials and some specialized tools and techniques. These operations should be left to a dealer service department or a shop specializing in glass work.

9   Radiator grille (2001 and later models) - replacement

1   Open the hood.

2   Remove the retaining screw in the center of the top edge of the grille.

3   Using a screwdriver, release the two clips and detach the grille by pulling straight out.

4   Press the grille into place until the clips click, then install the retaining screw.

10   Hood - removal, installation and adjustment

Note: *The hood is somewhat awkward to remove and install; at least two people should perform this procedure.*

Removal and installation

Refer to illustrations 10.3 and 10.4

1   Open the hood, then place blankets or

11

These photos illustrate a method of repairing simple dents. They are intended to supplement *Body repair - minor damage* in this Chapter and should not be used as the sole instructions for body repair on these vehicles.

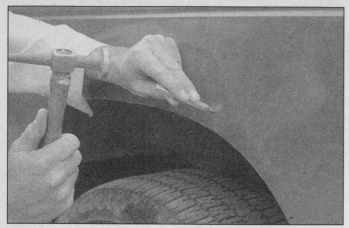

1   If you can't access the backside of the body panel to hammer out the dent, pull it out with a slide-hammer-type dent puller. In the deepest portion of the dent or along the crease line, drill or punch hole(s) at least one inch apart . . .

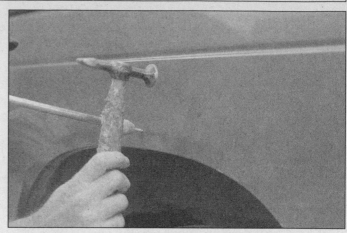

2   . . . then screw the slide-hammer into the hole and operate it. Tap with a hammer near the edge of the dent to help 'pop' the metal back to its original shape. When you're finished, the dent area should be close to its original contour and about 1/8-inch below the surface of the surrounding metal

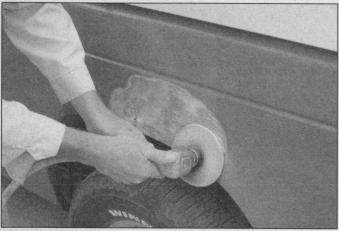

3   Using coarse-grit sandpaper, remove the paint down to the bare metal. Hand sanding works fine, but the disc sander shown here makes the job faster. Use finer (about 320-grit) sandpaper to feather-edge the paint at least one inch around the dent area

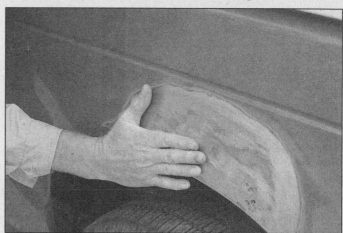

4   When the paint is removed, touch will probably be more helpful than sight for telling if the metal is straight. Hammer down the high spots or raise the low spots as necessary. Clean the repair area with wax/silicone remover

5   Following label instructions, mix up a batch of plastic filler and hardener. The ratio of filler to hardener is critical, and, if you mix it incorrectly, it will either not cure properly or cure too quickly (you won't have time to file and sand it into shape)

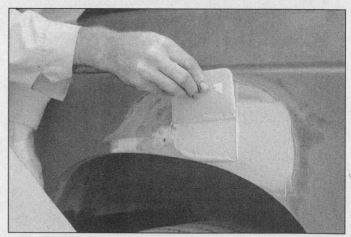

6   Working quickly so the filler doesn't harden, use a plastic applicator to press the body filler firmly into the metal, assuring it bonds completely. Work the filler until it matches the original contour and is slightly above the surrounding metal

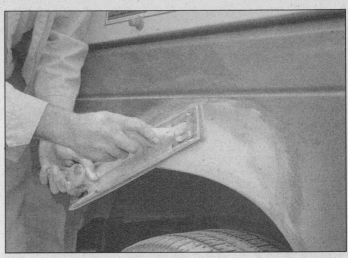

7 Let the filler harden until you can just dent it with your fingernail. Use a body file or Surform tool (shown here) to rough-shape the filler

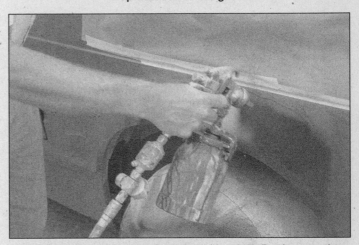

8 Use coarse-grit sandpaper and a sanding board or block to work the filler down until it's smooth and even. Work down to finer grits of sandpaper - always using a board or block - ending up with 360 or 400 grit

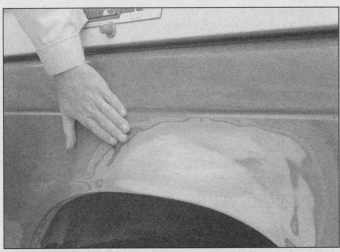

9 You shouldn't be able to feel any ridge at the transition from the filler to the bare metal or from the bare metal to the old paint. As soon as the repair is flat and uniform, remove the dust and mask off the adjacent panels or trim pieces

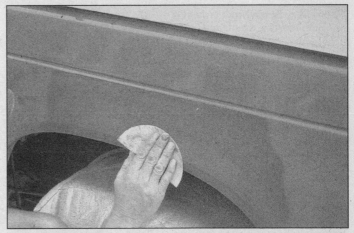

10 Apply several layers of primer to the area. Don't spray the primer on too heavy, so it sags or runs, and make sure each coat is dry before you spray on the next one. A professional-type spray gun is being used here, but aerosol spray primer is available inexpensively from auto parts stores

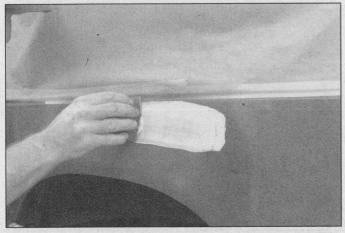

11 The primer will help reveal imperfections or scratches. Fill these with glazing compound. Follow the label instructions and sand it with 360 or 400-grit sandpaper until it's smooth. Repeat the glazing, sanding and respraying until the primer reveals a perfectly smooth surface

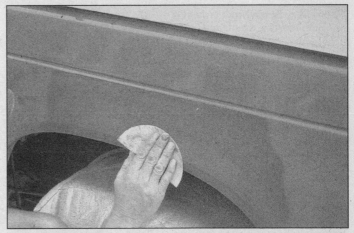

12 Finish sand the primer with very fine sandpaper (400 or 600-grit) to remove the primer overspray. Clean the area with water and allow it to dry. Use a tack rag to remove any dust, then apply the finish coat. Don't attempt to rub out or wax the repair area until the paint has dried completely (at least two weeks)

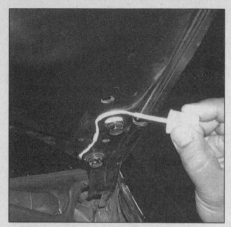

10.3 Scribe or draw alignment marks around the hood hinges to ensure proper alignment of the hood when it's reinstalled

10.4 With an assistant supporting one side of the hood, remove the bolts and lift the hood off

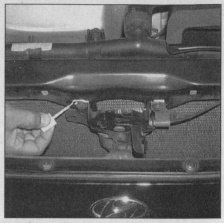

10.9 Before adjusting the hood latch horizontally or vertically, mark its position, then loosen the bolts

pads over the fenders and cowl area of the body. This will protect the body and paint as the hood is lifted off.

2   Disconnect any cables or wires that will interfere with removal. Disconnect the wind-

10.10 To adjust the vertical height of the front edge of the hood so that it's flush with the fenders, turn each hood bumper clockwise (to lower the hood) or counterclockwise (to raise the hood)

shield washer tubing from the nozzles on the hood.

3   Make marks or scribe a line around the hood hinge to ensure proper alignment during installation **(see illustration)**.

4   Have an assistant support one side of the hood. Take turns removing the hinge-to-hood bolts **(see illustration)**.

5   Installation is the reverse of removal. Align the hinge bolts with the marks made in Step 3.

Adjustment

Refer to illustrations 10.9 and 10.10

6   Fore-and-aft and side-to-side adjustment of the hood is done by moving the hinge plate slot after loosening the bolts or nuts.

7   Scribe a line around the entire hinge plate so you can determine the amount of movement **(see illustration 10.3)**.

8   Loosen the bolts or nuts and move the hood into correct alignment. Move it only a little at a time. Tighten the hinge bolts and carefully lower the hood to check the position.

9   If necessary after installation, the entire hood latch assembly can be adjusted up-

and-down as well as from side-to-side on the radiator support so the hood closes securely and flush with the fenders. Scribe a line or mark around the hood latch mounting bolts to provide a reference point, then loosen them and reposition the latch assembly, as necessary **(see illustration)**. Following adjustment, retighten the mounting bolts.

10   Finally, adjust the hood bumpers on the radiator support so the hood, when closed, is flush with the fenders **(see illustration)**.

11   The hood latch assembly, as well as the hinges, should be periodically lubricated with lithium-base grease to prevent binding and wear.

11 Hood latch and release cable - removal and installation

Warning: *The models covered by this manual are equipped with Supplemental Restraint systems (SRS), more commonly known as airbags. Always disable the airbag system before working in the vicinity of any airbag system component to avoid the possibility of accidental deployment of the airbag(s), which could cause personal injury* (see Chapter 12).

Latch

Refer to illustrations 11.1 and 11.2

1   Scribe a line around the latch to aid alignment when installing **(see illustration)**. Remove the retaining bolts and nut securing the hood latch to the radiator support. Remove the latch.

2   Disengage the cable from the latch assembly with a small screwdriver **(see illustration)**.

3   Installation is the reverse of removal. **Note:** *Adjust the latch so the hood engages securely when closed and the hood bumpers are slightly compressed.*

Cable

Refer to illustration 11.7

4   Disconnect the hood release cable from the latch assembly as described in Step 1.

11.1 Mark the position of the latch before removal

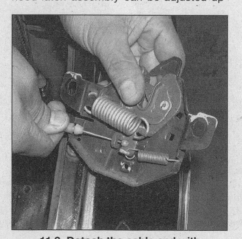

11.2 Detach the cable end with a small screwdriver

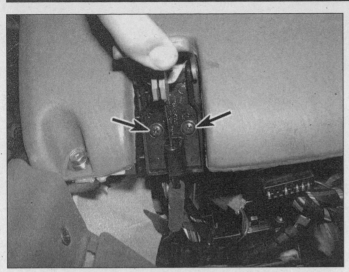

11.7 Remove the hood release handle retaining screws (arrows)

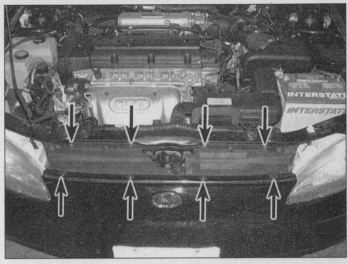

12.3 Remove the screws securing the air deflector and the top side of the bumper cover (arrows)

5   Attach a piece of thin wire or string to the end of the cable and unclip all remaining cable retaining clips at the radiator support.

6   Refer to Section 13 and remove the plastic inner fenderwell.

7   Working under the dash, remove the hood release handle mounting screws and detach the hood release handle and cable assembly (see illustration).

8   Pull the cable and grommet rearward into the passenger compartment until you can see the wire or string. Ensure that the new cable has a grommet attached, then remove the wire or string from the old cable and fasten it to the new cable.

9   With the new cable attached to the wire or string, pull the wire or string back through the firewall until the new cable reaches the latch assembly.

10   Working in the passenger compartment, install the new cable and handle assembly.

11   The remainder of installation is the reverse of removal.

12   Bumpers - removal and installation

Warning: *The models covered by this manual are equipped with Supplemental Restraint systems (SRS), more commonly known as airbags. Always disable the airbag system before working in the vicinity of any airbag system component to avoid the possibility of accidental deployment of the airbag(s), which could cause personal injury (see Chapter 12).*

Caution: *Some models are equipped with an anti-theft radio. Before performing a procedure that requires disconnecting the battery, make sure you have the activation code.*

Front bumper

Refer to illustrations 12.3, 12.5 and 12.6

1   Apply the parking brake, raise the vehicle and support it securely on jackstands.

2   Disconnect the negative battery cable,

then the positive battery cable and wait two minutes before proceeding any further.

3   Remove the retaining screws securing the air deflector and the upper side of the bumper (see illustration).

4   Remove the turn signal light (2000 and earlier models) or the headlight (2001 and later models) housings (see Chapter 12).

5   Detach the screws securing lower side of the bumper cover (see illustration).

6   Once the cover is removed, remove the retaining bolts or nuts and detach the bumper assembly. On 2000 and earlier models the bumper is retained by two bolts at each end (see illustration). On 2001 and later models the bumper is retained by four nuts and two bolts accessible from behind the bumper.

7   Installation is the reverse of removal. Make sure the alignment tabs on the bumper cover fit into the corresponding notches on the body before attaching the bolts and screws. An assistant is helpful.

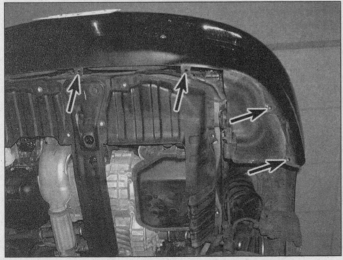

12.5 Remove screws along the bottom of the bumper cover (arrows)

12.6 Remove the bolts (arrows) and detach the front bumper (2000 and earlier model shown)

11

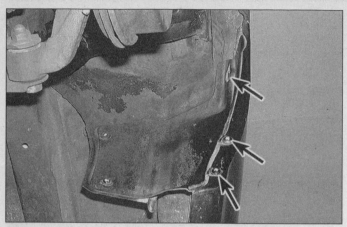

12.9a Remove the rear bumper cover retaining screws in the wheel wells (arrows)

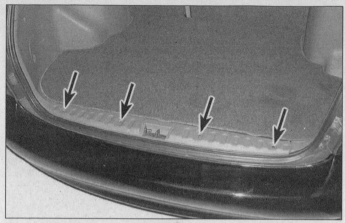

12.9b Remove the trim plate screws securing the top side of the bumper cover (arrows)

Rear bumper

Refer to illustrations 12.9a, 12,9b, 12.10a and 12.10b

8   If necessary for working clearance, raise the rear of the vehicle and support it securely on jackstands.

9   Remove the retaining screws in the wheel wells and along the upper and lower edges of the bumper cover **(see illustrations)**. On station wagons and 2001 and later sedan models, remove the tail light housings (Chapter 12). On all models, remove the rear trim plate and pull the luggage compartment trim out for access then remove the remaining bumper cover retaining screws **(see illustration)**. Remove the bumper bolts.

10   On station wagon models, remove the rear window washer fluid reservoir (see Chapter 1) for access to the bumper retaining bolts **(see illustration)**. The remaining bumper bolts are accessible from below **(see illustration)**.

11   On all models pull the bumper and cover assembly out and away from the vehicle.

12   Installation is the reverse of removal.

13 Front fender - removal and installation

Refer to illustrations 13.3, 13.4 and 13.5

1   Raise the vehicle, support it securely on jackstands and remove the front wheel.

2   Remove the turn signal housing (Chapter 12) and front bumper cover (see Section 12).

3   Detach the screws, then remove the inner fenderwell **(see illustration)**.

4   Open the hood and remove the fender-to-body bolts **(see illustration)**.

5   Detach the fender. It's a good idea to have an assistant support the fender while it's being moved away from the vehicle to prevent damage to the surrounding body panels.

6   Installation is the reverse of removal.

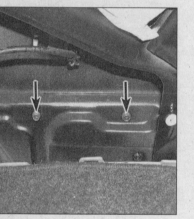

12.10a After removing the washer reservoir, remove the bumper cover screws on each side (arrows)

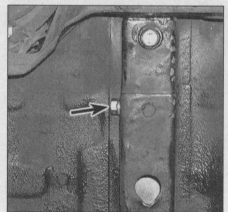

12.10b The remaining bumper bolts on station wagon models are located under the rear compartment on each side (arrow)

13.3 Remove the fenderwell screws (arrows)

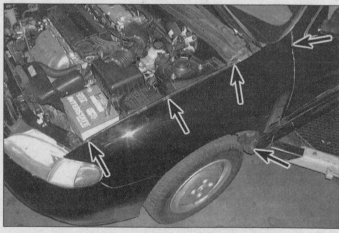

13.4 Remove the fender retaining bolts (arrows)

14.1 Remove the nuts and detach the wiper arms

14.2 Remove the screws (arrows) and detach the cowl cover

14 Cowl cover - removal and installation

Refer to illustrations 14.1 and 14.2
1   Remove the wiper arms **(see illustration)**.
2   Remove the screws securing the cowl cover to the vehicle **(see illustration)**.
3   Detach the cowl cover from the vehicle.
4   Installation is the reverse of removal.

15 Door trim panels - removal and installation

Refer to illustrations 15.3a, 15.3b, 15.3c, 15.3d, 15.3e and 15.4
Caution: *Wear gloves when working inside the door openings to protect against cuts from sharp metal edges.*

Removal

1   On manual window regulator equipped models, remove the window crank handle. A shop towel worked up between the handle and door panel will usually dislodge the clip,

15.3a Remove the inner door handle screw

15.3b Pry out the inner handle trim piece . . .

but it can also be removed with a hooked tool.
2   Remove the outside mirror (Section 20).
3   Detach the door handle trim piece and disconnect the linkage rod **(see illustrations)**. Remove the door pull mount-

ing screw **(see illustration)**. Unplug the electrical connector from the power window switch (if equipped) **(see illustration)**.
4   Remove the retaining screws and detach the panel by carefully prying it away from the door **(see illustration)**.

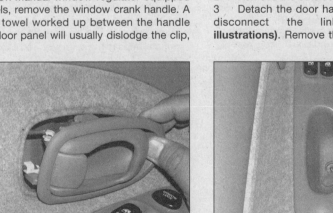

15.3c . . . rotate the handle assembly out of the trim panel, then disconnect the linkage rod

15.3d Remove the door pull screw

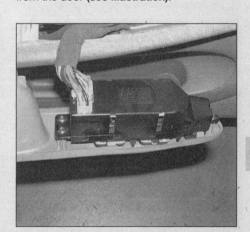

15.3e Lift the switch assembly out of the trim panel far enough to disconnect the electrical connector

11

5   For access to the door outside handle or the door window regulator inside the door, raise the window fully, remove the power window control unit (if equipped), the door panel bracket and the speaker, then carefully peel back the plastic water deflector shield (if equipped).

Installation

6   Prior to installation of the door trim panel, be sure to reinstall any clips in the panel which may have come out when you removed the panel.

7   Press the door panel into place and install the screws. Install the inner door handle and its screw and the pull-pocket and its screw. Install the power door lock switch assembly, if equipped, and the manual-regulator crank handle or power window switch assembly.

---

16   Door - removal, installation and adjustment

Note: *The door is heavy and somewhat awkward to remove and install - at least two people should perform this procedure.*
Caution: *Wear gloves when working inside the door openings to protect against cuts from sharp metal edges.*

Removal and installation

Refer to illustrations 16.6 and 16.8

1   Lower the window completely in the door and then disconnect the negative cable from the battery.

2   Open the door all the way and support it from the ground on jacks or blocks covered with rags to prevent damaging the paint.

3   Remove the door trim panel and water deflector as described in Section 15.

4   Disconnect all electrical connections, ground wires and harness retaining clips from the door. **Note:** *It is a good idea to label all connections to aid the reassembly process.*

5   From the door side, detach the rubber conduit between the body and the door. Then pull the wiring harness through conduit hole and remove from the door.

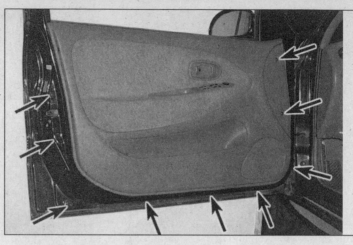

15.4 Locations of the door trim panel screws

6   Detach the door stop strut by removing the bolts **(see illustration)**.

7   Mark around the door hinges with a pen or a scribe to facilitate realignment during reassembly.

8   With an assistant holding the door, remove the hinge-to-door bolts **(see illustration)** and lift the door off. **Note:** *Draw a reference line around the hinges before removing the bolts.*

9   Installation is the reverse of removal.

Adjustment

Refer to illustration 16.13

10   Having proper door-to-body alignment is a critical part of a well-functioning door assembly. First check the door hinge pins for excessive play. Fully open the door and lift up and down on the door without lifting the body. If a door has 1/16-inch or more excessive play, the hinges should be replaced.

11   Door-to-body alignment adjustments are made by loosening the hinge-to-body bolts or hinge-to-door bolts and moving the door. Proper body alignment is achieved when the tops of the doors are parallel with the roof section, the front door is flush with the fender, the rear door is flush with the rear quarter panel and the bottom of the doors are aligned with the lower rocker panel. If these goals can't be reached by adjusting the hinge-to-body or hinge-to-door bolts, body

alignment shims may have to be purchased and inserted behind the hinges to achieve correct alignment.

12   To adjust the door closed position, scribe a line or mark around the striker plate to provide a reference point, then check that the door latch is contacting the center of the latch striker. If not adjust the up and down position first.

13   Finally adjust the latch striker sideways position, so that the door panel is flush with the center pillar or rear quarter panel and provides positive engagement with the latch mechanism **(see illustration)**.

---

17   Door latch, lock cylinder and handle - removal and installation

Caution: *Wear gloves when working inside the door openings to protect against cuts from sharp metal edges.*

Door latch

Refer to illustration 17.4

1   Raise the window, then remove the door trim panel and watershield (see Section 15).

2   Working through the access hole, disengage the outside door handle-to-latch rod, outside door lock-to-latch rod, the inside handle-to-latch rod, and the lock solenoid-to-latch rod.

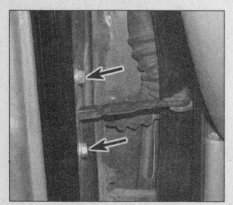

16.6 Remove the door stop strut bolts (arrows)

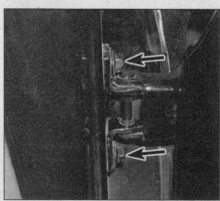

16.8 Remove the door hinge bolts (arrows) with the door supported

16.13 Adjust the door lock striker by loosening the mounting screws and gently tapping the striker in the desired direction

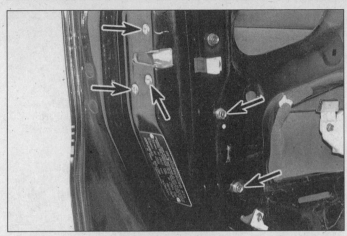

17.4 Remove the latch screws from the end of the door (and on some models the lock solenoid bolts) and withdraw the latch assembly through the access hole

17.8 Work through the access hole and detach the actuating rod and remove the outside door handle bolts (arrows)

3   All door lock rods are attached by plastic clips. The plastic clips can be removed by unsnapping the portion engaging the connecting rod and then pulling the rod out of its locating hole. On models with power door locks, disconnect the electrical connectors at the latch.

4   Remove the screws securing the latch to the end of the door **(see illustration)**. Remove the latch assembly from the door. On 2001 and later models, the latch is part of the door module assembly. On these models, remove the latch screws and the module retaining bolts, then remove the module from the door.

5   Installation is the reverse of removal.

Outside handle and door lock cylinder

Refer to illustration 17.8

6   To remove the outside handle and lock cylinder assembly, raise the window and remove the door trim panel and watershield (see Section 15). **Caution:** *Take care not to scratch the paint on the outside of the door. Wide masking tape applied around the handle opening before beginning the procedure can*

help avoid scratches.

7   Working through the access hole, disengage the plastic clips that secure the outside handle-to-latch actuating rod and the outside door lock-to-latch actuating rod.

8   Working through the access hole, remove the outside door handle retaining bolts **(see illustration)**.

9   Remove the handle/lock cylinder assembly from the vehicle.

10   Installation is the reverse of removal.

18   Door window glass - removal and installation

Refer to illustrations 18.3a, 18.3b and 18.5
Caution: *Wear gloves when working inside the door openings to protect against cuts from sharp metal edges.*

1   Remove the door trim panel and the plastic water deflector (see Section 15).

2   Lower the window glass all the way down into the door.

3   Remove the door window trim strip and pry out the rubber outer weatherstrip. On some models it will be necessary to remove

18.3a Remove the retaining screw (arrow) from the window outer rubber trim strip

the retaining screw in the end of the door, then pull the trim strip out **(see illustrations)**.

4   Raise the window just enough to access the window glass-to-bracket retaining bolts.

5   Place a rag over the glass to help prevent scratching the glass and remove the two glass-to-bracket retaining bolts **(see illustration)**.

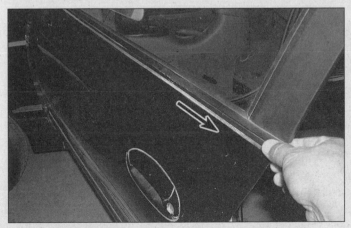

18.3b Grasp the trim strip and pull it out of the door

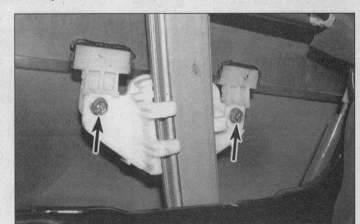

18.5 Remove the window glass-to-bracket retaining bolts (arrows)

11

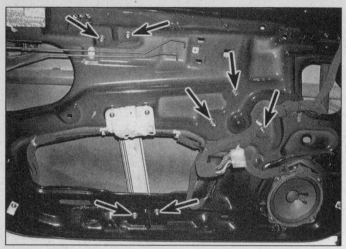

19.4 Remove the mounting bolts (arrows) retaining the regulator assembly to the door

20.1 Pry the mirror cover off

6   Remove the glass along with door opening weather stripping by pulling it up and out.
7   Installation is the reverse of removal.

19   Door window glass regulator - removal and installation

Refer to illustration 19.4
Caution: *Wear gloves when working inside the door openings to protect against cuts from sharp metal edges.*
1   Remove the door trim panel and the plastic watershield (see Section 15).
2   Remove the window glass assembly (see Section 18).
3   On power operated windows, disconnect the electrical connector from the window regulator motor.
4   Remove the regulator assembly mounting bolts **(see illustration)**.
5   Pull the regulator assembly through the service hole in the door frame to remove it.
6   Installation is the reverse of removal.

20.3 Remove the three mirror mounting bolts (arrows)

20   Mirrors - removal and installation

Outside mirrors

Refer to illustrations 20.1 and 20.3
1   Pry off the mirror trim cover **(see illustration)**.
2   Disconnect the electrical connector from the mirror (if equipped).
3   Remove the three mirror retaining bolts and detach the mirror from the vehicle **(see illustration)**.
4   Installation is the reverse of removal.

Inside mirror

5   The mirror base is retained to the mount on the windshield by a spring clip, and can be removed from the mount by pulling downwards (parallel to the windshield) and wiggling it side-to-side.
6   Install by sliding the base into the mount until it clicks in place.

21   Trunk lid (sedan models) - removal, installation and adjustment

Note: *The trunk lid is heavy and somewhat awkward to remove and install - at least two people should perform this procedure.*

Removal and installation

1   Open the trunk lid and cover the edges of the trunk compartment with pads or cloths to protect the painted surfaces when the lid is removed.
2   Scribe or draw alignment marks around the trunk hinges.
3   Remove the hinge-to-trunk lid bolts from both sides and lift off the trunk lid.
4   Installation is the reverse of removal. Be sure to align the hinge flanges with the marks made on the trunk lid during removal.
5   After installation, close the lid and see if

it's in proper alignment with the adjacent body surfaces. Fore-and-aft and side-to-side adjustments of the lid are controlled by the position of the hinge bolts in the slots. To adjust it, loosen the hinge bolts, reposition the lid and retighten the bolts.
6   The height of the rear of the lid in relation to the surrounding body panels when closed can be adjusted by turning the rubber trunk lid bumpers in or out.

22   Trunk lid latch and lock cylinder (sedan models) - removal and installation

Trunk lid latch

1   Open the trunk and scribe a line around the trunk lid latch assembly for a reference point to aid the installation procedure.
2   Disconnect the actuating cable.
3   Mark the position of the latch to the body, then unscrew the two retaining bolts and remove the latch.
4   Remove the end of the latch release cable from the latch.
5   Installation is the reverse of removal.

Trunk lock cylinder

6   Remove the lock cylinder rod (if equipped) from its clip and remove the lock's mounting clip.
7   Remove the lock cylinder from the trunk lid.
8   Installation is the reverse of removal.

23   Trunk/liftgate release and fuel door cables - removal and installation

Refer to illustration 23.2
1   Refer to Sections 22 and 25 for removal of the trunk latch and disengagement of the cable from the latch.

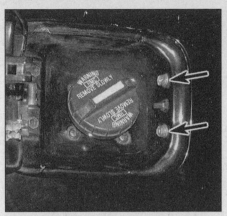

23.2 Remove the fuel door cable bolts (arrows)

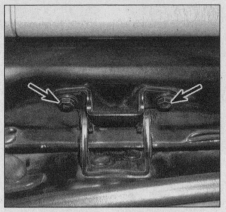

24.5 Remove the retaining bolts (arrows) on each side of the liftgate

25.3 Remove the liftgate latch retaining bolts (arrows), then detach the actuating rods and cable

2   Inside the trunk, remove the trim panels for access to the trunk release and fuel door cables. Disconnect the fuel door release cable bolts **(see illustration)**.

3   Detach all of the clips holding the cables to the body.

4   Detach the carpeting, remove the screw and detach the cover from the cable actuating lever housing next to the driver's seat. Remove the actuating lever housing and detach the cables from the lever.

5   Attach a piece of thin wire to the end of the cable.

6   Working in the trunk compartment, pull the cable assembly towards the rear of the vehicle until you can see the wire.

7   Attach the wire to the front of the new cable and fish it back through the body until it can be attached to the lever. The remainder of the installation is the reverse of removal.

24   Liftgate (station wagon models) - removal, installation and adjustment

Refer to illustration 24.5
Note: *The liftgate is heavy and somewhat awkward to hold - at least two people should perform this procedure.*

Removal and installation

1   Open the liftgate and support it securely.

2   Remove the upper trim moulding from the lift gate opening and disconnect all wiring harness connectors leading to the liftgate. On models equipped with a rear window washer, detach the roof headliner and disconnect the washer hose.

3   While an assistant supports the liftgate, detach the support struts (see Section 26).

4   Use a marking pen to mark the positions of the liftgate hinge plates to ensure proper alignment during installation.

5   Remove the hinge-to-liftgate bolts and remove the liftgate from the vehicle **(see illustration)**.

6   Installation is the reverse of removal.

Adjustment

7   The height of the liftgate in relation to the surrounding body panels when closed can be adjusted by loosening the liftgate latch bolts, moving the striker up or down, then re-tightening the bolts. **Note:** *Make a reference mark around the latch before making adjustments.*

25   Liftgate latch and lock cylinder (station wagon models) - removal and installation

Liftgate latch

Refer to illustration 25.3
1   Open the liftgate.
2   Scribe a line around the liftgate latch assembly for a reference point to aid the installation procedure.
3   Detach the retaining bolts and remove the latch **(see illustration)**.
4   Installation is the reverse of removal.

Lock cylinder

5   Remove the liftgate trim panel.
6   Detach the lock cylinder rod, then remove the lock's retaining clip.
7   Remove the lock cylinder.
8   Installation is the reverse of removal.

26   Liftgate support struts (station wagon models) - removal and installation

Refer to illustrations 26.2a and 26.2b
1   Open the liftgate and support it securely.
2   Unscrew the bolts from the brackets at each end of the support strut **(see illustrations)**.
3   Installation is the reverse of removal.

27   Center console - removal and installation

Refer to illustrations 27.2, 27.3a, 27.3b and 27.5
Warning: *The models covered by this manual are equipped with Supplemental Restraint systems (SRS), more commonly known as airbags. Always disable the airbag system before working in the vicinity of any airbag system component to avoid the possibility of accidental deployment of the airbag(s), which could cause personal injury (see Chapter 12).*
Caution: *Some models are equipped with an anti-theft radio. Before performing a proce-*

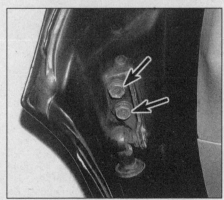

26.2a Use a wrench to remove the bolts (arrows) from the upper end of the support strut

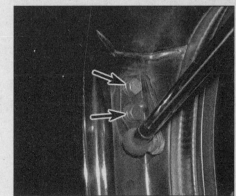

26.2b Remove the bolts (arrows) attaching the lower end of the strut

11

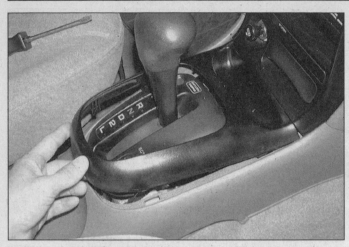

27.2 Detach the shift bezel and lift it out

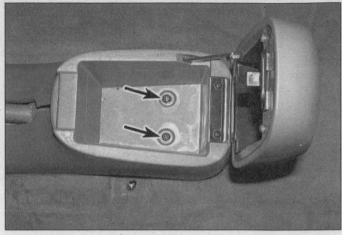

27.3a Open the console lid and remove the screws (arrows)

dure that requires disconnecting the battery, make sure you have the activation code.

1   Disconnect the battery cables (negative first, then positive; see the **Warning** above).

2   Use a screwdriver to pry out the gear selector trim bezel from the console **(see illustration).**

3   Remove the screws holding the console to the floor **(see illustrations).**

4   Lift the console up and over the shift lever. Disconnect any electrical connections and remove the console from the vehicle.

5   Installation is the reverse of removal. When installing the gear selector trim bezel, lower it into position and press down securely to seat the clips **(see illustration).**

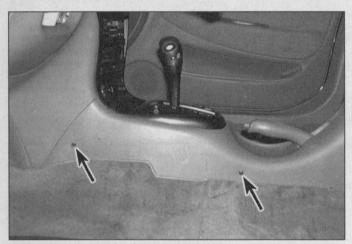

27.3b Remove the screws on both sides of the console (arrows)

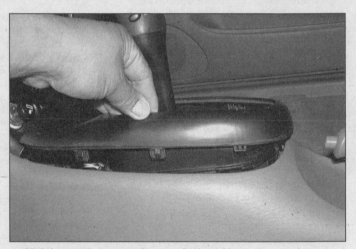

27.5 Lower the gear selector trim bezel into place and press down to seat the retaining clips

28.4a Remove the screws at the bottom and ...

28.4b ... and the top of the instrument cluster bezel (arrows) (2000 and earlier model shown)

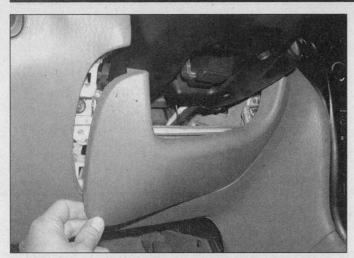

28.6 On 2000 and earlier models, the knee bolster cover can be detached by pulling it straight out

28.11a Remove the screws in the dashboard light control opening and at the base of the bezel (arrows) (2000 and earlier models)

28   Dashboard trim panels - removal and installation

Warning: *The models covered by this manual are equipped with Supplemental Restraint systems (SRS), more commonly known as airbags. Always disable the airbag system before working in the vicinity of any airbag system component to avoid the possibility of accidental deployment of the airbag(s), which could cause personal injury (see Chapter 12).*
Caution: *Some models are equipped with an anti-theft radio. Before performing a procedure that requires disconnecting the battery, make sure you have the activation code.*

1   Disconnect the negative battery cable (see the **Warning** above).

Instrument cluster bezel

Refer to illustrations 28.4a and 28.4b

2   If equipped with a tilt steering column, tilt the column all the way down.
3   Remove the steering column covers (see Section 29).

4   Remove the screws at the top and bottom of the instrument cluster bezel and detach it from the vehicle **(see illustrations)**.
5   Installation is the reverse of the removal procedure. Make sure any clips are engaged properly before pushing the bezel firmly into place.

Knee bolster

2000 and earlier models

Refer to illustration 28.6

6   Detach the bolster cover by pulling it straight out **(see illustration)**, then remove the bolster bracket by unscrewing the bolts. Installation is the reverse of removal.

2001 and later models

7   Remove the center console (see Section 27) and the hood release handle (see Section 11).
8   Pull the end cover from the end of the instrument panel, then remove the screws from the end of the panel and the two underneath, at each end of the knee bolster. Once the bolster has been removed, the reinforce-

ment behind it can be unbolted.
9   Installation is the reverse of removal.

Center instrument panel bezel

Refer to illustrations 28.11a and 28.11b

10   Remove the center console (see Section 27).
11   On 2000 and earlier models, pry the dashboard light control out of the bezel. Remove the screw in the light control opening and at the base of the bezel **(see illustration)**. Detach the bezel and pull it out, then disconnect the electrical connectors and remove the bezel **(see illustration)**.
12   On 2001 and later models, detach the ashtray for access. Remove the two screws in the ashtray opening and pry carefully on the bezel until the clips are disengaged, disconnect the electrical connectors and detach the bezel from the center instrument panel.
13   Installation is the reverse of removal.

Glove box

Refer to illustrations 28.14 and 28.15

14   Open the glove box door and remove the retaining screws **(see illustration)**.

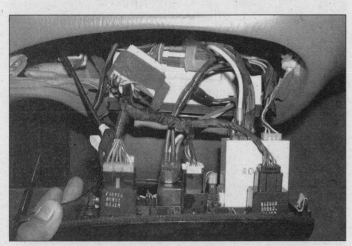

28.11b Pull the bezel out of the dashboard and unplug the electrical connectors

28.14 Remove the glove box screws (arrows)

11

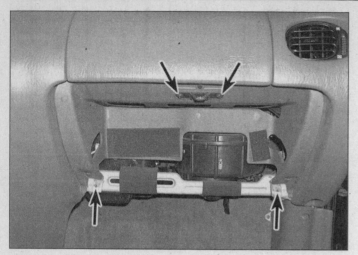

28.15 Remove the glove box housing screws (arrows)

29.2 Remove the screws under the lower column cover, then use a screwdriver to detach and remove the upper and lower covers

15   Remove the screws and detach the glove box housing from the instrument panel **(see illustration)**.
16   Installation is the reverse of removal.

29 Steering column covers - removal and installation

Refer to illustration 29.2
Warning: *The models covered by this manual are equipped with Supplemental Restraint systems (SRS), more commonly known as airbags. Always disable the airbag system before working in the vicinity of any airbag system component to avoid the possibility of accidental deployment of the airbag(s), which could cause personal injury* (see Chapter 12).
1   On tilt steering columns, move the column to the lowest position.
2   Remove the screws, then separate the halves and remove the upper and lower steering column covers **(see illustration)**.
3   Installation is the reverse of the removal procedure.

30 Instrument panel - removal and installation

Refer to illustration 30.8
Warning: *The models covered by this manual are equipped with Supplemental Restraint systems (SRS), more commonly known as airbags. Always disable the airbag system before working in the vicinity of any airbag system component to avoid the possibility of accidental deployment of the airbag(s), which could cause personal injury* (see Chapter 12).
1   Disconnect the negative battery cable (see the **Warning** above). Disable the airbag system (see Chapter 12).
2   Remove the dashboard trim panels (see Section 28) and the center console (see Section 27).
3   Remove the instrument cluster (see Chapter 12) and the glove box (see Section 28).
4   Disconnect the passenger's side airbag electrical connector.

5   Remove the audio unit from the center of the dashboard (see Chapter 12).
6   Remove the driver's knee bolster (see Section 28) for access, then remove the nuts/bolts securing the steering column and lower it away from the instrument panel.
7   A number of electrical connectors must be disconnected in order to remove the instrument panel. Most are designed so that they will only fit on one matching connector (male or female), but if there is any doubt, mark the connectors with masking tape and a marking pen before disconnecting them.
8   Remove all of the bolts holding the instrument panel to the body **(see illustrations)**. Once all are removed, lift the panel up, pull it away from the windshield and take it out through the driver's door opening.
9   Installation is the reverse of removal. Tighten the steering column mounting bolts to the torque listed in the Chapter 10 Specifications.

30.8a Remove the bolts (arrows) retaining the left side of instrument panel (2000 and earlier models shown)

30.8b Remove retaining bolts on the right side of the instrument panel (2000 and earlier models shown)

30.8c Pry off the grilles at the top corners of the instrument panel for access to . . .

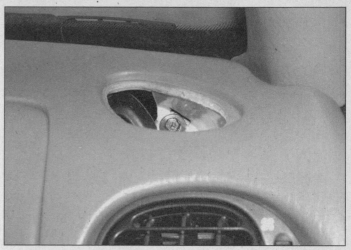

30.8d . . . the retaining bolts (2000 and earlier models shown)

31 Seats - removal and installation

Front seat

Refer to illustrations 31.2a and 31.2b

1   Position the seat all the way forward, then all the way to the rear to access the front seat retaining bolts.

2   Detach any bolt trim covers and remove the retaining nuts/bolts **(see illustrations)**.

3   Tilt the seat upward to access the underside; then disconnect any electrical connectors and lift the seat from the vehicle.

4   Installation is the reverse of removal.

Rear seat

5   On fixed seats, remove the bolts at base of the seat back side cushions and detach them. Remove the two bolts at the rear of the seat cushion and detach the cushion assembly. Remove the two bolts at the base and remove the seat backs.

6   On folding seats, remove the two bolts at the front of the seat cushions and detach the cushion assembly. Fold the seat backs forward, remove the bolts and lift the assembly out.

7   Installation is the reverse of removal.

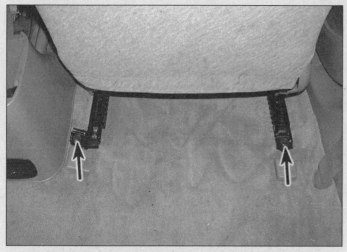

31.2a Move the seat all the way forward and unscrew the rear retaining nuts/bolts for the front seat (arrows) . . .

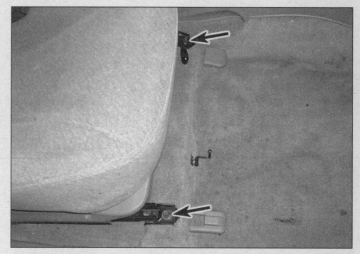

31.2b . . . then move the seat all the way to the rear and remove the front seat track retaining bolts (arrows)

11

Notes

Chapter 12
Chassis electrical system

Contents

1 General information

The electrical system is a 12-volt, negative ground type. Power for the lights and all electrical accessories is supplied by a lead/acid-type battery that is charged by the alternator.

This Chapter covers repair and service procedures for the various electrical components not associated with the engine. Information on the battery, alternator, distributor and starter motor can be found in Chapter 5. It should be noted that when portions of the electrical system are serviced, the negative battery cable should be disconnected from the battery to prevent electrical shorts and/or fires.

2 Electrical troubleshooting - general information

Refer to illustration 2.5a, 2,5b, 2.6, 2.9 and 2.15

A typical electrical circuit consists of an electrical component, any switches, relays, motors, fuses, fusible links or circuit breakers related to that component and the wiring and connectors that link the component to both the battery and the chassis. To help you pinpoint an electrical circuit problem, wiring diagrams are included at the end of this Chapter.

Before tackling any troublesome electrical circuit, first study the appropriate wiring diagrams to get a complete understanding of what makes up that individual circuit. Trouble spots, for instance, can often be narrowed down by noting if other components related to the circuit are operating properly. If several components or circuits fail at one time, chances are the problem is in a fuse or ground connection, because several circuits are often routed through the same fuse and ground connections.

Electrical problems usually stem from simple causes, such as loose or corroded connections, a blown fuse, a melted fusible link or a failed relay. Visually inspect the condition of all fuses, wires and connections in a problem circuit before troubleshooting the circuit.

If test equipment and instruments are going to be utilized, use the diagrams to plan

12

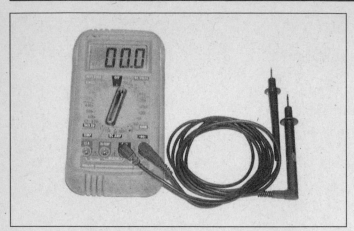

2.5a The most useful tool for electrical troubleshooting is a digital multimeter that can check volts, amps, and test continuity

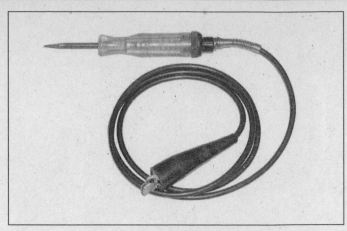

2.5b A test light is a very handy tool for checking voltage

ahead of time where you will make the necessary connections in order to accurately pinpoint the trouble spot.

The basic tools needed for electrical troubleshooting include a circuit tester or volt/ohmmeter (a 12-volt bulb with a set of test leads can also be used), a continuity tester, which includes a bulb, battery and set of test leads, and a jumper wire, preferably with a circuit breaker incorporated, which can be used to bypass electrical components **(see illustrations)**. Before attempting to locate a problem with test instruments, use the wiring diagram(s) to decide where to make the connections.

Voltage checks

Voltage checks should be performed if a circuit is not functioning properly. Connect one lead of a circuit tester to either the negative battery terminal or a known good ground. Connect the other lead to a connector in the circuit being tested, preferably nearest to the battery or fuse. If the bulb of the tester lights, voltage is present, which means that the part of the circuit between the connector and the battery is problem free. Continue checking the rest of the circuit in the same fashion. When you reach a point at which no voltage is present, the problem lies between that point and the last test point with voltage. Most of the time the problem can be traced to a loose connection. **Note:** *Keep in mind that some circuits receive voltage only when the ignition key is in the Accessory or Run position.*

Finding a short

One method of finding shorts in a circuit is to remove the fuse and connect a test light or voltmeter in place of the fuse terminals. There should be no voltage present in the circuit. Move the wiring harness from side-to-side while watching the test light. If the bulb goes on, there is a short to ground somewhere in that area, probably where the insulation has rubbed through. The same test can be performed on each component in the circuit, even a switch.

Ground check

Perform a ground test to check whether a component is properly grounded. Disconnect the battery and connect one lead of a self-powered test light, known as a continuity tester, to a known good ground. Connect the other lead to the wire or ground connection being tested. If the bulb goes on, the ground is good. If the bulb does not go on, the ground is not good.

Continuity check

A continuity check is done to determine if there are any breaks in a circuit - if it is passing electricity properly. With the circuit off (no power in the circuit), a self-powered continuity tester can be used to check the circuit. Connect the test leads to both ends of the circuit (or to the "power" end and a good ground), and if the test light comes on the circuit is passing current properly. If the light doesn't come on, there is a break somewhere in the circuit. The same procedure can be used to test a switch, by connecting the continuity tester to the switch terminals. With the switch turned On, the test light should come on.

Finding an open circuit

When diagnosing for possible open circuits, it is often difficult to locate them by sight because oxidation or terminal misalignment are hidden by the connectors. Merely wiggling a connector on a sensor or in the wiring harness may correct the open circuit condition. Remember this when an open circuit is indicated when troubleshooting a circuit. Intermittent problems may also be caused by oxidized or loose connections.

Electrical troubleshooting is simple if you keep in mind that all electrical circuits are basically electricity running from the battery, through the wires, switches, relays, fuses and fusible links to each electrical component (light bulb, motor, etc.) and to ground, from which it is passed back to the battery. Any electrical problem is an interruption in the flow of electricity to and from the battery.

Connectors

Most electrical connections on these vehicles are made with multi-wire plastic connectors. The mating halves of many connectors are secured with locking clips molded into the plastic connector shells. The mating halves of large connectors, such as some of those under the instrument panel, are held together by a bolt through the center of the connector.

To separate a connector with locking clips, use a small screwdriver to pry the clips apart carefully, then separate the connector halves. Pull only on the shell, never pull on the wiring harness as you may damage the individual wires and terminals inside the connectors. Look at the connector closely before trying to separate the halves. Often the locking clips are engaged in a way that is not immediately clear. Additionally, many connectors have more than one set of clips.

Each pair of connector terminals has a male half and a female half. When you look at the end view of a connector in a diagram, be sure to understand whether the view shows the harness side or the component side of the connector. Connector halves are mirror

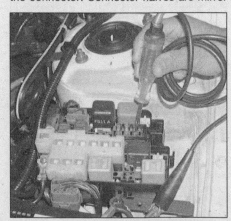

2.6 In use, a basic test light's lead is clipped to a known good ground, then the pointed probe can test connectors, wires or electrical sockets - if the bulb lights, the part being tested has battery voltage

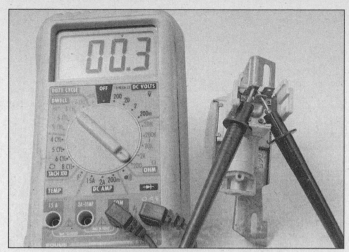

2.9 With a multimeter set to the ohms scale, resistance can be checked across two terminals - when checking for continuity, a low reading indicates continuity, a high reading indicates lack of continuity

2.15 To backprobe a connector, insert a small, sharp probe (such as a straight-pin) into the back of the connector alongside the desired wire until it contacts the metal terminal inside; connect your meter leads to the probes - this allows you to test a functioning circuit

images of each other, and a terminal shown on the right side end view of one half will be on the left side end view of the other half. When inserting a test probe into a female terminal, be careful not to distort the terminal opening. Doing so can lead to a poor connection and corrosion at that terminal later.

It is often necessary to take circuit voltage measurements with a connector connected. Whenever possible, carefully insert a straight pin into the rear of the connector shell to contact the terminal inside, then attach your meter lead to the pin. Shoving the meter's probe into the connector may spread or damage the connector. This kind of connection is called "backprobing" **(see illustration)**.

---

3 Fuses - general information

Refer to illustrations 3.1a, 3.1b and 3.3

1   The electrical circuits of the vehicle are protected by a combination of fuses and cir-

cuit breakers. The fuse blocks are located under the instrument panel and on the left side of the engine compartment **(see illustrations)**.
2   Each of the fuses is designed to protect a specific circuit (or circuits), and the various circuits are identified on the fuse panel cover.
3   Miniaturized fuses are employed in the fuse block. These compact fuses, with blade terminal design, allow fingertip removal and replacement. If an electrical component fails, always check the fuse first. To check the fuses, turn the ignition key to the On position and, using a test light, probe each exposed terminal of each fuse. If the test light glows on both terminals of a fuse, the fuse is good. If power is available on one side of the fuse but not the other, the fuse is blown. When removed, a blown fuse is easily identified through the clear plastic body. Visually inspect the element for evidence of damage **(see illustration)**.

3.1a Remove the plastic cover to access the interior fuse block located in the driver's side kick panel - the cover contains information on the fuse locations

3.1b The power distribution box is located in the engine compartment adjacent to the battery - it contains cartridge type fusible links, miniaturized fuses, and relays

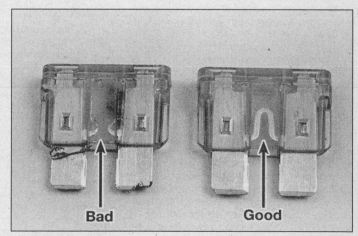

Bad   Good

3.3 When a fuse blows, the element between the terminals melts

4   Be sure to replace blown fuses with the correct type. Fuses of different ratings are physically interchangeable, but only fuses of the proper rating should be used. Replacing a fuse with one of a higher or lower value than specified is not recommended. Each electrical circuit needs a specific amount of protection. The amperage value of each fuse is molded into the fuse body.

5   If the replacement fuse immediately fails, don't replace it again until the cause of the problem is isolated and corrected. In most cases, the cause will be a short circuit in the wiring caused by a broken or deteriorated wire.

6   All models are equipped with a main fuse that protects all the circuits coming from the battery. If these circuits are overloaded, the main fuse blows, preventing damage to the main wiring harness. The main fuse consists of a metal strip that will be visibly melted when overloaded. Always disconnect the battery before replacing a main fuse. The main fuse is located in the engine compartment fuse box. If you have to replace a main fuse, make sure you install a replacement unit that's equivalent to the old fuse. In other words, if the old main fuse is an 80A unit, replace it with an 80A fuse; if it's a 100A unit, replace it with a 100A fuse. Don't switch amperage ratings on the main fuse!

4   Circuit breakers - general information

Circuit breakers protect components such as sunroof motors, power window motors and airbag inflator resistors.

On some models the circuit breaker resets itself automatically, so an electrical overload in a circuit-breaker-protected system will cause the circuit to fail momentarily, then come back on. If the circuit does not come back on, check it immediately. Once the condition is corrected, the circuit breaker will resume its normal function. Some circuit breakers must be reset manually.

5   Relays - general information and testing

General information

1   Many electrical accessories in the vehicle, such as the fuel injection system, horns, starter, cooling fans and fog lamps use relays to transmit the electrical signal to the component. Relays use a low-current circuit (the control circuit) to open and close a high-current circuit (the power circuit). If the relay is defective, that component will not operate properly. The various relays are mounted in the engine compartment fuse box and various other locations throughout the vehicle. If a faulty relay is suspected, it can be removed and tested using the procedure below or by a dealer service department or a repair shop. Defective relays must be replaced as a unit.

Testing

Refer to illustration 5.4

2   On most relays, two of the terminals are the relay control circuit (they connect to the relay coil which, when energized, closes the large contacts to complete the circuit). The other terminals are the power circuit (they are connected together within the relay when the control-circuit coil is energized).

3   Some relays may be marked as an aid to help you determine which terminals are the control circuit and which are the power circuit. If the relay is not marked, refer to the wiring diagrams at the end of this Chapter to determine the proper hook-ups for the relay you're testing.

4   To test a relay connect an ohmmeter across the two terminals of the power circuit, continuity should not be indicated **(see illustration)**. Now connect a fused jumper wire between one of the two control circuit terminals and the positive battery terminal. Connect another jumper wire between the other control circuit terminal and ground. When the connections are made, the relay should click and continuity should be indicated on the meter. On some relays, polarity may be critical, so, if the relay doesn't click, try swapping the jumper wires on the control circuit terminals.

5   If the relay fails the above test, replace it.

6   Turn signal/hazard flasher - check and replacement

Check

1   Turn signal and hazard flashers are controlled from a single electronic flasher unit that is located in the passenger compartment fuse block (Section 3). It can be located by listening for the clicks when the signals are on.

2   When the flasher unit is functioning properly, an audible click can be heard during its operation. If the turn signal flashes rapidly in one direction, a faulty turn signal bulb is indicated.

3   If both turn signals fail to blink, the problem may be due to a blown fuse, a faulty

flasher unit, a broken switch or a loose or open connection. If a quick check of the fuse box indicates that the turn signal fuse has blown, check the wiring for a short before installing a new fuse.

Replacement

4   To replace the flasher, unplug it from the relay panel directly above the fuse block, behind the driver's side of the dash.

5   Make sure that the replacement unit is identical to the original. Compare the old one to the new one before installing it.

6   Installation is the reverse of removal.

7   Multi-function switch - replacement

Refer to illustration 7.4

Warning: *The models covered by this manual are equipped with Supplemental Restraint systems (SRS), more commonly known as airbags. Always disable the airbag system before working in the vicinity of the airbag system components to avoid the possibility of accidental deployment of the airbag, which could cause personal injury (see Section 24).*

Caution: *Some models are equipped with an anti-theft radio. Before performing a procedure that requires disconnecting the battery, make sure you have the activation code.*

1   The multi-function switch is located on the top of the steering column. It incorporates functions of the turn signal, hazard and headlight dimmer into the stalk on the left side of the column, and the windshield wiper/washer and cruise control into the stalk on the right side of the column.

2   Disconnect the negative battery cable.

3   Position the front wheels and the steering wheel in the straight ahead position. Remove the steering wheel (see Chapter 10). Remove the knee bolster and steering column covers (see Chapter 11).

4   Remove the switch retaining screws, disconnect the electrical connectors, then detach the multi-function switch from the steering column **(see illustration)**.

5   Installation is the reverse of removal.

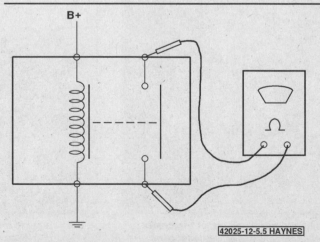

5.4 **To test a typical four-terminal normally open relay, connect an ohmmeter to the two terminals of the power circuit - the meter will indicate no continuity until battery power and ground are connected to the two terminals of the control circuit, then the relay will click and continuity will be indicated on the meter**

B+

42025-12-5.5 HAYNES

7.4 To remove the multi-function switch, remove the three screws (arrows) and unplug the electrical connector

8.3 The ignition switch is retained in the lock cylinder housing by one screw

8.5 Remove the lock cylinder/ignition switch shear-head mounting bolt(s) (arrows)

8   Ignition switch and key lock cylinder - replacement

Refer to illustrations 8.3 and 8.5

Warning: *The models covered by this manual are equipped with Supplemental Restraint systems (SRS), more commonly known as airbags. Always disable the airbag system before working in the vicinity of the airbag system components to avoid the possibility of accidental deployment of the airbag, which could cause personal injury (see Section 24).*

Caution: *Some models are equipped with an anti-theft radio. Before performing a procedure that requires disconnecting the battery, make sure you have the activation code.*

1   Disconnect the negative battery cable.

2   Remove the steering column covers and the lower instrument panel cover (see Chapter 11).

3   To remove the electrical portion of the ignition switch, follow the harness back and disconnect the electrical connector, then remove the screw and detach the switch from the lock cylinder housing **(see illustration)**.

4   Refer to Chapter 10 and lower the steering column.

5   The switch/lock cylinder housing is clamped to the steering column by shear-head bolts. Use a chisel and a hammer to tap the bolts in a counterclockwise direction to unscrew them **(see illustration)**.

6   Remove the lock cylinder/ignition switch assembly from the steering column.

7   Mount the new lock cylinder assembly on the steering column and install new shear-head bolts. Tighten the shear head bolts securely, but don't break the heads off at this time.

8   Insert the key and check the lock cylinder and steering column lock for proper operation. When you're satisfied the lock cylinder and steering column lock is operating properly, tighten the shear-head bolts until the heads break off.

9   The remainder of installation is the reverse of removal.

9   Instrument panel switches - replacement

Warning: *The models covered by this manual are equipped with Supplemental Restraint systems (SRS), more commonly known as airbags. Always disable the airbag system*

before working in the vicinity of the airbag system components to avoid the possibility of accidental deployment of the airbag, which could cause personal injury (see Section 24).

Dashboard light control

Refer to illustrations 9.2a and 9.2b

1   The dashboard light control unit is mounted on the left side of the center instrument panel fascia, to the right of the steering wheel. Within the control unit is a rheostat that varies the voltage to the instrument panel bulbs as the thumbwheel is turned. If the brightness doesn't vary, replace the light control switch.

2   Remove the light control unit on 2000 and earlier models by prying it out with a screwdriver **(see illustration)**. On 2001 and later models, remove the center bezel, unplug the connector and detach the switch **(see illustration)**.

Hazard warning switch

3   The hazard switch is marked with a triangle and is located in the instrument panel center bezel.

4   Replace the switch after removing the center bezel **(see illustration 9.2b)**.

9.2a Pry the dashboard light control unit out of the center instrument panel bezel (2000 and earlier model shown)

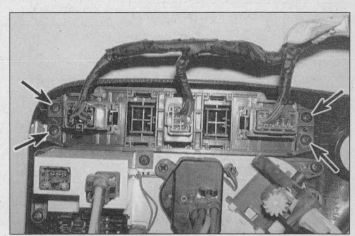

9.2b Remove the screws (arrows) to detach the switch panel from the instrument panel center bezel

Rear window defogger switch

5   The rear window defogger switch is mounted in the right side of instrument panel center bezel.
6   Remove the center bezel, then detach the switch **(see illustration 9.2b)**.

Rear wiper/washer switch

Refer to illustrations 9.8a and 9.8b

7   The rear wiper/washer switch is mounted on the left side of the instrument panel on station wagon models.
8   Carefully pry the switch out of the instrument panel with a screwdriver, disconnect the electrical connector and remove the switch **(see illustrations)**.

9.8a Use a screwdriver to pry the rear wiper/washer switch out . . .

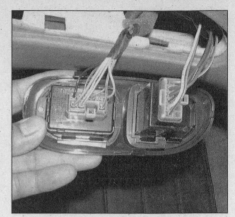

9.8b . . . then unplug the electrical connectors

---

10   Instrument cluster - removal and installation

Refer to illustrations 10.3a and 10.3b

Warning: *The models covered by this manual are equipped with Supplemental Restraint systems (SRS), more commonly known as airbags. Always disable the airbag system before working in the vicinity of the airbag system components to avoid the possibility of* accidental deployment of the airbag, which could cause personal injury (see Section 24).

1   Disconnect the negative cable from the battery.
2   Remove the instrument cluster bezel (see Chapter 11).
3   Remove the instrument cluster screws, pull out the cluster and unplug the electrical connectors **(see illustration)**.

4   Installation is the reverse of removal. Be sure to connect the positive cable to the battery first, then the negative cable.

---

11   Radio and speakers - removal and installation

Warning: *The models covered by this manual are equipped with Supplemental Restraint systems (SRS), more commonly known as airbags. Always disable the airbag system before working in the vicinity of the airbag system components to avoid the possibility of accidental deployment of the airbag, which could cause personal injury* (see Section 24).

Radio

Refer to illustrations 11.3a and 11.3b

1   Disconnect the negative battery cable.
2   Remove the instrument panel center bezel (see Chapter 11).
3   Remove the mounting screws and pull the radio out of the instrument panel **(see illustration)**.
4   Disconnect the electrical connectors and the antenna lead and remove the radio from the vehicle.
5   Installation is the reverse of removal.

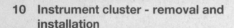

10.3a Remove the instrument cluster screws (arrows) then . . .

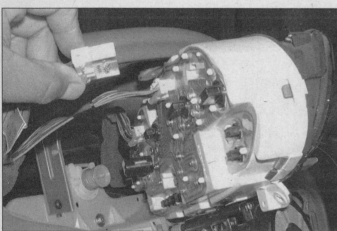

10.3b . . . pull the cluster out for access to the electrical connectors

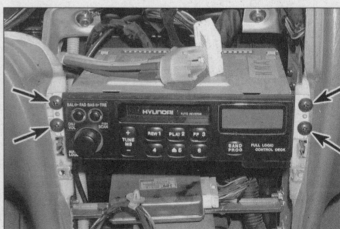

11.3a Remove the screws (arrows) to remove the radio

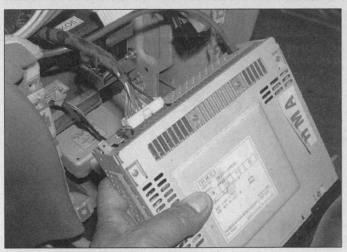

11.3b Pull the radio out and disconnect the electrical connectors

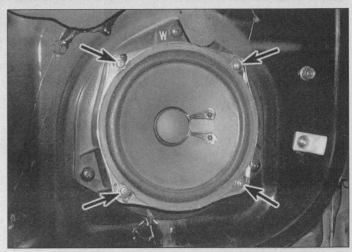

11.7 Remove the speaker mounting screws (arrows), pull the speaker away from the door and disconnect the electrical connector

Front speakers

Refer to illustration 11.7
6   Remove the front door trim panel (see Chapter 11).
7   Remove the speaker retaining bolts. Disconnect the electrical connector and remove the speaker from the vehicle **(see illustration)**.
8   Installation is the reverse of removal.

Rear speakers

Refer to illustrations 11.9 and 11.10
9   On sedan models, the rear speakers are under the package shelf behind the rear seat. Remove the seats and high mounted stop light, then detach the package tray panel for access to the mounting screws. On station wagon models, the rear speakers are in the cargo area. Remove the screws, detach the covers from the speakers for access to the mounting screws **(see illustration)**.
10   Remove the speaker retaining screws **(see illustration)**. Disconnect the electrical connector and remove the speaker from the vehicle.
11   Installation is the reverse of removal.

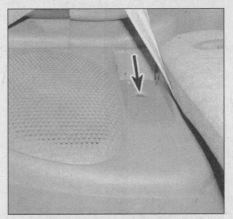

11.9 On station wagon models, remove the screw (arrow) and pry the cover up for access and . . .

12 Antenna - replacement

Refer to illustration 12.2 and 12.3
1   The vehicles covered by this manual are equipped with a fixed-mast antenna.
2   Use a wrench (on the hex portion of the

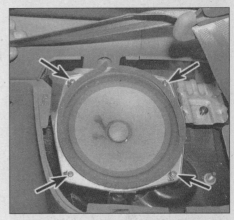

11.10 . . . remove the speaker screws

antenna mast) to remove the exterior antenna **(see illustration)**.
3   Remove the antenna nut/bezel with a large screwdriver **(see illustration)**.
4   The antenna base is accessed by removing the interior trim panel **(see illustration)**.

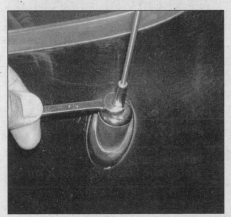

12.2 Use a small wrench on the hex portion to remove the antenna mast

12.3 With the mast off, use a screwdriver to remove the antenna nut and bezel

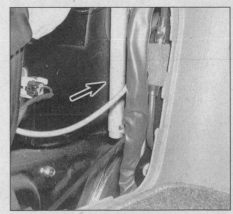

12.4 The antenna base is accessible with the trim panel removed

12

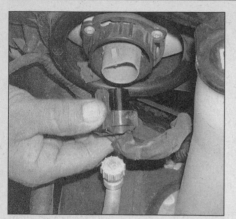

13.1 Disconnect the electrical connector from the bulb holder

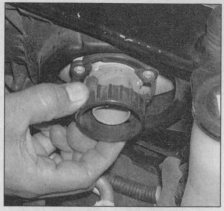

13.2a Rotate the knurled plastic collar counterclockwise and . . .

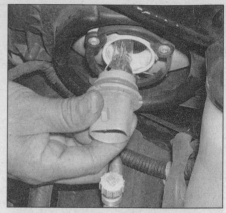

13.2b . . . withdraw the bulb holder from the headlight housing

5   Disconnect the antenna lead from the base of the antenna and remove the mounting bolt.
6   Installation is the reverse of removal.

13 Headlight bulb - replacement

Refer to illustration 13.1, 13.2a and 13.2b
Warning: *Halogen gas-filled bulbs are under pressure and may shatter if the surface is scratched or the bulb is dropped. Wear eye protection and handle the bulbs carefully, grasping only the base whenever possible. Do not touch the surface of the bulb with your fingers because the oil from your skin could cause it to overheat and fail prematurely. If you do touch the bulb surface, clean it with rubbing alcohol.*

1   Open the hood and from behind the headlight assembly, disconnect the electrical connector **(see illustration)**.
2   Rotate the knurled plastic collar counterclockwise, then withdraw the halogen bulb holder from the headlight housing **(see illustrations)**.
3   Without touching the glass with your bare fingers, insert the new bulb into the socket assembly, place the bulb holder in position and lock it in the place by rotating

the knurled plastic collar clockwise **(see illustration 13.2a)**.
4   Reinstall the electrical connector and test the headlight operation.

14 Headlights - adjustment

Refer to illustrations 14.1 and 14.2
Note: *The headlights must be aimed correctly. If adjusted incorrectly they could blind the driver of an oncoming vehicle and cause a serious accident or seriously reduce your ability to see the road. The headlights should be checked for proper aim every 12 months and any time a new headlight is installed or front end body work is performed. It should*

be emphasized that the following procedure is only an interim step which will provide temporary adjustment until the headlights can be adjusted by a properly equipped shop.
1   The headlights have two adjusting screws. The vertical screw is accessible from the top while the horizontal screw is located on the back of the housing **(see illustration)**. All adjusters are turned using a Phillips screwdriver.
2   The following adjustment method requires a level area and a blank wall. Position the vehicle with the headlights aimed squarely at the wall. Place masking tape vertically on the wall in reference to the vehicle centerline and the centerlines of both headlights **(see illustration)**.

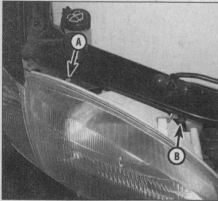

14.1 Headlight adjustment is made with a Phillips screwdriver at the vertical adjuster (A) and the horizontal adjuster (B)

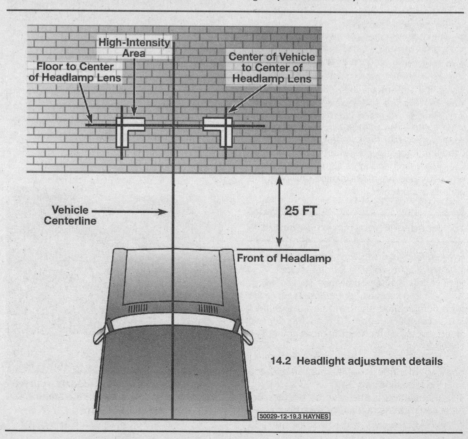

14.2 Headlight adjustment details

50029-12-19.3 HAYNES

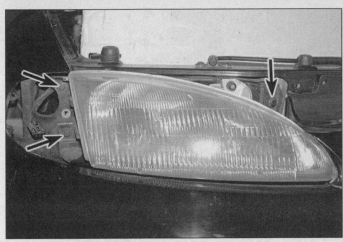

15.3 Remove the headlight housing screws (2000 and earlier model shown)

16.2a After removing the retaining screw . . .

3   Position a horizontal tape line in reference to the centerline of all the headlights. **Note:** *It may be easier to position the tape on the wall with the vehicle parked only a few inches away.*

4   Adjustment should be made with the vehicle parked 25 feet from the wall, sitting level, the gas tank half-full and no unusually heavy load in the vehicle.

5   Starting with the low beam adjustment, position the high intensity zone so it is two inches below the horizontal line and two inches to the side of the headlight vertical line, away from oncoming traffic. Adjustment is made by turning the top adjusting screw clockwise to raise the beam and counterclockwise to lower the beam. The inner adjusting screw should be used in the same manner to move the beam left or right.

5   With the high beams on, the high intensity zone should be vertically centered with the exact center just below the horizontal line. **Note:** *It may not be possible to position the headlight aim exactly for both high and low beams. If a compromise must be made, keep in mind that the low beams are the most used and have the greatest effect on safety.*

6   Have the headlights adjusted by a properly equipped headlight aiming facility at the earliest opportunity.

15   Headlight housing - replacement

Refer to illustration 15.3

1   Unplug the electrical connectors, and remove the halogen bulbs (see Section 14).

2   On 2000 and earlier models, remove the front combination (park and turn signal) light housing (see Section 16) and the screws along the top of the front bumper cover (see Chapter 11).

3   On all models, remove the headlight housing mounting bolts and remove the housing **(see illustration)**.

4   Installation is the reverse of removal. After you're done, adjust the headlights (see Section 14).

16   Bulb replacement

Warning: *Bulbs remain hot for up to twenty minutes after they're turned off. Be sure bulbs are off and cool before you touch them.*

Exterior lights

Front turn signal/park light

Refer to illustrations 16.2a and 16.2b

1   Remove the screw and pull the turn signal/parking light housing straight forward **(see illustrations)**.

2   Turn the bulb holder counterclockwise to remove it from the housing, then push in on the bulb, twist it counterclockwise and remove it from the holder.

3   Installation is the reverse of removal.

Rear turn signal, brake light and taillight bulbs

Refer to illustrations 16.5a 16.5b and 16.6

4   Open the trunk/liftgate. On sedan models, remove the cover for access to the housings that contain the bulbs for the brake, tail, turn and backup lights.

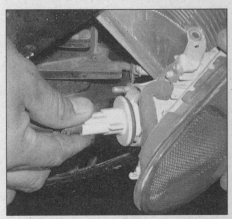

16.2b . . . pull the turn signal/park light housing straight out of the body

5   On station wagon models, remove the cover for access to the running lights. Remove three screws and rotate the housing away from the body for access to the brake, tail, turn and backup lights **(see illustrations)**.

6   To replace any rear bulb, rotate the bulb holder 1/8-turn counterclockwise and pull it

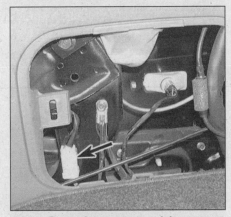

16.5a On station wagon models, remove the cover and disconnect the electrical connector (arrow) . . .

16.5b . . . remove the screws (arrows) and rotate the taillight housing out for access to the brake, tail, turn and backup lights

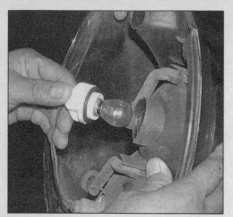

16.6 Rotate the bulb holder counterclockwise to remove it

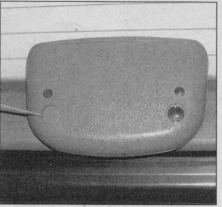

16.10a Pry off the covers, remove the screws and pull the light housing cover off to access the high-mounted brake light bulb (station wagon model shown)

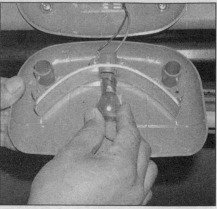

16.10b Push in on the bulb and rotate it counterclockwise to remove it

out of the housing, then push in on the bulb, turn it counterclockwise and remove it from the holder **(see illustration)**.

7   Installation is the reverse of removal.

High-mounted brake light

Refer to illustrations 16.10a and 16.10b

8   Open the trunk/liftgate.

9   On sedan models the light is mounted on the rear package tray shelf, while on station wagon models the high-mounted brake light is mounted to the underside of the liftgate glass at the top.

10   Remove the screws and detach the cover from the high-mount brake light to access the bulb **(see illustrations)**.

11   Twist the bulb holder counterclockwise to remove it, then pull the bulb straight out of the holder.

12   Installation is the reverse of removal.

License plate lights

Refer to illustration 16.13

13   On sedan models, use a screwdriver to pry the bulb holders down with for access to the bulb holder. On station wagon models, remove the screws and lower the two license plate housings from the liftgate **(see illustration)**.

14   Pull the bulb straight out of the holder.

15   Installation is the reverse of removal.

Interior lights

Dome/interior lights

Refer to illustration 16.16

16   Interior lights are accessed by removing their covers and extracting the bulb(s) **(see illustration)**. **Note:** *When replacing interior light bulbs, the battery should be disconnected or the doors kept shut while replacing the bulbs, since these bulbs will be illuminated (and hot) when the door is open.*

17   When handling the festoon-type interior bulbs (the type with contacts at each end that fit into spring clips), use gloves or a cotton cloth to hold them. Oil from your fingers could cause these hot-running bulbs to overheat.

Instrument panel lights

18   To gain access to the instrument panel lights, the instrument cluster will have to be removed first (see Section 10).

19   Rotate the bulb counterclockwise and remove it from the instrument cluster.

20   Pull the bulb straight out of the holder.

21   Installation is the reverse of removal.

Note: *Make sure you replace the bulb with one of the same wattage as the original bulb. The gauge bulbs have higher wattage than the indicator bulbs.*

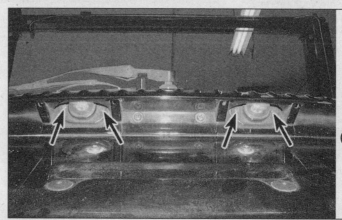

16.13 Remove the screws (arrows) and the two license plate light housings to access the bulbs (station wagon shown)

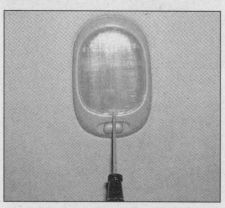

16.16 Pry off the translucent plastic cover to access the dome light bulbs

17   Wiper motor - replacement

Windshield wipers

Refer to illustration 17.4

1   Remove the wiper arms.

2   Remove the windshield wiper cowl cover (see Chapter 11).

3   Disconnect the electrical connector from the wiper motor and remove the motor.

4   Remove the wiper motor retaining bolts **(see illustration)**.

17.4 Unscrew the bolts (arrows) and remove the wiper motor

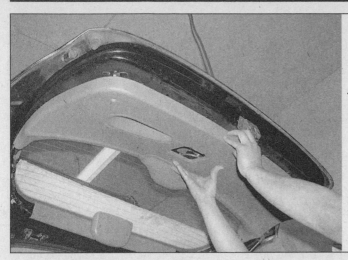

17.8 Remove this for access to the rear wiper motor

5   Pry the linkage arm off the wiper motor pin with a large screwdriver
6   Installation is the reverse of removal.

Liftgate wiper

Refer to illustrations 17.8 and 17.9
7   Remove the wiper arm.
8   Remove the liftgate trim cover **(see illustration)**.
9   Remove the wiper motor retaining bolts **(see illustration)**.
10   Disconnect the electrical connector from the wiper motor and remove the motor.
11   Installation is the reverse of removal.

18   Horn - check and replacement

Check

Refer to illustration 18.1
Note: *Check the fuses before beginning electrical diagnosis.*
1   Disconnect the electrical connector from the horn **(see illustration)**.
2   To test the horn(s), connect battery voltage to the horn terminals with a pair of jumper wires. If either horn doesn't sound, replace it.

3   If the horn does sound, check for voltage at the horn connector when the horn switch is depressed. If there's voltage at the connector, check for a bad ground at the horn.
4   If there's no voltage at the horn, check the relay (see Section 5).
5   If the relay is OK, check for voltage to the relay power and control circuits. If either of the circuits is not receiving voltage, inspect the wiring between the relay and the fuse panel.
6   If both relay circuits are receiving voltage, depress the horn switch and check the circuit from the relay to the horn switch for continuity to ground. If there's no continuity, check the circuit for an open circuit. If there's no open circuit, replace the horn switch.
7   If there's continuity to ground through the horn switch, check for an open or short in the circuit from the relay to the switch.

Replacement

8   To access the horn the left front turn signal/parking light housing must be removed. On models with two horns the bumper cover must first be removed for access to the right side horn (see Chapter 11).
9   Disconnect the electrical connectors

and remove the bracket bolts **(see illustration 18.1)**.
10   Installation is the reverse of removal.

19   Daytime Running Lights (DRL) - general information

The Daytime Running Lights (DRL) system used on Canadian models illuminates the headlights whenever the engine is running. The only exception is with the engine running and the parking brake engaged. Once the parking brake is released, the lights will remain on as long as the ignition switch is on, even if the parking brake is later applied.

The DRL system supplies reduced power to the headlights so they won't be too bright for daytime use, while prolonging headlight life.

20   Rear window defogger - check and repair

1   The rear window defogger consists of a number of horizontal heating elements baked onto the inside surface of the glass. Power is supplied through a large fuse from the power distribution box in the engine compartment. The heater is controlled by the instrument panel switch.
2   Small breaks in the element can be repaired without removing the rear window.

Check

Refer to illustrations 20.5, 20.6 and 20.8
3   Turn the ignition switch and defogger switches to the On position.
4   Using a voltmeter, place the positive probe against the defogger grid positive terminal and the negative probe against the ground terminal. If battery voltage is not indicated, check the fuse, defogger switch, defogger relay and related wiring. If voltage is indicated, but all or part of the defogger doesn't heat, proceed with the following tests.

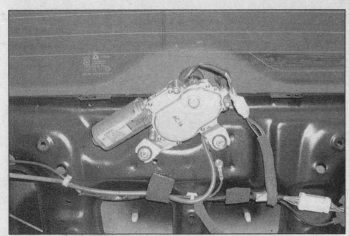

17.9 Remove the motor mounting bolts, disconnect the electrical connector and lower the wiper from the liftgate

18.1 Horn mounting bolt (A) and electrical connector (B)

12

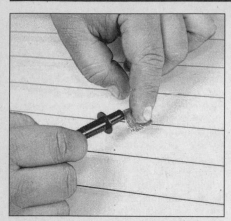

20.5 When measuring the voltage at the rear window defogger grid, wrap a piece of aluminum foil around the positive probe of the voltmeter and press the foil against the wire with your finger

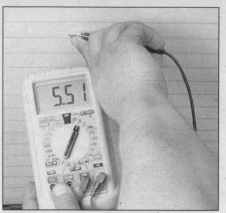

20.6 To determine if a wire has broken, check the voltage at the center of each wire. If the voltage is 5 to 6 volts, the wire is unbroken; if the voltage is 10 to 12 volts, the wire is broken between the center of the wire and the ground side; if the voltage is 0 volts, the wire is broken between the center of the wire and the power side

20.8 To find the break, place the voltmeter negative lead against the defogger ground terminal, place the voltmeter positive lead with the foil strip against the heat wire at the positive terminal end and slide it toward the negative terminal end - the point at which the voltmeter deflects from several volts to zero volts is the point at which the wire is broken

5   When measuring voltage during the next two tests, wrap a piece of aluminum foil around the tip of the voltmeter positive probe and press the foil against the heating element with your finger **(see illustration)**. Place the negative probe on the defogger grid ground terminal.

6   Check the voltage at the center of each heating element **(see illustration)**. If the voltage is 5 to 6 volts, the element is okay (there is no break). If the voltage is 0 volts, the element is broken between the center of the element and the positive end. If the voltage is 10 to 12 volts the element is broken between the center of the element and the ground side. Check each heating element.

7   If none of the elements are broken, connect the negative probe to a good chassis ground. The voltage reading should stay the same, if it doesn't the ground connection is bad.

8   To find the break, place the voltmeter negative probe against the defogger ground terminal. Place the voltmeter positive probe with the foil strip against the heating element at the positive side and slide it toward the negative side. The point at which the voltmeter deflects from several volts to zero is the point where the heating element is broken **(see illustration)**.

Repair

Refer to illustration 20.14

9   Repair the break in the element using a repair kit specifically for this purpose, such as Dupont paste No. 4817 (or equivalent). The kit includes conductive plastic epoxy.

10   Before repairing a break, turn off the system and allow it to cool for a few minutes.

11   Lightly buff the element area with fine steel wool; then clean it thoroughly with rubbing alcohol.

12   Use masking tape to mask off the area being repaired.

13   Thoroughly mix the epoxy, following the kit instructions.

14   Apply the epoxy material to the slit in the

masking tape, overlapping the undamaged area about 3/4-inch on either end **(see illustration)**.

15   Allow the repair to cure for 24 hours before removing the tape and using the system.

21   Cruise control system - description, check and cable adjustment

Refer to illustration 21.5

1   The cruise control system maintains vehicle speed with an actuator located in the engine compartment on the passenger's side fenderwell. This actuator is connected to the throttle linkage by a cable. The system consists of the actuator, brake switch (clutch switch on manual transmission models), con-

trol switches, speed sensors and relays. Some features of the system require special testers and diagnostic procedures that are beyond the scope of this manual. Listed below are some general procedures that may be used to locate common problems.

2   Check the fuses (see Section 3).

3   The brake light switch deactivates the cruise control system. Have an assistant press the brake pedal while you check the brake light operation.

4   If the brake lights do not operate properly, correct the problem and retest the cruise control.

5   Check the control cable between the cruise control actuator and the throttle linkage and adjust/replace as necessary **(see illustration)**.

6   The cruise control system uses a speed sensing device. The speed sensor is located

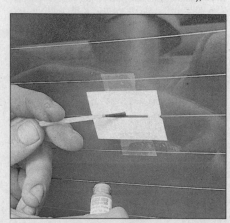

20.14 To use a defogger repair kit, apply masking to the inside of the window at the damaged area, then brush on the special conductive coating

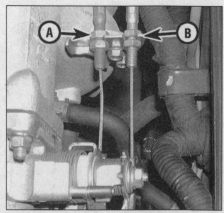

21.5 Make sure the accelerator cable (A) and cruise control cable (B) are not damaged and that they operate smoothly together when the throttle is opened

in the transaxle. To test the speed sensor, see Chapter 6.

7   Test drive the vehicle to determine if the cruise control is now working. If it isn't, take it to a dealer service department or an automotive electrical specialist for further diagnosis.

8   The Set/Resume functions are incorporated into the windshield wiper/washer combination switch (right side control stalk) (see Section 7) and the On/Off switch is located on the instrument panel or steering wheel.

Cable adjustment

9   Loosen both the accelerator and cruise cable adjusting nuts and locknuts until the throttle lever moves freely.

10   Without starting the engine, turn the ignition switch to the On position.

11   Tighten the cruise cable adjusting nut to remove any slack. With the cruise control lever just touching the throttle lever stopper, back off the adjusting nut one turn until there is 3 mm (1/8-inch) freeplay. Tighten the locknut securely. Repeat the procedure with the accelerator cable. After adjustment, check to make sure the idle switch touches the throttle lever.

22 Power window system - description and check

1   The power window system operates electric motors, mounted in the doors, which lower and raise the windows. The system consists of the control switches, the motors, regulators, glass mechanisms and associated wiring.

2   The power windows can be lowered and raised from the master control switch by the driver or by remote switches located at the individual windows. Each window has a separate motor that is reversible. The position of the control switch determines the polarity and therefore the direction of operation.

3   The circuit is protected by a fuse and a circuit breaker. Each motor is also equipped with an internal circuit breaker; this prevents one stuck window from disabling the whole system.

4   The power window system will only operate when the ignition switch is On. In addition, many models have a window lockout switch at the master control switch which, when activated, disables the switches at the rear windows and, sometimes, the switch at the passenger's window also. Always check these items before troubleshooting a window problem.

5   These procedures are general in nature, so if you can't find the problem using them, take the vehicle to a dealer service department or other properly equipped repair facility.

6   If the power windows won't operate, always check the fuse and circuit breaker first.

7   If only the rear windows are inoperative, or if the windows only operate from the master control switch, check the rear window

lockout switch for continuity in the unlocked position. Replace it if it doesn't have continuity.

8   Check the wiring between the switches and fuse panel for continuity. Repair the wiring, if necessary.

9   If only one window is inoperative from the master control switch, try the other control switch at the window. **Note:** *This doesn't apply to the driver's door window.*

10   If the same window works from one switch, but not the other, check the switch for continuity.

11   If the switch tests OK, check for a short or open in the circuit between the affected switch and the window motor.

12   If one window is inoperative from both switches, remove the trim panel from the affected door and check for voltage at the motor while the switch is operated. If a defective switch is suspected, check the switch as indicated.

13   If voltage is reaching the motor, disconnect the glass from the regulator (see Chapter 11). Move the window up and down by hand while checking for binding and damage. Also check for binding and damage to the regulator. If the regulator is not damaged and the window moves up and down smoothly, replace the motor. If there's binding or damage, lubricate, repair or replace parts, as necessary.

14   If voltage isn't reaching the motor, check the wiring in the circuit for continuity between the switches and motors. You'll need to consult the wiring diagram for the vehicle. If the circuit is equipped with a relay, check that the relay is grounded properly and receiving voltage.

15   Test the windows after you are done to confirm proper repairs.

23 Power door lock system - description and check

1   A power door lock system operates the door lock actuators mounted in each door. The system consists of the switches, actuators, and associated wiring. Diagnosis can usually be limited to simple checks of the wiring connections and actuators for minor faults that can be easily repaired.

2   Power door lock systems are operated by bi-directional actuators located in the doors. The lock switches have two operating positions: Lock and Unlock. On models with keyless entry the switches activate a module which in turn connects voltage to the door lock actuator. Depending on which way the switch is activated it reverses polarity, allowing the two sides of the circuit to be used alternately as the feed (positive) and ground side. On models without keyless entry, the switches directly activate the door lock actuators.

3   If you are unable to locate the trouble using the following general steps, consult your dealer service department or automotive electrical specialist.

4   Always check the circuit protection first. The battery voltage passes through fuse 2 in the drivers side interior fuse block.

5   Operate the door lock switches in both directions (Lock and Unlock) with the engine off. Listen for the faint click of the door lock relay operating.

6   If there's no click, check for voltage at the switches. If no voltage is present, check the wiring between the fuse block and the switches for shorts and opens.

7   If voltage is present but no click is heard, test the switch for continuity. Replace it if there's no continuity in both switch positions.

8   If the switch has continuity but the actuator doesn't click, check the wiring between the switch and actuator for continuity. Repair the wiring if there's not continuity.

9   If all but one lock actuators operates, remove the trim panel from the affected door (see Chapter 11) and check for voltage at the actuator while the lock switch is operated. One of the wires should have voltage in the Lock position; the other should have voltage in the unlock position.

10   If the inoperative actuator is receiving voltage, replace the actuator. **Note:** *It's common for wires to break in the portion of the harness between the body and door (opening and closing the door fatigues and eventually breaks the wires).*

24 Airbag system - general information

General information

1   All models are equipped with a Supplemental Restraint System (SRS), more commonly known as an airbag. There are two airbags, one for the driver and one for the front seat passenger. The SRS system is designed to protect the driver and front seat passenger from serious injury in the event of a head-on or frontal collision.

2   The SRS system consists of an SRS unit - which contains a safing sensor, impact sensor, self-diagnosis circuit and a back-up power circuit - located under the center console, an airbag assembly in the center of the steering wheel and a second airbag assembly for the front seat passenger, located in the top of the dashboard right above the glove box.

Operation

3   For the airbag(s) to deploy, the impact sensor and the safing sensor must be activated. When this condition occurs, the circuit to the airbag inflators is closed and the airbags inflate. If the battery is destroyed by the impact, or is too low to power the inflator, a back-up power unit provides power.

Self-diagnosis system

4   A self-diagnosis circuit in the SRS unit displays a light when the ignition switch is turned to the On position. If the system is

12

operating normally, the light should go out after about six seconds. If the light doesn't come on, or doesn't go out after six seconds, or if it comes on while you're driving the vehicle, there's a malfunction in the SRS system. Have it inspected and repaired as soon as possible. Do not attempt to troubleshoot or service the SRS system yourself. Even a small mistake could cause the SRS system to malfunction when you need it.

Servicing components near the SRS system

5   Nevertheless, there are times when you need to remove the steering wheel, radio or service other components on or near the dashboard. At these times, you'll be working around components and wire harnesses for the SRS system. Do not use electrical test equipment on any SRS wires or electrical connectors; it could cause the airbag(s) to deploy. **ALWAYS DISABLE THE SRS SYSTEM BEFORE WORKING NEAR THE SRS SYSTEM COMPONENTS OR RELATED WIRING.**

Disabling the SRS system

Warning: *Any time you are working in the vicinity of airbag wiring or components, DISABLE THE SRS SYSTEM.*
6   Disconnect the battery negative cable, then disconnect the positive cable and wait two minutes.

Driver's side airbag

7   Remove the access panel below the steering column and disconnect the electrical connector leading up the column to the driver's airbag.

Passenger's side airbag

8   Remove the glove box (see Chapter 11).
9   Disconnect the passenger's side airbag electrical connector.

Enabling the SRS system

10   After you've disabled the airbag and performed the necessary service, reconnect the electrical connector(s) to the airbag(s). Reinstall the lower panel and the glove box.

11   Turn the ignition switch to the Off position.
12   Reattach the positive battery cable first and then the negative cable.

25   Wiring diagrams - general information

Since it isn't possible to include all wiring diagrams for every year and model covered by this manual, the following diagrams are those that are typical and most commonly needed.

Prior to troubleshooting any circuits, check the fuse and circuit breakers (if equipped) to make sure they're in good condition. Make sure the battery is properly charged and check the cable connections (see Chapter 1).

When checking a circuit, make sure that all connectors are clean, with no broken or loose terminals. When unplugging a connector, do not pull on the wires. Pull only on the connector housings themselves.

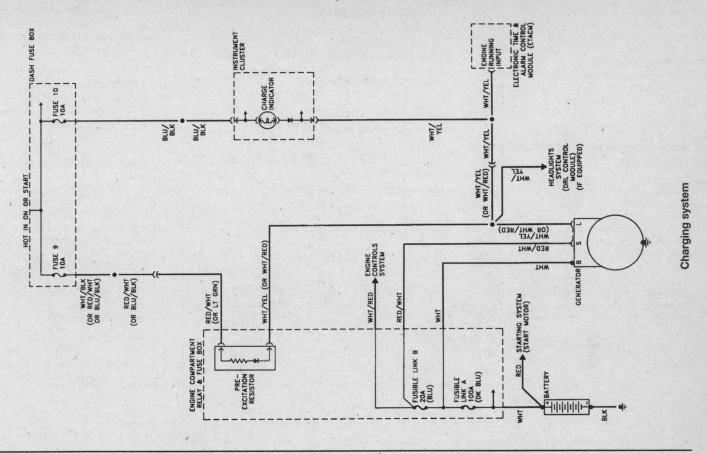

Charging system

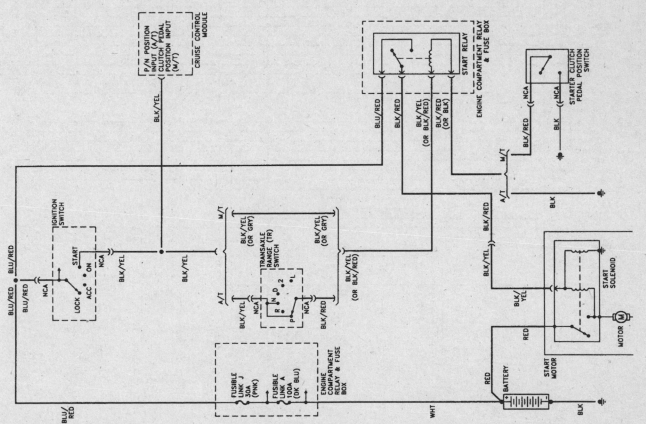

Starting system

12

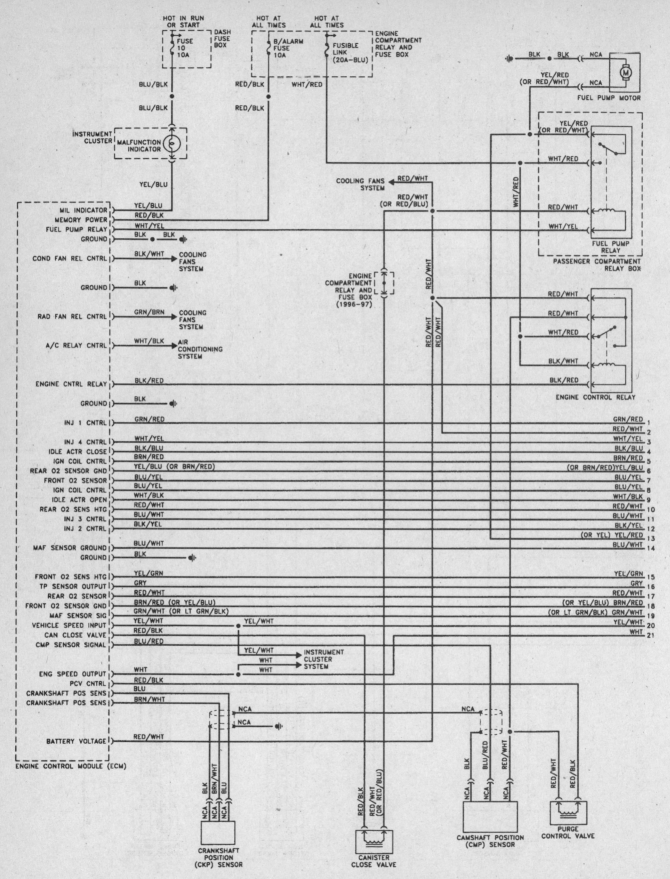

Engine control system - 1999 and earlier models (1 of 3)

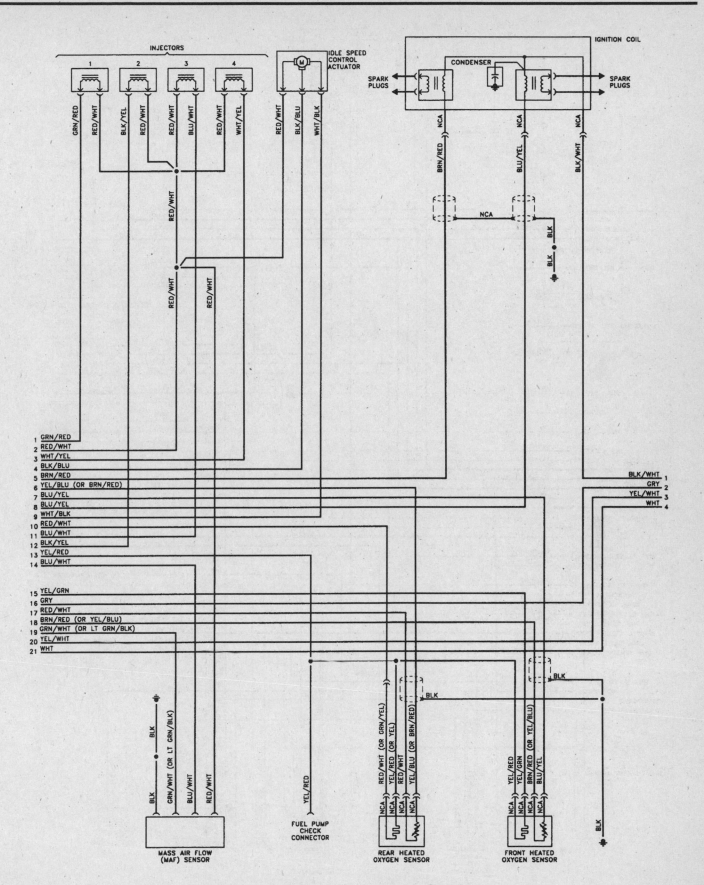

Engine control system - 1999 and earlier models (2 of 3)

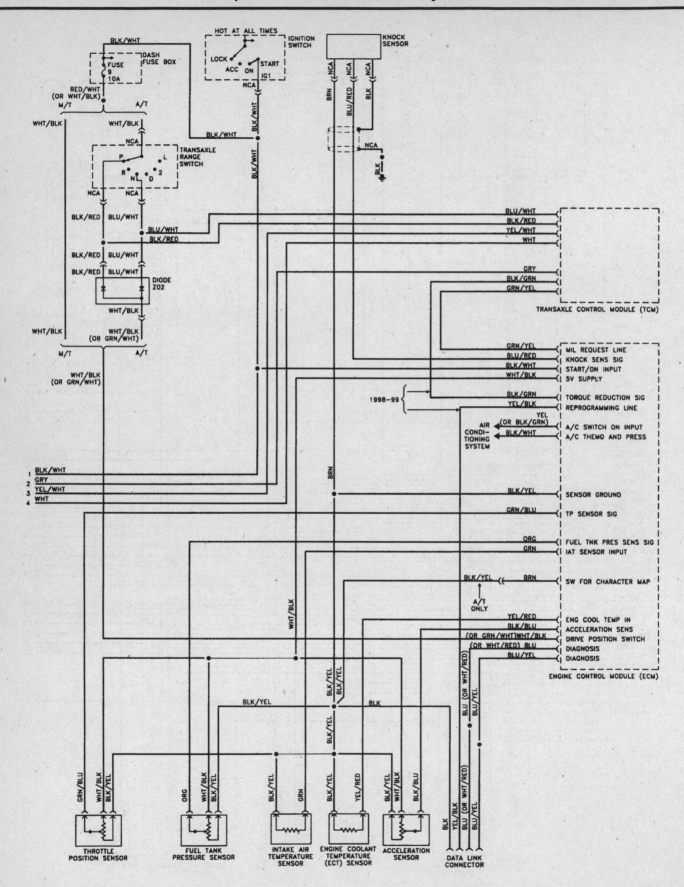

Engine control system - 1999 and earlier models (3 of 3)

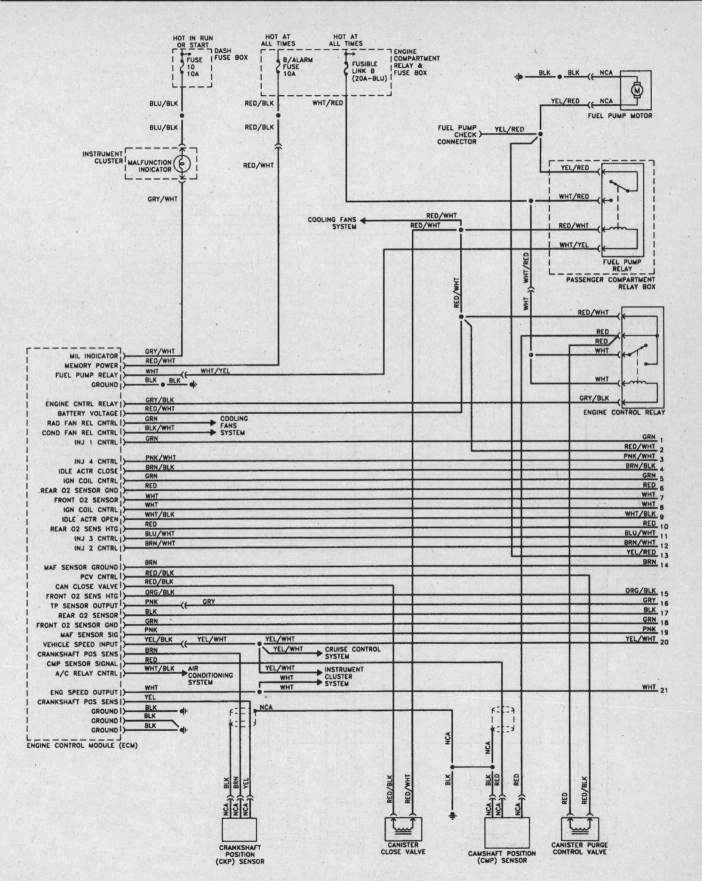

Engine control system - 2000 models (1 of 3)

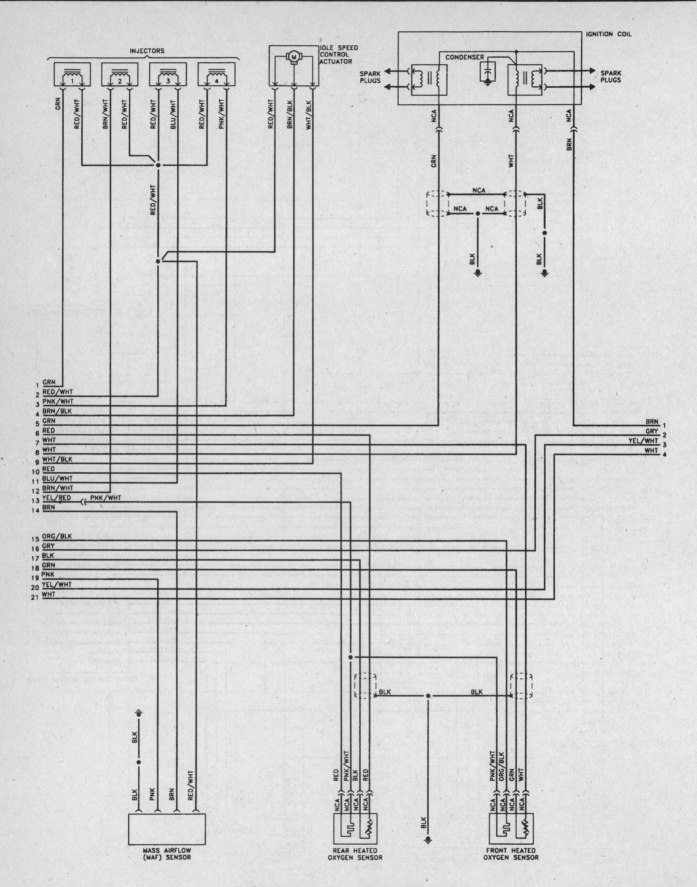

Engine control system - 2000 models (2 of 3)

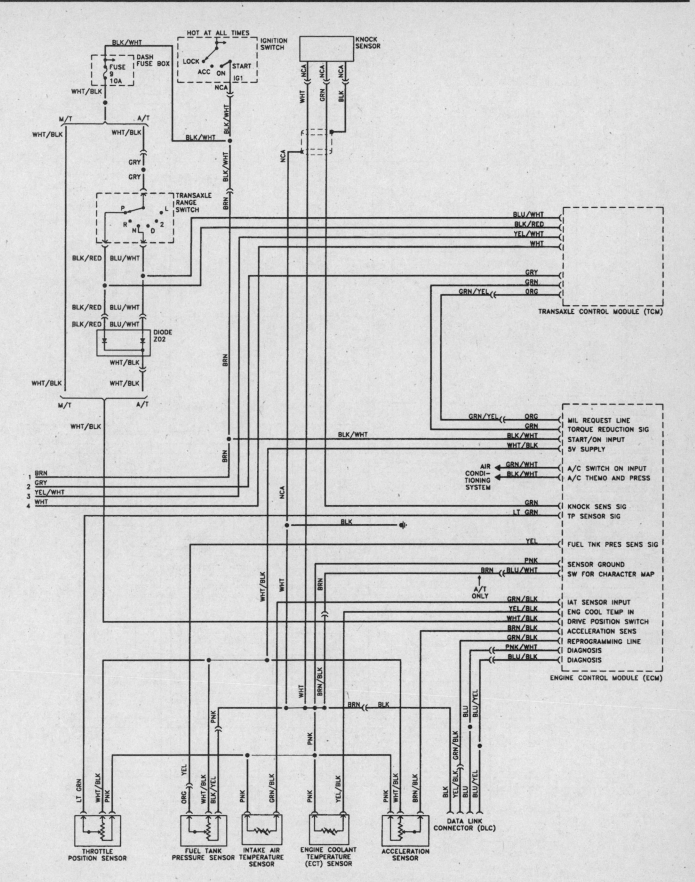

Engine control system - 2000 models (3 of 3)

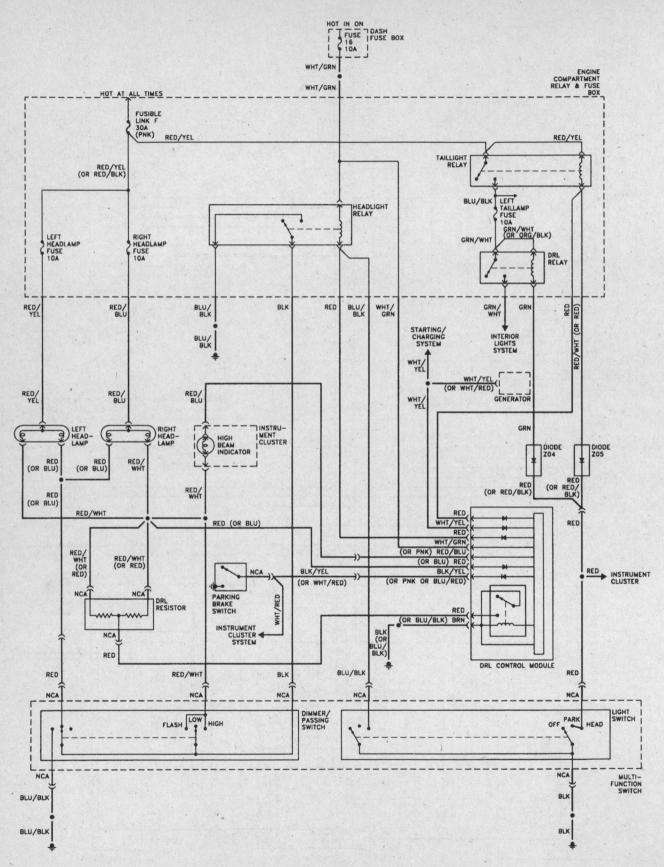

Headlight system - models with Daytime Running Lights

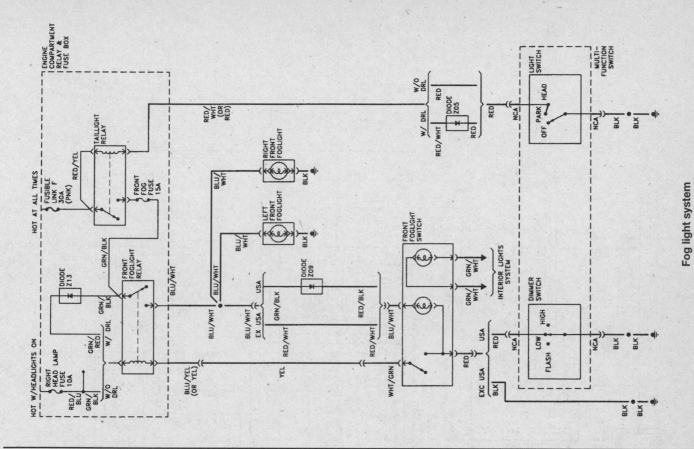

Fog light system

Headlight system - models without Daytime Running Lights

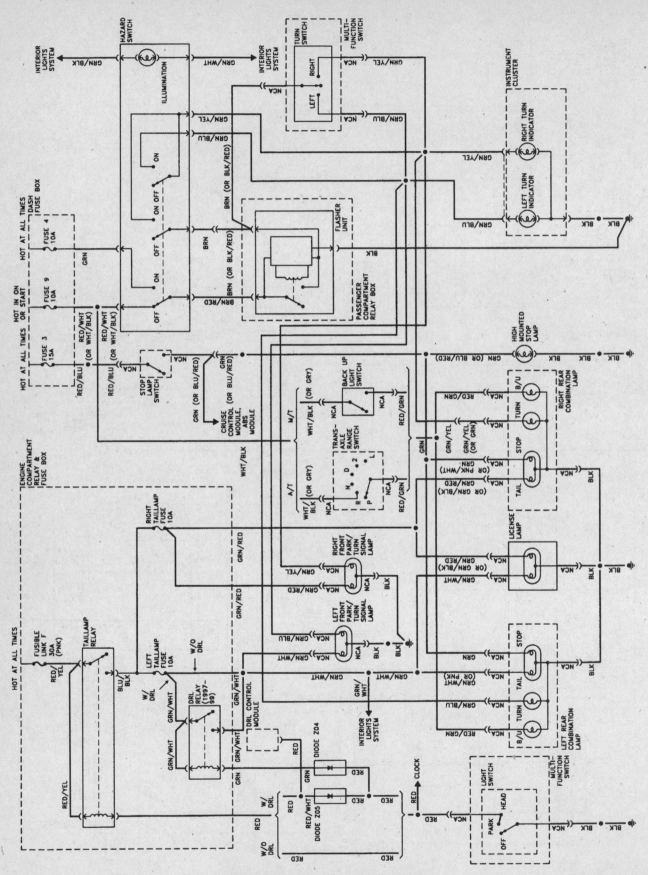

Exterior lighting system - sedan models

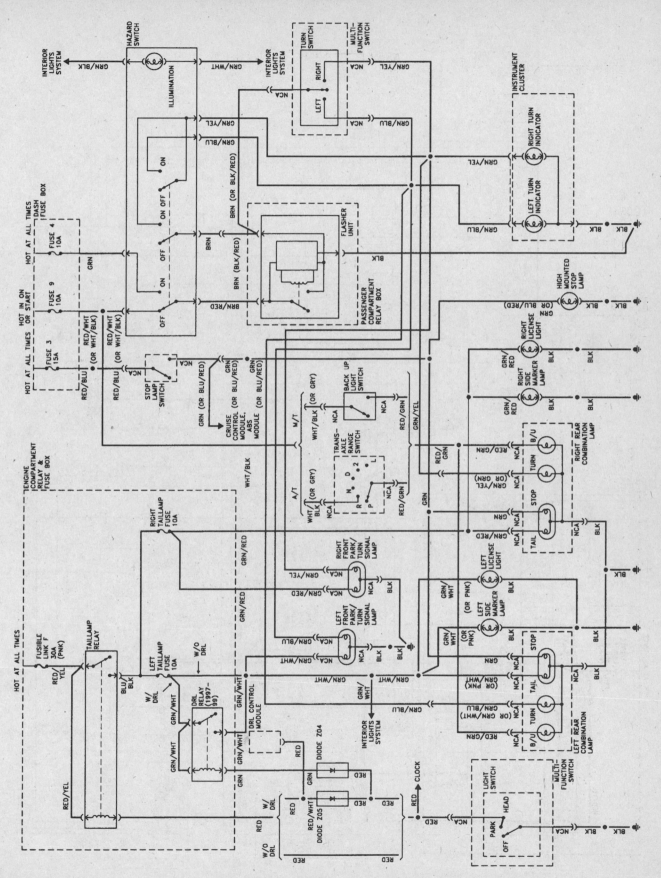

Exterior lighting system - station wagon models

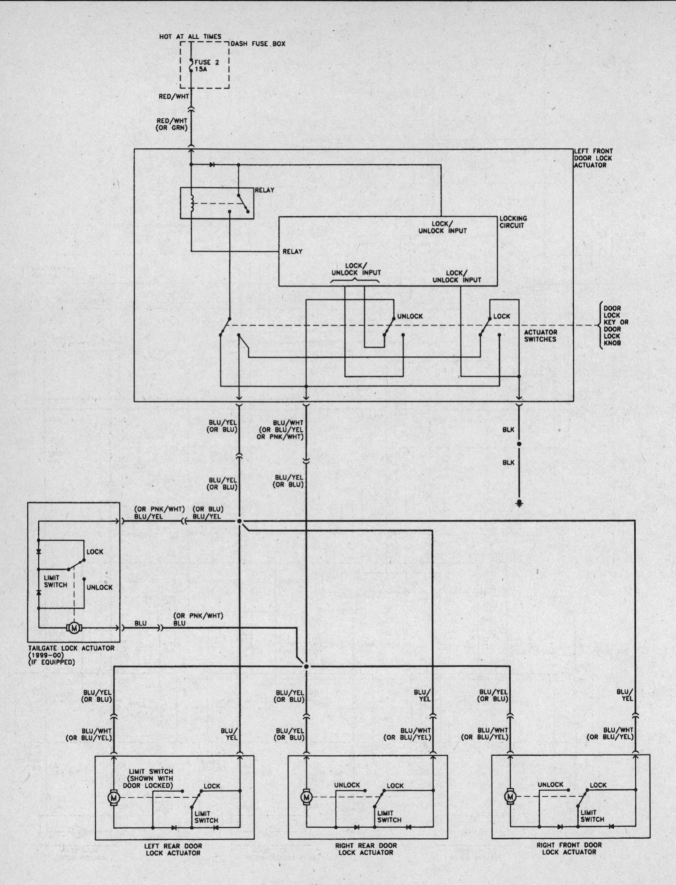

Power door lock system

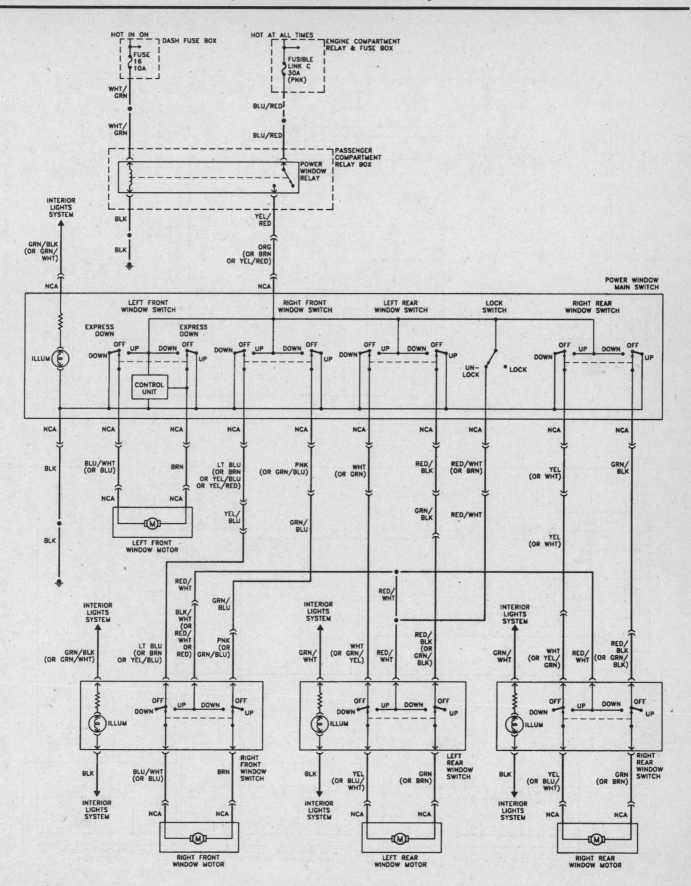

Power window system

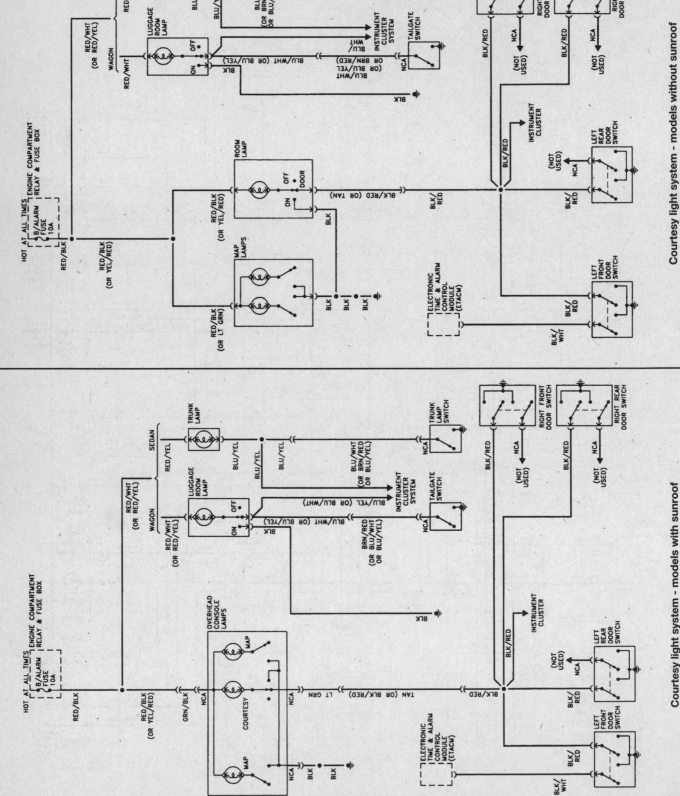

Courtesy light system - models without sunroof

Courtesy light system - models with sunroof

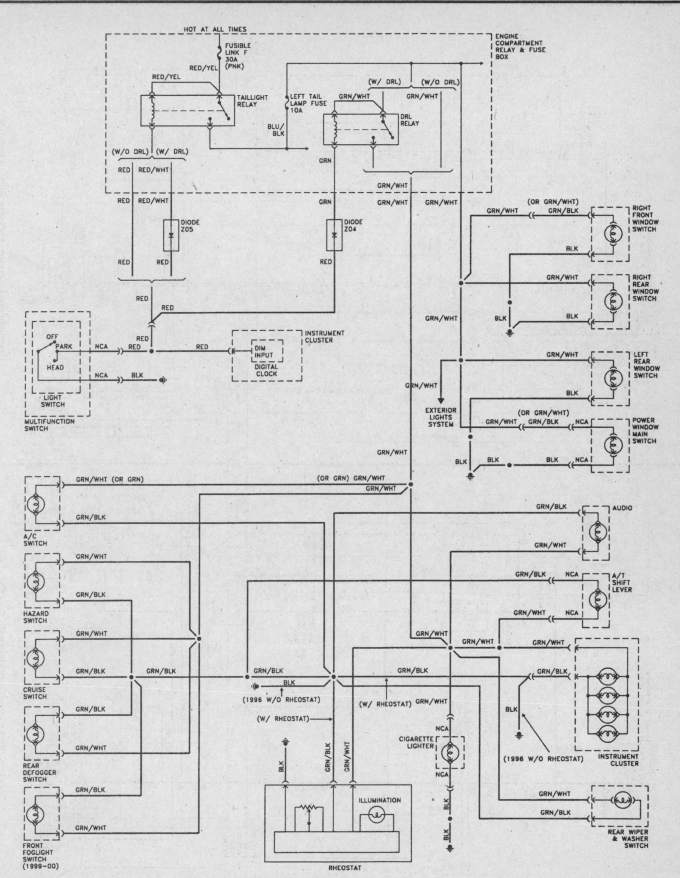

Instrument panel lighting system

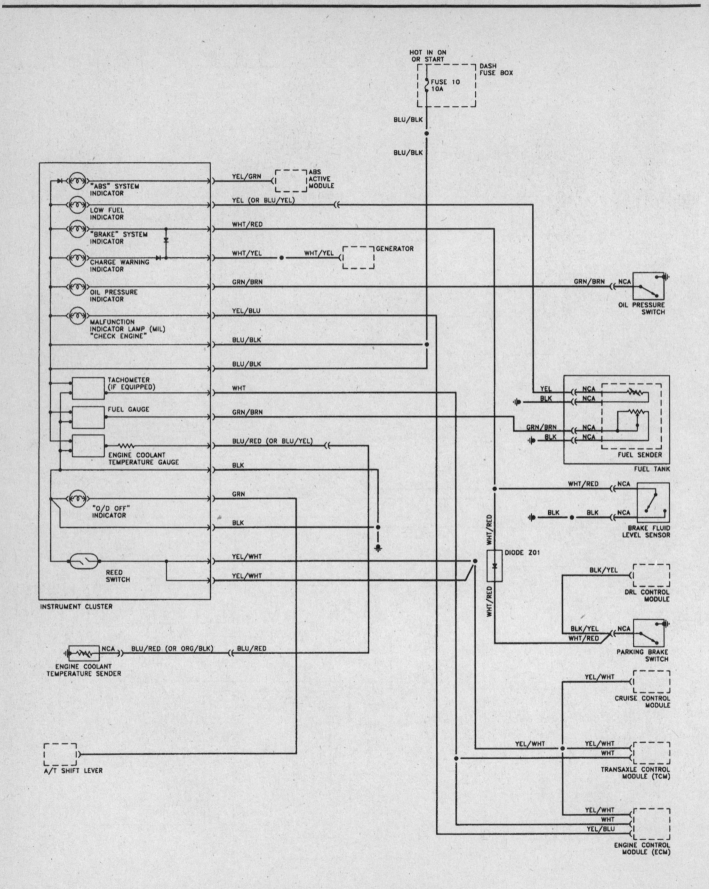

Instrument panel warning light system

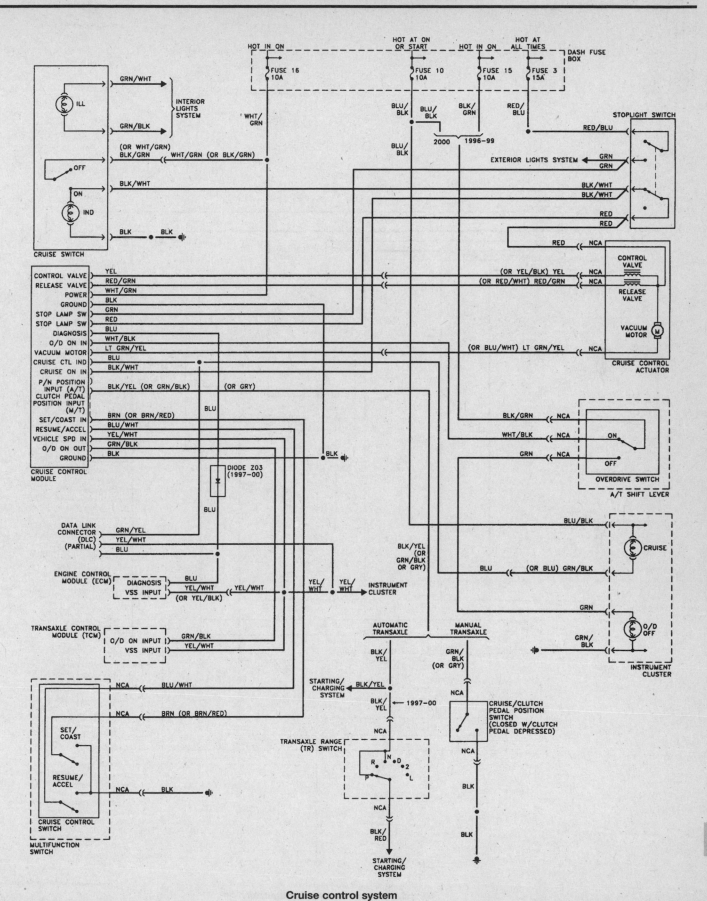

Cruise control system

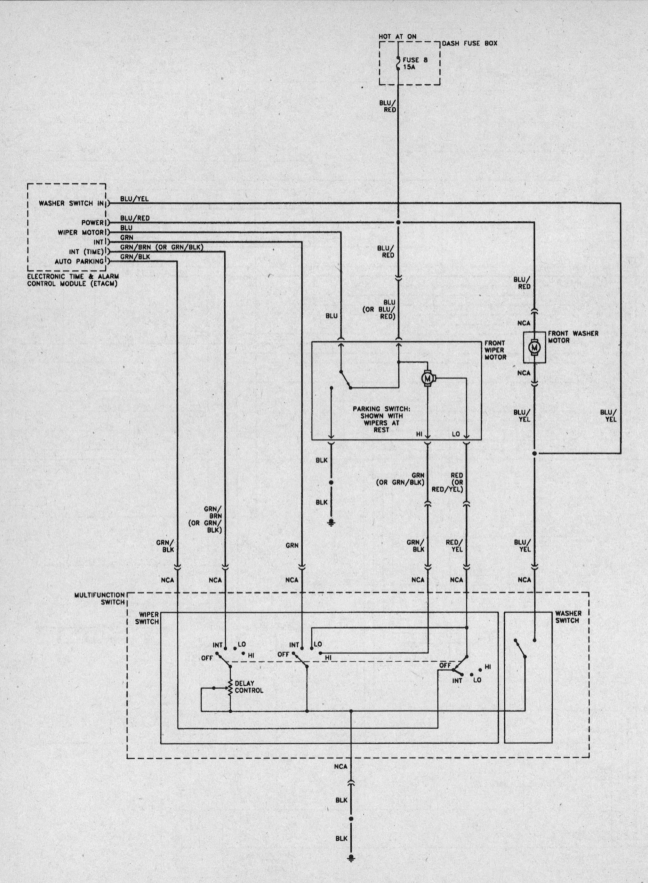

Windshield wiper and washer system

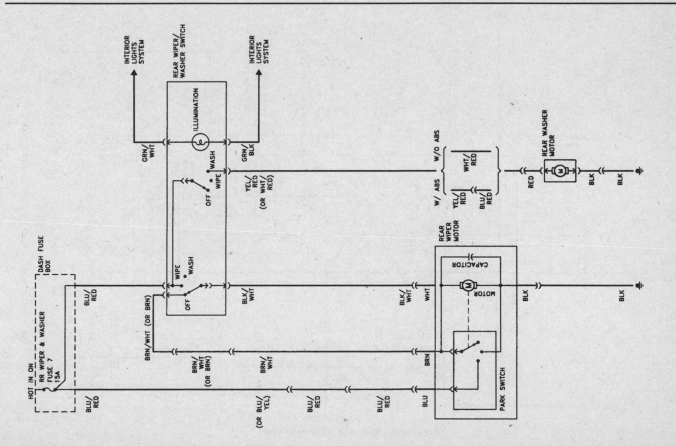

Rear wiper and washer system - 1997 and 1998 models

Rear wiper and washer system - 1996 models

12

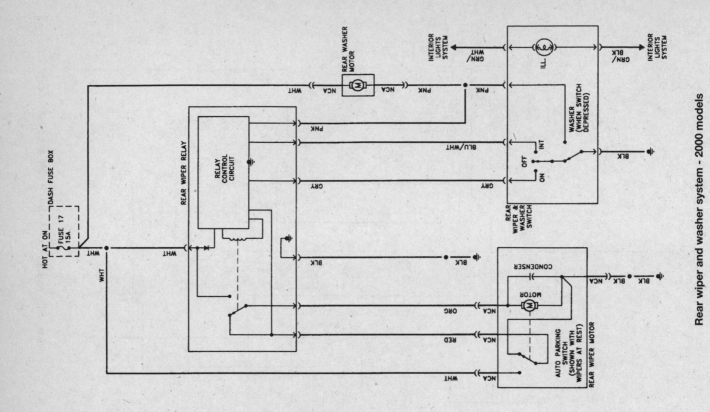

Rear wiper and washer system - 2000 models

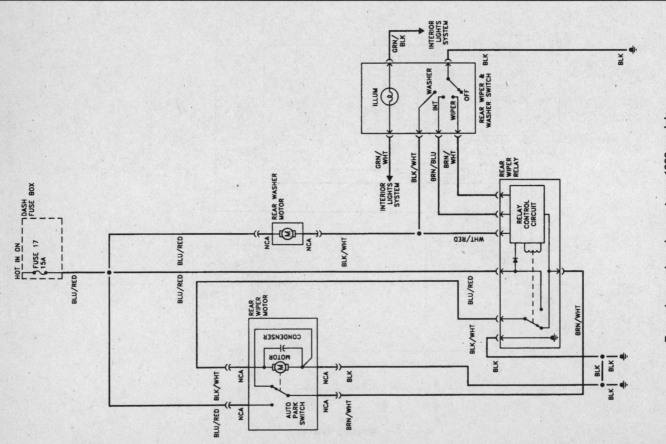

Rear wiper and washer system - 1999 models

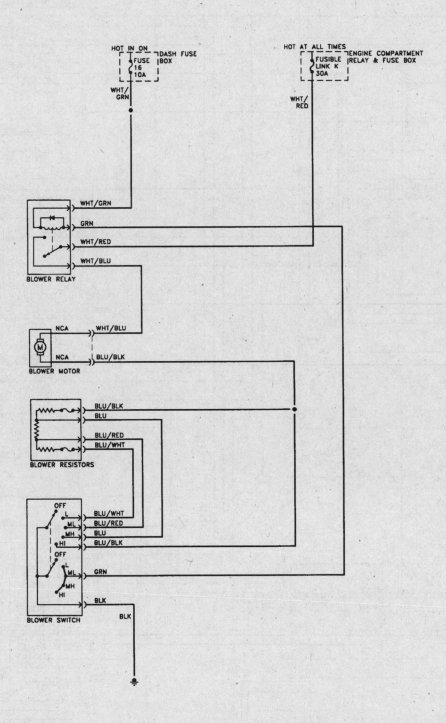

Heating system

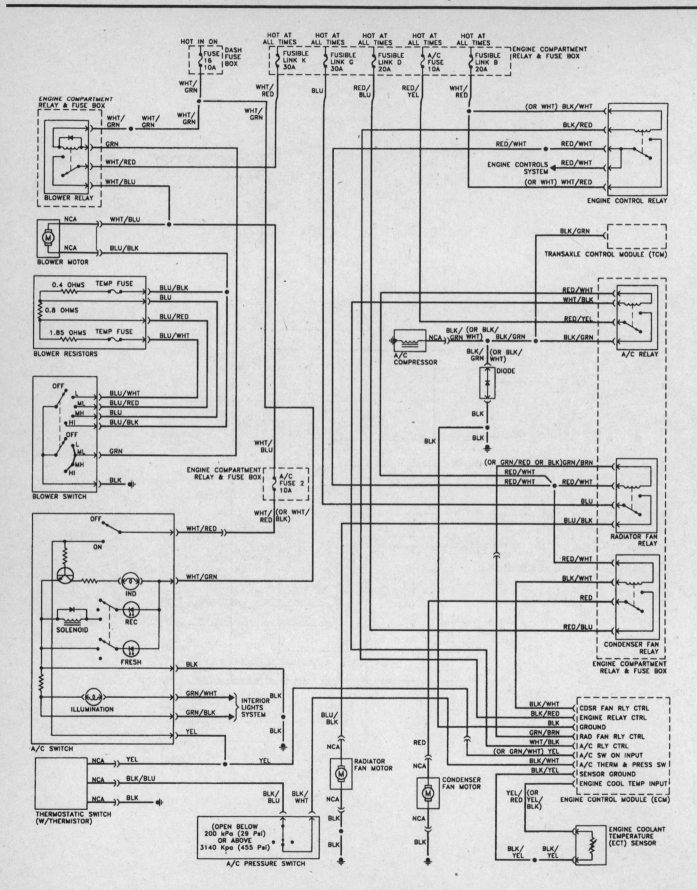

Air conditioning system

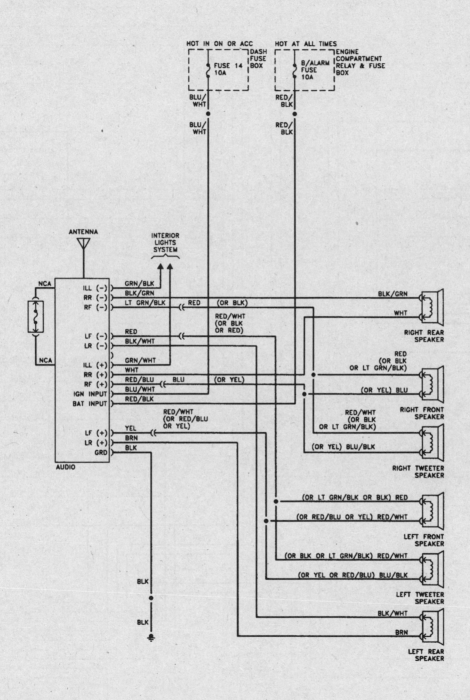

Typical stereo system

Notes

Index

NOTE: New manuals are added to this list on a periodic basis. If you do not see a listing for your vehicle, consult your local Haynes dealer for the latest product information.

ACURA
12020 Integra '86 thru '89 & Legend '86 thru '90
12021 Integra '90 thru '93 & Legend '91 thru '95

AMC
    Jeep CJ - see JEEP (50020)
14020 Mid-size models '70 thru '83
14025 (Renault) Alliance & Encore '83 thru '87

AUDI
15020 4000 all models '80 thru '87
15025 5000 all models '77 thru '83
15026 5000 all models '84 thru '88

AUSTIN-HEALEY
    Sprite - see MG Midget (66015)

BMW
*18020 3/5 Series not including diesel or all-wheel drive models '82 thru '92
18021 3-Series incl. Z3 models '92 thru '98
18025 320i all 4 cyl models '75 thru '83
18050 1500 thru 2002 except Turbo '59 thru '77

BUICK
*19010 Buick Century '97 thru '02
    Century (front-wheel drive) - see GM (38005)
*19020 Buick, Oldsmobile & Pontiac Full-size (Front-wheel drive) '85 thru '02
    Buick Electra, LeSabre and Park Avenue; Oldsmobile Delta 88 Royale, Ninety Eight and Regency; Pontiac Bonneville
19025 Buick Oldsmobile & Pontiac Full-size (Rear wheel drive)
    Buick Estate '70 thru '90, Electra '70 thru '84, LeSabre '70 thru '85, Limited '74 thru '79 Oldsmobile Custom Cruiser '70 thru '90, Delta 88 '70 thru '85, Ninety-eight '70 thru '84 Pontiac Bonneville '70 thru '81, Catalina '70 thru '81, Grandville '70 thru '75, Parisienne '83 thru '86
19030 Mid-size Regal & Century all rear-drive models with V6, V8 and Turbo '74 thru '87
    Regal - see GENERAL MOTORS (38010)
    Riviera - see GENERAL MOTORS (38030)
    Roadmaster - see CHEVROLET (24046)
    Skyhawk - see GENERAL MOTORS (38015)
    Skylark - see GM (38020, 38025)
    Somerset - see GENERAL MOTORS (38025)

CADILLAC
21030 Cadillac Rear Wheel Drive all gasoline models '70 thru '93
    Cimarron - see GENERAL MOTORS (38015)
    DeVille - see GM (38031 & 38032)
    Eldorado - see GM (38030 & 38031)
    Fleetwood - see GM (38031)
    Seville - see GM (38030, 38031 & 38032)

CHEVROLET
*24010 Astro & GMC Safari Mini-vans '85 thru '02
24015 Camaro V8 all models '70 thru '81
24016 Camaro all models '82 thru '92
24017 Camaro & Firebird '93 thru '00
    Cavalier - see GENERAL MOTORS (38016)
    Celebrity - see GENERAL MOTORS (38005)
24020 Chevelle, Malibu & El Camino '69 thru '87
24024 Chevette & Pontiac T1000 '76 thru '87
    Citation - see GENERAL MOTORS (38020)
24032 Corsica/Beretta all models '87 thru '96
24040 Corvette all V8 models '68 thru '82
24041 Corvette all models '84 thru '96
10305 Chevrolet Engine Overhaul Manual
24045 Full-size Sedans Caprice, Impala, Biscayne, Bel Air & Wagons '69 thru '90
24046 Impala SS & Caprice and Buick Roadmaster '91 thru '96
    Impala - see LUMINA (24048)
    Lumina '90 thru '94 - see GM (38010)
*24048 Lumina & Monte Carlo '95 thru '01
    Lumina APV - see GM (38035)
24050 Luv Pick-up all 2WD & 4WD '72 thru '82
    Malibu '97 thru '00 - see GM (38026)

24055 Monte Carlo all models '70 thru '88
    Monte Carlo '95 thru '01 - see LUMINA (24048)
24059 Nova all V8 models '69 thru '79
24060 Nova and Geo Prizm '85 thru '92
24064 Pick-ups '67 thru '87 - Chevrolet & GMC, all V8 & in-line 6 cyl, 2WD & 4WD '67 thru '87; Suburbans, Blazers & Jimmys '67 thru '91
24065 Pick-ups '88 thru '98 - Chevrolet & GMC, full-size pick-ups '88 thru '98, C/K Classic '99 & '00, Blazer & Jimmy '92 thru '94; Suburban '92 thru '99; Tahoe & Yukon '95 thru '99
*24066 Pick-ups '99 thru '01 - Chevrolet Silverado & GMC Sierra full-size pick-ups '99 thru '01, Suburban/Tahoe/Yukon/Yukon XL '00 thru '01
24070 S-10 & S-15 Pick-ups '82 thru '93, Blazer & Jimmy '83 thru '94,
*24071 S-10 & S-15 Pick-ups '94 thru '01, Blazer & Jimmy '95 thru '01, Hombre '96 thru '01
24075 Sprint '85 thru '88 & Geo Metro '89 thru '01
24080 Vans - Chevrolet & GMC '68 thru '96

CHRYSLER
25015 Chrysler Cirrus, Dodge Stratus, Plymouth Breeze '95 thru '00
10310 Chrysler Engine Overhaul Manual
25020 Full-size Front-Wheel Drive '88 thru '93
    K-Cars - see DODGE Aries (30008)
    Laser - see DODGE Daytona (30030)
25025 Chrysler LHS, Concorde, New Yorker, Dodge Intrepid, Eagle Vision, '93 thru '97
*25026 Chrysler LHS, Concorde, 300M, Dodge Intrepid, '98 thru '03
25030 Chrysler & Plymouth Mid-size front wheel drive '82 thru '95
    Rear-wheel Drive - see Dodge (30050)
*25035 PT Cruiser all models '01 thru '03
*25040 Chrysler Sebring, Dodge Avenger '95 thru '02

DATSUN
28005 200SX all models '80 thru '83
28007 B-210 all models '73 thru '78
28009 210 all models '79 thru '82
28012 240Z, 260Z & 280Z Coupe '70 thru '78
28014 280ZX Coupe & 2+2 '79 thru '83
    300ZX - see NISSAN (72010)
28016 310 all models '78 thru '82
28018 510 & PL521 Pick-up '68 thru '73
28020 510 all models '78 thru '81
28022 620 Series Pick-up all models '73 thru '79
    720 Series Pick-up - see NISSAN (72030)
28025 810/Maxima all gasoline models, '77 thru '84

DODGE
    400 & 600 - see CHRYSLER (25030)
30008 Aries & Plymouth Reliant '81 thru '89
30010 Caravan & Plymouth Voyager '84 thru '95
*30011 Caravan & Plymouth Voyager '96 thru '02
30012 Challenger/Plymouth Saporro '78 thru '83
30016 Colt & Plymouth Champ '78 thru '87
30020 Dakota Pick-ups all models '87 thru '96
*30021 Durango '98 & '99, Dakota '97 thru '99
30025 Dart, Demon, Plymouth Barracuda, Duster & Valiant 6 cyl models '67 thru '76
30030 Daytona & Chrysler Laser '84 thru '89
    Intrepid - see CHRYSLER (25025, 25026)
*30034 Neon all models '95 thru '99
30035 Omni & Plymouth Horizon '78 thru '90
30040 Pick-ups all full-size models '74 thru '93
*30041 Pick-ups all full-size models '94 thru '01
30045 Ram 50/D50 Pick-ups & Raider and Plymouth Arrow Pick-ups '79 thru '93
30050 Dodge/Plymouth/Chrysler RWD '71 thru '89
30055 Shadow & Plymouth Sundance '87 thru '94
30060 Spirit & Plymouth Acclaim '89 thru '95
*30065 Vans - Dodge & Plymouth '71 thru '03

EAGLE
    Talon - see MITSUBISHI (68030, 68031)
    Vision - see CHRYSLER (25025)

FIAT
34010 124 Sport Coupe & Spider '68 thru '78
34025 X1/9 all models '74 thru '80

FORD
10355 Ford Automatic Transmission Overhaul
36004 Aerostar Mini-vans all models '86 thru '97
36006 Contour & Mercury Mystique '95 thru '00
36008 Courier Pick-up all models '72 thru '82
*36012 Crown Victoria & Mercury Grand Marquis '88 thru '00
10320 Ford Engine Overhaul Manual
36016 Escort/Mercury Lynx all models '81 thru '90
36020 Escort/Mercury Tracer '91 thru '00
36024 Explorer & Mazda Navajo '91 thru '01
36028 Fairmont & Mercury Zephyr '78 thru '83
36030 Festiva & Aspire '88 thru '97
36032 Fiesta all models '77 thru '80
*36034 Focus all models '00 and '01
36036 Ford & Mercury Full-size '75 thru '87
36040 Granada & Mercury Monarch '75 thru '80
36044 Ford & Mercury Mid-size '75 thru '86
36048 Mustang V8 all models '64-1/2 thru '73
36049 Mustang II 4 cyl, V6 & V8 models '74 thru '78
36050 Mustang & Mercury Capri all models Mustang, '79 thru '93; Capri, '79 thru '86
*36051 Mustang all models '94 thru '03
36054 Pick-ups & Bronco '73 thru '79
36058 Pick-ups & Bronco '80 thru '96
*36059 F-150 & Expedition '97 thru '02, F-250 '97 thru '99 & Lincoln Navigator '98 thru '02
*36060 Super Duty Pick-ups, Excursion '97 thru '02
36062 Pinto & Mercury Bobcat '75 thru '80
36066 Probe all models '89 thru '92
36070 Ranger/Bronco II gasoline models '83 thru '92
*36071 Ranger '93 thru '00 & Mazda Pick-ups '94 thru '00
36074 Taurus & Mercury Sable '86 thru '95
*36075 Taurus & Mercury Sable '96 thru '01
36078 Tempo & Mercury Topaz '84 thru '94
36082 Thunderbird/Mercury Cougar '83 thru '88
36086 Thunderbird/Mercury Cougar '89 thru '97
36090 Vans all V8 Econoline models '69 thru '91
*36094 Vans full size '92 thru '01
*36097 Windstar Mini-van '95 thru '03

GENERAL MOTORS
10360 GM Automatic Transmission Overhaul
38005 Buick Century, Chevrolet Celebrity, Oldsmobile Cutlass Ciera & Pontiac 6000 all models '82 thru '96
*38010 Buick Regal, Chevrolet Lumina, Oldsmobile Cutlass Supreme & Pontiac Grand Prix (FWD) '88 thru '02
38015 Buick Skyhawk, Cadillac Cimarron, Chevrolet Cavalier, Oldsmobile Firenza & Pontiac J-2000 & Sunbird '82 thru '94
*38016 Chevrolet Cavalier & Pontiac Sunfire '95 thru '01
38020 Buick Skylark, Chevrolet Citation, Olds Omega, Pontiac Phoenix '80 thru '85
38025 Buick Skylark & Somerset, Oldsmobile Achieva & Calais and Pontiac Grand Am all models '85 thru '98
*38026 Chevrolet Malibu, Olds Alero & Cutlass, Pontiac Grand Am '97 thru '00
38030 Cadillac Eldorado '71 thru '85, Seville '80 thru '85, Oldsmobile Toronado '71 thru '85, Buick Riviera '79 thru '85
*38031 Cadillac Eldorado & Seville '86 thru '91, DeVille '86 thru '93, Fleetwood & Olds Toronado '86 thru '92, Buick Riviera '86 thru '93
38032 Cadillac DeVille '94 thru '02 & Seville - '92 thru '02
38035 Chevrolet Lumina APV, Olds Silhouette & Pontiac Trans Sport all models '90 thru '96
*38036 Chevrolet Venture, Olds Silhouette, Pontiac Trans Sport & Montana '97 thru '01
    General Motors Full-size Rear-wheel Drive - see BUICK (19025)

GEO
    Metro - see CHEVROLET Sprint (24075)
    Prizm - '85 thru '92 see CHEVY (24060), '93 thru '02 see TOYOTA Corolla (92036)

(Continued on other side)

Listings shown with an asterisk (*) indicate model coverage as of this printing. These titles will be periodically updated to include later model years - consult your Haynes dealer for more information.

Haynes North America, Inc., 861 Lawrence Drive, Newbury Park, CA 91320-1514 • (805) 498-6703

Haynes Automotive Manuals (continued)

NOTE: New manuals are added to this list on a periodic basis. If you do not see a listing for your vehicle, consult your local Haynes dealer for the latest product information.

40030 Storm all models '90 thru '93
Tracker - see SUZUKI Samurai (90010)

GMC
Vans & Pick-ups - see CHEVROLET

HONDA
42010 Accord CVCC all models '76 thru '83
42011 Accord all models '84 thru '89
42012 Accord all models '90 thru '93
42013 Accord all models '94 thru '97
*42014 Accord all models '98 and '99
42020 Civic 1200 all models '73 thru '79
42021 Civic 1300 & 1500 CVCC '80 thru '83
42022 Civic 1500 CVCC all models '75 thru '79
42023 Civic all models '84 thru '91
42024 Civic & del Sol '92 thru '95
*42025 Civic '96 thru '00, CR-V '97 thru '00, Acura Integra '94 thru '00
42040 Prelude CVCC all models '79 thru '89

HYUNDAI
*43010 Elantra all models '96 thru '01
43015 Excel & Accent all models '86 thru '98

ISUZU
Hombre - see CHEVROLET S-10 (24071)
*47017 Rodeo '91 thru '02; Amigo '89 thru '94 and '98 thru '02; Honda Passport '95 thru '02
47020 Trooper & Pick-up '81 thru '93

JAGUAR
49010 XJ6 all 6 cyl models '68 thru '86
49011 XJ6 all models '88 thru '94
49015 XJ12 & XJS all 12 cyl models '72 thru '85

JEEP
50010 Cherokee, Comanche & Wagoneer Limited all models '84 thru '00
50020 CJ all models '49 thru '86
*50025 Grand Cherokee all models '93 thru '00
50029 Grand Wagoneer & Pick-up '72 thru '91 Grand Wagoneer '84 thru '91, Cherokee & Wagoneer '72 thru '83, Pick-up '72 thru '88
*50030 Wrangler all models '87 thru '00

LEXUS
ES 300 - see TOYOTA Camry (92007)

LINCOLN
Navigator - see FORD Pick-up (36059)
*59010 Rear-Wheel Drive all models '70 thru '01

MAZDA
61010 GLC Hatchback (rear-wheel drive) '77 thru '83
61011 GLC (front-wheel drive) '81 thru '85
61015 323 & Protegé '90 thru '00
*61016 MX-5 Miata '90 thru '97
61020 MPV all models '89 thru '94
Navajo - see Ford Explorer (36024)
61030 Pick-ups '72 thru '93
Pick-ups '94 thru '00 - see Ford Ranger (36071)
61035 RX-7 all models '79 thru '85
61036 RX-7 all models '86 thru '91
61040 626 (rear-wheel drive) all models '79 thru '82
61041 626/MX-6 (front-wheel drive) '83 thru '91
61042 626 '93 thru '01, MX-6/Ford Probe '93 thru '97

MERCEDES-BENZ
63012 123 Series Diesel '76 thru '85
63015 190 Series four-cyl gas models, '84 thru '88
63020 230/250/280 6 cyl sohc models '68 thru '72
63025 280 123 Series gasoline models '77 thru '81
63030 350 & 450 all models '71 thru '80

MERCURY
64200 Villager & Nissan Quest '93 thru '01
All other titles, see FORD Listing.

MG
66010 MGB Roadster & GT Coupe '62 thru '80
66015 MG Midget, Austin Healey Sprite '58 thru '80

MITSUBISHI
68020 Cordia, Tredia, Galant, Precis & Mirage '83 thru '93
68030 Eclipse, Eagle Talon & Ply. Laser '90 thru '94
*68031 Eclipse '95 thru '01, Eagle Talon '95 thru '98
68040 Pick-up '83 thru '96 & Montero '83 thru '93

NISSAN
72010 300ZX all models including Turbo '84 thru '89
72015 Altima all models '93 thru '01
72020 Maxima all models '85 thru '92
*72021 Maxima all models '93 thru '01
72030 Pick-ups '80 thru '97 Pathfinder '87 thru '95
*72031 Frontier Pick-up '98 thru '01, Xterra '00 & '01, Pathfinder '96 thru '01
72040 Pulsar all models '83 thru '86
Quest - see MERCURY Villager (64200)
72050 Sentra all models '82 thru '94
72051 Sentra & 200SX all models '95 thru '99
72060 Stanza all models '82 thru '90

OLDSMOBILE
73015 Cutlass V6 & V8 gas models '74 thru '88
For other OLDSMOBILE titles, see BUICK, CHEVROLET or GENERAL MOTORS listing.

PLYMOUTH
For PLYMOUTH titles, see DODGE listing.

PONTIAC
79008 Fiero all models '84 thru '88
79018 Firebird V8 models except Turbo '70 thru '81
79019 Firebird all models '82 thru '92
79040 Mid-size Rear-wheel Drive '70 thru '87
For other PONTIAC titles, see BUICK, CHEVROLET or GENERAL MOTORS listing.

PORSCHE
80020 911 except Turbo & Carrera 4 '65 thru '89
80025 914 all 4 cyl models '69 thru '76
80030 924 all models including Turbo '76 thru '82
80035 944 all models including Turbo '83 thru '89

RENAULT
Alliance & Encore - see AMC (14020)

SAAB
*84010 900 all models including Turbo '79 thru '88

SATURN
*87010 Saturn all models '91 thru '02

SUBARU
89002 1100, 1300, 1400 & 1600 '71 thru '79
89003 1600 & 1800 2WD & 4WD '80 thru '94

SUZUKI
90010 Samurai/Sidekick & Geo Tracker '86 thru '01

TOYOTA
92005 Camry all models '83 thru '91
92006 Camry all models '92 thru '96
*92007 Camry, Avalon, Solara, Lexus ES 300 '97 thru '01
92015 Celica Rear Wheel Drive '71 thru '85
92020 Celica Front Wheel Drive '86 thru '99
92025 Celica Supra all models '79 thru '92
92030 Corolla all models '75 thru '79
92032 Corolla all rear drive models '80 thru '87
92035 Corolla all front wheel drive models '84 thru '92
92036 Corolla & Geo Prizm '93 thru '02
92040 Corolla Tercel all models '80 thru '82
92045 Corona all models '74 thru '82
92050 Cressida all models '78 thru '82
92055 Land Cruiser FJ40, 43, 45, 55 '68 thru '82
92056 Land Cruiser FJ60, 62, 80, FZJ80 '80 thru '96
92065 MR2 all models '85 thru '87
92070 Pick-up all models '69 thru '78
92075 Pick-up all models '79 thru '95
*92076 Tacoma '95 thru '00, 4Runner '96 thru '00, & T100 '93 thru '98
*92078 Tundra '00 thru '02 & Sequoia '01 thru '02

92080 Previa all models '91 thru '95
*92082 RAV4 all models '96 thru '02
92085 Tercel all models '87 thru '94

TRIUMPH
94007 Spitfire all models '62 thru '81
94010 TR7 all models '75 thru '81

VW
96008 Beetle & Karmann Ghia '54 thru '79
*96009 New Beetle '98 thru '00
96016 Rabbit, Jetta, Scirocco & Pick-up gas models '74 thru '91 & Convertible '80 thru '92
96017 Golf, GTI & Jetta '93 thru '98 & Cabrio '95 thru '98
*96018 Golf, GTI, Jetta & Cabrio '99 thru '02
96020 Rabbit, Jetta & Pick-up diesel '77 thru '84
96023 Passat '98 thru '01, Audi A4 '96 thru '01
96030 Transporter 1600 all models '68 thru '79
96035 Transporter 1700, 1800 & 2000 '72 thru '79
96040 Type 3 1500 & 1600 all models '63 thru '73
96045 Vanagon all air-cooled models '80 thru '83

VOLVO
97010 120, 130 Series & 1800 Sports '61 thru '73
97015 140 Series all models '66 thru '74
97020 240 Series all models '76 thru '93
97040 740 & 760 Series all models '82 thru '88
97050 850 Series all models '93 thru '97

TECHBOOK MANUALS
10205 Automotive Computer Codes
10210 Automotive Emissions Control Manual
10215 Fuel Injection Manual, 1978 thru 1985
10220 Fuel Injection Manual, 1986 thru 1999
10225 Holley Carburetor Manual
10230 Rochester Carburetor Manual
10240 Weber/Zenith/Stromberg/SU Carburetors
10305 Chevrolet Engine Overhaul Manual
10310 Chrysler Engine Overhaul Manual
10320 Ford Engine Overhaul Manual
10330 GM and Ford Diesel Engine Repair Manual
10340 Small Engine Repair Manual, 5 HP & Less
10341 Small Engine Repair Manual, 5.5 - 20 HP
10345 Suspension, Steering & Driveline Manual
10355 Ford Automatic Transmission Overhaul
10360 GM Automatic Transmission Overhaul
10405 Automotive Body Repair & Painting
10410 Automotive Brake Manual
10411 Automotive Anti-lock Brake (ABS) Systems
10415 Automotive Detaiing Manual
10420 Automotive Eelectrical Manual
10425 Automotive Heating & Air Conditioning
10430 Automotive Reference Manual & Dictionary
10435 Automotive Tools Manual
10440 Used Car Buying Guide
10445 Welding Manual
10450 ATV Basics

SPANISH MANUALS
98903 Reparación de Carrocería & Pintura
98905 Códigos Automotrices de la Computadora
98910 Frenos Automotriz
98915 Inyección de Combustible 1986 al 1999
99040 Chevrolet & GMC Camionetas '67 al '87 Incluye Suburban, Blazer & Jimmy '67 al '91
99041 Chevrolet & GMC Camionetas '88 al '98 Incluye Suburban '92 al '98, Blazer & Jimmy '92 al '94, Tahoe y Yukon '95 al '98
99042 Chevrolet & GMC Camionetas Cerradas '68 al '95
99055 Dodge Caravan & Plymouth Voyager '84 al '95
99075 Ford Camionetas y Bronco '80 al '94
99077 Ford Camionetas Cerradas '69 al '91
99083 Ford Modelos de Tamaño Grande '75 al '87
99088 Ford Modelos de Tamaño Mediano '75 al '86
99091 Ford Taurus & Mercury Sable '86 al '95
99095 GM Modelos de Tamaño Grande '70 al '90
99100 GM Modelos de Tamaño Mediano '70 al '88
99110 Nissan Camioneta '80 al '96, Pathfinder '87 al '95
99118 Nissan Sentra '82 al '94
99125 Toyota Camionetas y 4Runner '79 al '95

Over 100 Haynes motorcycle manuals also available

8-03

---

* Listings shown with an asterisk (*) indicate model coverage as of this printing. These titles will be periodically updated to include later model years - consult your Haynes dealer for more information.

Haynes North America, Inc., 861 Lawrence Drive, Newbury Park, CA 91320-1514 • (805) 498-6703